COMPUTER SYSTEM PERFORMANCE

McGraw-Hill Computer Science Series

Richard W. Hamming
Bell Telephone Laboratories

Edward Feigenbaum
Stanford University

Computer System Performance

Herbert Hellerman
State University of New York at Binghamton

Thomas F. Conroy
IBM Corporation
Education Center

McGraw-Hill Book Company

New York   St. Louis   San Francisco   Auckland   Düsseldorf
Johannesburg   Kuala Lumpur   London   Mexico   Montreal   New Delhi
Panama   Paris   São Paulo   Singapore   Sydney   Tokyo   Toronto

Computer System Performance

1 2 3 4 5 6 7 8 9 0   K P K P   7 9 8 7 6 5

This book was set in Press Roman by Scripta Graphica.
The editors were Kenneth J. Bowman and Michael Gardner;
The production supervisor was Charles Hess.
The drawings were done by J & R Services, Inc.
Kingsport Press, Inc. was printer and binder.

Library of Congress Cataloging in Publication Data

Hellerman, Herbert, date
  Computer system performance.

  (McGraw-Hill computer science series)
  Includes bibliographical references.
    1. Electronic digital computers—Evaluation.
I. Conroy, Thomas F., joint author. II. Title.
QA76.5.H447   001.6'4'044   74-19029
ISBN 0-07-027953-5

Contents

Preface

Assessing the performance of a complex and expensive computer system is both a practical necessity and a formidable technical challenge. Performance is characterized by a set of precisely defined descriptors of efficiency that help determine how closely a system comes to meeting stated objectives. Because these may differ from system to system, and even conflict within the same system, it is important to understand not only the descriptors, but also the relationships between them and how they are influenced by choices that must be made in system architecture, design, and operations. The study of performance involves not only mastery of certain special definitions and techniques, like measurement and simulation, but also a deep understanding of many themes that thread the entire fabric of computer science and technology.

This book is concerned primarily with performance as opposed to function. The reader is assumed already to be familiar with functional aspects of machine organization and programming. However, some complex topics like operating systems are discussed, beginning with basic concepts. A performance viewpoint offers a splendid opportunity to cap an academic program in computer science or engineering, since it brings together considerations of hardware, software, human, and management factors. This book is therefore intended for senior undergraduate or graduate courses. It should also be of interest to working computer professionals in research, development, and operations.

The first chapter is an overview of major performance issues in computer systems. It is designed to introduce some of the terminology and problems in characterizing performance and to motivate interest in the subject.

The next two chapters cover selected topics in statistics and discrete mathematics. They supply all tools needed later and other material useful in reading the literature. A major objective is to explain fundamental concepts and to develop important skills in statistics, set notation, and applied probability. For the most part, the formulas given in text are supplied with their assumptions and derivations. For readers having a weak background in these subjects, Chap. 2 and 3 are essential and help make the book self-contained. This material and the Appendixes are also valuable for review and reference.

Chapters 4 and 5, in the middle of the book, deal with job processing and queueing models from three viewpoints: intuitive, simulation, and mathematical. Some of this material may be familiar to industrial engineers and operations-research specialists, but it should also be at the fingertips of computer professionals.

The last six chapters are concerned with performance issues that are very specific to computer systems. Chapter 6 discusses the relatively simple class of cases involving a single job or a single component. The material includes mix and kernal techniques of CPU evaluation, compiler performance, software measurement methods, and a simple model of a single job where processing and input-output are overlapped in various ways.

Since computer performance is intimately related to the way its resources are managed, especially by its operating system, Chap. 7 describes major design options of operating systems including relocation, loading, scheduling, and deadlock-handling features. Chapter 8 discusses the various versions of the complex IBM OS/360 operating system and illustrates the principles discussed in Chap. 7.

Chapter 9 is devoted to timesharing systems, beginning with the user viewpoint, proceeding to general architecture considerations, and finally to specific cases including MIT-CTSS, IBM-TSO, and IBM-APL.

Chapters 10 and 11 examine the theory and practice of virtual storage, which includes some of the most sophisticated and dynamic resource-allocation strategies in computer systems. The two design contexts of a fast CPU with a cache store and the main-store/drum-disk memory hierarchy are both discussed with most examples from IBM System/370 systems.

A set of exercises for each chapter is supplied at the end of the book. For those chapters covering mathematical-analytic techniques, these exercises include numerical and algebraic problems. For the last few chapters, which involve primarily descriptive material, most of the exercises require word answers. These are intended not only to help focus attention on important points in the text but also to stimulate critical thinking and familiarity with terminology, and to give readers practice in developing their skills of expression and exposition. The final exercises in many of the chapters are major projects, some of which require considerable library work and nontrivial programs to be written.

We have used the manuscript as a text in a two-semester sequence in system performance. Since our particular curriculum required a separate course in probability and stastics, Chap. 2 and 3 were used only for a quick review, and thereafter for reference. Most of the first half of the first semester was spent on Chap. 4 and 5, where the simulation and mathematical job processing models were developed. Here, we found the use of the SIMJOB simulator program (outlined in Chap. 4) to be useful for student experimentation. Chapter 6 was then covered rather quickly and the last half of the term was devoted mainly to Chap. 7 and 8, which concern modern conventional operating systems, and a part of Chap. 9, which introduces timesharing systems. The second semester began with timesharing systems and continued with the final chapters on virtual storage. The last four weeks were reserved for student seminars on papers selected from the references or reports on student projects, most of which were of the simulation type. Depending on the interests and needs of the students and the preferences of the instructor, different orderings and selections from the text are, of course, possible.

We are pleased to acknowledge the diligent proofreading work of Mr. Steven Lake at State University of New York at Binghamton. We also wish to express our appreciation to Mrs. Shanna McGoff for her excellent efforts and patience in typing the manuscript.

Herbert Hellerman
Thomas F. Conroy

COMPUTER SYSTEM PERFORMANCE

CHAPTER 1

The Nature of Computer-Performance Evaluation

The evaluation of a computer system involves the following classes of considerations:

1. Performance (defined loosely as *measures of system speed* and resource use)
2. Cost
3. User convenience
4. Reliability

Perhaps the most fundamental property of modern data-processing systems is their generality. The theoretical basis of this generality is due to the work of A.M. Turing (1936). It can be shown that most commercially available computers are logically equivalent to each other, since they can compute the same wide class of *computable* functions, conditional only on the character-sets they can accept and print and on the size of storage available (but not fundamentally on the technologies or speed properties of the storage devices). This extreme generality of function is the source of many of the greatest difficulties in computer evaluation. This is because any system can be evaluated only with respect to its functions; the wider the class of functions, the more difficult the task of characterizing its "goodness."

The fact that performance varies in the same direction as cost is understandable, although the quantitative relationship is often not at all clear. The relation of user convenience to performance is also very difficult to quantify. Like most desirable properties, user convenience usually has its price in both system cost and performance, but this can be more than offset by increased human productivity. One reason for a speed penalty is that convenience requires the physical system to be disguised to user-oriented objectives through the use of resources in an indirect manner that is not the best match to their physical structure. Also, user convenience is achieved at least in part by system programs that automatically do tasks otherwise left to the individual programmer. It is difficult to design such facilities to perform optimally for the particular needs of all possible user programs. However, with care, system programs can often perform at least as well as corresponding programs written by most programmers.

It would be most desirable to have *quantitative* measures of the value of system features to user convenience. Unfortunately, these are rarely obtainable. For example, even today we have no measure of the worth of say the FORTRAN language over coding in Assembly language, although there is little doubt that the benefits in human productivity are very great. This kind of gap is a major obstacle in developing a science of system evaluation.

Since about 1969, the literature on computer performance has burgeoned. This reflects in part the maturing of the data-processing industry. Increasing attention is now being given to making wise selections from among several available devices and software components with comparable functions. The strong incentive of system economies coupled with considerable technical effort has not yet produced a science of system performance. Some of the obstacles still to be overcome include considerable differences among workers in performance in the definitions of various performance measures, the scarcity of analytic methods for relating various performance measures to each other, and the lack of general methods of scaling performance measures from one system to another. In other words, we do not have a *theory* of performance evaluation. Progress toward such a theory has been slow, not only because of technical problems in definitions and analysis, but also because performance, user convenience, reliability, and cost have important business implications. Many tools and results are consequently being held proprietary to the business firm that developed them.

In the remainder of this chapter, we shall briefly touch on several computer performance issues, many of which will be discussed in greater detail later in the book.

1-1 MOTIVATIONS FOR EVALUATION

Computer system evaluation is of interest to several classes of people, each with its own perspective. A rough classification is:

1. Hardware-software architects and designers
2. Managers of system installations and their system programmers
3. Users (application programmers and analysts)

The scope narrows in the order of the above listing. The designer must deal with factors influenced by the entire spectrum of possible system use; the manager at a particular installation is concerned with many users, but only in a restricted environment; and the individual user is interested in his single program or a small collection of programs. As the width of interest becomes more specific, performance objectives and measures can be stated more precisely. However, less freedom is also available to manipulate resources and meet particular objectives. Thus the designers have a relatively large number of choices, while the installation manager working with a delivered system is confined to available resources. However, many modern computers are delivered with "open" parameters in their operating systems so that each installation can make important efficiency decisions, such as the devices to be used for program residence and *scheduling* options, in accordance with the properties of its workload. Judicious setting of these can be a major factor in good performance. Although at present most of this "tuning" is done manually, future operating systems will be "adaptive," i.e., they will sense the resources available, monitor activity, and assign resources automatically. However, even here it will still be necessary for users (e.g., installation managers) to convey their performance objectives to the system.

The individual user is most constrained in resource allocation, yet he often has a vital influence on performance. A recent specific case in our personal experience showed an improvement (by a *factor* of 50) in run time for a certain program by changing the iteration scheme. This factor is comparable to the average internal speed ratio between many large and small machines! Almost any experienced observer can give similar examples. The fact is that the range of program quality is in practice exceedingly large; this reflects the great differences in human skill in problem solving, which is really what programming is all about.

1-2 THE SYSTEM AS A COLLECTION OF RESOURCES

A modern computer system is best considered as a collection of *resources*. These and their typical present implementations include:

1. *Storages:*
    (*a*) Registers and buffers; logic circuitry, logic arrays, and small fast core, film arrays.
    (*b*) Main storage; film core, integrated transistor circuits.
    (*c*) Auxiliary storage; core, drum, disk, delay line, tape.
2. *Processing Units:*
    (*a*) Arithmetic-logical and program control operations.
    (*b*) Transmission controllers.
3. *Transducers* (converters of one physical form of information to another):
    (*a*) Card-tape readers, punches.
    (*b*) Typewriters, printers, displays.
4. *System Programs*:
    (*a*) Subroutine libraries.
    (*b*) Language processors.
    (*c*) Resource-management utilities.

The economics of technology has thus far resulted in system structures that are heterogeneous in speed and cost of substructures, especially storages. Although technology is changing, the fact that different technologies yield different cost-speed characteristics seems to be a safe extrapolation from all past experience. It follows that whatever the particular values of speed-cost improvement, future (like past) systems will consist of mixed technologies. Management of this hierarchy will remain a central issue of system performance.

Since resource allocation is programmable, it has traditionally been left to each individual user in each of his programs. This is a "fair" although burdensome task in a nonshared system where each user has all resources available to him during his run. In a shared (multiprogrammed) system, multiple-user demands converge at unpredictable times on common resources. Careful space allocation is now essential, since too large a share given to one user deprives others of this vital resource. These conflicts must be resolved by the *system*, since the individual user lacks the knowledge of resource states and the incentive and responsibility to manage resources for other users. Major resources are thus allocated and scheduled by a system program which we shall call the *supervisor*. To the user this program might as well be part of the hardware, and although many options are available to him and his installation, important performance factors are determined by the organization of the supervisor. The system-supplied programs mentioned above are used extensively by most programs, often in ways not obvious to the programmer. A realistic evaluation must take into account the performance of these facilities.

Finally, it is well to recognize the important role of the human operator as a "component" of system performance. Manual operations in the machine room (tape-disk mounting, printer-paper bursting, etc.) as well as console interaction can and do have significant effects on overall system performance.

1-3 PERFORMANCE MEASURES   [Refs. BA,GO,HE2,LU]

Quantitative measures of performance are meaningful only when the following are clearly specified:

1. The system configuration (all device and software parameters)
2. The workload or job stream
3. The definition of the measures

The first of these is obvious, and little can be said in general. Configuration information can be very voluminous, although most of the performance effects are usually due to a small fraction of the total number of parameters. The difficulties in specifying and extrapolating workloads was mentioned earlier and will be a recurring theme of this book (see Sec. 1-4). For now, job i in a stream will be specified by a number-pair (A_i, X_i) giving its arrival and execute or service time. If all A_i are omitted, all jobs arrive at time $= 0$.

The definition of performance measures involves careful consideration of the objectives of the system, especially with regard to human expectations. Two measures in very common use are *thruput* and *response time*.

Thruput is a commonly used measure for "batch" systems and is expressed in units of jobs per minute, that is, the number of jobs in a stated job stream divided by the total time to process the stream:

$$H = \frac{n}{T}$$

This would seem to be simple enough, but in fact it is far from simple. For example, the ordering of the jobs can be of great importance in a multiprogramming system, as can their times of arrival. Thruput also says nothing about when each job is finished; it only tells us, in effect, when the *last* job is completed.

Response time for job i is the time difference $(Q_i - A_i)$ between completion time and arrival time. Mean response time is

$$\bar{t}_e = \frac{1}{n} \sum_{i=1}^{n} (Q_i - A_i)$$

Mean response time, because it is an average, must suppress certain details that are often of importance. For example, consider the following 5-job stream processed by two systems (both with no overhead); the systems differ in the sequencing of their service.

		Job→				
		1	2	3	4	5
	Execute time	2	20	2	8	3
System A:	Response time	2	22	24	32	35
	Thruput = 5/35 = 0.143; Mean Response = 115/5 = 23					
	Execute time	2	20	2	8	3
System B:	Response time	6	35	8	23	13
	Thruput = 5/35 = 0.143; Mean Response = 85/5 = 17					

Although both systems have the same thruput, the mean response time is much better for system *B*. Also, notice that the response times for three of the jobs are better in system *B* than in *A*, while the reverse is true for only two jobs.

Thruput gives only a measure of the time to process the entire stream and says nothing about the times individual jobs are completed or the order in which they are completed. This lack of sensitivity to order-of-completion makes thruput of less importance for fast response environments (e.g., timesharing) than for batch systems. Mean response time is then a better measure of the desired objectives. However, even when response time is most significant, thruput is still of interest. This is true because thruput is usually closely correlated with the efficient use of system resources; hence it has a direct bearing on costs, even when its relevance to immediate user satisfaction is not as important as response time.

Important general factors influencing thruput are:

1. Speeds of components
2. The workload
3. Overlap (concurrency) permitted in use of components
4. Scheduling method of assigning resources to workload

The first factor is obvious. The workload has a profound effect on thruput or on any other useful performance measure, a fact that is so important that it will be repeated often throughout this book. However, the *sensitivity* of various measures need not be the same with respect to the same set of workloads. To illustrate, let the thruput of system i on workload W_j be written $H_i(W_j)$. Now suppose that two systems are to be compared on two different workloads. The four thruput values can be compared in a number of different ways, of which we cite two: (1) thruput ratios and (2) thruput differences. We now compare these in order to investigate their sensitivity to workload.

$$\text{Difference of ratios} = \frac{H_2(w_2)}{H_1(w_2)} - \frac{H_2(W_1)}{H_1(W_1)} = a - b$$

$$\text{Ratio of differences} = \frac{H_2(W_2) - H_1(W_2)}{H_2(W_1) - H_1(W_1)} = \frac{H_1(W_2)}{H_1(W_1)} \frac{a-1}{b-1}$$

It is usually the case that the first of these is smaller than the second; that is, thruput ratios of two systems tend to be more workload independent than thruput differences.

Overlap, i.e., permitting more than one resource to work concurrently, can have a major effect on thruput. A simple analysis shows an extreme upper bound. Consider an n-resource system and a job that, run sequentially (i.e., without any overlap), requires t_j seconds of resource j. The time to run the job sequentially is then

$$T_s = \sum_{j=1}^{p} t_j$$

Assuming the best possible overlap conditions (which is *not* possible for every workload), all resources are used at the same time and the job time is then

$$T_v = \text{Max}.(t_j)$$

The improvement factor over nonoverlap is then

$$\frac{T_s}{T_v} = \frac{\sum_{j=1}^{p} t_j}{\text{Max }(t_j)}$$

The t_j are, of course, determined by both the system and the job. However, the best possible case for the ratio occurs where all components of t_j are equal, since then each term of the sum is the maximum value of 1. Hence,

$$\text{Max}\left(\frac{T_s}{T_v}\right) = p$$

This establishes the principle:

> *With all resource use overlapped as much as possible for the most favorable possible workload, the thruput improvement factor over a nonoverlap system with the same resources is equal to the number of resources.*

For example, a system containing two I/O channels and a CPU (three resources) can *at best* be three times faster than a nonoverlap system. Aside from the sequence dependency of most jobs that preclude ideal overlap, there is another factor: The time advantages of overlapped operations usually require space sharing (e.g., for buffers), which affects program and data organization. This tends to work against the overlapped system relative to the sequential.

1-4 WORKLOAD SELECTION: BENCHMARKS
[Refs. BU2,DO,DR2,GO,JO,RO,SR,WA]

Every measure of performance requires some specification of the workload that is to be handled. As indicated in our introduction, the general-purpose nature of most computing systems means that a very wide variety of jobs can be processed by a computer. Practical considerations require that only a few of the many possible jobs be selected as *benchmarks*, i.e., representative of the work expected of the system. What guidelines may be used to select benchmarks? Three criteria (of many) are:

1. Jobs run most frequently
2. Jobs that account for most of the system's time
3. Jobs with response (completion) time requirements that are most critical to the system's mission

The distinction between the first and second class is worth particular attention. For example, it is possible that 80 percent of the *number* of jobs run in a typical period consists of many short jobs, but that these account for (say) only 30 percent of the system *time*. The remaining 70 percent of the time is due to only three long-run jobs. Clearly, a representative workload for this system must include some short jobs to represent "most jobs," and some long jobs to represent "most time."

Often in evaluation work we seek knowledge to help make decisions about *future* performance, either as improvement of existing performance on the same system, or to decide on a new configuration. How are we to select a workload representative of the future? In most cases, this is done by selecting jobs run in the past. This is often quite valid. In other cases it may be of doubtful value, as for example when an installation that has run only batch workloads is to be converted to a mixed batch and timesharing operation. Certainly, every effort should be made to identify the workload the system *will* encounter. If this is not feasible, then at least the limitation should be acknowledged.

It is not an exaggeration to say that workload selection is the trickiest item in most system evaluation studies. When the system configurations being compared are functionally very similar, the considerations discussed above apply. In the case where different functional features (like different machine instruction-sets or different programming languages) are also part of the picture, then even greater caution must be used in formulating the workload and in interpreting the results. For example, if the systems being compared use different languages, then the programming skills and styles of the people writing the workload programs are real and subtle factors influencing the results.

In the past few years there has been a growing interest in *synthetic workloads*, i.e., specially constructed artificial jobs whose resource-use properties reflect properties of the workload. (See Refs. BU2, SR, and also Sec. 4-2.)

1-5 RESOURCE EXERCISERS: KERNELS   [Refs. CA,DO,DR2,SM]

Resource exercisers are programs designed for the purpose of exercising selected system resources in a carefully controlled regimen. This method has considerable merit from the viewpoint of scientific methodology. Some analysts feel that it can give meaningful answers useful in system comparison. However, it suffers from the defect that each exerciser is itself an incomplete measure, and it is usually difficult to relate the performance found with an exerciser to the performance of the same system on any particular real problem of interest.

Nevertheless, at least one type of exerciser, the "kernel," has been frequently used in evaluation studies, especially in scientific computation. Here a program segment, usually one representing the inner loop or loops of a frequently used program, is programmed for the machines of interest. Using instruction timings of the machines, times to execute the kernels are computed. The data used to apply the kernel method is relatively easy to obtain compared to, say, the mix method (see Sec. 1-6) and is particularly valuable in early stages of CPU design for the evaluation of different proposed instruction-sets, addressing, and indexing features. Although useful for this purpose, it completely neglects input-output operations and is, therefore, not a complete system-performance analysis technique. It may be possible to extend the kernel idea to include I/O operations, although this seems to have been rarely done. Yet something like a kernel that includes I/O activity has been used, as for example, the simple model of workload to investigate I/O and compute overlap described in Chap. 6.

1-6 INSTRUCTION MIXES   [Refs. DR2,G1]

It is natural to seek measures of performance that are less specifically workload dependent than thruput or response time (or kernel times), especially since the general-purpose nature of a system makes the number of potential workloads very large. One way to do this, which has proved of some value in the evaluation of the CPU part of the computer, is an averaging technique called the *instruction-mix* method. Here, one or more programs are run (usually interpretively) and each time a given instruction type is executed, a counter of its frequency is increased by 1. The list of frequencies may then be weighted by the instruction execution times of each instruction type. The weighted sum is an "average instruction execution time" for the machine (see Fig. 1-6.1). The same frequency distribution may then be used with the instruction execution times of another system to obtain its average instruction time. The two averages can then be compared to get some measure of the relative performances of the two systems. This method has the most validity if the instruction-sets are very similar.

The instruction-mix method has some disadvantages and limitations. It only gives a useful measure of CPU performance of machines with similar instruction-sets, and it neglects input-output performance. It is very expensive in machine time to do the tracing; a traced program may well run 50 times slower than the program without tracing. For large systems with various degrees of instruction overlap, frequencies of individual instructions may not reflect many overlap effects. Finally, the frequency

Instruction or operation	Frequency[3]	Time/OP	Product
Floating point ADD/SUBTRACT[1]	0.095	15	1.425
Floating point multiply[1]	0.056	10	0.560
Floating point divide[1]	0.020	10	0.200
Load/store	0.285	4	1.140
Indexing	0.225	0	0
Conditional branch	0.132	4	0.528
Miscellaneous[2]	0.187	4	0.748
	1.000		
Mean instruction time			4.501

Notes:

1. These instructions have variable execution times. Average times are often used for the time weights.
2. This category includes shifts, immediate, and logical instruction types.
3. This table was generated from traces of IBM 7090 object programs of the "scientific application" type.

Fig. 1-6.1 Illustrative instruction-mix computation.

distribution depends on the programs traced to obtain it; it is most advisable to trace several classes of programs and to develop a separate table for each (e.g., FORTRAN compile and some commonly executed application programs). Other subtle questions can also arise; e.g., if system $S1$ contained a clever compiler, the object code produced might have a different frequency distribution than system $S2$ shows with the code produced by its compiler.

The mix method is one illustration of the powerful statistical technique of frequency analysis of data. The major limitation of such a method is that frequency counting cannot include the sequence relationships contained within the data. In many cases, especially smaller computers, the sequencing information is not too important. However, in larger systems such as those like the IBM System/370 Models 155, 165, which use a storage hierarchy within the CPU, performance will depend upon the ordering of the instruction and data references, not only on the counts of activity. The mix method is least applicable here.

1-7 MEASURING AND DEDUCING SYSTEM ACTIVITY
[Refs. AP,DR2,KO,LU,STA1]

Three basic classes of tools are available for performance studies.

1. Analysis
2. Simulation
3. Measurement

In this section, emphasis is on measurements. Measurement may be done with special equipment, such as a hardware-activity monitoring device, or by software, e.g., event-recording programs such as are incorporated in many modern operating systems.

Hardware monitors have the great advantage of "portability." The same hardware monitor, say one consisting of several event counters, can be physically connected to a wide variety of machines executing any programming system. The counters are usually attached to record times when the CPU, channels, and devices are busy, idle, or overlap in various combinations. Although versatile in recording activities of equipment parts, it is often most difficult to correlate the recorded activity from hardware monitors with the programs that constituted the workload during the measurement interval.

Software monitors are programs that are usually called into execution at each "interrupt" of the CPU. Interrupts in most systems are generated whenever significant events occur, since they are the principal means of notifying the system of resource or program-part completion. Thus by intercepting interrupts, the software monitor program can (by access to the system's clock or interval timer) record a time stamp of every significant event. With care, this recording can place but a slight burden on the system; data reduction of these recordings (usually from a magnetic tape record) can be done as a normal user program. The results of this data analysis can yield information describing where each program spends most of its time and the frequency of access to devices and data-sets, etc. This information is invaluable in deciding on reallocation of storage devices so that the more frequently accessed information is on the faster devices. Contention conflicts on common paths, like disk arms, is thus minimized. This kind of data is not only of great value in "tuning" an installed system, but also in identifying "performance bugs" and "hot spots" (areas of intense activity) during system development. Another important use of a software monitor is to supply data to drive a performance simulator program that models the system and its options. Such a simulator can be a most valuable tool in helping answer "what-if" questions in performance tuning, new purchasing, and system design.

1-8 OPERATING SYSTEM CLASSES

An operating system is a collection of programs responsible for allocating and monitoring the use of equipment and program resources. The last few chapters of this book discuss some operating systems from the performance viewpoint. Our aim is not to convey the formidable details of these example systems, but rather to illustrate important performance categories and issues using timely examples.

As can be seen by the chapter and section titles, three distinct classes of operating system features may be identified:

1. Multiprogramming
2. Timesharing
3. Virtual storage

We now give brief, simple, and informal definitions of these and then consider them in combination.

Multiprogrammed systems are those in which several user programs space-share storage, especially main storage. Usually, there is also time sharing of resources among user programs.

Timeshared systems are designed for use by several people concurrently, each of whom can construct, debug, and use programs *interactively*, i.e., with convenience and delay times that are comfortable for direct man-machine interaction.

Virtual storage systems are those in which a storage hierarchy, consisting of two or more devices that differ in logical properties and speed, are automatically managed so that users see them as a single logical store.

The perceptive reader may well detect that there is no *essential* connection between these categories. Although this is true in a strictly logical sense, many modern systems combine them in various ways. The Venn diagram (Fig. 1-8.1) can help organize our thinking on this. The above three categories are shown as three intersecting circles; there are of course eight possible intersections, i.e., possible combinations of the categories. Under the diagram we list each of these together with some brief remarks and examples. More detail will be found in the last part of this book.

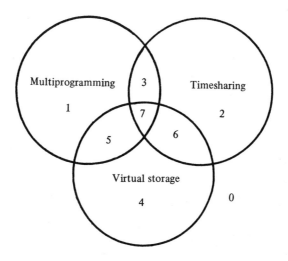

Type	Remarks and Examples
0	Early systems and small modern systems
1	Modern batch systems (e.g., IBM OS/360/370 MVT)
2	MIT/CTSS; some stand-alone timesharing systems
3	Most timesharing systems before 1972 (IBM TSO, GE Information Services network)
4	Rare, since most virtual systems are also multiprogrammed
5	IBM VS systems announced in 1972; early Ferranti-ATLAS system
6	Rare, since most virtual systems are multiprogrammed
7	GE/MIT MULTICS, U. of Michigan MTS, IBM TSS, IBM CP/67, IBM VM system

Fig. 1-8.1 Illustrating categories of operating system and combinations.

1-9 CONCLUDING REMARKS

System-performance evaluation is still in its infancy as a sound technical discipline. Evaluation information is required by at least three broad groups of people: system designers, installation managers and system programmers, and application programmers. Each group has its own needs and requires a different degree of freedom to choose resources or to control them to meet its needs.

The very wide class of problems executable by a computer system, the mixed-speed resource structure of systems, and the differences in resource use by different jobs require that any performance measures include a specification of the workload. This is a most delicate process. One reason is that we have no theory of performance evaluation that permits us to deduce system performance on one workload from known performance on another.

A promising future direction for workload specification is a stochastic representation of jobs, rather than requiring actual jobs for the workload. It is possible to envision a workload designated by a few statistical parameters. A job-stream generator program would then produce a synthetic job stream that would be fed into the system as an actual workload, or else it would generate a job-stream skeleton suitable for feeding a system simulator. This technique is commonly used today in simulators, but has not yet been widely used in measurement studies.

Statistical and probabilistic methods, already in wide use in complex technical and social-system evaluations, will certainly be of increasing importance in computer systems as they service more users in more unpredictable ways (as in timesharing and information-processing utility systems). This is the reason why the first part of this book is concerned with the methods of statistics and probability. Finally, we must emphasize that there is really no such thing as a simple "general" evaluation of a structure as complex as a computer system; each performance study must first decide on its goals and then specifically reflect these in the choice of workload and performance measures. Performance results, whether they are obtained by measurements, simulation, or analysis (or some combination) are meaningful only with respect to these choices. Not only performance numbers, but also the rankings of these numbers between systems, may well change if any of the goal definitions change.

REFERENCES AND BIBLIOGRAPHY

1. [AP] Apple, C.T.: The Program Monitor—A Device for Program Performance Measurement, *Proc. ACM 20th Natl. Conf.*, August, 1965, pp. 66-75.
2. [AR] Aaron, J.D.: Real Time Systems in Perspective, *IBM Systems Journal*, vol. 6, no. 1, 1967.
3. [BA] Bagley, P.R.: Two Think Pieces: Item 2: Establishing a Measure of Capability of a Data Processing System, *Comm. ACM*, vol. 3, no. 1, p. 1, January, 1960.
4. [BU1] Bucholz, W.: A Selected Bibliography on Computer System Performance Evaluation, *IEEE Computer Group News*, vol. 2, no. 8, March, 1969.
5. [BU2] Bucholz, W.: A Synthetic Job for Measuring System Performance, *IBM Systems Journal*, vol. 8, no. 4, pp. 309-318, 1969.
6. [CA] Calingaert, P.: System Performance Evaluation: Survey and Appraisal, *Comm. ACM*, vol. 10, no. 4, pp. 12-18, April, 1967.

7. [DO] Dopping, O.: Test Problems Used for Evaluation of Computers, *BIT*, vol. 2, no. 4, pp. 197-202, 1962.

8. [DR1] Drummond, M.E.: A Perspective on System Evaluation, *IBM Systems Journal*, vol. 8, no. 4, p. 252, 1969.

9. [DR2] Drummond, M.E.: "Evaluation and Measurement Techniques for Digital Computer Systems," Prentice-Hall, New York, 1973.

10. [GI] Gibson, J.C.: The Bigson Mix, *IBM Technical Report* TROO. 2043, June, 1970.

11. [GO] Gosden, J.A. and R.L. Sisson: Standardized Comparisons of Computer Performance, *Information Processing 1962* (Proc. IFIP Congress 62), pp. 57-61.

12. [HE1] Hellerman, H.: "Digital Computer System Principles," (2nd Ed) McGraw-Hill Book Company, New York, 1973.

13. [HE2] Hellerman, H.: Some Principles of Time Sharing Scheduler Strategies, *IBM Systems Journal*, vol. 8, no. 2, 1969.

14. [HEN] Hendrie, G.C. and R.W. Sonnenfeldt: Evaluating Control Computers, *ISA J.*, vol. 10, no. 8, pp. 73-78, August, 1963.

15. [IB1] IBM Corp.: *IBM Systems Journal*, vol. 5, no. 3, 1966. (Contains six articles on the design of teleprocessing systems.)

16. [IB2] IBM Corp.: *IBM Systems Journal*, vol. 8, no. 4, 1969. (This issue contains several articles summarizing the state-of-the-art, as of date of article, on performance measurement and evaluation.)

17. [JO] Joslin, E.O.: "Computer Selection," Addison-Wesley Publishing Company, Reading, Mass., 1968.

18. [KI] Kittel, H. and P. Mertens: Einige Quantitative Untersuchungen zur Groessendegression von Datenverarbeitungsanlagen. (On the economy of scale of data processing systems.) *Elektronische Datenverarbeitung*, vol. 7, no. 6, pp. 255-262, December, 1965.

19. [KO] Kolence, K.W.: A Software View of Measurement Tools, *Datamation*, January, 1971.

20. [LU] Lucas, H.C.: Performance Evaluation and Monitoring, *Computing Surveys*, vol. 3, no. 3, pp. 79-91, September, 1971.

21. [MA] Martin, J.: "Design of Real Time Computer Systems," Prentice-Hall Book Company, New York, 1967.

22. [RO] Rosin, R.F.: Determining a Computing Center Environment, *Comm. ACM*, vol. 8, no. 7, pp. 463-468, 1965.

23. [SO] Solomon, M.B. Jr.: Economies of Scale and IBM System/360, *Comm. ACM*, vol. 10, no. 2, pp. 435-440, June, 1966.

24. [SM] Smith, J.M.: A Review and Comparison of Certain Methods of Computer Performance Evaluation, *The Computer Bulletin*, pp. 13-18, May, 1968.

25. [STA1] Stanley, W.I.: Measurement of System Operational Statistics, *IBM Systems Journal*, vol. 8, no. 4, pp. 299-308, 1969.

26. [STA2] Statland, N.: Methods of Evaluating Computer System Performance, *Computers and Automation*, vol. 12, no. 2, pp. 18-23, 1964.

27. [STE] Stevens, D.F.: System Evaluation on the Control Data 6600, *Proc. IFIP Congress 1968*, pp. 542-547.

28. [STI] Stimler, S.: "Real Time Data Processing Systems," McGraw-Hill Book Company, New York, 1969.

29. [WA] Walter, E.S. and V.L. Wallace: Further Analysis of a Computing Center Environment, *Comm. ACM*, vol. 10, no. 5, pp. 266-272, 1967.

30. [WH] White, P.: Relative Effects of Central Processor and Input-Output Speeds Upon Thruput on the Large Computer, *Comm. ACM*, vol. 7, no. 12, December, 1964.

CHAPTER 2

Principles of Statistics

The word *statistics* is derived from the same root as the word "state." This fact gives us a glimpse of the origin of the subject that arose in its modern form in seventeenth-century England from the needs of government and commerce. For example, insurance firms cannot function without reliable well-organized data on human life span together with techniques for predicting the future life expectancies of a population.

Statistics is a branch of mathematics concerned with the precise description of data. A vital early stage in the rational design of most modern systems is, or at least should be, gathering and organizing data. This is so because no system can be intelligently specified without a clear statement of the nature of its inputs and desired outputs. Such a statement must usually be derived from many observations of the behavior of perspective users and their programs and the resulting response of existing systems. Although our interest will be in computing systems, statistics is becoming an increasingly essential ingredient of many other kinds of systems. Thus, voting statistics in an election help the candidate and the party decide how to design the next system (their next campaign).

In the case of a computing system, intelligent design requires voluminous data on many levels of detail. At the hardware level, choice of instruction-set and addressing methods should reflect the statistical demands for resources, especially storages observed from running programs. The design of storage hierarchies that include virtual storage organizations has also depended on the use of such information. In all cases, the general objective is to identify the patterns of frequent activity so that these may receive their due weight in the design process.

Most statistical calculations and even some data gathering is done today by computers. Certainly as far as its own operations are concerned, a computer system can easily monitor the resource demands of its users and its own response to these demands. Thus, the computer system is an admirable place to apply statistics. This may be done at two distinct epochs of time.

1. *Design time:* to determine the "parameter values" of a design, such as specific instruction types, sizes, and speeds of storage devices.
2. *Execution time:* to record "actual behavior" during system operation that can serve as input to scheduling algorithms for resource allocations. Such algorithms are designed to optimize some measure of good service.

The above ideas are already in some use, but there is little doubt that we have only begun to tap the potential of statistical design. Increasingly, the world of systems is a statistical world!

At some risk of dampening the enthusiasm for statistical techniques, it must be emphasized that the subject is full of traps and opportunities for error. The most common ones are (1) faulty data gathering, and (2) the indiscriminate use of formulas and results of statistical theory by applying them to situations that violate the assumed model from which they were derived. There are plenty of opportunities for innocent errors of both kinds. In addition, because great economic and social issues may be at stake, fallacies are sometimes inserted deliberately to produce some desired result. Although this has tended to give the subject a bad name with the general public, the direction for improvement is clear, i.e., better understanding and clearer exposition of methods and how they are applied, as well as built-in checks wherever possible.

The main idea of statistics is simple but profound: organize and precisely describe large collections of data in order to extract its significance for some intended purpose, such as input and stimulus for rational and prudent action. By *precisely describe* we sense the use of numbers; much of statistics may be understood as information-compression techniques for judiciously defining a small set of numbers that can characterize a much larger set of data values. For this reason we begin by defining some *measures of central tendency* such as the mean, mode, and standard deviation. We then go on to discuss the frequency-distribution functions and some of their properties. We conclude with ways of characterizing data by finding polynomial curves that "best fit" the data in the least square sense. Perhaps the most common case is where the fitting polynomial is a straight line. This is called linear regression and is used to interpolate data and to search for trends.

2-1 MODE, MEAN, AND STANDARD DEVIATION

Suppose we have a data-set or data vector named X consisting of N numbers. We shall use the following numbers as an example

$$X = 1,3,14.5,16.4,18,7,14.6,2,0.5,6$$

The *range* of X is the pair of numbers which are its smallest and largest values.*

$$R_X = \text{Min}\,(X), \text{Max}\,(X) = 0.5, 18 \tag{1}$$

The *mode* of X in the simplest (unimodal) case is that value of X which occurs most frequently. If more than one value occurs with the same highest frequency, then the data is said to be *multimodal* and the mode is then the vector of all distinct values having the highest frequency.

The *arithmetic mean*, also called simply the *mean* or *average* of X, is defined as the sum of the elements of X divided by the number of elements

$$M = M_X = \bar{X} = \frac{1}{N}\sum_{i=1}^{N} X_i = \frac{1}{N}\sum X = \tfrac{1}{10}\,(83) = 8.3 \tag{2a}$$

On the left are some common symbols for the mean; we shall use the unsubscripted M unless a subscript is required to specify which of two or more data-sets is being discussed. The rightmost form of the summation that suppresses detail on the subscripts will also be used as a convenient shorthand; the subscript is then assumed to range over all its values.

If the same constant c is introduced to every element of X, the mean is affected as follows [the proofs follow easily using Eq. $(2a)$]:

$$M_{X+c} = M_X + c \quad \text{also} \quad M_{X-c} = M_X - c \tag{2b}$$

$$M_{cX} = cM_X \quad \text{also} \quad M_{X/c} = \frac{M_X}{c} \tag{2c}$$

Although the mean is the most widely used measure of central tendency, it does not give any information about the *variability* of data values. For example, the two data collections

$X = 2, 3, 59, 24$

$Y = 22, 25, 19, 22$

have the same mean (22), so that their means cannot indicate that Y seems clustered about values of 20 or so while X is not. If it is suspected that the data clusters around some value h, or even if we simply wish to investigate the deviations of X values from h, it is reasonable to take the difference D between each X value and h and develop some simple function of these differences as the measure of deviation of the entire data-set from the h value. The sum of the squares of the differences is a reasonable choice for the form of our measurement function, since squaring the differences will ensure that positive and negative differences do not cancel when taking the sum. The sum will tend to grow larger for larger data-sets merely because there are more data numbers, not necessarily because there is more spread in the values. To avoid this we divide the sum by the number of data elements that makes our measurement the *mean of the squares of the differences:*

*Some authors define the range as $(\text{Max}(X) - \text{Min}\,(X))$.

$$M_{D^2} = \frac{1}{N} \sum_{i=1}^{N} D_i^2 = \frac{1}{N} \sum_{i=1}^{N} (X_i - h)^2 = \frac{1}{N} \sum (X - h)^2 \tag{3}$$

Now we must ask: How is the value of h, the reference number for taking differences, to be chosen? Of course there is no single answer, but one reasonable criterion is that h be selected so that the mean of the square of the deviations (M_{D^2}) is a *minimum*. Using this condition, a formula for h may be derived by applying the calculus technique of finding the minimum of a function with respect to a variable (h) by setting the derivative to zero. When this is done on Eq. (3), it is found that the resulting h equals the mean of the data. In other words:

> *when the common reference for differences is the mean of the data, the mean-square difference is smaller than for any other possible reference value.*

This minimum mean square of differences from the mean is called the *variance* and its square root is the *standard deviation* S_X

$$S^2 = S_X^2 = \frac{1}{N} \sum_{i=1}^{N} (X - M)^2 \quad \text{or} \quad S = \sqrt{1/N \, \Sigma (X - M)^2} \tag{4}$$

For any given set of data, Eq. (4) can be used to calculate the standard deviation. This requires two program loops, one for the sum required to compute the mean, the other for the sum of squared differences from the mean. A worthwhile saving in computation can be gained by first using a little algebra on Eq. (4). Expanding the square, factoring out M and its square from the sums, and using Eq. (2), the result is

$$S^2 = \left(\frac{1}{N} \sum X^2\right) - M_X^2 = \left(\frac{1}{N} \sum X^2\right) - \left(\frac{1}{N} \sum X\right)^2 \tag{5a}$$

The second form on the right indicates the promised improvement in efficiency, since values of X and X^2 may be summed within a single program loop.

The mean and standard deviation have the same physical units as the data values. It is worth noting, however, that neither need coincide with any of the data values.

If the same constant c is introduced arithmetically to every value of X, the variance is affected as follows as can be proved using Eq. (5a):

$$S_{X \pm c}^2 = S_X^2 \tag{5b}$$

$$S_{X/c}^2 = \frac{1}{c^2} S_X^2 \tag{5c}$$

A useful way to express the standard deviation is as the *coefficient of variation* that compares (by division) the standard deviation to the mean:

$$CV = \frac{S}{M} \tag{6}$$

It is sometimes necessary to merge two separate vectors of data X and Y into a single collection X,Y. What is the relation between the means of X and Y and the mean of the combined data? Similarly, what is the new standard deviation in terms of the individual ones? We shall derive the equation for the case of the mean and then state the result for the standard deviation. First, by definition, the mean of the joint data is

$$M_{X,Y} = \frac{\Sigma X + \Sigma Y}{N_X + N_Y} \tag{7}$$

Of course

$$M_X = \frac{1}{N_X}\sum X \quad \text{and} \quad M_Y = \frac{1}{N_Y}\sum Y \tag{8}$$

Solving for the sums in Eqs. (8), then substituting these into Eq. (7) gives

$$M_{X,Y} = \frac{N_X M_X + N_Y M_Y}{N_X + N_Y} \tag{9}$$

This basic rule for combining mean values also extends to more than two sets of data. The following special cases of interest follow from Eq. (9):

Equal means: $M_X = M_Y$

$$M_{X,Y} = M_X = M_Y \tag{10}$$

Equal number of data values: $N_X = N_Y$

$$M_{X,Y} = \frac{M_X + M_Y}{2} = \text{mean of the means} \tag{11}$$

To combine squared standard deviations, first note the definition

$$S_{X,Y}^2 = \frac{\Sigma(X - M_{X,Y})^2 + \Sigma(Y - M_{X,Y})^2}{N_X + N_Y} \tag{12}$$

By a process similar (although more involved algebraically) to that given above for mean values, the following is obtained for the squared standard deviation

$$S_{X,Y}^2 = \frac{N_X S_X^2 + N_Y S_Y^2}{N_X + N_Y} + \frac{N_X N_Y (M_X - M_Y)^2}{(N_X + N_Y)^2} \tag{13}$$

Some special cases follow from this general equation:

Equal means: $M_X = M_Y$

$$S_{X,Y}^2 = \frac{N_X S_X^2 + N_Y S_Y^2}{N_X + N_Y} \tag{14}$$

Note the similarity to Eq. (9) for means

Equal number of data values: $N_X = N_Y$

$$S_{X,Y}^2 = \frac{S_X^2 + S_Y^2}{2} + \frac{(M_X - M_Y)^2}{4} \tag{15}$$

Example The following statistics are available for a certain computing center for the months of February, March, and April:

Month	No. Jobs	Mean Job Time	Std. Dev.
February	2000	10 min	4 min
March	3000	12 min	5 min
April	3000	15 min	6 min

(a) Find the mean and standard deviation of job times for the two-month period of February-March.

(b) Find the mean and standard deviation of job times for the three-month period February-March-April.

Solution

(a) Using Eq. (9)

$$M_{F,M} = \frac{(2000)(10) + (3000)(12)}{2000 + 3000} = 11.2 \text{ min}$$

Using Eq. (13)

$$S_{F,M}^2 = \frac{(2000)(4)^2 + (3000)(5)^2}{2000 + 3000} + \frac{(2000)(3000)(10 - 12)^2}{(2000 + 3000)^2}$$

$$S_{F,M} = 4.7$$

(b) Exercise for reader: [*Hint:* Consider (February-March) as one "pseudomonth" using above values calculated in (a).]

2-2 STANDARDIZED VARIABLES

Comparing data and functions of data can sometimes be greatly simplified by standardizing the form of the data values to better focus attention on certain differences. The following translation of X data, i.e., of every element of X, produces a new vector Z called a *standardized variable*

$$Z = \frac{X - M}{S} \tag{1}$$

Thus Z is the difference between X and mean X divided by the standard deviation. Since X,M,S have the same physical units, Z is dimensionless (without physical units).

Two further important properties of the standardized variable are

$$M_Z = 0 \tag{2}$$

$$S_Z = 1 \tag{3}$$

These may be easily established by substituting Eq. (1) into the previously stated definitions of mean and variance.

2-3 TYPES OF MEANS

The arithmetic mean is the most widely used of many kinds of mean values. Some other kinds of means are sometimes defined:

Geometric mean: $G = \sqrt[N]{X_1, X_2, \ldots, X_N}$ (1)

Harmonic mean: $H = \dfrac{N}{\Sigma 1/X} = \dfrac{1}{1/N\Sigma 1/X}$ (2)

Quadratic mean (root mean square or rms): $\text{rms} = \sqrt{M_{X^2}} = \sqrt{1/N\Sigma X^2}$ (3)

The rms is closely related to the standard deviation and arithmetic mean by the equation

$$\text{rms} = \sqrt{S_X^2 + M_X^2}$$ (4)

2-4 FREQUENCY-GROUPED DATA

One very important way to organize data for analysis is by use of the *frequency technique*. This can be done by the following procedure (Fig. 2-4.1):

1. Make a list of all distinct (nonduplicate) values of X and arrange them in increasing order. Call this vector of N' values X'. Thus

   $$X'_{i+1} > X'_i \quad i = 1, 2, \ldots, N'-1$$

2. Count the number of appearances (frequency) of each X'_i value in the data vector X. Call this count f_i.

   The *frequency distribution* consists of a pair of vectors $(X';f)$, the first vector giving all *distinct* data values in ascending order, and the second the number of times each value appears in the data. An alternative approach to obtaining the frequency function is first to *sort* the data X in nondecreasing order. Since repeating values will now be adjacent, it is a simple matter to count repetitions to obtain f and then to

Original data

$X = 1, 4, 12, 9, 3, 5, 4, 12, 9, 3, 4, 12, 1, 9, 3, 12$

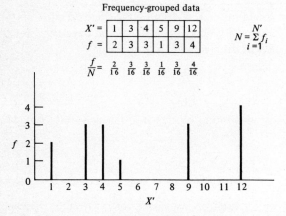

Fig. 2-4.1 Frequency-grouped data.

delete repetitions to obtain X'. Data organized in frequency distribution form is said to be *grouped*.

Since the sum of all f values counts all the values in the original data X, it follows

$$\sum_{i=1}^{N'} f_i = \sum f = N \tag{1}$$

$$\sum_{i=1}^{N'} \frac{f_i}{N} = \frac{1}{N}\sum f = 1 \tag{2}$$

The vector f/N is called the relative frequency vector and the function formed by vectors $(X'; f/N)$ is called the *relative frequency distribution*. Figure 2-4.1 shows some illustrative examples.

The *cumulative relative frequency* distribution is obtained by replacing f/N by the vector of partial sums of f/N. Its i component C_i gives, therefore, the fraction of the number of data values that are "less than or equal to" X_i

$$C_i = \frac{1}{N} \sum_{j=1}^{i} f_j \qquad i = 1, 2, \ldots, N' \tag{3a}$$

Another useful form easily obtainable from Eq. 3(a) is

$$C_i = C_{i-1} + \frac{f_i}{N} \qquad i = 1, 2, \ldots, N' \tag{3b}$$

where $C_0 = 0$. It follows from Eq. (2) that $C_{N'} = 1$.

If data is already in grouped form, the labor to compute various measures of central tendency can be significantly reduced. We now give some equations applicable to grouped data. Since the X' are ordered (sorted) it follows that

Range: $R_X = X'_1, X'_{N'}$ $\tag{4}$

Since each X'_i value is found f_i times in X, the sum of all such values is $f_i X'_i$. It then follows that

Mean: $M = \dfrac{1}{N} \displaystyle\sum_{i=1}^{N'} f_i X'_i = \dfrac{\Sigma f X'}{\Sigma f}$ $\tag{5}$

Standard deviation (squared): $S^2 = \dfrac{1}{N} \displaystyle\sum_{i=1}^{N'} f_i (X'_i - M)^2$

$$= \left(\frac{1}{N}\sum f X'^2\right) - M^2 \tag{6}$$

Mode: $\text{Mode} = X'_{\underset{j}{\text{Max}}\,(f_j)}$ $\tag{7}$

The mode is (are) the value(s) of X' at the peak(s) of the frequency distribution.

Before considering further details of frequency grouping, we might well ask what are its advantages and disadvantages. One fundamental disadvantage is that in reorganizing the data, the original ordering is lost (unless of course a separate copy is made). Whether the original ordering is of any importance is another question whose answer must depend upon particular circumstances. A major advantage of frequency grouping is the reduction in storage space required to hold the data. As a simple extreme example, take the case where the data consists of 1000 numbers that happen to be identical in value. Stored as vector X, this requires 1000 cells of storage; in grouped form, only 2 cells are required—one for data value and one for the frequency (1000).

In most practical situations it is not necessary to develop frequencies of all actual data values—it suffices to count the occurrences in only certain *ranges* of data values. For example, suppose we expect the values of each X_i to lie in the range

$$0 \leqslant X \leqslant 1.00$$

and are willing to accept frequencies of those values that fall into intervals of say 0.1. It is helpful to visualize 10 buckets, each corresponding to an interval (class interval) of possible X values (Fig. 2-4.2). Associated with each bucket, say bucket i, will be three numbers:

L_i = lower limit of bucket interval

U_i = upper limit of bucket interval

f_i = count of number of data values falling in the bucket interval

Any given data value X_j will "fall into" the range of some bucket i where

$$L_i \leqslant X_j < U_i \tag{8}$$

Note that bucket i accounts for all values that would fall on the lower limit or above, up to but *not* including the upper limit value. The reason for not considering values equal to U_i as falling in bucket i is to avoid double counting, since U_i will also be L_{i+1}; i.e., the upper limit of each bucket is the lower limit of the next (Fig. 2-4.2). The final bucket is, however, defined to include its upper limit, since there is no bucket beyond and hence no danger of double counting.

Once the bucket limits have been established, it is conceptually simple to see how the frequency counters f_i are determined as the data vector X is processed. We

Original data

X = 0, .15, .20, .11, .77, .24, .70, .23, .28, .52, .10, .15, .75, .88, 1.0

Bucket organization: $R_1 = 0; R_2 = 1.0; \Delta = .1; m = 10$

Bucket # ➤	1	2	3	4	5	6	7	8	9	10
L	0	.1	.2	.3	.4	.5	.6	.7	.8	.9
U	.1	.2	.3	.4	.5	.6	.7	.8	.9	1.0
f	1	4	4	0	0	1	0	3	1	1

Fig. 2-4.2   Bucket (class) organized frequency-grouped.

shall say more about this shortly. For the moment, let us recapitulate a process of *bucket setup* in general terms:

1. Determine the *range* of the data

$$R_1 = \text{Min } X \quad R_2 = \text{Max } X \tag{9}$$

   If one or both range values are unknown, and a separate pass through the data is not feasible, R_1 and R_2 may be estimated and two extra buckets, one below R_1 and one above R_2, may be established to record the two frequencies of overflows.
2. Specify the bucket interval Δ (assumed the same for all buckets).
3. The total number of buckets is then given by

$$m = \lceil \frac{(R_2 - R_1)}{\Delta} \quad \text{where } \lceil \text{ means } \textit{nearest equal} \text{ or } \textit{higher integer} \tag{10}$$

4. The limits of each bucket are obtained by

$$L_1 = R_1 \tag{11}$$

$$L_i = L_{i-1} + \Delta = R_1 + (i - 1)\Delta \quad i = 2, 3, \ldots, m$$

$$U_i = \text{Min } (R_2, (L_i + \Delta)) \tag{12}$$

This particular setup process requires the user to specify the range of data values and the bucket interval—all else in the bucket setup is computed from these. In practice, the range may not be known by the user at setup time, in which case it may be found from search of the data or else estimated by some "feel" for data values. In some cases, the user would like to specify directly the number of buckets (m) rather than the interval. The interval is then determined by

$$\Delta = \frac{R_2 - R_1}{m} \tag{13}$$

Afterwards, the limits are computed by the above step 4.

It is worth noting that the bucket setup process, while requiring some crude knowledge of the properties of the data, has the nice feature that it is independent of the number of data values.

Suppose the bucket intervals have already been defined and all bucket frequencies initially set to zero. Consider two ways of actually constructing a frequency distribution of data X. In the *search method*, each X_k is used to search the numbers L (the lower end of each bucket range) until the last bucket is reached whose L value is less than or equal to the data value X_k. The f value corresponding to this bucket is then increased by 1. In symbols:

$$j \leftarrow \underset{i}{\text{Max}} (L_i \leqslant X_k) \tag{14a}$$

$$f_j \leftarrow f_j + 1 \tag{14b}$$

The *index transformation method* is another technique that is, however, only applicable where buckets are of equal width. In this common case, it completely avoids searching the bucket ranges and thus saves computer time. Instead, each data value is transformed into an integer index identifying the bucket; the frequency for this bucket is then incremented by 1. To be more precise, to construct the frequency vector for data X, first initialize all counters to zero ($f = 0$). Then for *each* data number X_k, compute i, the bucket index, as the smaller of m (and 1 plus the nearest equal or lower integer to $(X_k - R_1)/\Delta$)

$$i = \text{Min}\left[m, \left[1 + \llcorner\left(\frac{X_k - R_1}{\Delta}\right)\right]\right] \qquad (15a)$$

then update the frequency of bucket i

$$f_i \leftarrow f_i + 1 \qquad (15b)$$

The bucket idea may also be used for functions other than the frequency. For example, each bucket may be used to hold the running sum of the data values that lie in the range of the bucket. This permits easy computation of the mean value for the bucket interval.

Certain conventions and terminology are commonly used for plotting or displaying frequency functions. A *histogram* (Fig. 2-4.3) is a plot with the following characteristics:

1. The horizontal (X' or X) axis is labeled with the midpoints of each bucket range.
2. The frequency of each bucket is plotted as a rectangle with its width equal to the bucket interval; its lower base on the X axis is centered on the midpoint value.
3. The rectangle *area* is proportional to the frequency. For equal-range buckets, the widths of all rectangles will be the same and the heights can be simply the frequency values (or else relative frequencies). If straight lines are used to connect the center points of the tops of successive rectangles of the histogram, the resulting continuous (but jerky) curve is called a *frequency polygon.*

The same kind of rectangular plot may be applied to display cumulative frequency information. (The polygon version is called an *ogive* plot.) The vertical coordinate then gives the fraction of the number of data points whose values are less than the value at the upper end of the bucket range.

Example Suppose we are given a tree structure, as shown in Fig. 2-4.4, that may be encountered in keeping records on parts needed for assemblies, subassemblies, sub-subassemblies, etc. Each node represents a disk storage address (pointer) to data and also pointers to successor nodes in the tree structure. The structure is used by a program which is passed a node label; the program then searches the structure for the match with the given label. Assuming

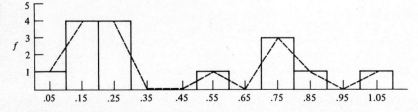

Fig. 2-4.3 Histogram for data of Fig. 2-4.2.

one access when passing through each node, the number of accesses needed to reach any given node is easily determined from the diagram and is recorded as vector A. Suppose now that after observing 100 searches, the number of times each node was requested is recorded in vector F. Find, for the number of accesses:

1. Mean
2. Median (see Sec. 2-6)
3. Standard deviation
4. Coefficient of variation
5. Frequency distribution
6. Cumulative relative frequency distribution

The solution to this problem is shown in Fig. 2-4.4.

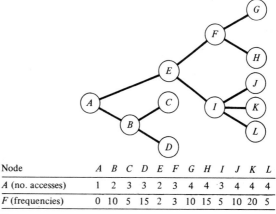

Node	A	B	C	D	E	F	G	H	I	J	K	L
A (no. accesses)	1	2	3	3	2	3	4	4	3	4	4	4
F (frequencies)	0	10	5	15	2	3	10	15	5	10	20	5

Mean

$$M_A = \frac{\Sigma FA}{\Sigma F} = \frac{348}{100} = 3.48 \qquad [\text{by Eq. (5)}]$$

Median

A' (distinct values in order) →	1	2	3	4
F →	0	12	28	60
Cumulative relative frequency	0	.12	.4	1.0

From A', F, the mid value (median) is 4

Standard deviation

$$N = \Sigma F = 100$$

$$S = \sqrt{1/N \, \Sigma F(A' - M_A)^2} \quad = .6697 \;\; [\text{by Eq. (6)}]$$

Coefficient of variation

$$CV = \frac{S}{M_A} = .20107$$

Fig. 2-4.4 Some tree search statistics (example).

```
C    RANDOM NUMBER GENERATOR
C    IX=123 (SAY) FOR FIRST CALL ON RANDU
C       USE IY FOR IX FOR SUBSEQUENT CALLS
C    IY=INTEGER RANDOM NO. GENERATED (BETW. 0 AND 2**31)
C    YFL=FRACTION RANDOM NO. GENERATED (BETW. 0 AND 1)
     SUBROUTINE RANDU(IX,IY,YFL)
     IY=IX*65539
     IF(IY) 5,6,6
   5 IY=IY+2147483647+1
   6 YFL=IY
     YFL=YFL*.4656613E-9
     RETURN
     END
```

Fig. 2-5.1 Random-number generator (IBM scientific subroutine package
　　　　(H20–0205)).

2-5 SIMULATION OF OBSERVATIONS FROM FREQUENCY FUNCTIONS
　　　[Refs. IB,KN]

As discussed previously, a frequency function is a compact way of representing voluminous data for many purposes. It is, however, sometimes necessary to do the inverse of such compaction, i.e., to generate data values *from* a frequency function. For example this need arises if we wish to *simulate a system* whose workload is described by one or more distribution functions. The simulation requires simulated data values describing each unit of work to be sent through the simulator's program. For example, the simulator may require the arrival time and service time for each simulated job. These are to be obtained from distribution functions received from prior measurement. We now turn to the mechanics of using a frequency function to generate such data. Assume that a *cumulative relative frequency* function $C(X)$ is available for data values X. The X values may lie in any range, but $C(X)$, being a relative frequency, ranges from 0 to 1. From a programming viewpoint, X and $C(X)$ may be represented as a table of *number pairs*. We now wish to use $C(X)$ to generate random instances of X values in such a way that, if enough values are so generated, their cumulative relative frequency distribution will approach $C(X)$.

　　　To generate random X values satisfying this condition, first assume that a standard type of random-number generator is available which generates, on each call, a random number in the interval

$$0 \leqslant y \leqslant 1$$

Each random number has a *flat* distribution, i.e., its relative frequency distribution is a horizontal line which indicates that the probabilities of every possible number in the interval are equal. The subject of random-number generators is quite profound.† Figure 2-5.1 shows a FORTRAN random-number generator. The y value produced by the random-number generator is then used to generate a synthetic data value as follows (see Fig. 2-5.2):

† See the article by D. E. Knuth, Ref. 8.

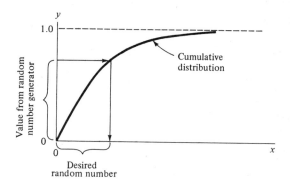

Fig. 2-5.2 Generating random numbers from a given
(cumulative) distribution.

1. Call the flat random-number generator. We designate the value it produces as y.
2. Use y to find the matching (or interpolated) value of $C(x)$.
3. The corresponding value of x is then a desired synthetic data value.

In the case where the cumulative distribution is available analytically, a process similar to that above can be done as follows:

Example   Consider the analytically specified exponential distribution

$$C(x) = y = 1 - e^{-0.04\,x}$$

To generate a synthetic data value x from this distribution, it is convenient first to solve *analytically* for x and to obtain the *inverse function*

$$x = -25\ \ln(1 - y)$$

It is then easy to follow the above stated procedure:

1. Call the flat random-number generator. Suppose it gives a value of, say, $y = 0.2$.
2. Substitute 0.2 for y in the inverse function and obtain x:

$$x = -25\ \ln(1 - 0.2)$$
$$= (25)(0.22314) = 5.5785$$

2-6 MEDIAN AND QUANTILES

The median of X is that value for which there are as many values equal or larger as there are equal or smaller. To find the median, sort the values of X in increasing (more accurately nondecreasing) order; call the result vector X''. It follows that

$$X''_{i+1} \geqslant X''_i \quad \text{for} \quad 1 \leqslant i \leqslant N \tag{1}$$

The median of X is then defined as a single expression covering the cases of N even or odd

$$\text{Median} = \frac{X''_{1 + \llcorner N/2} + X''_{\llcorner (N+1)/2}}{2}$$

where $\llcorner$ means "nearest equal or lowest integer." That is,

$$\text{Median} = X''_{\frac{N+1}{2}} \qquad \text{for } N \text{ odd} \tag{2a}$$

$$= \frac{X''_{N/2} + X''_{N/2+1}}{2} \qquad \text{for } N \text{ even} \tag{2b}$$

In other words, after sorting X values, the median is the value in the center position in the case of an odd number of values and the average of the two center values in the case of an even number of values. For N even, the median need not be a member of X.

The median is often a better single descriptor than the mean when the data contains a few very large values as is often the case, for example, with incomes. Thus, consider a committee of five people with salaries $8,000, $9,000, $11,000, $12,000, and $85,000. The mean salary is $25,000 and the median is $11,000. Clearly the median gives a much better indication of the salary composition of this committee than the mean.

Suppose now that the original data has been organized into a relative frequency distribution and a cumulative relative frequency distribution, using some specified bucket scheme. All this information can be represented by the following vectors, which may be visualized as columns of a table:

L lower limits of buckets
U upper limits of buckets
f/N relative frequencies
C cumulative relative frequencies

If we are presented with a data value x and are then asked: To which bucket does it belong? The answer is bucket j, given by Eq. (14a) of Sec. 2-4.

$$j = \operatorname*{Max}_i (L_i \leqslant x)$$

If we wish to know what fraction of the total number of data values are less than or equal to x, we proceed as will now be described. A crude first estimate to this percentage is C_{j-1}. This is the cumulative relative frequency for bucket $j-1$ (for $j-1=0$, take $C_0 = 0$). But, C_{j-1} is almost always an underestimate, since it really gives the fraction of the total number of data values that lie in all buckets below the bucket containing x. In bucket j, which includes x, f_j data values are counted, but we cannot tell from the distribution exactly how many of these are less than or equal to the x value. However, an estimate of this number is possible by linear interpolation, which amounts to assuming that the f_j values are uniformly spread throughout the bucket j range. With this assumption, the interpolation giving the number of values in the bucket below or equal to x is f_j times the fraction of the bucket interval below x. The complete formula for F, the fraction of values less than or equal to x, is then

$$j = \operatorname*{Max}_i (L_i \leqslant x) \tag{3a}$$

$$F = C_{j-1} + \frac{(x - L_j)f_j}{U_j - L_j} = C_{j-1} + \frac{x - L_j}{U_j - L_j}(C_j - C_{j-1}) \tag{3b}$$

Instead of expressing the relative ranking of a data value as the fraction or decimal F, it is common practice and often convenient to give this ranking information in terms of the integer q, which specifies the bucket number in which it falls in a Q-way bucket scheme. The most popular Q values are $Q = 4,10,100$, which are called respectively: quartiles, deciles, and percentiles. To convert a fraction or decimal rank F to a q value

$$q = 1 + \lfloor FQ \tag{4}$$

To illustrate, if data x is such that it is found by Eq. (3) to have an $F = 0.3$, Eq. (4) expresses with $Q = 4,10,100$ the relative rank of x as being in the second quartile, fourth decile, or thirty-first percentile. Clearly, the choice of Q value for expression is arbitrary, although the above mentioned schemes are by far the most common. The generic term for the possible Q values is *quantiles*.

2-7 MEASURES OF SYMMETRY

Plots of frequency distributions often exhibit certain general characteristics such as:

1. *Modality* (number of peaks)
2. *Skewness* (degree of asymmetry)

Skewness usually shows up as a less rapid decrease in frequency values to one side of the peak (mode) than the other. The less rapidly decreasing region is called the *longer tail*.

Two common quantitative measures of skewness involve the difference between the mean and a central value (mode or median). These are called Pearson's first and second coefficients of skewness

$$P_1 = (\text{mean} - \text{mode})/\text{standard deviation} \tag{1}$$

$$P_2 = 3\,(\text{mean} - \text{median})/\text{standard deviation} \tag{2}$$

For example, a distribution that is skewed to the right, i.e., falls off slower to the right of the peak (mode) than to the left, may be expected to have its mean to the right, and hence higher than the mode. P_1 is then seen to be positive. It will be zero when mode and median coincide, and negative when the mode is higher than the mean.

2-8 MEAN AND VARIANCE OF THE SUM OF TWO VARIABLES: CORRELATION

Consider two vectors of data X and Y with equal number of values in each. Suppose now we add the corresponding values of the two vectors, i.e., $X + Y$. This results in a new data vector with its own mean and variance. These will be denoted M_{X+Y} and S_{X+Y}^2. We now seek to express M_{X+Y} and S_{X+Y}^2 in terms of M_X, M_Y, S_X, S_Y.

The case of the mean is fairly easy: simply apply the definition of the mean to the case at hand and do some simple algebra

$$M_{X+Y} = \frac{1}{N}\Sigma(X + Y)$$

$$= \frac{1}{N}\Sigma X + \frac{1}{N}\Sigma Y$$

It follows that the mean of the sum distribution equals the sum of the means

$$M_{X+Y} = M_X + M_Y \tag{1}$$

For standardized variables, since the means are zero

$$M_{Z_{X+Y}} = M_{Z_X} + M_{Z_Y} = 0 + 0 = 0 \tag{2}$$

The variance of the sum of two variables is a bit more complex to derive. Start with the general definition for variance and then substitute the sum $X + Y$ for the variable

$$S_{X+Y}^2 = \frac{1}{N}\Sigma(X + Y - M_{X+Y})^2$$

Using Eq. (1) for M_{X+Y}, regroup terms

$$S_{X+Y}^2 = \frac{1}{N}\Sigma[(X - M_X) + (Y - M_Y)]^2$$

By expanding the square, but in so doing keeping the differences intact,

$$S_{X+Y}^2 = \frac{1}{N}\Sigma[(X - M_X)^2 + (Y - M_Y)^2 + 2(X - M_X)(Y - M_Y)]$$

By distributing the summation through the sum and using the definitions

$$S_X^2 = \frac{1}{N}\Sigma(X - M_X)^2 \quad \text{and} \quad S_Y^2 = \frac{1}{N}\Sigma(Y - M_Y)^2$$

plus a new definition, the *covariance* of X, Y,

$$\text{COV}(X, Y) = \frac{1}{N}\Sigma(X - M_X)(Y - M_Y) \tag{3}$$

we can then express the variance of a sum as

$$S_{X+Y}^2 = S_X^2 + S_Y^2 + 2\,\text{COV}(X, Y) \tag{4}$$

Using Eq. (3), the definition of the covariance, but substituting the standardized variables for X and Y,

$$\text{COV}(Z_X, Z_Y) = \frac{1}{N}\Sigma(Z_X - M_{Z_X})(Z_Y - M_{Z_Y}) \tag{5}$$

Since the means of the standardized variables are zero

$$\text{COV}(Z_X, Z_Y) = \frac{\Sigma Z_X Z_Y}{N} \tag{6}$$

We are now ready to derive the relationship between the covariance of two variables X, Y and the corresponding covariance of the standardized variables Z_X, Z_Y. Recalling the definitions of the standardized variables

$$X - M_X = S_X Z_X \quad \text{and} \quad Y - M_Y = S_Y Z_Y \tag{7}$$

substitute these into Eq. (5) while factoring out the common factors S_X, S_Y to obtain

$$\text{COV}(X, Y) = \frac{S_X S_Y \Sigma Z_X Z_Y}{N} = S_X S_Y \text{ COV}(Z_X, Z_Y) \tag{8}$$

where the last simplification uses Eq. (6).

The covariance of the standardized variables is called the *correlation r*. Thus

$$r = \text{COV}(Z_X, Z_Y) = \frac{\text{COV}(X, Y)}{S_X S_Y} \tag{9}$$

Another form for r, called the *product-moment formula*, is then seen to be

$$r = \frac{\Sigma(X - M_X)(Y - M_Y)}{N S_X S_Y} = \frac{\Sigma(X - M_X)(Y - M_Y)}{\sqrt{[\Sigma(X - M_X)^2][\Sigma(Y - M_Y)^2]}}$$

$$= \frac{\Sigma xy}{\sqrt{\Sigma x^2 \Sigma y^2}} \tag{10}$$

where $x = X - M_x$ and $y = Y - M_y$. The values of r lie in the range

$$-1 \leqslant r \leqslant 1$$

If $r = 0$, the X and Y data are said to be *uncorrelated*.

Equation (9) may be used to express Eq. (4) in the form

$$S_{X+Y}^2 = S_X^2 + S_Y^2 + 2r S_X S_Y \tag{11}$$

This equation bears a striking algebraic resemblance to the law of cosines in geometry that relates c^2 (the square of the length of one side of a triangle) to the sum of squares of the other sides a, b and to the cosine of the angle C opposite side c.

As a special case of Eq. (11), if two variables have the same distributions and hence the same standard deviations, but are uncorrelated ($r = 0$),

$$S_{X+Y} = \sqrt{2} S_X \tag{12}$$

More generally, for the sum of K-uncorrelated distributions all with the same standard deviation, the standard deviation of the distribution of the sum variable is

$$S = \sqrt{K} S_X \tag{13}$$

2-9 LEAST SQUARE CURVE FITTING: REGRESSION [Refs. DA,DR]

It is recalled that one purpose of statistics is to represent many numbers by a few numbers. One way to do this is to "fit" an analytic function like a polynomial to the data. Once this is done, only the few coefficients of the polynomial need be stored to represent the data, at least for some purposes; pseudodata values may be computed as needed using the polynomial. This section derives a common method for fitting polynomials (including a straight line) to data.

Let us begin with two data vectors X, Y each containing the same number (N) of data elements. Usually, the data is such that we suspect some relationship between the vectors, as for example, run time and the number of bytes of a program. Each X_i value and the corresponding Y_i value can be considered coordinates of a point on an X,Y plot. The entire collection of points is called a *scatter plot* (Fig. 2-9.1).

Suppose now it is desired to draw a straight line on the scatter plot in such a way that it is a "best" fit to the points of data. The notion of "best" arises because it is clearly impossible for a straight line to pass through *all* the points (except for the very rare case where the data points all fall on the line). Hence, no matter how the line is drawn, there will in general be some error (or difference) between each Y data value and the corresponding ordinate on the line. We now proceed to define what we mean by one kind of "best" fit. The equation of *any* line used to estimate the data will have the *form*

$$Y_e = a_0 + a_1 X \qquad (1)$$

where Y_e is the estimated ordinate corresponding to X. Note that the parameters a_0, a_1 are at the moment unknown in value.

The mean-square error between the line and the data is also called the *standard error of estimate* and is given by the mean of the squared differences between the data values Y and the corresponding Y_e values on the approximating line

$$E^2 = \frac{1}{N} \Sigma (Y - Y_e)^2 \qquad (2)$$

Using Eq. (1) for Y_e

$$E^2 = \frac{1}{N} \Sigma (Y - a_0 - a_1 X)^2 \qquad (3)$$

We now seek to find those values of a_0, a_1 such that the mean-square error is minimized. This can be done, using calculus, by setting the two partial derivatives of E^2 (with respect to a_0 and a_1) to zero. The a_0, a_1 that result are then found to be the solutions to the linear equations (in a_0, a_1) called *normal equations*

$$\Sigma Y = a_0 N + a_1 \Sigma X \qquad (4)$$

$$\Sigma YX = a_0 \Sigma X + a_1 \Sigma X^2 \qquad (5)$$

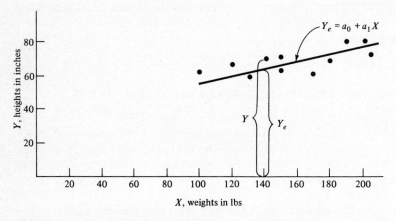

Fig. 2-9.1   Scatter plot and regression line.

Solving these two linear equations for a_0 and a_1:

$$a_0 = \frac{(\Sigma Y)(\Sigma X^2) - (\Sigma XY)(\Sigma X)}{D} \tag{6}$$

and

$$a_1 = \frac{(N\Sigma YX) - (\Sigma X)(\Sigma Y)}{D} \tag{7}$$

where

$$D = (N\Sigma X^2) - (\Sigma X)(\Sigma X) \tag{8}$$

Using Eqs. (6), (7), and (8) for a_0, a_1 in Eq. (1), the line thus determined is called the *regression line*. It is that line, of all possible straight lines, whose mean-square deviation from all data points is a minimum. The regression line has a number of interesting and useful properties.

Theorem 2-9.1 The regression line passes through the intersection of the X, Y mean values (M_X, M_Y).

Proof
1. The first normal equation Eq. (4) may be divided by N giving

$$M_Y = a_0 + a_1 M_X$$

2. From Eq. (1), M_X, M_Y is then a point on the regression line.

Theorem 2-9.2 The standard error of estimate, i.e., the mean-square error between data Y and the line Y_e is

$$E^2 = \frac{1}{N}\Sigma(Y - Y_e)^2 = \frac{1}{N}(\Sigma Y^2 - a_0\Sigma Y - a_1\Sigma XY) \tag{9}$$

Proof
1. By definition

$$E^2 = \frac{1}{N}\Sigma(Y - Y_e)^2 = \frac{1}{N}\Sigma(Y - a_0 - a_1 X)^2$$

2. Expanding the square

$$E^2 = \frac{1}{N}[\Sigma Y(Y - a_0 - a_1 X) - a_0\Sigma(Y - a_0 - a_1 X)$$
$$- a_1\Sigma X(Y - a_0 - a_1 X)]$$

3. The second and third sums are zero by substitution of the normal equations, Eqs. (4) and (5), hence Eq. (9).

Theorem 2-9.3 With the new variables x, y defined by

$$x = X - M_X \tag{10}$$

and

$$y = Y - M_Y \tag{11}$$

the regression line may be written

$$y = a_1 x \quad \text{or} \quad Y - M_Y = a_1(X - M_X) \tag{12}$$

where

$$a_1 = \frac{\Sigma xy}{\Sigma x^2} \tag{13}$$

$$a_0 = M_Y - a_1 M_X \tag{14}$$

The proof follows from algebraic manipulation, using the above defining equations of x and y in the equations for a_0 and a_1. Theorem 2-9.3 expresses the fact that, since the point M_X, M_Y lies on the regression line, the origin of the coordinate system can be shifted to the point (M_X, M_Y) with resulting simplification of the equation of the regression line.

If a *parabola* rather than a straight line is used as the fitting curve, then the form of the approximating curve is

$$Y = a_0 + a_1 X + a_2 X^2 \tag{15}$$

The normal equations in this case are

$$\Sigma Y = a_0 N + a_1 \Sigma X + a_2 \Sigma X^2$$

$$\Sigma YX = a_0 \Sigma X + a_1 \Sigma X^2 + a_2 \Sigma X^3 \tag{16}$$

$$\Sigma YX^2 = a_0 \Sigma X^2 + a_1 \Sigma X^3 + a_2 \Sigma X^4$$

The above principle may be extended to a curve represented by a polynomial of any degree. The first normal equation is always the sum over the elements of the approximating curve. The second equation is the sum of products of X and the terms of the approximating curve. Each successive normal equation is obtained by multiplying the approximating equation by successive powers of X and summing over the products. This rule is easily seen to be satisfied for the cases of approximating line and parabola, as shown above.

Another type of generalization over the simple regression line is where a "linear fit" is sought, but where there are now several variables (instead of just X and Y). For the case of three variables X, Y, Z, the scatter plot is in three dimensions and the linear approximation is a *plane* whose equation is

$$Z = a_0 + a_1 X + a_2 Y \tag{17}$$

where a_0, a_1, and a_2 satisfy the normal equations

$$\Sigma Z = a_0 N + a_1 \Sigma X + a_2 \Sigma Y$$

$$\Sigma ZX = a_0 \Sigma X + a_1 \Sigma X^2 + a_2 \Sigma YX \tag{18}$$

$$\Sigma ZY = a_0 \Sigma Y + a_1 \Sigma XY + a_2 \Sigma Y^2$$

Note that these equations may be remembered as following a similar rule stated above for the case of two variables with an approximating polynomial instead of a straight line.

For generalization of the simple two-variable linear fit to either a higher-degree curve or to a linear relation between many variables, the coefficients in the equations for the approximating curve or surface are found by solving linear simultaneous equations, as seen above.

2-10 MORE ON REGRESSION LINES AND CORRELATION

The mean-square difference of data Y from its mean M_Y may be expressed in the form

$$\Sigma(Y - M_Y)^2 = N S_Y^2 \tag{1}$$

The sum on the left may be shown (by algebra) to be expressible as two sums:

$$\Sigma(Y - M_Y)^2 = \Sigma(Y - Y_e)^2 + \Sigma(Y_e - M_Y)^2 \tag{2}$$

where the first sum on the right is sometimes called the *unexplained variation*, and the second term is called the *explained variation*. These designations may be understood as follows. After the a_0, a_1 have been found for data Y, the regression line, and hence all points on it, is completely determined. The differences $Y_e - M_y$ are then between the law of a straight line and the mean value. The differences $(Y - Y_e)$, however, represent the deviations of actual data Y and the regression line, which need follow no definite law (and hence is "unexplained").

The ratio of explained variation to total variation is

$$r^2 = \frac{\text{explained variation}}{\text{total variation}} = \frac{\Sigma(Y_e - M_Y)^2}{\Sigma(Y - M_Y)^2} \tag{3}$$

This ratio will now be shown to be none other than the square of the correlation coefficient (also called r) discussed in Sec. 2-8 and given in Eq. (10) of that section. To show this, we start with Eq. (3) above and manipulate it algebraically to equal the product-moment formula for r^2 [Eq. (10), Sec. 2-8]. First note that the denominator of Eq. (3) is Σy^2. The squared difference in the numerator sum of Eq. (3) may be expressed in terms of the x, y variables using Eq. (12) of Sec. 2-8. Equation (3) may then be written

$$r^2 = \frac{\Sigma a_1^2 x^2}{\Sigma y^2} = \frac{a_1^2 \Sigma x^2}{\Sigma y^2} \tag{4}$$

Substituting the x, y form for a_1^2 from Eq. (13) of Sec. 2-9 and simplifying gives

$$r^2 = \frac{(\Sigma xy)^2}{(\Sigma x^2)(\Sigma y^2)} \tag{5}$$

which is equal to Eq. (10) of Sec. 2-8. Note the symmetry with respect to x and y, which means that the correlation coefficient for X vs. Y is the same as for Y vs. X.

Although Eq. (5) is a relatively simple algebraic form for r^2, since it is in terms of x, y that require prior computation of the means of X and Y, at least two program loops are required. An alternative form enables r^2 to be computed from the data vectors X and Y within a single loop that also can include calculation of the means and standard deviations:

$$r = \frac{(N\Sigma XY) - (\Sigma X)(\Sigma Y)}{\sqrt{[(N\Sigma X^2) - (\Sigma X)^2][(N\Sigma Y^2) - (\Sigma Y)^2]}} \tag{6}$$

The following is a valuable property of the correlation coefficient.

Theorem 2-10.1: The standard error of estimate E, i.e., the root-mean squared difference of the data from the regression line may be expressed in terms of only the correlation coefficient and standard deviation

$$E^2 = (1 - r^2)S_y^2 \tag{7}$$

Proof By definition

$$E^2 = \frac{1}{N}\Sigma(Y_e - Y)^2 = \frac{1}{N}\Sigma(y_e - y)^2 \tag{8}$$

where $y_e = Y_e - M_y$ and $y = Y - M_y$. Also, from Eq. (12) of Sec. 2-9

$$y_e = a_1 x \tag{9a}$$

$$a_1 = \frac{\Sigma xy}{\Sigma x^2} \tag{9b}$$

Expanding the square on the right of Eq. (8) and substituting Eqs. (9)

$$E^2 = \frac{1}{N}\left[\frac{(\Sigma xy)^2}{\Sigma x^2} - \frac{2(\Sigma xy)^2}{\Sigma x^2} + \Sigma y^2\right] \tag{10}$$

Combining like terms and using the product-moment formula for r [Eq. (5)], Eq. (10) may be written

$$E^2 = \frac{1}{N}(1 - r^2)\Sigma y^2 = (1 - r^2)S_y^2 \quad \text{QED} \tag{11}$$

From Eq. (7), it is seen that

1. If $r = 1$ or -1, $E^2 = 0$; that is, all data points fall on the regression line.
2. If $r = 0$, then the standard error of estimate equals the standard deviation of Y.

The term *correlation coefficient* for r suggests that r can be interpreted as some sort of measure of relatedness between X and Y data. The following points should be made about this; verify them using the above formulas and their derivations.

1. The range of r is
   $$-1 \leqslant r \leqslant 1$$
2. If r is close to 1, this means that as X increases, Y tends to increase linearly. If r is close to -1, as X increases, Y tends to decrease linearly. (In either case, there is *no implication that X is the cause of Y or vice versa*. However, if they are causally related in a linear way, then r will be close to $+1$ or -1.)
3. If r is close to 0, this means that there is a poor *linear* relationship between X and Y data. However, there may still be a relationship through a type curve other than a straight line.

REFERENCES AND BIBLIOGRAPHY

1. [DA] Daniel, C. and F.S. Wood: "Fitting Equations to Data," John Wiley and Sons, Inc., New York, 1971.
2. [DR] Draper, N.R. and H. Smith: "Applied Regression Analysis," John Wiley and Sons, Inc., New York, 1967.
3. [FR] Freiberger, W. (Ed): "Statistical Computer-Performance Evaluation," Academic Press, New York, 1972.
4. [HA] Hahn, G.J. and S.S. Shapiro: "Statistical Models in Engineering," John Wiley and Sons, Inc., New York, 1968.
5. [HAN] Hanssmann, F., W. Kistler, and H. Schultz: Modelling for Computing Center Planning, *IBM Systems Journal*, vol. 10, no. 4, 1971.
6. [HI] Hickman, E.P. and J.G. Hilton: "Probability and Statistical Analysis," Intext Publ. Co., 1971.
7. [IB] IBM Corp.: "Random Number Generation and Testing," Document #C20-8011, IBM Corp., 112 E. Post Rd., White Plains, N.Y.
8. [KN] Knuth, D.E.: "The Art of Computer Programming," vol. 2, Seminumerical Algorithms, Chapter 3, Random Numbers, Addison-Wesley Publishing Company, Reading, Mass., 1969.
9. [MA] Margolin, B.H., R.P. Parmalee, and M. Schatzoff: Analysis of Free-Storage Algorithms, *IBM Systems Journal*, vol. 10, no. 4, 1971.
10. [PA] Parzen, E.: "Modern Probability Theory and Its Applications," John Wiley and Sons, Inc., New York, 1960.
11. [SP] Spiegel, M.R.: "Statistics," Schaum's Outline Series, McGraw-Hill Book Company, New York, 1961.
12. [ST] Stanley, W.I. and H.F. Hertel: Statistics Gathering and Simulation for the Apollo Real-Time Operating System, *IBM Systems Journal*, vol. 7, no. 2, pp. 85-102, 1968.

CHAPTER 3

Topics in Discrete Mathematics and Applications

The digital computer is essentially a processor of discrete symbols arranged into various types of "strings." For example, the representation of a number is a string of digit, sign, and punctuation symbols; even an entire program may be considered as a long string of symbols. Discrete mathematics is the area of mathematics that deals with various theories of strings of symbols, each symbol being a member of some prespecified alphabet. In computer work we call an alphabet a *character-set*. Topics in discrete mathematics include permutations, combinations, recursion, and some (but not all) of the theories of sets and probability. It is also of interest to note that proofs of theorems are also strings of symbols, and hence the theory of proofs is a topic of discrete mathematics.

In this chapter we present a brief but serious account of selected topics in discrete mathematics; there will also be occasions when we shall use continuous mathematical techniques such as calculus. Our aims are

1. To illustrate the kind of thinking that underlies much of the theory of system analysis, including computer performance.
2. To derive and list certain notation and results. Some of these will be used later in this book; others, which are not used here, are nevertheless of general interest and will help the reader in the study of theoretical papers in the literature.

The first few sections discuss principles of combinatorial analysis, i.e., methods of counting symbol strings constructed according to certain rules. We next go on to the theory of sets, from which we consider functions and recursion. Both combinatorial analysis and sets are not only important subjects in their own right, they are also essential to the major topic of this chapter—probability theory. Throughout, we shall use examples from everyday life as well as from computer systems. The final sections of this chapter focus on a single system-analysis application of probability— the theory of reliability.

3-1 ELEMENTARY COMBINATORIAL ANALYSIS: PERMUTATIONS AND COMBINATIONS

In all that follows, we assume there is a prespecified alphabet that lists all possible single symbols to be used to form strings. By the *size* of the alphabet, we simply mean the number of symbols it contains. For example, for symbol strings that are the recordings of the up-face from the tossing of a single die, the alphabet is

$\{1, 2, 3, 4, 5, 6\}$

and the alphabet size is 6.

Suppose some rule is stated for forming symbol strings. How many distinct strings can be formed using this rule? By *distinct* we mean that for any given rule, we never count identical strings more than once. Unless otherwise stated, the term *number of strings* shall mean *number of distinct strings*. Although there are innumerable possible rules of string formation, there are two properties that occur so frequently that they are worth highlighting:

1. *Symbol repetition*: The same symbol is (is not) permitted to appear more than once in a string.
2. *Ordering significance*: Different orderings of the same symbols are (are not) considered as distinct strings to be counted.

Although these properties are important and helpful, the reader is cautioned that there are no universal panaceas in solving combinatorial problems. The subject is full of traps; a seemingly slight change in the statement of a problem can not only alter the answer significantly, it can require a different solution method.

A basic idea is the *product rule*, since with care, several of the subsequent formulas may be derived from it.

Theorem 3-1.1 Product rule Given two alphabets A and B with n_1 and n_2 symbols, respectively. The number of strings of length 2 that can be formed with the first symbol from alphabet A and the second from B is

$$N = n_1 n_2 \tag{1}$$

This formula for the number of strings (we shall always mean distinct strings) may be understood by imagining a process for generating strings. The first symbol may be chosen as any of n_1 symbols; for *each* of these, the second may be chosen from any of n_2. Hence we have n_1 times n_2 possible 2-strings.

Example In how many ways can a coin-toss *followed by* a throw of a die show their faces?

Solution For the coin, the alphabet is $\{h, t\}$. For the die, it is $\{1,2,3,4,5,6\}$.
Hence $n_1 = 2$, $n_2 = 6$. By Eq. (2)

$$N = 2 \times 6 = 12$$

Enumeration of these 12 strings:

$$\{h1, h2, h3, h4, h5, h6, t1, t2, t3, t4, t5, t6\}$$

Note that this model and the above results require each trial to be in the order "coin toss followed by die throw." This is why a string like $1h$ never appears.

The natural generalization of Theorem 3-1.1 is the following theorem.

Theorem 3-1.2 Given k alphabets of sizes $n_1, n_2, \ldots, n_k$. The number of strings of length k that may be formed by choosing each symbol from successive alphabets in a definite order is

$$N = \prod_{i=1}^{k} n_i \tag{2}$$

A very important special case of this result is where all the n_i are equal because all of the alphabets are the same. In that case, we use the same alphabet throughout.

Theorem 3-1.3 The number of strings k long that can be formed *with repetitions* from an alphabet of n symbols is

$$N = n^k \tag{3}$$

The importance of this case is illustrated by the following example. Consider the alphabet consisting of the 10 decimal digit symbols ($n = 10$)

$$D = \{0,1,2,3,4,5,6,7,8,9\}$$

If k is (say) 3, Eq. (3) then says that there are 10^3 possible strings. They are: $000,001,\ldots,999$, i.e., all possible 3-digit decimal numbers. Theorem 3-1.3 is then seen to be at the heart of the method of enumeration implicit in our positional number systems. As another example, consider a book with the following:

No. pages = 500
No. lines per page = 44
No. characters per line = 72
Alphabet size = 70

Here the alphabet includes lower- and uppercase letters, digits, blank, and various punctuation marks. Any such book can be considered as a long symbol string whose length is

$$k = 500 \times 44 \times 72 = 1{,}584{,}000 \text{ symbols}$$

The number of possible books of this class is then

$$N = 70^{1584000}$$

The size of this number is beyond human comprehension. It is very much larger than the number of electrons in the solar system! Yet it *is* a finite number. Further, we know how to enumerate all such strings systematically, and hence all such books, although it would require eons of time to do so. These books would include all the books of length k and of alphabet size 70 ever written or that ever will be written!

Theorem 3-1.3 counted strings in which repetitions of symbols are permitted; all strings containing the same number of each symbol in different orderings are counted as distinct. We next turn to the case where repetitions are again permitted, but where we do not count reordering.

Theorem 3-1.4 The number of strings k long that can be formed with repetitions from an alphabet of n symbols, but where different orderings of the same symbols do *not* count as distinct, is

$$D(n,k) = \frac{(n + k - 1)!}{k!(n - 1)!} \tag{4}$$

This number is sometimes called *the number of combinations of n things taken k at a time with repetitions*. In this case, two strings A and B are counted as distinct only if the number of appearances of at least one of their symbols is different in one string from the other. For example, the following strings are *not* both counted

abcbc
accbb

Consider next the formation of strings with *no repetitions* of the same symbol permitted in the same string.

Theorem 3-1.5 Permutations The number of strings of length k that can be formed from an alphabet of size n, with *no repetitions* permitted in any string and different orderings counted as distinct, is

$$P(n,k) = n(n - 1)(n - 2), \ldots, (n - k + 1) \quad \text{where } 0 \leqslant k \leqslant n \tag{5}$$

This result is easily understood using the product rule of Eq. (1). To begin to form a string, we can choose the first symbol as any of n in the alphabet. For any such choice, since repetitions are not permitted, the second symbol can be chosen in only $n - 1$ ways. By the product rule, the first two symbols can therefore be chosen in n times $(n - 1)$ ways. This same idea applied to successive symbols yields Eq. (5).

$P(n,k)$ of Eq. (4) is sometimes called *the number of permutations of n things taken k at a time* (*without repetition*). Its formula is often expressed in terms of the factorial function

$$P(n,k) = \frac{n!}{(n - k)!} \quad \text{where } 0 \leqslant k \leqslant n \tag{6}$$

A recursion form for Eq. (6) is easily derived

$$P(n,0) = 1$$

$$P(n,k) = (n - k + 1)P(n - k - 1) \quad \text{where } 1 \leqslant k \leqslant n$$

Example: In a certain computer installation, 20 jobs are run in a certain hour. A sample job stream consisting of 5 of these 20 jobs in a definite order is to be selected. How many such sample streams are there?

Solution: Consider the jobs labelled 1,2, . . . ,20 so that this is our alphabet. The number of strings of length 5 is then by Eq. (6)

$$P(20,5) = \frac{20!}{(20-5)!} = \frac{20!}{15!} = 20 \cdot 19 \cdot 18 \cdot 17 \cdot 16 = 1,860,480$$

A special but important case of Eq. (6) is when we wish to know the *number of ways* it is possible to order *n distinct things* (*no repetitions*). Using Eq. (6) with $k = n$:

$$P(n,n) = \frac{n!}{0!} = \frac{n!}{1} = n! \tag{7}$$

The scheme for forming permutations may be visualized as a tree (Fig. 3-1.1). Each string is enumerated by reading the node labels in a path from the far left to far right of the tree.

Another variation of permutations is where you wish the number of permutations in a circle with no particular symbol designated as the first. Then the number of such strings n long is $(n-1)!$

No symbol in any single string that is counted in permutations appears more than once. Different orderings of the same symbols are counted as distinct. The latter property is omitted to obtain *combinations* (without replacement).

Theorem 3-1.6 Combinations The number of strings of length k that can be formed from an alphabet of size n, with *no repetitions* permitted in any string and no string having all of the symbols found in any other (i.e., different orderings of the same symbols are *not* permitted), is found by

$$C(n,k) = \frac{n!}{k!(n-k)!} \qquad 0 \leqslant k \leqslant n \tag{8}$$

Also

$$C(n,k) = \frac{P(n,k)}{k!} \tag{9}$$

A recursion form for combinations is:

$$C(n,0) = 1 \tag{10a}$$

$$C(n,k) = \frac{n-(k-1)}{k} C(n,k-1) \qquad \text{where } 1 \leqslant k \leqslant n \tag{10b}$$

Several other notations for $C(n,k)$ sometimes found in the literature are

$$C(n,k) = \binom{n}{k} = {}_nC_k = \{k\}_n$$

$C(n,k)$ is a widely used primitive function in combinatorial analysis. It appears in a surprising number of different contexts, only a few of which will be discussed here.

To understand how Eq. (8) is derived, recall from Theorem 3-1.5 that the number of strings k long (without repetitions), counting ordering as distinct, is $P(n,k)$.

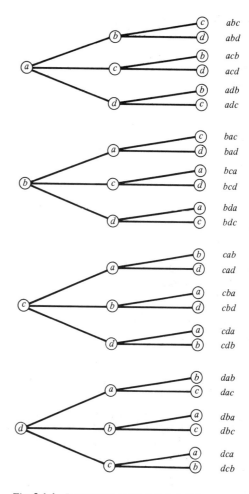

Fig. 3-1.1 Permutation tree $n = 4$, $k = 3$.

Now consider any particular string in the enumeration of permutations. The k-distinct symbols in this string may then be considered an alphabet of size k, and hence can be rearranged by Eq. (7) in $k!$ ways. Each string with the same symbols then belongs to a *set* of $k!$, such strings having different orderings of the same symbols. Dividing $P(n,k)$ by $k!$ then gives the number of such *sets*, and hence Eq. (9).

Example   Given five pigeonholes and three objects: One object is to be placed in one pigeonhole. In how many ways can this be done?

Solution   Label the pigeonholes 1,2,3,4,5. A "way" is then a string of three labels chosen from the label alphabet of five symbols without repetition, since there is no more than one object per pigeonhole.
Hence, by Eq. (9)

$$C(5,3) = \frac{5!}{3!\,2!} = 10$$

Another viewpoint of this problem is first to list all of the occupancy states of the pigeonholes. This is done by setting down a kind of truth table (Fig. 3-1.2) with column headings as the pigeonhole labels (1,2,3,4,5 in the above example). Each occupancy state is a row of the table composed of 0,1 values, the 1s designating which pigeonholes are occupied. The set of states with exactly three 1s then represents all of those with exactly three pigeonholes occupied. Hence

$C(n,k)$ = number of possible bit vectors n bits in length
      with exactly k 1s and $n - k$ 0s

The complete truth table listing for a given n and all k also justifies the important formula

$$\sum_{k=0}^{n} C(n,k) = 2^n \tag{11}$$

Yet another important meaning of $C(n,k)$ is the coefficient of the kth term (k starts at zero for the leftmost term) of the expansion of the binomial $(x + y)^n$

$$(x + y)^n = \sum_{k=0}^{n} C(n,k)x^{n-k}y^k \tag{12}$$

Example:

$$(x + y)^4 = 1x^4 + 4x^3y + 6x^2y^2 + 4xy^3 + y^4$$

The above property of $C(n,k)$ is why it is sometimes called the *binomial coefficient*.

The French mathematician Blaise Pascal (1623-1662) suggested an interesting way to display $C(n,k)$ values in the form of a triangle (pyramid). Row n (counting $n = 0$ at top) gives all the $C(n,k)$ for the $n+1$ values $k = 0,1,\dots,n$. When properly drawn, each entry (except those at the ends) is the sum of its two nearest neighbors in the row above (see Fig. 3-1.3).

Occupancy states: 3 of 5 pigeonholes filled

1	2	3	4	5	← Pigeonholes
0	0	1	1	1	
0	1	0	1	1	
0	1	1	0	1	
0	1	1	1	0	
1	0	0	1	1	Occupancy states
1	0	1	1	0	
1	0	1	0	1	
1	1	0	0	1	
1	1	0	1	0	
1	1	1	0	0	

No. of occupancy states for $n = 5$, $k = 3$
$C(5,3) = 10$

Fig. 3-1.2 States of occupancy of five pigeon-holes by three objects.

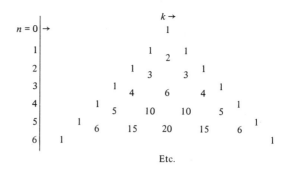

Fig. 3-1.3 Pascal's triangle for $C(n,k)$.

One generalization of the number of combinations of n things taken k at a time is embodied in the following theorem.

Theorem 3-1.7 Multinomial Strings of length k are to be formed from an alphabet of n symbols where each string must contain exactly k_1 repetitions (copies) of the first symbol, k_2 repetitions of the second, etc. The number of such distinct strings is

$$M(k_1, k_2, \ldots, k_n) = \frac{k!}{k_1! k_2!, \ldots, k_n!} \tag{13a}$$

where

$$k = \sum_{i=1}^{n} k_i \tag{13b}$$

A special case of the multinomial is where all the k_i are equal, say to m. Then Eq. (13a) becomes

$$N(m,n) = \frac{(nm)!}{(m!)^n} \tag{14}$$

Note the use of Eq. (13b) for k (since all $k_i = m$).

Example A bridge tournament of 20 people is to be divided into five groups of four people each. In how many ways can this be done?

Solution Imagine that each group is assigned a letter A through E. A "way" is a string of $nm = 20$ symbols (one per person), each chosen from an alphabet of $n = 5$ with $m = 4$ repetitions of each symbol. The number of such strings is then, using Eq. (14),

$$N(4, 5) = \frac{(20)!}{(4!)^5}$$

However, this is not quite the answer, since it counts as distinct strings, assigning people to the same groups but with the groups merely labelled differently. Since there are 5! ways of labelling five groups, our answer is

$$\frac{(20)!}{(5!)(4!)^5}$$

3-2 SETS: DEFINITIONS, SPECIFICATION, EQUALITY, EQUIVALENCE
[Ref. ST]

The theory of sets deals with precise properties of collections of objects. Because of its primary position in the hierarchy of mathematical structure, sets are often introduced in a formal and axiomatic manner. We shall faintly reflect this approach, but mainly treat sets as primitive data structures on which certain operators are defined.

DEFINITION

A set S is any collection of definite distinguishable objects of our intuition or of our intellect to be conceived as a whole. The objects are called elements or members of S.

The definition permits wide latitude as to what are permitted to be members of a set. Most of our examples will consider sets as *collections of symbols*. In other discourses, they may be points on a line, geometric figures, people, etc. The word *definite* means that given an object x and a set S, it is always possible to determine whether or not x is a member of S. This idea may be made more precise by defining an operator $\in$ such that the statement $x \in S$ results in the value *true* if x is indeed a member of S, and a value *false* otherwise. This operator is a primitive in set theory, i.e., it cannot be defined in terms of more basic operators. The statement $x \in S$ is, however, most commonly used in a somewhat different sense, which we shall adopt: It asserts that x "is an element of" S. Also, $x \notin S$ specifies that x "is *not* an element of" S.

A few basic ways to specify sets are:

1. *Listing elements:*

   Example: $A = \{a, b, 1, c, d\}$
   Elements are usually written as lowercase letters or digits and set names are given by capital letters. Set elements are separated by commas within a listing and the set listing is delimited by curly brackets.

2. *A statement of property satisfied by all elements of the set:*
   Example: $A = \{$all boys in the local high school graduating class$\}$
   This type of specification is much more convenient than listing when the number of elements is large, and it is essential if the number is infinite. Thus we may speak of

   $Z = \{$all integers$\}$

   But, of course, we cannot list all elements of Z.

   The property type of specification is usually organized using the following notation scheme:

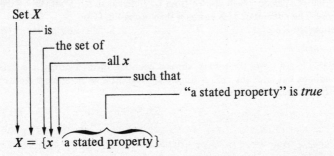

Example: $X = \{x \mid x > 5\}$

means: X is the set of all x such that "x is greater than 5" is true, i.e., X is the set of all x greater than 5.

3. A set may be specified as the result of any of certain operators applied to existing sets. (These operators will be discussed shortly.)
4. Two special sets are given unique names:
   - ϕ the *empty* or *null* set, i.e., the set containing no elements
   - U the *universe* set containing all elements of all sets in a given discourse.

Two sets are defined to be *equal* ($A = B$) iff (if and only if) they have the same elements. If $A = B$, then every element of A is an element of B and every element of B is an element of A. It follows that the order of listing the elements of a set is *not* significant. Also, a set that lists some elements repetitively is equal to the set with only a single appearance of the same elements. We shall assume from now on that all sets of interest have nonrepetitive elements. The properties just discussed may be illustrated:

$$\{a,b,c\} = \{a,c,b\} = \{a,c,c,b,a\}$$

A set may be a single element of another set. This has simple but subtle consequences:

$$\{a,b,c\} \neq \{a,\{b,c\}\}$$

since the set on the left has three elements, a,b,c, but the set on the right has only two elements: a and the *set* $\{b,c\}$. Also, c is an element of the left set, but not of the right set. As another example,

$$\{\{a\}\} \neq \{a\}$$

since the left set has one element, the set $\{a\}$, while the right set has one element, a.

Two sets are defined to be *equivalent* if each element of one set can be paired or associated with one element of the other, i.e., be placed in one-to-one correspondence in the sense that no elements of either set are "left over." To illustrate the definitions of equality and equivalence, let

$$A = \{a,b,c\} \quad B = \{c,b,a\} \quad C = \{p,r,q\} \quad \text{and} \quad D = \{a,b,c,q\}$$

Then, sets A and B are equal, sets A,B,C are equivalent, and set D is neither equal or equivalent to the other sets.

Equivalence is used directly to define the *cardinal numbers*. All sets that are equivalent to each other are defined by this property to have the same cardinal number. Thus the sets "three computers, three students, and three politicians" are equivalent in the sense of set theory, and the cardinality of these sets is *three*. Each cardinal thus corresponds to an integer, and each integer may be considered to be the name of an equivalence class of sets. The cardinality of the empty set is the number zero.

3-3 SET OPERATORS AND EXPRESSIONS

Three simple but very common operators on sets will now be defined. Later it will be shown how these may be linked together to form expressions and thus provide a very powerful precise language for combining sets to form new sets.

The definitions may be stated concisely using the notation described earlier:

Union: $A \cup B = \{x \mid x \in A \ or \ x \in B\}$

Intersection: $A \cap B = \{x \mid x \in A \ and \ x \in B\}$

Relative complement: $A \sim B = \{x \mid x \in A \ and \ x \notin B\}$

Absolute complement: $\sim B = U \sim B$ (U is the universe set)

In words these may be stated as follows: the union of two sets A,B is the set of all elements contained in A *or* B (or both); the intersection of two sets A,B is the set of all elements common to both A *and* B; the complement of B relative to A is the set of all elements of A *not* in B; if, as is often the case, set A is the universe set, then it may be omitted from explicit mention, and we speak of the absolute complement of B.

A popular pictorial scheme for visualizing the set operators is the Venn diagram (Fig. 3-3.1). Sets are shown as simple geometric figures (like circles), and the results of a stated set operator or expression is shown shaded. It is useful to identify all subsets of the given sets; a scheme for labelling these for the case of three sets is shown in the figure, where the integer labels correspond to the subset labelling scheme, using bit vectors described earlier.

The statement of inclusion: "A is a subset of B" (written $A \subset B$) can be shown to be equivalent to $A \cup B = B$, or $A \cap B = A$, or $A \cap \sim B = \phi$ or $B \cup \sim A = U$. The basic set operators may be used to define an algebra of sets. To this end, the commutative, associative, and distributive laws, as well as other properties shown in Fig. 3-3.2, are most important.

Sets, set names, and set operators may be linked together to form expressions in much the same kind of way as is done in ordinary algebra. The following precedence rules simplify the writing of complex expressions:

1. Complement operations are done first.
2. Intersection operations are done next.
3. Union operations are done next.
4. Parenthesis pairs may be used to delimit subexpressions within an expression. The above rules then apply within each subexpression and also in using the result of a subexpression in the rest of the entire expression.
5. Expression scanning is done from left to right.

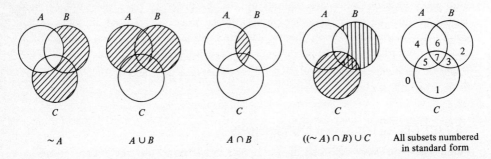

Fig. 3-3.1   Venn diagrams illustrating set operations and standard numbering.

					Remarks
(a)	$A \cup \phi = A$	(a')	$A \cap \phi = \phi$		ϕ is identity set for union
(b)	$A \cup U = U$	(b')	$A \cap U = A$		U is identity set for intersection
(c)	$A \cup A = A$	(c')	$A \cap A = A$		idempotent laws of union and intersection
(d)	$A \cup \sim A = U$	(d')	$A \cap \sim A = \phi$		
(e)	$A \cup (A \cap B) = A$	(e')	$A \cap (A \cup B) = A$		Absorption properties
(f)	$\sim \sim A = A$				Double application of $\sim$ returns original set
(g)	$A \cup B = B \cup A$	(g')	$A \cap B = B \cap A$		Commutative laws for union and intersection
(h)	$A \cup (B \cup C) = (A \cup B) \cup C$				Associative laws for union and intersection
(h')	$A \cap (B \cap C) = (A \cap B) \cap C$				
(i)	$A \cup (B \cap C) = (A \cup B) \cap (A \cup C)$				Distributive laws: union over intersection
(i')	$A \cap (B \cup C) = (A \cap B) \cup (A \cap C)$				intersection over union
(j)	$\sim (A \cup B) = \sim A \cap \sim B$				DeMorgan's laws
(j')	$\sim (A \cap B) = \sim A \cup \sim B$				

Fig. 3-3.2   Listing of some properties of set operators.

If only single-letter names are permitted (unless stated otherwise), the intersection operator may be implicit, so we may write $AB = A \cap B$. To illustrate the above rules, we show an expression on the left and its fully parenthesized equivalent on the right.

$$A \sim B(C \cup A \sim C) = (A \cap (\sim B)) \cap (C \cup (A \cap (\sim C)))$$

Since operators produce new sets from given arts, it is of interest to see how the *number* of elements in the result sets are related to the number of elements in the operand sets. We denote the number of elements in a set A by $N(A)$. For the three operators defined above:

$$N(\sim A) = N(U) - N(A) \tag{1}$$

$$N(A \cap B) \leqslant \text{Min } (N(A), N(B)) \tag{2}$$

$$N(A \cup B) = N(A) + N(B) - N(A \cap B) \tag{3}$$

The equation in the case of the complement operator follows directly from the definition of complement. For intersection, only a bound (but no precise relation) can be stated in general; the number of elements in the result set is at most as large as the smaller of the number of elements in the two original sets. The number of elements in the set resulting from the union of two sets is the sum of the numbers in each set minus the number in the intersection between the sets. The reasoning behind this rule should be clear from the Venn diagram for union (see Fig. 3-3.1) which shows that if the number of elements in A and B are added, those in the intersection are counted twice; thus the number of these twice-counted elements must be subtracted, as seen in the above expression. Two sets whose intersection is the null set are said to be *disjoint*. It is seen from the expression for $N(A \cup B)$ that only for the union of disjoint sets is the number of elements of the result set equal to the sum of the numbers of elements in the two operand sets.

3-4 SUBSETS

One set A is said to be included in another set B (written $A \subseteq B$) if every element of A is also an element of B. An equivalent reading of $A \subseteq B$ is "A is a subset of B." The null set ϕ is included in every set, and every set is included in the universe set. A set A is said to be a *proper subset* of B (written $A \subset B$) if $A \subseteq B$ *and* $A \neq B$, that is, iff B includes every element of A and at least one other element. Thus all elements of A constitute a subset, but not a proper subset of A.

Systematic listing of all subsets of a given listed set is easily done with the aid of a table in which each column is labelled by one set element and each row represents one subset as a string of 1,0 entries; a 1 indicates the element heading the column is included in the subset, 0 means it is not. For example, if the set is $\{a,b,c,d\}$, the subset $\{a,c,d\}$ is represented by the row 1011. For n elements in the given set, the table is easily constructed by recognizing that the rows are the binary (base 2) representations of the integers. This is one way to understand that the number of subsets of a set of n elements is 2^n. The set consisting of all 2^n subsets of a given set A is called the *power set* of A and is written $P(A)$.

Example: $A = \{a,b,c\}$

$$P(A) = \{\phi, \{c\}, \{b\}, \{b,c\}, \{a\}, \{a,c\}, \{a,b\}, \{a,b,c\}\}$$

The systematic listing of subsets is a useful technique in many problems. Consider the following simple problem, which is representative of a class of such problems.

Example In a certain graduate-school class in computer science, of the 100 students, 40 were engineers and the remainder liberal-arts majors. An honors grade was earned by 25 students of which 10 were nonengineers. Find:
(*a*) The number of liberal-arts students that did not receive an honors grade.
(*b*) The number of engineers that received an honors grade.

Solution The process starts by identifying the pertinent classifications which, although specifying sets of students, became the set elements for this problem. Thus E will denote the engineering students and H the students receiving an honors grade. The possible subsets are displayed in the following table, which also assigns an identifier number to each:

Subset No.	E	H
0	0	0
1	0	1
2	1	0
3	1	1

In words, subset 2 is "the set of students that are engineers *and* that did not receive an honors grade." All other subsets may be stated in similar fashion. The number of students in subset i will be denoted by n_i. The statement of the problem can then be expressed as the following equations:

$$n_0 + n_1 + n_2 + n_3 = 100 \quad \text{(100 students)}$$
$$n_2 + n_3 = 40 \quad \text{(40 engineers)}$$
$$n_1 + n_3 = 25 \quad \text{(25 honors grades)}$$
$$n_1 = 10 \quad \text{(10 nonengineers honors grades)}$$

Solving the above equations: $n_0 = 50$ and $n_3 = 15$.

The above technique is valuable in the analysis of overlapped use of computer system resources. See Sec. 4-6 for an example.

Two or more sets with no element in common are said to be *disjoint*. Two sets are disjoint if

$$A \cap B = \phi$$

Three (or more) sets are disjoint only if *all* possible set *pairs* are disjoint. (*Caution*: because $A \cap B = \phi$ and $B \cap C = \phi$, it does *not* necessarily follow that $A \cap C = \phi$ or that A,B,C are disjoint. This can easily be seen from a Venn diagram showing A,C overlap, but with B isolated.)

There are many ways to form subsets from a given set X. One kind of collection of subsets is of particular interest. A *partition* of X is any set of disjoint subsets of X whose union equals X.

> *Example*: $X = \{a,b,c,d,e\}$

One possible partition of X is the set $S = \{\{a,b,e\},\{c,d\}\}$. A partition thus contains all the elements of X, but the subsets constituting the partition have no elements in common.

The number of partitions of a set of n elements will be designated as B_n, which has long been of interest to mathematicians. As n increases, the B_n constitute a sequence called the *exponential numbers*. One way of giving the B_n is by its generating function, i.e., implicitly in the following equation (see Ref. RO)

$$\sum_{n=0}^{\infty} \frac{B_n}{n!} x^n = e^{e^x - 1} \quad \text{where } B_0 = 1$$

However, obtaining actual values of the B_n from this formula is a nasty process involving expanding the right side in a power series in x and matching terms with the left side. The following is a recursive formula more suitable to computation

$$B_{n+1} = \sum_{k=0}^{n} C(n,k) B_k$$

The first few values are:

n	0	1	2	3	4	5	6	7	8	9	10
B_n	1	1	2	5	15	52	203	877	4140	21147	115975

From this table we find for example that for a set of six elements, there are 203 possible partitions, i.e., 203 ways of listing subsets of the six elements. For each way, no two subsets have any element in common, and all subsets together include all six elements.

3-5 ORDERED PAIRS, CARTESIAN PRODUCT, MAPPINGS, AND FUNCTIONS

An *ordered pair* is designated

$$(x,y)$$

It specifies two quantities in one: x is "first" and y is "second." The ordered pair (x,y) is *not* the same as the set $\{x,y\}$, since no ordering (positioning) is implied for a set, while positioning is essential to an ordered pair. Thus,

$$\{x,y\} = \{y,x\}$$

but, in general,

$$(x,y) \neq (y,x)$$

It is possible to use only set notation to give the same information as is given by an ordered pair. Thus,

$$(x,y) = \{\{x\},\{x,y\}\}$$

The simplicity of the parenthesis notation should now be evident. The ordered pair may be extended to the ordered triple by the definition:

$$(x,y,z) = ((x,y),z)$$

In a similar way, ordered n-tuples may be defined. They are also called *vectors*.

The *cartesian product* set of two given sets A,B is designated $A \times B$ and is defined as the set of all distinct ordered pairs obtained when the first element of a pair is an element of A and the second an element of B. Thus, forming a cartesian product of two sets is a way of associating or forming a *correspondence* of each element of set A with each element of set B. The following is a formal definition of the product:

$$A \times B = \{(x,y) \mid x \in A \quad \text{and} \quad y \in B\}$$

Example: $A = \{a,b,c\}$ $B = \{1,2\}$

$$A \times B = \{(a,1),(a,2),(b,1),(b,2),(c,1),(c,2)\}$$

The number of elements in $A \times B$ is clearly the product of the number of elements in A and the number in B. This may be seen either by simple reasoning or by use of the product rule given in Sec. 3-1.

Mappings (or *functions*) are certain kinds of subsets of cartesian products. Let A and B be any two nonempty sets. Let M be a subset of the cartesian product $A \times B$. Thus M is a listing of ordered pairs, all of which come from $A \times B$. M is called a *mapping of A into B* if each member of A is a first element of exactly one ordered pair of M. To better understand this definition, imagine that the ordered pairs of M constitute a two-column table. If M is a mapping of A into B, every element of set A will appear only once in the left column. Thus we have complete coverage of all elements of A and also uniqueness of these elements in the left column. A discrete function is, therefore, a correspondence between two sets of values. The left set is called the function's *domain* and the right set is called the *range*. An element of the domain is called an *argument*, or a value of the independent variable. An element of the range is called a value of the dependent variable.

If M is a mapping of A into B such that each member of B is a second term of *at least* one member of M, then M is said to be a *mapping of A onto B*. Thus a mapping *onto* is a particular kind of mapping *into* whereby there is complete coverage (and perhaps repetitions) of every element of B in the second column of our table representation of the mapping.

Examples: Let $A = \{a, b, c\}$ $B = \{1, 2\}$

then $A \times B = \{(a, 1), (a, 2), (b, 1), (b, 2), (c, 1), (c, 2)\}$

Clearly $A \times B$ is *not* itself a mapping of A into B since, for example, b appears more than once as a left element. However,

$\{(a, 1), (b, 1), (c, 1)\}$

is a mapping of A *into* B, but *not onto* B, since there is no coverage of set B. (The element 2 is missing as a right member of the pairs.) However,

$\{(a, 1), (b, 2), (c, 2)\}$

is a mapping of A *into* and *onto* B.

3-6 RECURSIVE FUNCTIONS [Refs. BA,KL,MC]

The essence of the recursion idea may be stated informally as follows: The computation of any function may be accomplished by repeated computation of a few simpler functions together with a rather general scheme of variable substitutions, the latter applying over a wide class of functions. One example is the function giving the number of permutations (see Sec. 3-1).

$$P(n, 0) = 1 \tag{1}$$

$$P(n, k) = \frac{n!}{(n - k)!} \quad 1 \leqslant k \leqslant n \tag{2}$$

Here the function is expressed in terms of the primitives: factorial, subtraction, and division. We usually expect to see functions defined in terms of the usual primitives of arithmetic. In the above example, to compute, say, $P(5,2)$

$$P(5, 2) = \frac{5!}{(5 - 2)!} = \frac{5!}{3!} = \frac{5 \times 4 \times 3 \times 2 \times 1}{3 \times 2 \times 1} = 20$$

This process is seen to require one subtraction, six multiplications, and three divisions.

Consider now an alternative computation scheme for the same function. This is derived with the use of a little algebra.

$$P(n,0) = 1 \qquad\qquad\qquad\qquad\qquad\qquad\qquad\qquad\qquad\qquad *(1)$$

$$P(n,k+1) = (n-k) \times P(n,k) \qquad 0 \leqslant k < n \qquad\qquad\qquad (3)$$

In this *recursive* form, the function name (P) appears on both sides of the = sign. For the example $P(5,2)$, the above recursion equations are interpreted as describing the following scheme of substitutions:

$$P(5,2) = (5-1) \times P(5,1) \text{ by Eq. (3)} \qquad\qquad\qquad\qquad (4a)$$

$$P(5,1) = (5-0) \times P(5,0) \text{ by Eq. (3)} \qquad\qquad\qquad\qquad (4b)$$

$$\text{recognizing } P(5,0) = 1 \qquad \text{by Eq. (1)}$$

$$P(5,1) = 5 \times 1 = 5 \quad \text{[back substitution into Eq. } (4b)] \qquad\qquad (4c)$$

$$P(5,2) = 4 \times 5 = 20 \quad \text{[back substitution into Eq. } (4a)] \qquad\qquad (4d)$$

Comparing counts of operations, only two multiplications and no divisions are required, but the substitutions are more complex and two subtractions are also required. Also notice that the process automatically computes the intermediate values $P(5,0)$ and $P(5,1)$. Since the substitutions are made in a regular order, first calling the function with decreasing argument values and then back-substituting in the order of last-encountered-first or last-in-first-out (LIFO), there is a suggestion of using a single substitution scheme for many functions. In programming, the "piling up" of arguments in the forward process and their use in back substitution is said to be a *stack* or pushdown *store*. Of course this type of structure may be explicitly programmed in any programming language, but some languages (including APL, PL/I, and ALGOL) give the ability in the language syntax to call functions recursively with the stack referencing mechanism supplied automatically. For example in APL, the above P function may be programmed as shown in Fig. 3-6.1, which also shows the sequence of calls on the function generated at line [4], which is seen to contain the name of the function (PERM). The first time line [4] is executed, the PERM encountered there may be considered to call a "fresh copy" of the PERM program and pass it the value of $k-1$. Execution of this copy may well then reach *its* line [4], which again calls PERM and thus activates a new copy, etc. Note that each of these copies remains "stalled" at the point just to the left of the name PERM as the *new* copy is called. When the copy with the argument value of 0 is called, the test and branch at line [1] results in progression to line [2], where R is set to 1, and then to line [3], which exits the current PERM copy to the previously called copy of PERM. This uses the value of R thus passed back in *its* line [4] and then exits to the previously called copy, etc. In this way the back substitutions are implemented. As a practical matter, only the stack of argument values is held in storage; a single physical copy of the function serves for all logical copies referred to above.

*An equivalent form is
$$P(n,0) = 1 \qquad\qquad\qquad\qquad\qquad\qquad\qquad\qquad (1^*)$$
$$P(n,k) = (n-k+1) \times P(n,k-1) \qquad 1 \leqslant k \leqslant n \qquad (3^*)$$

$$\nabla R \leftarrow N \ PERM \ K$$

[1] $\rightarrow (K \neq 0)/LAST$
[2] $R \leftarrow 1$
[3] $\rightarrow 0$
[4] $LAST: \ R \leftarrow (N-(K-1)) \times N \ PERM \ K-1$
       ∇

If this function is called by

    6 *PERM* 2

The APL programming system implements as follows:

For
$K=2$	$R \leftarrow (6\text{-}1) \times 6\ PERM\ 1$	Line[4]	First copy (original)
$K=1$	$R \leftarrow (6\text{-}0) \times 6\ PERM\ 0$	Line[4]	Second copy
$K=0$	$R \leftarrow 1$	Line[2]	Third copy
$K=1$	$R \leftarrow (6\text{-}0) \times 1$	Line[4]	Second copy
$K=2$	$R \leftarrow (6\text{-}1) \times 6$	Line[4]	First copy
	Exit	Line[3]	First copy

ANSWER PRINTED: 30   (Since $R \leftarrow$ was omitted in call)

Fig. 3-6.1 Illustration of APL system execution of recursive function PERM with arguments 6,2.

A comparison of efficiency of the recursion with the direct method of evaluating functions will now be considered. Suppose the function $F(X,Y)$ is to be computed for $Y = S, S + 1, \ldots, S + N$ given $F(X,S) = C$, where $X, C,$ and N are constant. Two basic approaches may be contrasted:

1. *Direct method* The computation is done only in terms of "universal" primitives (such as addition, subtraction, multiplication, and division), in which case if K_{F_i} of these operations are required to compute F_i,

$$\sum_{i=1}^{N} K_{F_i}$$

    operations are required to compute N values.

2. *Recursion method* The computation is done by the equations

$$F(X,S) = C \tag{5}$$

$$F(X, Y + 1) = G(X, Y, F(X, Y)) \tag{6}$$

This requires analysis to discover the new function G, whose arguments are seen to be X, Y and the *previous* F value. If K_{G_i} primitive operations are required to compute G_i, then the N values of F require

$$\sum_{i=1}^{N} K_{G_i}$$

primitive operations (plus substitutions).

If ΣK_{G_i} is smaller than ΣK_{F_i}, as is frequently the case, the indirect method is more efficient (at least using operation count as the efficiency measure). The improved operation count may be understood to arise from the fact that instead of reverting to universal primitives to compute each function value, recursion instead uses the function itself as a primitive! In this way the particular complexity contained in the previous value of the function is available to compute the next value. Note that in general there is no "cookbook" method of finding the G function given an F function [see Eq. (6)]. This mainly requires ingenuity.

3-7 PROBABILITY CONCEPTS: SAMPLE SPACES AND AXIOMS
[Refs. FE,FR,MO]

The beginnings of a theory of probability go back at least as early as the seventeenth century in attempts to analyze the odds in certain games of chance. The nineteenth century saw much of physics move towards probabilistic models through the work of Gibbs, Maxwell, and Boltzmann. This development continued into the twentieth century with the quantum theories of M. Planck and E. Schroedinger.

Systems science and engineering also make much use of probability. Shannon's information theory and queuing models, first introduced by A.K. Erlang in 1909 for the design of telephone systems, are all probability-based (see Chap. 5).

Statistics is concerned with the analysis and description of data. Probability theory deals with a kind of abstraction of processes that could account for the appearance of certain properties of data. Even these rather vague statements should indicate that the two subjects are closely related, since we usually seek not only the quantitative description of data, but also a system model that could have generated the observed data. Once available, such a model can be used to investigate relationships among system parameters. Much of modern statistics is concerned with the analysis of data to determine whether the data fits some assumed model. Thus statistics and probability theory are intimately related.

Probability, like most theories, deals with a *model* of the real world, *not* the real world itself. No model is completely comprehensive, but is only useful for certain rather limited purposes. For example, in the design of a timesharing system, it is often a good assumption, borne out by measurement, that the users are statistically similar; i.e., in each small time interval, each user not already being served is as likely to make a request as any other. Now this assumption does *not* say that every user behaves in the same way in all aspects of his system usage. Various traits, like size of main storage used and processing time, are indeed different for different customers. Yet the assumption of equally probable request time is a good one and greatly simplifies the formulation of an analytic model (this particular model is treated in depth in Chap. 5).

As far as we are concerned, there are two aspects of probability theory: (1) the methodology and ways of reasoning so essential to model construction and solution, and (2) results of analysis of a few models like the binomial, Poisson, and normal that have been found to fit many real-world situations. The first of these is the more fundamental, and ultimately more important. In the study of the few famous models we find many examples, some of which are valuable in themselves, all of which are important as illustrations of model building and solution.

In this book, probability theory of discrete random variables is discussed in this chapter and used in later chapters. A brief account of the fundamentals of continuous probability is given in Appendix B.

Consider an experiment with a finite number of distinct outcomes called *elementary events*, each identified by a unique label. This *set* of labels, constituting an alphabet of possible outcomes, is called the *sample space* or *state space* of the experiment.

Examples:

1. For the experiment "tossing a coin once," the sample space has two points: *head* and *tail*, so the space is the set:

$$X = \{h, t\}$$

2. For the experiment "tossing a coin three times," each sample point is conveniently labelled by a string of three symbols. Thus the elementary event: "first heads, then head, then tail" is labelled *hht*, and the entire sample space is

$$X = \{hhh, hht, hth, htt, thh, tht, tth, ttt\}$$

An event is a subset of sample points. Thus the event "two tails" is the subset of X: $\{htt, tht, tth\}$. Since probability theory is concerned with events, the language of set theory is a powerful tool. The universe set in probability problems is the entire sample space. The labels of the sample points need not be numbers (as was seen in the coin-tossing example). They must, however, be distinct and all together account for all possible experimental outcomes of the probability model.

A *probability* is a number assigned to each point x or event A (set of points) of a sample space X. The probability of event A denoted by $P(A)$ must satisfy the following axioms:

A1: *Range* $0 \leqslant P(A) \leqslant 1$ The range of probabilities is the positive numbers from 0 to 1 inclusive.

A2: *Certainty* $P(X) = 1$ The probability of the entire sample space is 1. This axiom together with A1 normalizes the probability numbers.

A3: *Union*   If A and B are mutually exclusive (disjoint) events, i.e., if they have no point in common ($A \cap B = \phi$), then $P(A \cup B) = P(A) + P(B)$.

Axiom A3 may be extended to three or more sets using the associative and distributive laws of union and intersection. We leave the proof as an exercise and state the result:

If S_1, S_2, S_3 denotes three disjoint subsets of a sample space, i.e.,

$$S_1 \cap S_2 = \phi \quad \text{and} \quad S_2 \cap S_3 = \phi \quad \text{and} \quad S_1 \cap S_3 = \phi$$

then

$$P(S_1 \cup S_2 \cup S_3) = P(S_1) + P(S_2) + P(S_3)$$

As a special but important illustration, consider each S_i to consist of one sample point X_i. Since these are all distinct, they are disjoint. The probability of all points of the sample space is then the sum of the sample point probabilities, and by A2 this sum is 1.

$$P(X) = \sum_{i=1}^{n} P(X_i) = 1 \tag{1}$$

If A and B are not necessarily disjoint, the probability of the union of A and B is

$$P(A \cup B) = P(A) + P(B) - P(A \cap B) \tag{2}$$

This equation is seen to resemble the count-of-elements for the union of two sets (see Sec. 3-3). Again the last term corrects for double counting in the intersection of A and B. The probability of the null event is zero

$$P(\phi) = 0 \tag{3}$$

Constructing the sample space is a vital step in formulating a probability model of an experiment or process. It is here where the most delicate abstractions are made of the real-world phenomena, with all its complexities, to the simpler symbolic structure that sometimes permits mathematical solution. There are no firm rules for this procedure; each case requires judgment and ingenuity. Construction of the sample space has two aspects:

1. Enumerating and labelling the sample points
2. Assigning a probability to each sample point

The reader is encouraged to study the remainder of this chapter with an eye to these two tasks which must be done in such a way that the axioms are satisfied.

Although a sample point or an event need not be characterized by a number, in most cases of interest, an event like "the number of successes in n trials" *is* a number which is then designated as a value assumed by a *random variable*. Since to each value of a random variable there is a corresponding probability, we may then speak of a random variable and its *probability function* (or *distribution*). Thus the symbolic pair $(X,P(X))$ denotes the set of values of the random variable X and its distribution function $P(X)$.

3-8 INDEPENDENT EVENTS: THE PRODUCT PRINCIPLE

Two events A, B are said to be *independent* iff

$$P(A \cap B) = P(A)P(B) \tag{1}$$

Independent events are *not* mutually exclusive events. In fact, mutually exclusive events cannot be independent, as can be seen by the following reasoning: If A and B are mutually exclusive, by definition, $A \cap B = \phi$ and hence $P(A \cap B) = 0$. But if A and B are independent, and $P(A)$ and $P(B)$ are nonzero, $P(A \cap B) \neq 0$ by Eq. (1). Hence events A and B cannot be mutually exclusive and also independent.

Let the sample space and associated probabilities of an experiment be symbolically represented by the pair $(X,P(X))$. Consider also an independent experiment $(Y,P(Y))$, where "independent" intuitively means that either experiment is not influenced by the other. Suppose we now define another experiment, *each* of whose outcomes is a particular *pair* of X, Y outcomes, i.e., first one from X and then one from Y. The new sample space Z can then be labelled by the cartesian product set

$$Z = X \times Y \tag{2}$$

The probability of each point in this new sample space Z is the product of the probabilities of the X, Y events constituting the point. These properties will be called the *product principle*. It is not difficult to show that Z and its probabilities satisfy the axioms.

Example:
1. One toss of a "fair" coin has a sample space and probabilities

$$X = \{h, t\} \quad \tfrac{1}{2}, \tfrac{1}{2}$$

2. One throw of a "fair" six-sided die has sample space and probabilities

$$Y = \{1, 2, 3, 4, 5, 6\} \quad \tfrac{1}{6}, \tfrac{1}{6}, \tfrac{1}{6}, \tfrac{1}{6}, \tfrac{1}{6}, \tfrac{1}{6}$$

3. The experiment "toss a coin and then throw a die" has sample points and probabilities

$$Z = \{h1, h2, h3, h4, h5, h6, t1, t2, t3, t4, t5, t6\}$$
$$p = \tfrac{1}{12}, \tfrac{1}{12}, \ldots, \tfrac{1}{12}$$

In some cases the experiment cannot be simply characterized by the cartesian product of sample spaces (see Sec. 3-5), since the product of probabilities of elementary events must be applied differently for various classes of sample points.

Example   A fair coin is tossed up to five times until two heads have turned up. Find the sample space and associated probabilities.

Solution   The sample space can be enumerated with the aid of a tree diagram showing the various possibilities of experimental outcome (see Fig. 3-8.1). The tree has two roots (head or tail for the first toss) and branches according to the possible toss possibilities until two heads have appeared. Once constructed, the label for a sample point is read by recording the node labels for the path from a root to a leaf of the tree. Each node corresponds to probability of one-half, since it represents one toss of the coin; the probability of a sample point is then the product of one-half as many times as there are nodes in its path in the tree.

3-9   EQUIPROBABLE SAMPLE SPACES

In some sample spaces, sample points are known or can be assumed to be of *equal probability*, i.e., $p_i = p$ for all i. Then, since the sum of all probabilities is 1,

$$P(X) = \sum_{i=1}^{n} p_i = np = 1 \tag{1}$$

and hence

$$p = \frac{1}{n} \tag{2}$$

Since an event is some subset of sample points, an event containing j elements of an *equiprobable sample space* of n elements has the probability j/n. In other words:

$$P(A) = \frac{\text{Number of elements of } A}{\text{Number of elements in } X} \qquad (3)$$

or

$$P(A) = \frac{\text{Number of ways } A \text{ can occur}}{\text{Number of ways } X \text{ can occur}} \qquad (4)$$

It must be emphasized that these simple relations hold only for equiprobable sample spaces.

One great analysis convenience of equiprobable sample spaces is that since event probabilities are computed by simply counting sample points in the event set, and each point is labelled by a symbol string, the problem becomes one of counting symbol strings that satisfy certain stated conditions. This is precisely the kind of problem considered by combinatorial analysis (Secs. 3-1 and 3-2).

Example   A birthday problem.

> *Given:* n people in a room ($n \leq 365$).
> *Assume:* 1. All birth dates are equally likely.
>   2. A year of 365 days.
> *Find:* The probability that all birthdays are different.

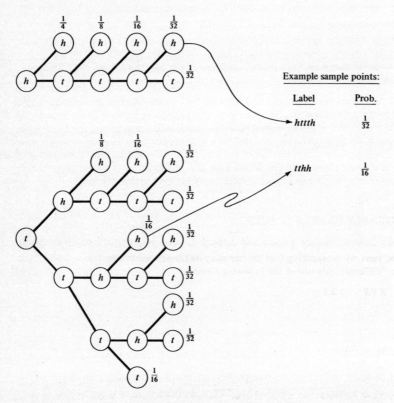

Example sample points:

Label	Prob.
$httth$	$\frac{1}{32}$
$tthh$	$\frac{1}{16}$

Fig. 3-8.1 Sample space for tossing coin until two heads appear; up to five tosses.

Solution An elementary event here consists of one possible collection of n birthdays, i.e., a string of n symbols each chosen from an alphabet of $r = 365$ symbols. Hence the sample space has r^n points each with probability $1/r^n$. The event of interest is the set of points each of whose labels have no repetitions of any symbol. The number of such strings is the number of permutations without replacement (repetition) of n symbols from an alphabet of r symbols, i.e., $P(r,n)$. Hence our event probability is this many sample-point probabilities, or

$$p = P(r,n)\frac{1}{r^n} = \frac{r!}{(r-n)!r^n}$$

Example A certain computer system has four disk drives, and it may be assumed in this particular problem that each drive is as likely to be referenced as any other. Find the probabilities that in three references:
1. All references will be to a single drive.
2. All references will be to different drives.
3. Exactly two references will be to the same drive.

Solution The single-reference sample points and probabilities are

A,B,C,D $\frac{1}{4}, \frac{1}{4}, \frac{1}{4}, \frac{1}{4}$

For three references, the sample space consists of $4^3 = 64$ sample points that may be labelled as follows, with each point probability $1/4^3 = 1/64$:

AAA
AAB
etc.
DDD

The event specified in part 1 of the above example consists of the four sample points (AAA,BBB,CCC,DDD). The event probability is then

Probability $= \frac{4}{64}$

The event specified in part 2 requires us to count the number of sample points as the number of ways a string three symbols long can be chosen without replacement from an alphabet of four symbols:

$$P(4,3) = \frac{4!}{(4-3)!} = 24 \text{ sample points}$$

Hence

Probability $= \frac{24}{64}$

The event specified in part 3 has a probability that is somewhat more difficult to compute. Here we start by recognizing that the sample-point labels containing two symbols "alike" and one "different" has one of the following forms:

XXY   XYX   YXX

For each of these, we can choose the X in four ways and then the Y in three remaining ways. Hence there are $(3 \times 4 \times 3) = 36$ such sample points, and hence

Probability $= \frac{36}{64}$

Note that the parts 1, 2, and 3 of this problem constitute a *partition* of the sample space (all points are included, i.e., no overlap of points in the events). For this reason, the event probabilities sum to 1.

3-10 HIERARCHY OF SAMPLE SPACES

Suppose we have a sample space X and a set of events S, where each event S_i is a subset of X. If S is a *partition* of X (i.e., all S_i disjoint, but their union equals X), then we can consider each *event* S_i as a sample point in a new sample space S. The reader should check for himself that if $P(X)$ satisfied the axioms, so will $P(S)$. This property is very useful, since it often happens that probabilities for events of interest are not directly available, while those of a simpler related experiment are known. If the sample space for the events of interest can be formed by disjoint subsets of the more primitive experiment, this will permit computation of the desired event probabilities (usually using Axiom 3 or its generalization).

Example

Given: the sample space for "three tosses of a coin"

$X = \{hhh,hht,hth,htt,thh,tht,tth,ttt\}$

with all point probabilities = 1/8
Find: the sample space and associated probabilities of the events "none,one,two,three heads" labelled, $0h,1h,2h,3h$

Solution First list the events of interest in set form.

$0h = \{ttt\}$ $1h = \{htt,tht,tth\}$ $2h = \{hht,hth,thh\}$ $3h = \{hhh\}$

A check will show that these sets are disjoint and their union is the original sample space X. Hence, we have a valid new sample space:

$H = \{0h, 1h, 2h, 3h\}$

We now calculate the probabilities of these events using Axiom 3:*

$P(0h) = \frac{1}{8}$ since $P(ttt) = \frac{1}{8}$ as given

$P(1h) = P(htt,tht,tth) = P(htt \cup tht \cup tth)$

$\qquad = P(htt) + P(tht) + P(tth)$

$\qquad = \frac{1}{8} + \frac{1}{8} + \frac{1}{8} = \frac{3}{8}$

$P(2h) = \frac{3}{8}$ by a similar process to $P(1h)$

$P(3h) = \frac{1}{8}$ by same reason as $P(0h)$

The idea of generating new sample spaces from others can often be carried to several levels, as is illustrated by the following example.

Example

Given: the sample space X for the tossing of three coins (see above)
Find: the probability of *two or more heads*

Solution   The first step in our new problem is the entire previous example problem yielding its sample space and probabilities. Next, using this sample space, we enumerate a new sample space that includes the event of interest

---

*In designating sets as the arguments of probabilities as in $P(\ldots)$, we omit the curly brackets usually used to delimit set listing.

$\{h \geqslant 2\} = \{2h, 3h\}$

$\{h < 2\} = \{0h, 1h\}$

The event of interest is only the first of these, so

$P(h \geqslant 2) = P(2h \cup 3h)$

By Axiom 3:

$P(h \geqslant 2) = P(2h) + P(3h)$

Using the probabilities from the previous example

$P(h \geqslant 2) = \dfrac{3}{8} + \dfrac{1}{8} = \dfrac{4}{8}$ (Ans.)

Sometimes, as in the last example, it is not necessary to list all elements of a sample space to solve a specific problem [i.e., listing $P(h < 2)$ was not of direct interest]. However, it is often valuable, especially when first learning the subject, to be aware of all the sample points and spaces. With more practice and sophistication, many shortcuts are possible.

3-11 CONDITIONAL PROBABILITY

Given a sample space X with each of its n points assigned a probability so that

$$\sum_{i=1}^{n} p_i = 1 \tag{1}$$

let us focus attention on event B composed of the first k sample points of X (we can always number the points in this way)

$$P(B) - \sum_{i=1}^{k} p_i \tag{2}$$

Also consider event A, some of whose sample points intersect event B. Now suppose we obtain information that event B has actually occurred. The question now raised is: What is the *new* probability of event A, written $P(A|B)$ and meaning the probability of A conditional on the occurrence of B? Receiving the information that B has occurred amounts to creating a new sample space containing only all the elements of B. Although this B still is composed of k sample points, their probabilities, now called p_i', must satisfy the axiom for all sample spaces:

$$\sum_{i=1}^{k} p_i' = 1 \tag{3}$$

It would seem reasonable to require that the p_i' bear the same ratios to each other as the p did, i.e., that p_i' and p_i be related by a fixed constant v

$$p_i' = v p_i \tag{4}$$

Substituting into Eq. (3) and then using Eq. (2)

$$v = \frac{1}{\displaystyle\sum_{i=1}^{k} p_i} = \frac{1}{P(B)} \tag{5}$$

Thus, the probabilities now associated with each element of B is the factor $1/P(B)$ times the corresponding probabilities (p) before we knew that B had occurred. The event corresponding to A, now called $(A|B)$, is the set of sample points belonging to A, but also in B; that is, this event is the set $A \cap B$. The probability of this event is then $P(A \cap B)$ multiplied by the factor $1/P(B)$. Hence we have the formula

$$P(A|B) = \frac{P(A \cap B)}{P(B)} \tag{6}$$

This holds only if $P(B)$ is nonzero, i.e., as long as B is not the null event.

Example

> *Given:* four computer firms A,B,C,D bidding for a certain contract. A survey of past bidding success of these firms on similar contracts shows the following probabilities of winning:
>
> $P(A) = 0.3, P(B) = 0.2, P(C) = 0.4,$ and $P(D) = 0.1$
>
> Before the decision is made to award the contract, firm B withdraws its bid.
> *Find:* the new probabilities of A,C,D winning the bid

Solution Label the event "B has withdrawn" as Y and recognize that it is also the event "B does *not* win." Then $P(Y) = 1 - P(B) = 0.8$. The sets $A \cap Y$, $C \cap Y$, and $D \cap Y$ equal, respectively, the sets A,C,D, since A,C,D are all subsets of Y. Hence by Eq. (6)

$$P(A|Y) = \frac{P(A)}{P(Y)} = \frac{0.3}{0.8} = \frac{3}{8}$$

$$P(C|Y) = \frac{P(C)}{P(Y)} = \frac{0.4}{0.8} = \frac{4}{8}$$

$$P(D|Y) = \frac{P(D)}{P(Y)} = \frac{0.1}{0.8} = \frac{1}{8}$$

The principle of conditional probability may be generalized to the following theorem.

Bayes, theorem   Given S, an n-way partition of sample space X, that is, all of the n events S_i are disjoint and their union equals X. The probability $P(S_i)$ is often called the "a priori" or prior probability of event S_i. If information is then received that some event E has occurred, $P(S_i|E)$ the new (or a posteriori) probability of S_i is given by

$$P(S_i|E) = \frac{P(S_i \cap E)}{P(S_1 \cap E) + P(S_2 \cap E) + \cdots P(S_n \cap E)}$$

Example A certain firm has plants A,B,C with percent outputs of the total 20, 30, and 50, respectively. The probabilities of nondefective products are, respectively, 0.85, 0.90, and 0.95. A customer receives a defective product. What is the probability it came from plant C?

Solution Let E equal a defective product. An $E = AE$ equals a defective product from plant A (similarly for BE,CE). Then $P(AE) = 0.2(1 - 0.85) = 0.03$; $P(BE) = 0.3(0.1) = 0.03$; and $P(CE) = 0.5(0.05) = 0.025$. These were obtained using the product rule, since the source of the defective parts and the output probabilities are independent. By Bayes theorem

$$P(C\ E) = \frac{P(CE)}{P(AE) + P(BE) + P(CE)} = \frac{25}{85} = \frac{5}{17}$$

3-12 FREQUENCY RATIO: LAW OF LARGE NUMBERS

One insight into a meaning of probability follows from a situation typified by the following experiment. Consider some process (whose mechanics need not be known) that produces for each experimental trial an integer x known to be in the range, say

$$10 \leqslant x \leqslant 60$$

The sample space of the experiment then has $(60 - 10) + 1 = 51$ sample points. Now if the experiment is repeated say 10 times, one might typically observe the following 10 outcomes:

39,41,20,40,41,12,36,60,41,38

Even a cursory inspection of this string shows that most values tend to cluster around the value 40 (or 41), but there are also some values like 20, 12, and 60 that are quite distant from 40. In any case, the process that is generating our numbers seems to indicate that the experiment outcome "tends toward" the value 40 (with some less strong tendency toward numbers distant from 40). Our problem is to give a precise statement to this intuitive idea. To this end, for any sequence of trials, we can construct a frequency table (see Chap. 2) that lists all sample points and the number of occurrences of each, as well as the ratio of each such number to the total number of numbers (experiment trials).

If the experiment is repeated many more than just 10 times, we may expect that (provided each repetition of the experiment is independent of all others) the underlying (and unknown) process generating the numbers will exhibit its consistency in the following manner: Although each possible outcome may be expected to appear more times in 100 trials than in 10 trials, and more times in 1000 trials than 100 trials, the *proportion* (ratio) of the number of appearances of any particular outcome to the total number of trials tends towards a limiting value as the number of trials increases (say from 10 to 100 to 1000, as discussed above). To state this precisely, let $N_m(x)$ denote the number of appearances of x in a sequence of m trials. Let $P_m(x)$ be defined as

$$P_m(x) = \frac{N_m(x)}{m} = \frac{\text{number of appearances of outcome } x}{\text{number of trials}}$$

The ratio $P_m(x)$ as m becomes indefinitely large is one interpretation of the probability of the outcome x. The belief that the ratio will approach a limit p is just that, a *belief* based on many (but not all) observable phenomena. This property, also called the *law of large numbers* may be expressed mathematically as:

Given any $\epsilon > 0$, no matter how small,

$$\underset{m \to \infty}{\text{Probability}} \left(\left| \frac{N_m}{m} - p \right| < \epsilon \right) = 1$$

The law of large numbers should *not* be considered a law of the physical world, but rather a property of an abstract model that seems however to fit a large variety of systems (as judged by observing their behavior). A rigorous proof of the equation for certain mathematical probability models is also available (see Sec. 3-14).

A careful reading of the law of large numbers shows that it does *not* claim that the frequency ratio N_m/m approaches the probability p as m becomes large, but rather that the *probability* of the ratio being close to p is very close to 1. Thus even though m is extremely large, there is always some chance that the frequency ratio will be significantly different from p.

3-13 EXPECTATION AND VARIANCE

In a manner quite analogous to that used in statistics (Chap. 2), and for much the same reason, we seek descriptor numbers of random variables. Since the concepts are similar to those developed for statistics, we only list some results for random variables. It is worth noting, however, in the case of random variables, that most sums are over *sample-point values*, not over actual experiment sequences. We denote the random variable values as X_j and, according to the Axioms,

$$\sum_{j=1}^{n} P(X_j) = 1$$

Expectation (mean or expected value)

$$E(X) = \mu = \sum_{j=1}^{n} X_j P(X_j) \tag{1}$$

Thus, the expectation of a random variable is the weighted sum of its sample-point values, each point being weighted by its probability.

Suppose we now consider m random variables $X_1, X_2, \ldots, X_m$. Note the different use of the subscript from Eq. (1). There X_j meant one value in a sample space; now it means one random variable, i.e., the entire set of sample values for space j. Then, if the variables have expected values $\mu_1, \mu_2, \ldots, \mu_m$, we have the following theorem on the expectation of a sum.

Theorem 3-13.1

$$E(X_1 + X_2 + \cdots X_m) = E(X_1) + E(X_2) + \cdots E(X_m) = \sum_{i=1}^{m} \mu_1 \qquad (2)$$

An important special case is where all of the variables have the same mean μ_1. Then

$$E(mX) = m\mu_1 \qquad (3)$$

The *variance* of a random variable X is

$$V(X) = \sigma^2 = E((X - E(X))^2)$$

$$= \sum_{j=1}^{n} (X_j - \mu)^2 P(X_j) = \left(\sum_{j=1}^{n} X_j^2 P(X_j) \right) - \mu^2 \qquad (4)$$

The *standard deviation* σ is the square root of the variance.

If we now consider the variance of the random variable formed by summing several random variables, the applicable theorem, here stated without proof (see Ref. 1) is the companion to Theorem 3-13.1.

Theorem 3-13.2 Variance of sum If $X_1, X_2, \ldots, X_m$ are m random variables with variances $\sigma_1^2, \sigma_2^2 \ldots \sigma_m^2$ and S_m is the sum random variable $S_m = X_1 + X_2 + \cdots X_m$ then the variance of S_m is

$$V(S_m) = \sum_{i=1}^{m} \sigma_i^2 + 2 \sum_{j,\,k} \text{COV}(X_j, X_k) \qquad (5)$$

where the last sum contains each of the possible $C(m,2)$ pairs (X_j, X_k) with $j \neq k$ once, and only once.

An important special case is where the variables X_j are *mutually independent*; then the covariances are all zero and

$$V(S_m) = \sigma_1^2 + \sigma_2^2 + \cdots \sigma_m^2 \qquad (6)$$

If further, the variances are all equal say to σ_1^2,

$$V(S_m) = m\sigma_1^2 \qquad (7a)$$

and hence

$$\sigma_{S_m} = \sqrt{m}\, \sigma_1 \qquad (7b)$$

An application of the above theorems is to derive the formula for the mean number of probes in a binary search (Fig. 3-13.1). The binary search is a technique of efficiently searching a *sorted list* (file) X of distinct (nonduplicate) numbers for the position number of that element in X that matches (equals) a given argument value A.

Probe # → 1   2   3   4

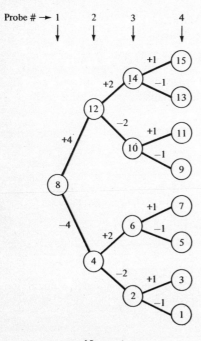

Probe # (k)	# cells reachable	Cell prob.	Product
1	1	$\frac{1}{15}$	$\frac{1}{15}$
2	2	$\frac{1}{15}$	$\frac{4}{15}$
3	4	$\frac{1}{15}$	$\frac{12}{15}$
4	8	$\frac{1}{15}$	$\frac{32}{15}$
k	2^{k-1}	$\frac{1}{15}$	$k2^{k-1}(1/n)$

$$E(k) = (\tfrac{1}{15})(1 + 4 + 12 + 32)$$
$$= \tfrac{49}{15} = 3.27$$

$n = 15;\ m = 4$

Increment magnitudes: 8, 4, 2, 1

Fig. 3-13.1 Binary search.

We will here assume that n, the number of elements in X, is one less than an integer power of 2

$$n = 2^m - 1 \quad \text{or} \quad m = \log_2(n + 1)$$

The search algorithm generates a succession of index values in X, the first index at the midpoint of the file. Each successive index I is used to compare $X[I]$ with A. If these are equal, the search is complete. Otherwise, if $X[I] > A$, a positive increment is added to I, and if $X[I] < A$, a negative increment is added to I. Each increment magnitude is half of the previous increment. The new I is then used in the next probe, etc. The process may be visualized with the aid of a tree diagram whose nodes are all possible I values (see Fig. 3-13.1 for the case of $m = 4$). Each connecting line is labelled with the positive or negative increment used to obtain the next index value from the current index.

To derive a formula for the mean number of probes to complete a search, assume equal probabilities of all items in X. The number of probes required to reach various items of X may be tabulated with the aid of the table. Thus on the kth probe, 2^{k-1} items can be reached. The mean number of probes is then

$$E(k) = \sum_{k=1}^{m=\log_2(n+1)} k2^{k-1}\left(\frac{1}{n}\right)$$

The heart of the expression on the right may be expressed as

$$\sum_{k=1}^{j} k2^k = 2(1 + (j - 1)2^j)$$

Using this and some algebra

$$E(k) = \left(\left(\frac{n + 1}{n}\right) \log_2 (n + 1)\right) - 1 \tag{8}$$

For a large list to be searched, $n \gg 1$, and then

$$E(k) \doteq (\log_2 n) - 1 \tag{9}$$

Thus the mean number of probes is only one less than the maximum number.

3-14 MARKOV AND CHEBYSHEV INEQUALITIES

These important general formulas give bounds on probabilities in terms of the mean and variance. They are independent in form of the particular probability function and are useful in both practical work and in proving theorems in probability theory.

Given a sample space with points x, assumed here to be nonnegative numbers, then, if t is any positive number, the expected value may be written

$$E(X) = \sum_{\cdot x} xP(x) = \sum_{x < t} xP(x) + \sum_{x \geq t} xP(x) \tag{1}$$

where the sum(s) extend over all x values. Since all x are nonnegative, both sums on the right are nonnegative as well. If only the second sum is retained, this is then clearly at most as large as $E(X)$, so that

$$E(X) \geq \sum_{x \geq t} xP(x) \tag{2}$$

Since the sum is over $x \geq t$, the inequality remains true if every x is replaced by the smaller value t

$$E(X) \geq \sum_{x \geq t} tP(x) = t \sum_{x \geq t} P(x) = tP(x \geq t) \tag{3}$$

The form at the right uses a concise kind of set specification to indicate the part of the sample space to which P refers. Transposing, we obtain *Markov's inequality*

$$P(x \geq t) \leq \frac{E(X)}{t} \tag{4}$$

Example Suppose the expected number of successes in 1000 trials of an experiment is 420. The probability of 800 or more successes is then *at most*

$$P(x \geq t) \leq \frac{420}{800} = 0.525$$

If we replace X by $(X - E(X))^2$ and t by t^2, then since $E((X - E(X))^2)$ is the variance, Markov's inequality becomes *Chebyshev's inequality*

$$P((X - E(X))^2 \geqslant t^2) \leqslant \frac{V(X)}{t^2} \tag{5}$$

where $V(X)$ is the variance of X. Another form is

$$P(|X - E(X)| \geqslant t) \leqslant \frac{V(X)}{t^2} \tag{6}$$

where $|X - E(X)|$ is the absolute value of the difference.

One important use of Chebyshev's inequality is to prove the "law of large numbers" stated in Sec. 3-12 and given here for proof.

Theorem 3-14.1 The (weak) law of large numbers Given a random variable X with mean μ and variance σ^2. Consider sample values $x_1, x_2, \ldots, x_n$ drawn from X and their sample average $M_n = (X_1 + X_2 + \cdots X_n)/n$. Then, given any ϵ value, no matter how small,

$$\underset{n \to \infty}{\text{limit}}\ P(|M_n - \mu| \geqslant \epsilon) = 0$$

Proof
1. Since $X_1, X_2 \ldots X_n$ are from the same population

   $$E(X_1) = E(X_2) \ldots E(X_n) = \mu$$

2. Using Eq. (3) of Sec. 3-13

   $$E(M_n) = \frac{n\mu}{n} = \mu$$

3. Since

   $$V\left(\frac{X}{n}\right) = \frac{1}{n^2 V(X)}$$

   then using Eq. (6) of Sec. 3-13

   $$V(M_n) = V\left(\frac{X_1 + X_2 + \cdots X_n}{n}\right) = \frac{n\sigma^2}{n^2} = \frac{\sigma^2}{n}$$

4. Applying Chebyshev's inequality to the random variable M_n, we then have

   $$P(|M_n - \mu| \geqslant \epsilon) \leqslant \frac{\sigma^2}{n\epsilon}$$

5. However small an ϵ is given (as n increases without limit), the right side approaches zero, and the theorem is proved.

3-15 BERNOULLI TRIALS: BINOMIAL, MULTINOMIAL, AND GEOMETRIC DISTRIBUTIONS

The Bernoulli trial is a representation of almost the simplest kind of experiment, since only two outcomes are permitted: one is called success (*s*), and the other failure (*f*). The probability of *s* is *p* and the probability of failure is then $q = 1 - p$. A Bernoulli trial may then be visualized as the toss of a biased coin, where *p* is the probability of head and $1 - p$ the probability of tail.

The Bernoulli trial is the experiment model for the fundamental binomial probability-distribution function, which includes as special cases the Poisson and normal distributions.

The binomial probability function is denoted by $B(k;n,p)$, which may be read: the probability of *k* successes in *n* Bernoulli trials where *p* is the probability of success in a single trial. Since the outcome of a sequence of *n* Bernoulli trials may be expressed as a string of *n* symbols, each from alphabet $\{s,f\}$ some sample points, for say $n=7$, would be labelled, for example,

   ssfssff   ffsfsss

Since each trial is independent of the others, the probability of a sample point representing *k* successes (and therefore $n - k$ failures) is, by the product rule,

   $p^k(1 - p)^{n-k}$

The number of these sample points may be found by identifying each with a bit vector of length *n* with *k* values 1. The number of such bit vectors was found to be $C(n,k)$ in Sec. 3-1. Hence

$$B(k;n,p) = C(n,k)p^k(1 - p)^{n-k} \tag{1}$$

or

$$B(k;n,p) = \left(\frac{n!}{k!(n - k)!}\right)p^k(1 - p)^{n-k} \tag{2}$$

where $B(k; n,p)$ = probability of *k* successes in *n* trials, and *p* = probability of success in one trial. Usually, *n* and *p* are fixed values, while *k* is the random variable.

Example What is the probability that in five throws of a fair die, the number 2 will appear
   (*a*) three times
   (*b*) at least three times

Solution Since the die is fair, $p = 1/6$ for any face. The solution to (*a*) is then $P(3; 5, 1/6) = (1/6)^3 (5/6)^2 (5!/2!3!)$. The solution to (*b*) is found by summing the sample-point probabilities in the event "at least three successes"

$$P\text{ (at least three successes)} = \sum_{k=3}^{5} B\left(k; 5, \frac{1}{6}\right)$$

The sum of all B values from $k = 0$ through $k = n$ must of course equal 1. This is easily demonstrated by recognizing that Eq. (1) is the kth term of the binomial expansion of

$$(p + (1 - p))^n = 1^n = 1$$

The sum of the B values is then this binomial, and hence also equals 1.

The mean of the binomial distribution may be derived starting with the definition

$$E(k) = \sum_{k=0}^{n} k \, B(k;n,p) = \sum_{k=1}^{n} k \, B(k;n,p) \tag{3}$$

Since the term for $k = 0$ is zero

$$E(k) = \sum_{k=1}^{n} \frac{n!}{k!(n-k)!} \, p^k (1-p)^{n-k}$$

substitute $k = j + 1$. Then, after some algebra,

$$E(k) = pn \sum_{j=0}^{n-1} \frac{(n-1)!}{j!(n-1-j)!} \, p^j (1-p)^{n-1-j}$$

Another substitution of $r = n - 1$ gives

$$E(k) = pn \sum_{j=0}^{r} \frac{r!}{j!(r-j)!} \, p^j (1-p)^{r-j}$$

The sum is 1, since it is the sum of *all B*. Hence

$$E(k) = pn \tag{4}$$

A somewhat more tedious process gives, for the variance of k,

$$V(k) = pn(1 - p) \tag{5}$$

The binomial distribution may be generalized to the *multinomial*. This applies to an experiment where in *each* trial there are n possible outcomes, the ith with probability p_i. Then

$$\sum_{i=1}^{n} p_i = 1 \tag{6}$$

Any sequence of m such trials is an *experiment* whose outcome can then be represented as a string of m symbols, each belonging to an n alphabet. The multinomial distribution gives the probability that such a string has k_1 appearances of the first member of the outcome alphabet, k_2 appearances of the second, etc. This probability may be derived using analogous reasoning to the binomial

$$P(k_1,k_2,\ldots,k_n;p_1,p_2,\ldots,p_n) = \frac{m!}{k_1!,k_2!,\ldots,k_n!}p_1^{k_1}p_2^{k_2}\ldots p_n^{k_r} \qquad (7)$$

where clearly

$$\Sigma k_i = k_1 + k_2 + \cdots k_n = m \qquad (8)$$

The expected (mean) number of occurrences of the ith outcome is

$$E(k_i) = np_i \qquad (9)$$

and the variance for this outcome is

$$V(k_i) = m(1 - p_i) \qquad (10)$$

The multinomial is useful for analyzing frequency distributions arising from sampling a process with replacement. A frequency distribution gives the number of occurrences of each possible outcome. If each outcome is designated as a distinct symbol, any given frequency distribution is then a string of symbols that fits the multinomial model. This fact is the basis of the chi-squared test (see Appendix B) for comparing an observed frequency distribution to some other one, such as one arising from some abstract probabilistic model.

The binomial distribution is not the only probability function that can be defined by a sequence of Bernoulli trials. Consider, for example, the following experiment that leads to the *geometric distribution:*

A sequence of Bernoulli trials to the *first* success. The probability that k trials are required is

$$G(k;p) = (1 - p)^{k-1}p \qquad (11)$$

This is readily verified since there is only one sample point for a given k; it may be labelled with its first $k - 1$ symbols f (failures) and the last symbol an s. Since the trials are independent, the product rule then gives Eq. (11). Note that the sample space contains an infinite number of points, since we may have to make this many trials until the *first* success. Thus

$$\sum_{k=1}^{\infty}(1 - p)^{k-1}p = 1 \qquad (12)$$

That the sum equals 1 may be established algebraically using the formula for the sum of the geometric progression.

The *negative binomial* distribution results from a sequence of Bernoulli trials *until* the rth success (where k, the number of required trials, is now the random variable). A sample-point label will then have k symbols; the first $k - 1$ will contain $r - 1$ s symbols, and hence $(k - r)$ f symbols, and the kth symbol must be an s. For any given k, using the product rule on such a configuration gives a sample-point probability of $p^r(1 - p)^{k-r}$. The number of such sample points is the number of ways of assigning the $r - 1$ s symbols to the first $k - 1$ positions. Hence

$$N(k;r,p) = C(k - 1, r - 1)p^r(1 - p)^{k-r} \qquad (13)$$

and

$$\sum_{k=1}^{\infty} N(k;r,p) = 1 \tag{14}$$

3-16 THE POISSON DISTRIBUTION

The Poisson distribution function that arises in many physical models may be derived in a number of ways. In this section we show how to obtain it as a special case of the binomial distribution. It will be most convenient to start with the recursion form of this function, which may be derived by simple algebra from the closed form of Eq. (2) of Sec. 3-15.

$$B(0;n,p) = (1 - p)^n \tag{1a}$$

$$B(k + 1;n,p) = \left(\frac{p}{1 - p}\right)\left(\frac{n - k}{k + 1}\right) \, B(k;n,p) \tag{1b}$$

Equation (1a) is the case of $k = 0$. Taking logarithms of both sides

$$\ln B(0;n,p) = n \ln (1 - p) \tag{2}$$

and substituting the series expansion of $\ln (1 - p)$ about $p = 0$

$$\ln B(0;n,p) = n\left(-p - \frac{p^2}{2} - \frac{p^3}{3} \cdots \right)$$

Suppose now that

$$p \ll 1 \tag{3a}$$

$$k \ll n \tag{3b}$$

$$\lambda = pn \tag{3c}$$

Then, since p is small, all terms of the series except the first may be dropped, and

$$\ln B(0;n,p) \doteq -np = -\lambda$$

Taking antilogs

$$B(0;n,p) = P(0;\lambda) = e^{-\lambda} \tag{4}$$

If the approximations of Eqs. (3) are now applied to the recursion form of Eq. (1b)

$$B(k + 1;n,p) = \left(\frac{\lambda}{k + 1}\right) B(k;n,p) \tag{5}$$

Using Eq. (4) for $B(0;n,p)$, a few successive substitutions into Eq. (5) gives

$$B(1;n,p) = \left(\frac{\lambda}{1}\right) e^{-\lambda} \tag{6a}$$

$$B(2; n, p) = \left(\frac{\lambda^2}{1 \cdot 2}\right)e^{-\lambda} \tag{6b}$$

etc., so that in general, for any k

$$P(k; \lambda) = \left(\frac{\lambda^k}{k!}\right)e^{-\lambda} \tag{7}$$

This is the Poisson distribution function, which may also be written in recursion form

$$P(0; \lambda) = e^{-\lambda}$$

$$P(k + 1; \lambda) = \left(\frac{\lambda}{k + 1}\right)P(k; \lambda) \tag{8}$$

As for any probability function

$$\sum_{k=0}^{\infty} P(k; \lambda) = \sum_{k=0}^{\infty} \left(\frac{\lambda^k}{k!}\right)e^{-\lambda} = 1 \tag{9}$$

This may be seen algebraically since $e^{-\lambda}$ may be factored out from the sum; the sum is then recognized as the series expression for e^{λ}. The product of $e^{-\lambda}e^{\lambda} = 1$.

The mean and variance of the Poisson distribution may be obtained from the expressions for the binomial by applying the approximations of Eq. (3). Thus

$$E(k) = pn = \lambda \tag{10}$$

$$V(k) = pn(1 - p) \doteq pn = \lambda \tag{11}$$

Hence the Poisson distribution is characterized by the mean and variance, both of which are equal to each other and to the parameter λ.

It is of interest at this point to examine the "physical" or model conditions implied by the approximation. Equations (3) suggests that the Poisson distribution applies to an experiment characterized by a long sequence of Bernoulli trials, where p (the success probability in a single trial) is very small; the long sequence (large n) yields an expected (mean) value of $\lambda = pn$ that may be moderately large, even though p is very small. Then p, n "merge" into the parameter λ. If it is known that we have a Poisson process, then only the single parameter λ, which is the mean of the distribution, suffices to determine the entire probability function.

It is also worth noting that

$$P(0; \lambda) = e^{-\lambda} = \text{probability of no successes}$$

and

$$1 - P(0, \lambda) = 1 - e^{-\lambda} = \text{probability of } at \text{ } least \text{ one success}$$

The last form shows that in a Poisson process, the probability of "at least one success" is an exponential. Tables of the Poisson distribution are available (see Appendix Table C-1).

Example In a certain communications system there are 100 statistically similar users that can request service. In a given interval, the probability that any particular user makes a request is 0.05 (and the same for any user). Find:

(*a*) expected number of requests
(*b*) the probability of at least one request
(*c*) the probability that three or more users make a request

Solution Consider each user's "request/no request" as a Bernoulli trial. Then

$$p = 0.05 \quad n = 100 \quad pn = (0.05)(100) = 5$$

Since $p \ll 1$, the model is considered as Poisson. Then

(*a*) $E(k) = \lambda = 5$

(*b*) $P(k \geqslant 1; 5) = 1 - P(0; 5) = 1 - e^{-5}$

$$= 1 - 0.0067$$

$$= 0.9933$$

(*c*) $P(k \geqslant 3; 5) = 0.8753$ (from tables)

3-17 MARKOV CHAIN MODELS

Discrete Markov chains are conceptually similar in many ways to the finite-state machine models familiar to computer scientists. Figure 3-17.1 shows an example to illustrate the basic concepts. Consider a "rat maze" of four chambers, each representing a state of the system. From each chamber there are various exits to other chambers. Associated with each exit is a probability of the rat taking this exit.

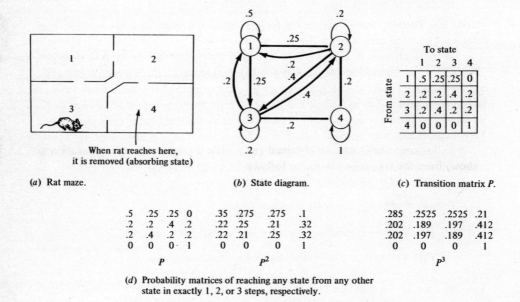

(*a*) Rat maze. (*b*) State diagram. (*c*) Transition matrix *P*.

						To state			
							1	2	3	4

From state:

	1	2	3	4
1	.5	.25	.25	0
2	.2	.2	.4	.2
3	.2	.4	.2	.2
4	0	0	0	1

$$
P = \begin{array}{cccc}
.5 & .25 & .25 & 0 \\
.2 & .2 & .4 & .2 \\
.2 & .4 & .2 & .2 \\
0 & 0 & 0 & 1
\end{array}
\qquad
P^2 = \begin{array}{cccc}
.35 & .275 & .275 & .1 \\
.22 & .25 & .21 & .32 \\
.22 & .21 & .25 & .32 \\
0 & 0 & 0 & 1
\end{array}
\qquad
P^3 = \begin{array}{cccc}
.285 & .2525 & .2525 & .21 \\
.202 & .189 & .197 & .412 \\
.202 & .197 & .189 & .412 \\
0 & 0 & 0 & 1
\end{array}
$$

(*d*) Probability matrices of reaching any state from any other state in exactly 1, 2, or 3 steps, respectively.

Fig. 3-17.1 A simple Markov chain model.

(Different probabilities may be due to the sizes of the exit holes.) Since the exits connect chambers which are states, the probabilities of exit are the probabilities of state transitions. Also, in this particular model, we assume that if the rat reaches chamber 4, it is removed from the maze. Such a state, from which the probability of reaching any and all other states is zero, is called an *absorbing* state.

Suppose that a rat is placed in some chamber (state) initially. What is the probability that it will be in some other specified state after 1, 2, 3, etc., steps? By a *step* we mean a state transition. To begin to answer such questions, consider two representations of the maze problem shown in Fig. 3-17.1. The first is a state diagram where the rat's presence in a chamber is a state shown by a circle, and the probability of exit to another state is shown as a "directed line" labelled with the probability. Note the "self-loops," each labelled with the probability of the rat remaining in the same state. A matrix form of the problem statement is also shown. The matrix P is called the *transition matrix* and the typical element P_{ij} is the probability of a transition from state i to state j in a single step. P_i, denoting row i of P, then accounts for all exit lines from state i, and hence the sum of all elements of P_i must be 1.

Let us now return to a basic question of the type posed earlier. Given that the rat is now in state 3, what is the probability that in the next step it will be in state 1? Clearly, this is easily found from the state diagram by locating the edge from state 3 to state 1 and reading its label, which is seen to be 0.2. Now suppose we ask: What is the probability that, 2 steps after starting in state 3, the rat will be in state 1? To answer this, we carefully trace all 2-step paths from state 3 to state 1. Along each path, the probabilities are multiplied (since the transitions are independent) and the products are then added:

Path	Probability
$3 \rightarrow 1 \rightarrow 1$	$(0.2)(0.5) = 0.10$
$3 \rightarrow 2 \rightarrow 1$	$(0.4)(0.2) = 0.08$
$3 \rightarrow 3 \rightarrow 1$	$(0.2)(0.2) = \underline{0.04}$
Probability of transition from state 3 to state 1 in 2 steps	$= 0.22$

The same result can be obtained (as a little thought and experimentation will show) from the transition matrix, as follows:

$$\sum_{k=1}^{4} P_{3k} P_{k1}$$

or, in matrix-vector notation, as the inner product of row 3 and column 1:

$$P_3 P_{,1}$$

More generally, the matrix product of P with itself has the following meaning:

$$P^1 = P = \text{probabilities of states after 1 transition}$$
$$P^2 = PP^1 = \text{probabilities of states after 2 transitions (steps)}$$

Also

$$P^n = PP^{n-1} = \text{ probabilities of states after } n \text{ transitions}$$

We now shall record some fundamental definitions and theorems of Markov chains, occasionally commenting on these.

DEFINITION

A regular Markov chain is one whose transition matrix, when raised to some power, has all of its elements nonzero.

It follows that for a regular chain, it is possible to reach every state from any state in some finite number of steps. As we step through a Markov process, we naturally are interested in the matrix of powers of P whose elements give, as seen previously, the probabilities of reaching each state from any other state as a function of the number of steps taken. The following theorems assure us that, for regular chains, there is a "steady state" reached.

Theorem 3-17.1 If P is a transition matrix for a regular chain, then
1. As n increases, P^n approaches some matrix T.
2. Each row of T equals the same vector W.
3. All components of W are nonzero.

Theorem 3-17.2 The steady-state probability vector W of Theorem 3-17.1 is unique and satisfies the vector-matrix equation $WP = W$.

A regular chain (see Definition) is a subclass of an *ergodic* chain.

DEFINITION

An ergodic chain is a Markov chain such that it is possible to reach every state from every other state in some sequence of steps.

The ergodic class is wider than the regular class; i.e., every regular chain is ergodic, but not every ergodic chain is regular. For example, consider the transition matrix for a two-state system where state 2 can be reached from state 1 (and vice versa) in only an odd number of steps. Then

$$P = \begin{pmatrix} 0 & 1 \\ 1 & 0 \end{pmatrix} \qquad P^2 = \begin{pmatrix} 1 & 0 \\ 0 & 1 \end{pmatrix} \qquad P^3 = \begin{pmatrix} 0 & 1 \\ 1 & 0 \end{pmatrix} \text{etc.}$$

Here, every state is reachable in one or two steps from every other, and hence the chain is ergodic. However, the powers of P are seen always to contain some O elements so the chain is not regular. We now list some important theorems for ergodic chains.

Theorem 3-17.3 If P is a transition matrix for an ergodic chain, then
1. There is a unique probability vector W such that $WP = W$. W is called the steady-state probability vector.

2. All components of W are nonzero.
3. If $h_j^{(n)}$ is the average number of times the process is in state s_j in the first n steps, then for any $\epsilon > 0$

Probability $(|h_j^{(n)} - W_j| > \epsilon) \to 0$

(no matter what the starting state).

This theorem is a "law of large numbers" for Markov chains, since it states roughly that as the number of state transitions increase, the average number of times the system is in any given state (i.e., its relative frequency of being in the state) approaches the steady-state probability of its being in the state.

A Markov process, in stepping from state to state, will often leave some state only to return to it in some later step. The number of steps to return to a state is called the *recurrence time* for the state.

Example Suppose a job is represented as having only two possible states: the first is CPU processing, and the second is I/O processing. Assume that the probabilities of all state transitions are available. Find expressions for the steady-state probabilities for the CPU and I/O states in terms of the transition probabilities.

Solution Transition matrix is

$$P = \begin{pmatrix} P_{11} & P_{12} \\ P_{21} & P_{22} \end{pmatrix}$$

Since all P_{ij} are nonzero, the chain is regular and ergodic. If W_1 and W_2 are the steady-state probabilities, then from Theorem 3-17.3

$$(W_1, W_2) \begin{pmatrix} P_{11} & P_{12} \\ P_{21} & P_{22} \end{pmatrix} = (W_1, W_2)$$

from which we get the first two of the following equations, which is augmented by the third,

$$P_{11} W_1 + P_{21} W_2 = W_1$$
$$P_{12} W_1 + P_{22} W_2 = W_2$$
$$W_1 + W_2 = 1$$

Since there are three equations in two unknowns, the equations are not independent. Since the last one *must* hold, we choose the last two equations. Upon solving them both, we obtain

$$W_1 = \frac{1 - P_{22}}{1 + P_{21} - P_{22}}$$

$$W_2 = \frac{P_{21}}{1 + P_{21} - P_{22}}$$

It follows from Theorem 3-17.3 that W_1, W_2 are the average number of times the system is in the CPU and I/O states, respectively.

Theorem 3-17.4 For an ergodic Markov chain, the mean recurrence time for state i is $1/W_i$, where W_i is the ith component of the steady-state probability vector.

An absorbing state was illustrated in the "rat-maze" example and was seen to be a state with no exit to another state. Its row of the transition matrix is all zeros, except for a "one" on the main diagonal position. If a process ever reaches an absorbing state, it is blocked (i.e., no further states can then be reached). A chain is said to be absorbing if it contains an absorbing state and it is possible to reach this state. A Markov chain with one or more absorbing states can always be represented by a standard or *canonical* form of its transition matrix:

$$P = \begin{array}{cc} & r \text{ states} \quad s \text{ states} \\ \begin{array}{c} r \\ s \end{array} & \left(\begin{array}{c|c} I & O \\ \hline R & Q \end{array} \right) \end{array}$$

Here, the first r states are the absorbing ones; the remaining s states are not. Then

$I = r$ by r identity matrix (all O elements except 1s on main diagonal)
$O = r$ by s matrix of zeros
$R = s$ by r matrix for transitions from nonabsorbing to absorbing states
$Q = s$ by s matrix of transitions from nonabsorbing to nonabsorbing states

It can be easily shown that the nth power of P may be written

$$P^n = \begin{pmatrix} I & O \\ * & Q^n \end{pmatrix}$$

where $*$ denotes a matrix of no immediate interest. Note the similarity of P and P^n. In particular, Q^n gives the probabilities of being in nonabsorbing states after n steps, having started in any nonabsorbing state. With this in mind, we now list two important theorems:

Theorem 3-17.5 For an absorbing Markov chain, the probability of the absorbing state being reached is 1.

Theorem 3-17.6 Let N be the matrix related to the submatrices of the canonic form of P, as follows:

$$N = (I - Q)^{-1}$$

Then the elements of N give the mean number of times the process reaches each nonabsorbing state, starting from each possible nonabsorbing state.

3-18 RELIABILITY MODELS: SERIES-PARALLEL STRUCTURES

System-reliability considerations have the following aspects:

1. Estimation of failure (or reliability)
2. Minimization of probability of failure

3. Detection of failure
4. Recovery from failure

Our concern in this chapter is with the first of these items, more precisely the computation of system reliability from the reliability of the components. The mathematical models that will be developed are valuable in gaining certain insights into the reliability performance of various configurations. However, reliability data of the components (like tape, disk, storage, CPU, etc.) are rarely available, which is clearly a limitation to the practical value of any prediction methodology.

Reliability has been an essential consideration in computer planning from the earliest days of electronic machines. Modern system design includes reliability considerations from device to system fabrication to programming. Examples include selection of the simplest and most reliable two-state operation of devices, worst-case design of circuits, parity checking in I/O, storage and data-flow paths, and more elaborate methods, such as *echoing* and automatic retry on some mechanical devices. (*Echoing* is a technique for checking information entered into a device by copying it from that device and comparing this with the original.)

Like most other desirable commodities, reliability is costly; the most reliable system may not be the best practical system if the cost is too great. Naturally, where national security, human life, or key operations of a firm depend critically on the system, a higher investment in reliability is wise, if not essential; one factor in deciding on the size of investment in reliability improvement is the estimated cost of failure to the users of the system.

Recently, the subject of reliability of general systems has become a full-fledged technical discipline, as evidenced by the appearance of textbooks, numerous technical papers, and professional organizations for workers in this field. A theory of reliability is developing which draws heavily on combinatorial mathematics, probability theory, and statistics. As in most theories, the mathematical techniques are applied to certain idealized models of the real world. In the rest of this chapter, a few such models are discussed.

Any well-defined part of a system that can be classified at all times as either working or else nonworking (failed) will be called a *component*. The *reliability* of a component will be defined as the probability that it will work (will not fail) over some specified time interval. If r is the reliability of a component, then $1 - r$ is the probability of failure (sometimes called the *unreliability*) of the component. A system consists of an interconnection of components. Notice that a system or subsystem is technically also a component. We assume throughout that all component failures are independent. For this discussion, we are not interested directly in the physical interconnections, but in a reliability structure which can often be represented as a network-like diagram that displays the behavior of the system from a reliability viewpoint. Two basic reliability structures, each containing n components, may be contrasted. The first, called a *series* system, has the property that if any one of its components fails, the system fails. An alternative statement is: A series structure is one so connected that all its components must work for the system to work. The reliability of the series structure is the *product* of its component reliabilities. In general, a reliability structure containing n components in series, the ith having reliability r_i, will have a system reliability R

$$R = \prod_{i=1}^{k} r_i \tag{1}$$

Another simple reliability structure is called *parallel* and has the property that the system fails only if all its components fail. In this case, the probability of failure of the system, equal to one minus the reliability of the system, is the product of the unreliabilities of the components

$$R = 1 - \prod_{i=1}^{n} (1 - r_i) \tag{2}$$

Many system reliability structures can be considered to be composed of combinations of series and parallel substructures. The above fundamental relations are then applied to each such substructure until an expression is derived for the system reliability in terms of the component reliability. An example is shown in Fig. 3-18.1 in step-by-step form. The reliability of the parallel substructure r_1, r_2 is called a; the

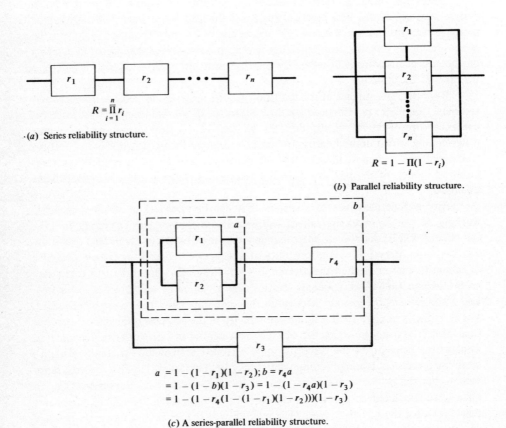

(a) Series reliability structure.

$$R = \prod_{i=1}^{n} r_i$$

$$R = 1 - \prod_{i}(1 - r_i)$$

(b) Parallel reliability structure.

$$a = 1 - (1 - r_1)(1 - r_2); b = r_4 a$$
$$= 1 - (1 - b)(1 - r_3) = 1 - (1 - r_4 a)(1 - r_3)$$
$$= 1 - (1 - r_4(1 - (1 - r_1)(1 - r_2)))(1 - r_3)$$

(c) A series-parallel reliability structure.

Fig. 3-18.1   Series-parallel structures.

expression for this is combined with r_4 to form the series substructure whose reliability is called b. Finally, b and r_3 are combined as a parallel structure to obtain the expression for p.

As another example, consider a computer system with the following component reliabilities:

One core-storage unit with reliability r_1
One arithmetic unit with reliability r_2
Two disk-file units, each with reliability r_3
Three tape units, each with reliability r_4

For this system to work, the core storage, arithmetic unit, at least one disk file, and at least two tape units must work. What is the reliability of the system? It should be clear that the reliability structure contains r_1 in series with r_2, and this in series with two r_3's in parallel. This substructure is in series with a substructure involving r_4. To derive the reliability representation for the "two-out-of-three" tapes specification, make an eight-row truth table representing the three tapes; place a "one" in the function column wherever the corresponding row has at least two 1s. These rows and their corresponding reliability expressions are

$$011 \rightarrow (1 - r_4)r_4 r_4 = r_4^2 - r_4^3$$
$$101 \rightarrow r_4(1 - r_4)r_4 = r_4^2 - r_4^3$$
$$110 \rightarrow r_4 r_4(1 - r_4) = r_4^2 - r_4^3 \qquad (3)$$
$$111 \rightarrow r_4 r_4 r_4 = r_4^3$$

The reliability of the tape part of the system is the sum of the above expressions:

$$t = 3r_4^2 - 2r_4^3 \qquad (4)$$

This reliability should then be combined in series with the rest of the system as described earlier. The expression for total system reliability is then

$$R = r_1 r_2 (1 - (1 - r_3)^2) r_4^2 (3 - 2r_4) \qquad (5)$$

3-19 MORE GENERAL RELIABILITY STRUCTURES

Many reliability statements can be easily translated to a series-parallel structure as seen above. One type that cannot is the "at least j-out-of-m components-must-work" type of statement seen in the last example of Sec. 3-18. There we resorted to a truth-table technique that may be generalized as follows: Given m components, each with reliability r. If at least j must work for the system to work, the reliability is

$$R = \sum_{i=j}^{m} C(m, i) r^i (1 - r)^{m-i}$$

This formula may be derived using the truth-table representation, the product rule, and the discussion of $C(n,i)$ in Sec. 3-1.

3-20 REDUNDANCY

Thus far only the reliability analysis problem, i.e., the computation of reliability of a given system, has been considered. The problem of improving reliability with specified components will now be explored.

If a system is specified with n components and the system has a reliability p, it will usually be necessary to add components in order to improve the reliability. The system then contains *redundancy*. In practice, the additional components may, with proper design, also be employed to increase performance. With such a system, highest performance (e.g., speed) is available when all components work. When failure occurs, at least up to some limiting number of components, the system suffers performance degradation, but it is still operational. Such a system is said to "fail softly."

Consider now an elementary question of how best to use a given amount of redundant equipment. If a system originally requires s components in series, each with reliability r, and we are willing to use ms components, there are two schemes that may be contrasted; these are called *component standby* and *system standby*. With component standby, each component is in parallel with $m - 1$ components, and these parallel structures are connected in series. Reliability is then

$$R = (1 - (1 - r)^m)^s \tag{1}$$

With system standby m systems are in parallel, and each is a copy of the original system containing s components in series. System reliability is

$$R = 1 - (1 - r^s)^m \tag{2}$$

It can be shown that for any reliability r and given values of s and m (amount of equipment), the component-standby scheme is at least as reliable as system standby. The component-standby system, however, requires more connections and hence tends to be more costly. Also, the reliability of the switching processes must be considered.

3-21 MEAN TIME TO FAILURE

Thus far, component reliability has been represented by the symbol r. In practice r will be a function of time. Theoretical models exist that are particularly suitable for deriving theoretical results and performing computations. Needless to say, the results from these models should be applied with caution to practical situations.

Before discussing a common analytic expression for $r(t)$, it is well to consider qualitatively a more practical case, as shown in Fig. 3-21.1. The shape of the curve is typical of vacuum-tube and many mechanical components. The curve has three regions: the first is called *burn-in* or *infant mortality,* which lasts from installation time to time t_1; after which there follows a period of constant failure rate to t_2; and finally there is the *wear-out* region. Although this function is fairly typical of many actual systems, it is difficult to represent analytically. The theory below applies to the flat constant failure-rate region.

Consider the observation of a large number n_0 of identical components over a long time period. As time progresses, some components will fail, and hence the

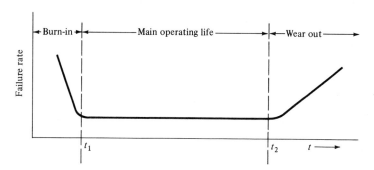

Fig. 3-21.1   Typical form of failure rate vs. time.

number surviving, n_s, will be a function of time. The reliability of the component at time t will be defined as the fraction of the original number that survive at time t:

$$r(t) = \frac{n_s(t)}{n_0} \tag{1a}$$

Suppose that the components fail in such a way that in the interval from t to $t + dt$, the number that fail, dn_f, is proportional to both the number surviving at the start of the interval and to the length of the interval

$$dn_f = an_s dt \tag{1b}$$

Since $n_f \equiv n_0 - n_s$ and n_0 is independent of t, (1b) becomes

$$- dn_s = an_s dt \tag{1c}$$

By Eq. (1a), $n_s \equiv n_0 r$ and Eq. (1c) can be written

$$\frac{dr}{r} = - a\, dt \tag{1d}$$

Integrating both sides and determining the integration constant with condition $r(0) = 1$, the exponential law is obtained:

$$r(t) = e^{-at} \tag{1e}$$

The reliability and failure densities are the derivatives of r and $1-r$

$$r' = \frac{dr}{dt} = - ae^{-at} \tag{2a}$$

$$(1 - r)' = ae^{-at} \tag{2b}$$

The mean time to failure (MTF) is the average overall time of the failure density

$$\text{MTF} = \int_0^\infty t(1 - r)'\, dt \tag{3}$$

using Eq. (2b) to find $(1 - r)$

$$\text{MTF} = \int_0^\infty tae^{-at}\, dt \tag{4}$$

Integrating by parts

$$\text{MTF} = \frac{1}{a} \tag{5}$$

For n identical components in *series*, exponential distribution of component reliability yields

$$R(t) = [r(t)]\,n = e^{-nat} \tag{6}$$

The mean time to failure of the system is then

$$\text{MTF} = \frac{1}{na} \tag{7}$$

From Eq. (5), this is seen to be $1/n$ times the mean time to failure of a single component.

More generally, if n components with nonidentical reliabilities are in series, the ith having a reliability r_i and a mean time to failure of $t_i = 1 \div a_i$, Eq. (6) becomes a product, and for the exponential distribution, the sum of the a_i, appears in the exponent. For this more general case, Eq. (7) becomes

$$\text{MTF} = 1 \div \sum_{i=1}^n a_i = 1 \div \sum_{i=1}^n 1 \div t_i \tag{8}$$

The mean time to failure of a parallel system of identical components can be derived by a process similar to that for obtaining Eq. (7), although the algebraic manipulation is more involved. Using Eq. (2) of Sec. 3-18 and substituting into the definition of Eq. (3),

$$\text{MTF} = \frac{n}{a} \int_0^\infty at(1 - e^{-at})^{n-1} e^{-at}\, d(at) \tag{9}$$

Using the binomial expansion for the $1 - e^{-at}$ raised to the $(n - 1)$st power and then integrating and simplifying gives

$$\text{MTF} = \frac{1}{a} \sum_{j=1}^n (-1)^{j-1} \frac{C(n,j)}{j} \tag{10}$$

where $C(n,j)$ is the binomial coefficient (number of combinations of n things taken j at a time). Equation (10) can be shown to simplify to

$$\text{MTF} = \frac{1}{a} \sum_{j=1}^n \frac{1}{j} \tag{11}$$

3-22 A FAILURE/REPAIR RELIABILITY MOₗ

All of the models considered thus far have b₍ only with failure probabilities. In practice, failures of machines (reliabᵢ `)` are followed by repairs, including diagnostic activities. We now consiₔ t includes both failure and repair.

It is a Markov model that is called the *machine* odel in the literature of queuing theory. The same mathematical techₙ `cations to multiuser systems of various types, as will be shown in Ch₎ eliability context, there are n machines in all, i of them working and ₗ e., not working and being repaired. It is assumed that the probabilitᵧ any working machine is the same as any other, and also that the probaₗ led machine completing repair is the same for all machines. Furthermₒ d that the failure and repair probabilities of each machine are constanₗ depend on their time of failure or previous history. All failures and repaiₗ are also assumed independent of each other.

The model may be visualized as a queuing situation with the repair faₓ ., the server(s), and each failure a request for service. Then let

n = total number of machines

P_i = probability that i machines are in repair (not working)

$\lambda_i h$ = probability of some single working machine failing in the short interval h

$\mu_i h$ = probability of some single failed machine completing repair in the short interval h

Note that λ_i and μ_i, representing failure and service rates respectively, are functions of the number of machines currently failed (i). We shall later suggest specific functions for λ_i, μ_i, but for the present we keep the analysis general.

We now consider a Markov type representation, as suggested in Fig. 3-22.1. State i means i machines awaiting repair, and of course also $n - i$ machines working. State

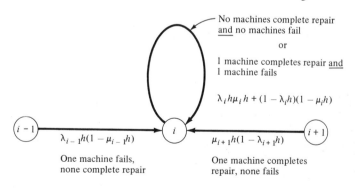

No machines complete repair and no machines fail

or

1 machine completes repair and 1 machine fails

$$\lambda_i h \mu_i h + (1 - \lambda_i h)(1 - \mu_i h)$$

$\lambda_{i-1} h(1 - \mu_{i-1} h)$

One machine fails, none complete repair

$\mu_{i+1} h(1 - \lambda_{i+1} h)$

One machine completes repair, none fails

$\lambda_i h$ = probability of failure of some one machine when i machines have failed
$\mu_i h$ = probability of repair of some one machine when i machines have failed

Fig. 3-22.1 Markov nodes for failure-repair model.

transitions occur only at time intervals h, which must be short enough that there is negligible probability that more than one machine will either fail or emerge repaired in this interval. As will be seen shortly, h is not a parameter of the problem, but it must be assumed to be very small, as indicated above for Fig. 3-22.1, since only transitions involving one-state transitions from $i-1$ and $i+1$ to i are considered. From Fig. 3-22.1, the probability of state i may be found by summing the lines in node i; in recording the result, we neglect terms with h^2 in them (since h is assumed small as noted earlier).

$$P_i = P_{i-1}\lambda_{i-1}h + P_i(1 - \lambda_i h - \mu_i h) + P_{i+1}\mu_{i+1}h \tag{1}$$

Subtracting the common P_i from both sides, dividing by h, and solving for P_{i+1}

$$P_{i+1} = \frac{1}{\mu_{i+1}}(P_i(\lambda_i + \mu_i) - P_{i-1}\lambda_{i-1}) \tag{2}$$

Since no machines can complete repair when none have failed

$$\mu_0 = 0 \tag{3}$$

Also, when all n machines are in repair, none can fail, so

$$\lambda_n = 0 \tag{4}$$

Using those, for $i = 0$, Eq. (2) yields

$$P_1 = \frac{\lambda_0}{\mu_1}P_0 \tag{5}$$

Then, Eq. (2) may be used successively to find first

$$P_2 = P_0 \frac{\lambda_0 \lambda_1}{\mu_1 \mu_2} \tag{6}$$

and then the general pattern

$$P_j = P_0 \frac{\lambda_0}{\mu_j}\prod_{i=1}^{j-1}\left(\frac{\lambda_i}{\mu_i}\right) \quad 1 \leqslant j \leqslant n \tag{7}$$

Since P_j is the probability that j machines are in repair, it is also the probability that $n-j$ machines are working. The mean number working is then

$$\bar{n} = \sum_{j=0}^{n}(n-j)P_j = n - \sum_{j=1}^{n}jP_j \tag{8}$$

where we have here used

$$\sum_{i=0}^{n}P_j = P_0 + \sum_{j=1}^{n}P_j = 1 \tag{9}$$

Using Eq. (7) in Eq. (9) and solving for P_0

$$P_0 = \cfrac{1}{1 + \displaystyle\sum_{j=1}^{n} \frac{\lambda_0}{\mu_j} \prod_{i=1}^{j-1} \left(\frac{\lambda_i}{\mu_i}\right)} \tag{10}$$

To get further specific results, we need explicit expressions for λ_i, μ_i as functions of i. Several "reasonable" such functions can be suggested, each corresponding to a different crude but hopefully usable representation of a failure/repair mechanism. For example, because the machines, failure probabilities are identical and independent, the probability of the failure of some one machine when $n - i$ machines are working would seem to be

$$\lambda_i = (n - i)\lambda \tag{11}$$

where $\lambda =$ the failure rate of any single machine. Similarly, if we assume i machines being repaired and no preference for any machine completing repair

$$\mu_i = i\mu \tag{12}$$

This last assumption is the most difficult to swallow, but let us press on anyway! The reliability of the system R is defined as the probability that at least 1 machine is not in repair, i.e.,

$$R = 1 - P_n$$

Using Eq. (2) for P_n and Eqs. (11) and (12), we find after algebraic simplification

$$R = 1 - \cfrac{1}{1 + \displaystyle\sum_{j=1}^{n} \left(\frac{\mu}{\lambda}\right)^j C(n,j)} \tag{13}$$

where

$$C(n,j) = \frac{n!}{j!(n-j)!}$$

Figure 3-22.2 gives some values for R for up to 10 machines with various μ/λ ratios.

This and the preceding sections have introduced the theory of reliability. Several assumptions were implicit in the mathematical models. A major one is that the failure properties of each component were independent of all others. Also, no account was taken of preventive and other types of maintenance.

N	$\frac{\mu}{\lambda}$ = time-to-failure/time-to-repair					
	0.1	0.5	1	2	5	10
1	0.091	0.333	0.500	0.667	0.833	0.909
2	0.174	0.556	0.750	0.889	0.972	0.992
3	0.249	0.704	0.875	0.962	0.995	0.999+
4	0.317	0.802	0.938	0.988	0.999+	0.999+
5	0.379	0.868	0.969	0.996	0.999+	0.999+

Fig. 3-22.2 System reliability with various numbers of machines and failure-repair times.

The assumption of exponential reliability dependence on time is important in theoretical work because it is convenient for mathematical treatment, especially in obtaining bounds on reliability improvement as a function of component configuration. The *exponential law* is equivalent to the assumption that the reliability for any given time interval is independent of the age of the component at the beginning of the interval. The reliability literature also treats distributions other than the exponential.

Early work of von Neumann and Moore and Shannon established some theoretical methods of building reliable structures from unreliable components.

The theory of reliability is related to information theory, especially coding theory. There is strong evidence that these two disciplines will continue to influence each other productively.

REFERENCES AND BIBLIOGRAPHY

1. [BA] Barlow, R., and F. Proschan: "Mathematical Theory of Reliability," John Wiley and Sons, Inc., New York, 1965.
2. [BAR] Barron, D.W.: "Recursive Techniques in Programming," American Elsevier Publ. Co., Inc., New York, 1968.
3. [BAZ] Bazovsky, I.: "Reliability Theory and Practice," Prentice-Hall, Inc., Englewood Cliffs, N.J., 1961.
4. [CA] Calabro, S.R.: "Reliability Principles and Practices," McGraw-Hill Book Company, New York, 1962.
5. [DR] Drenick, R.F.: The Failure Law of Complex Equipment, *J. Appl. Math,* vol. 8, p. 680, 1960.
6. [FE] Feller, W.: "An Introduction to Probability Theory and Its Applications," vol. I, (2nd edition), John Wiley and Sons, Inc., New York, 1957.
7. [FL] Flehinger, B.J., and P.A. Lewis: Two-Parameter Lifetime Distributions for Reliability Studies of Renewal Processes, *IBM J. Res. Dev.,* vol. 3, 1959.
8. [FR] Fry, T.C.: "Probability and its Engineering Uses," (2nd edition), D. Van Nostrand Co., New York, 1965.
9. [KE] Kemeny, J.G., H. Mirkil, J.L. Snell, and G.L. Thompson: "Finite Mathematical Structures," Prentice-Hall, Inc., Englewood Cliffs, N.J., 1965.
10. [KL] Kleene, S.C.: "Introduction to Metamathematics," D. Van Nostrand, New York, 1950.
11. [MC] McCarthy, J.: Recursive Functions of Symbolic Expressions and Their Computation by Machine, Part 1, *Comm. ACM,* vol. 3, no. 4, pp. 184-195, April, 1960.
12. [MO] Moore, E.F., and C.E. Shannon: Reliable Circuits Using Less Reliable Elements, *J. Franklin Inst.,* vol. 262, pp. 191, 281, September-October, 1956.
13. [MO1] Moskowitz, F., and J.B. McLean: Some Reliability Aspects of Systems Design, *IRE Trans. PGRQC,* vol. 8, no. 7, 1956.
14. [MO2] Mosteller, F., R.E.K. Rourke, and G.B. Thomas, Jr.: "Probability with Statistical Applications," Addison-Wesley Publishing Company, Reading, Mass., 1970.
15. [NE] Neumann, J. von: "Probabilistic Logics and Synthesis of Reliable Organisms from Unreliable Components," Princeton University Press, Princeton, N.J., 1956.
16. [P1] Pierce, W.H.: "Failure-Tolerant Computer Design," Academic Press, Inc., New York, 1965.
17. [RO1] Roberts, N.H.: "Mathematical Methods in Reliability Engineering," McGraw-Hill Book Company, New York, 1964.
18. [RO2] Rota, G. C.: The Number of Partitions of a Set, *Math Monthly,* May, 1964.
19. [ST] Stoll, R.R.: "Sets, Logic and Axiomatic Theories," W. H. Freeman and Co., San Francisco, Calif., 1961.
20. [WI] Winograd, S., and J.D. Cowan: "Reliable Computation in the Presence of Noise," MIT Press, Cambridge, Mass., 1963.

CHAPTER 4

Job-Processing Models: Informal and Simulation Viewpoints

Modern industrial societies are replete with systems for servicing large numbers of jobs. The nature of the jobs vary from manufacturing products, to processing banking transactions, to work submitted to a computing center (to name but a few). Some service facilities are almost completely automated, as in a telephone system, while others like banking transactions at a teller's window are mostly manual, and still others like some machine shops usually combine manual and machine services. Yet despite these and other differences, at a fundamental level, there is much in common to most of these systems. All are characterized by having only a few service processing resources, "few" meaning relative to the number of jobs they must process. The voluminous stream of jobs converging on the scarce resources will therefore find them busy, much if not all the time. We are interested in the relationships between job arrival and service demand characteristics, resource properties and resource management strategies, and definite measures of system performance. The purpose of this chapter is to give an informal, intuitive "gut" feeling for such systems using some rather idealized models that capture some of their important and common traits.

An informal approach is valuable in solving new practical problems by common-sense study and simulation methods. In Chap. 5 we shall consider analytic methods, i.e., formal models for which mathematical formulas for *some* performance measures for *some* systems can be derived. It must be emphasized, however, that most real systems (and many useful measures of performance) cannot be handled by existing analytic models. Some of the methods and results of the rest of this chapter are therefore more general and widely applicable, if less precise, than those of Chap. 5. Nevertheless, where applicable, analytic methods yielding equations that relate parameters of workload, resources, and scheduling to performance can give deep insights into system behavior, as well as suggest algorithmic design procedures that carry the assurance of mathematical proof.

Some explanation is now in order about terminology in discussing job-processing systems. The word "job" will here be used to denote some identifiable piece of work that is *logically independent* of all other jobs. Thus, the work on one job is never dependent on the work of another; the only way the jobs interact with each other is by their independent needs for the same resources. Within each job there may (in principle) be *tasks* that are units of work with logical dependencies between them However, unless otherwise stated, each job here shall consist of a single task.

Our primary aim in this chapter is to discuss mostly abstract models for which we use a single terminology reflecting the most common usage. Later, when we turn to more specialized systems like timesharing, the word *tract* (short for *transactions*) will be used in the same sense as the more generic term *job*.

4-1 NATURE OF A SYSTEM MODEL

By a *system model* we mean an abstract representation of an interconnected configuration of resources supplied with a workload of jobs. A complete description of a system model consists of the following types of information:

1. Workload description
2. System structure
3. Scheduling
4. Performance indices

The *workload description* states how jobs are to be characterized, as for example, by arrival and required-execution times. By *system structure* we mean the individual resources and the paths by which jobs may be moved into, out of, and within the system. The *scheduling* rules specify how jobs are selected for movement within the structure; common examples are FCFS (first-come-first-served, also called FIFO) and SXFS (shortest-execution-first-served). *Performance indices* define one or more ways in which the "goodness" of the system is to be measured. Two classes of performance indices may be distinguished:

1. Job-stream performance
2. Resource performance

Job-stream performance indices include: mean elapsed or response time, thruput, response-time frequency distribution for various execution time ranges, etc. This kind of measure is oriented toward the user who supplies the workload, rather than the system operator or manager who directly pays for the resources. In contrast, *resource performance* includes such factors as resource utilizations and overlaps.

In the following sections we shall consider each aspect of the system model in some detail.

4-2 WORKLOAD DESCRIPTIONS   [Refs. BU2, SR]

Every performance study requires first a way to describe a workload, and then the data to supply values to the description parameters.

The description method depends on the nature of the study. For actual performance runs, as are frequently made in late stages of system development for finding performance bugs, in running acceptance tests or in bidding by vendors, it is common to use a sampling of actual jobs which is called a *benchmark*. The jobs are usually selected from current activity of a system similar to the one under consideration. Some important criteria in selecting jobs for a benchmark are:

1. Those jobs that are run most frequently (jobs representative of the largest number of jobs).
2. Those jobs that account for most of the system's time and resource use.
3. Those jobs whose completion-time requirements are most critical to the system's mission.

Usually, the set of jobs that best fits one of these criteria does not fit the others, so a many-criteria selection process is indicated.

Another problem in benchmark selection is *scaling*, i.e., selecting a set of jobs, say according to the above criteria, with the constraint that their total running time be reasonable (say several hours), although the jobs are to reflect a month's or several months' activity.

In recent years, considerable attention has been given to the method of *synthetic workloads*. Here, a profile of system activity is constructed such as units of CPU time, units of various types of I/O time, etc. The profile is usually obtained from the analysis of real system activity. However, the test workload is a pseudoworkload that induces the same system activity (at least as far as the profile descriptors are concerned) as the workload used in constructing the profile. The advantage of the synthetic-workload approach is that its implementation modules are easily modified for scaling purposes, and the same ones are also useful with a variety of profiles.

Aside from the technical problems of benchmark selection and profile construction, there are other important considerations in constructing a workload for performance studies. For example, the job base can, with care, adequately represent the job activity of the past, but are these the jobs of the future? Naturally, there is no general technical answer to this type of question. There is, however, a management answer: *Those doing the analysis and simulation of the system should obtain advance agreement (by those who will use the results) of the actual job stream to be used as representative of the workload.* Although the analyst can help identify the significant components of workload, the initiative here should lie with the people responsible for buying and running the installation. Also, agreement on the workload should culminate in a definite document confirming the decision, and this should ideally be done before the results of any modelling are available. This is especially important if it is suspected that the people calling for the performance study have a conscious or unconscious bias toward some particular system, since the outcome of the study can usually be nudged in any direction desired with an appropriate selection of workload.

A computer system is usually embedded in a human system, and this simple but profound fact can seriously influence the service that users will experience from the system. Among those factors that can directly affect this service are:

1. Time for the manual operations to take individual job decks from their submission point in order to compose the next batch of jobs, time to mount and demount tapes and disk packs, etc.
2. Time to manually process output, including bursting of printer pages and dispersing the output listings and decks to the bins where the users can pick them up.
3. Information of job-arrival times and even order-of-arrival are often not given careful attention in job-stream specification.

The first two of these factors are easy to understand, but are often forgotten. Manual mechanisms of gathering the jobs for the input stream and distributing them to the actual users can account for much user dissatisfaction, even though the automatic part of the system is performing well. The last point about job ordering is quite complex. For example, a collection of n jobs can be ordered in $n!$ different ways of which any particular job-stream deck is only one. The effect of job ordering once the stream enters the system (i.e., after the jobs have been batched) may or may not be important, depending upon whether the system overlaps resource use, the nature of the scheduling process, and the performance measure used. If scheduling is done on parameters other than order-of-arrival and the scheduler can scan the stream without regard to order in making its scheduling decisions, then original job-stream order is not terribly important. This is indeed the case in modern operating systems like IBM OS/360, which scans a job stream for priority and class numbers and schedules jobs to resources based on these (FCFS is, however, still used to resolve "ties").

The use of a real benchmark job stream or the synthetic-job method is appropriate for performance tests of a system that already exists. To study the nature of performance dependence on a variety of different resource configurations and to contribute to theories of computer performance, it is necessary to construct mathematical and simulation models which are fed models of a workload. One such model requires:

1. Time of arrival of job i to the system
2. Time of required service of each system resource for job i
3. Sequence in which resources are required by job i

The first is a single number A_i, the time stamp of when the job request arrives. If the entire system is considered as a single resource, then one number, X_i, is the resource time required for job i, and there is no need for sequence information for job i. Note that an X_i value depends on the processing speed of the system. For example, to model a job that is the inversion of a 50 by 50 matrix, X_i is the time for this job on the particular system being modelled.

DEFINITION

A Type I workload model characterizes each job i by the number pair A_i, X_i, designating arrival and required processing time, respectively. We shall assume that the A_i vector is sorted in nondecreasing order of its values.

A Type I workload model, although simple, can represent enough of reality to be useful. A *job-stream model* then consists of the pair of vectors A and X whose corresponding elements refer to the same job. Two ways to represent Type I data are

(1) explicit and (2) probabilistic. By *explicit* we mean directly specified arrival and execute time values for each job. By *probabilistic* we mean values of these times generated from frequency distributions constructed from historical data gathered from the system (or a similar system) using the method described in Sec. 2-5. A method of generalizing a Type I workload using Markov chains is indicated in Sec. 3-17.

A Type II workload representation generalizes the Type I so that it also includes a *setup* time. We shall also assume a setdown time equal to setup time.

DEFINITION

A Type II workload model characterizes each job by a number triple A_i, X_i, S_i designating job arrival, execution, and setup times, respectively.

The above workload descriptions are very simple and are concerned only with the *time* characteristics of the jobs. In a computer system, every job also requires *space* (storage), both in high-speed memory and also in auxiliary storage (such as disks). In most of this chapter we shall concentrate solely on time scheduling, for reasons of simplicity. Also, time scheduling has a considerable body of theory and experience that has built up over several years in noncomputing environments. Space scheduling is applicable mainly to multiprogrammed computer systems. We shall consider *time and space* scheduling models later when discussing timesharing and virtual systems.

4-3 SIMPLEST SINGLE-SERVER MODEL

The single-server model is the simplest and most widely understood. It displays many of the characteristics of all system models. (See Fig. 4-3.1.) Job requests characterized by arrival and execution times are assumed to flow into a queuing area that has a maximum capacity of q jobs. Any jobs arriving when the queue area is full are assumed lost and do not enter the system. In most cases, and unless otherwise stated, it will be assumed that q is large enough to accommodate whatever queue builds up. The single processor always obtains its work from the queue of waiting jobs, selecting one at a time in a way specified by the scheduling rule. For the time being, assume that the scheduler is FCFS; jobs are selected for service in order of arrival, and each job is finished before the next is started (other scheduling rules will be considered in Sec. 4-4).

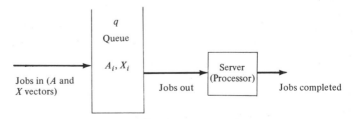

Fig. 4-3.1 Simple single-server model.

If jobs arrived at equally spaced intervals of time and required the same processing times, the dynamics and performance analysis of the model would be rather trivial. In practice, and in our model, these not only differ from job to job, but we shall also often assume that they are unpredictable. However, even when job arrival and execution times are individually unpredictable, their distribution functions will be assumed known (as discussed in Sec. 4-2).

Figure 4-3.2 summarizes in concise form most of the definitions and considerations in a single-server system. The reader is advised to consult this chart throughout the chapter. Whatever the particular distributions of arrival and execute times, if we focus attention on their *mean* rates, under steady state conditions, let

α = mean arrival rate (jobs per second)
ω = mean execute rate (jobs per second)

We can then identify the following mutually exclusive complete set of cases:

case 1. $\alpha > \omega$ or $r = \dfrac{\alpha}{\omega} > 1$
case 2. $\alpha = \omega$ or $r = 1$
case 3. $\alpha < \omega$ or $r < 1$

Thus r is the ratio of mean arrival to mean execution rate. To get a "feel" for these cases, it is helpful to picture a fluid-flow analogy wherein jobs are a fluid that flows from an input pipe into the queuing area, represented by a tank, and flows out into the processor via another pipe. The instantaneous rates of flow are unpredictable, but their mean rates are α and ω. Case 1 then means that on the average, jobs arrive faster than they can be processed. The excess job "fluid" then accumulates in the tank, causing the queue length (number of jobs in the queue) and the waiting times to tend to grow without bound as time passes. This is true even though the instantaneous queue length may sometimes decrease from one particular moment to the next. In case

Job descriptors and performance

n = number of jobs in stream
A = job arrival times
X = job execution times
D = job deadline times
Q = job completion times
$Q - A$ = job elapsed (= response) times
$Q - D$ = delay of due times
$\bar{t}_e = 1/n\ \Sigma(Q\text{-}A)$ = mean elapsed (response) time
$H = n/(\text{Max}(Q)\text{-}\text{Min}(A))$ = thruput

Resource descriptors and performance

m = number of resources (= 1 for single server)
T = Total elapsed time = $\text{Max}(Q) - \text{Min}(A)$
u = resource utilization time
u/T = resource utilization fraction
t_j = total time queue length is j
$\bar{j} = (\Sigma jt_j)/T$ = mean queue length

Fig. 4-3.2 Definitions and notation.

3, since the mean service rate is greater than the mean arrival rate, the server can keep up with the load, at least in the long term over which the mean is defined. The queue length and wait times will fluctuate from time to time, but their mean values should be finite numbers that are functions of α and ω. All of these results will be confirmed rigorously (at least under certain conditions) in the analytical solution of this model given in Chap. 5.

Some simple formulas may be derived for the performance of the single-server FCFS system. First, it is of interest to know for a given Type I workload whether the server will ever have idle periods caused by all-arrived-work completed and the next job not yet arrived. A condition for no idle time over an n-job stream is

$$A_i \leqslant A_1 + \sum_{j=1}^{i-1} X_j \quad i = 2, 3, \ldots, n \tag{1}$$

These inequalities ensure that no job arrives after all previous jobs have been executed. A very simple and special case is where all the jobs arrive together, say at $A_i = 0$. Then, the elapsed time of job i is the sum of the execution times of the jobs previous to and including job i

$$Q_i - A_i = Q_i = \sum_{j=1}^{i} X_j \tag{2}$$

The mean elapsed time is then the sum of partial sum of X_j, divided by n

$$\bar{t}_e = \frac{1}{n} \sum_{i=1}^{n} \sum_{j=1}^{i} X_j \tag{3}$$

Equation (3) is valuable for computing the mean elapsed time for any given ordering of the X_j. A given collection of n jobs can be ordered in $n!$ ways, each being a distinct job stream with its own $\bar{t}_e$ value. The mean of these means, over all possible $n!$ orderings may be shown to be given by

$$\bar{\bar{t}}_e = \left(\frac{n+1}{2n}\right) \sum_{i=1}^{n} X_i \tag{4}$$

Figure 4-3.3 (p. 98) shows a tableau for a simple example job stream. Part (a) of the figure shows a case of five jobs arriving at the same time, so Eqs. (1) and (3) hold.

4-4 SCHEDULING

There is no single "correct" objective function of performance; depending upon the kind of service for which the system is designed, many criteria are possible (some conceivable ones are, however, impossible). Each precise statement of "optimum" may well yield a different scheduler.

A	0	0	0	0	0
X	12	4	3	5	2
Q	12	16	19	24	26
$t_e = Q - A$	12	16	19	24	26

Mean elapsed time: $\bar{t}_e = \dfrac{\Sigma Q - A}{n} = \dfrac{97}{5} = 19.4$

(*a*) Simultaneous arrivals.

A	1	2	18	20	22
X	12	4	3	5	2
Q	13	17	21	26	28
$t_e = Q - A$	12	15	3	6	6

Mean elapsed time: $\bar{t}_e = \dfrac{\Sigma Q - A}{n} = \dfrac{42}{5} = 8.4$

(*b*) Staggered arrivals (with idle time).

Fig. 4-3.3 Job-stream tableaus (FCFS single server).

DEFINITION

A scheduler is an algorithm that uniquely specifies which job is to receive next service by a resource.

The selections are made in such a way that some stated objective function of good performance is optimized.

The following conventions will simplify the discussion of several particular schedulers:

V = scheduling vector; V_i designates the value of the scheduling variable for job i
n = number of jobs in the system ($= \rho V$ = number of values in V)
j^* = the job selected by the scheduler

The optimization will always be expressed as a minimization (maximization could just as well have been chosen):

$$j^* = \underset{i}{\text{Min}} \ (V_i) \qquad i = 1, 2, \ldots, n \tag{1}$$

Two specific examples are:

FCFS scheduler Since this scheduler selects jobs in order-of-arrival, the scheduling vector V is the arrival time vector A.
SXFS scheduler Since this scheduler selects the job with shortest execution first, the scheduling vector V is the vector of execution times X.

The V_i may either be a single variable, as in the above examples, or a stated function of one or more variables, as shall be illustrated later. In any case, using Eq. (1), a scheduler is identified by the procedure for obtaining V values. This may still not be a complete definition of a scheduler because it does not necessarily ensure a unique selection of the next job for service, since Eq. (1) can result in *ties*. This occurs when more than one job has the same minimum V_j value. For example, suppose that for the FCFS scheduler, the scheduling vector of arrival times is

$$V = A = 2, 2, 2, 4, 4, 7, 8$$

Then from Eq. (1), the minimum V value is 2 and the three jobs that arrived at time 2 are tied, so that j is a vector

$$j^* = 1, 2, 3$$

By definition, a complete scheduling algorithm must always come up with a *unique* job and, unless ties are impossible, must include some tie-breaking rule as well as the primary selection rule. One simple tie-breaker is to select the first job appearing in the tie vector j^*. Another is to use the FCFS rule on the jobs specified by the vector j^*, but note that this may generate ties also. The unique job finally selected for service is said to have the "highest priority."

An important general distinction to be made between schedulers is whether or not they are preemptive.

DEFINITION

A preemptive scheduler is capable of making its selection and assignment of a job to a server at times that are not necessarily job-completion times.

By implication, a nonpreemptive scheduler does all its selections and assignments only when a job is finished. Thus, a preemptive scheduler assumes that jobs are *interruptible* and will indeed interrupt a job to permit the resource to work on another that has become highest priority. This implies that for preemptive schedulers, the ranking of a job's scheduling variable can vary even after the job starts. Also, the resources (servers) must be capable of capturing all necessary information about a job so that it can be interrupted and then completed some indefinite time later. Preemption tends to improve scheduling flexibility, which in itself tends to improve performance. However, a setup "overhead" time penalty is often the price that must be paid each time the server changes jobs. In a machine shop, setup consists of initial alignment of tools and work. In a computer system, it typically consists of loading and storing registers or parts of high-speed memory. For a nonpreemptive scheduler, this is done only once per job, but for a preemptive scheduler, setup overhead is also required twice for *each job interruption* (once at interruption and once at resumption). Setup overhead may be included in the scheduler by making V_i a function of this time.

When a preemptive scheduler detects the necessity to switch jobs, it is most advisable, in view of setup-time overhead associated with job switching, to give the new job some minimum use of the processor before considering the next scheduling decision. This short unit of time is called the *quantum*; in a computing system it is typically on the order of 100 milliseconds. Thus, scheduling is done only at "quantum end" or job end.

An LCFS scheduler, for example, may be described as "least-completed-first service" because the high-priority job is that job which has had the least of its execution time completed. Thus new jobs (with zero execution time completed) are automatically highest priority, and the scheduler will interrupt any work in progress to get *some* work done on newly arrived jobs. It will also interrupt a job as soon as more work is completed for it than the least work completed on any other job (see below for further discussion of this scheduler).

We have now stated the major considerations in a simple but useful model of scheduling. To discuss specific schedulers better, Fig. 4-4.1a lists six important variables that often appear in scheduling functions. Of these, three (arrival time, deadline time, and static priority) can be known as soon as the job enters the system. The required execution time X_i may or may not be known at that time. In a computer system, X_i is almost never known precisely since it often depends on some data values that are computed by the job itself, and hence cannot be known before the job is run. Execution times estimated by the user or by previous history of the job may be used. However, schedulers can be defined to (say) favor short jobs, even without explicit estimation of job times (see below).

Two of the variables (P_i and L_i) change their values as the system runs. P_i is the part of X_i already completed, and L_i is the time that job i started its *last* quantum. Both these variables are useful only with preemptive schedulers.

Figure 4-4.1b lists six primitive schedulers (primitive in the sense that each uses one of the six variables as the scheduling variable). The first three schedulers (FCFS, SXFS, and LCFS) have already been described. We now comment briefly on the others.

The EDFS scheduler (earliest-due-time-first) requires a desired deadline or *due time* to be declared for each job and selects that job for next service with the earliest due time. For the HSFS scheduler (highest-static-priority), a static (fixed) priority number is declared for each job prior to entry time, and these numbers are the scheduling vector. Although both of these schedulers tend to have a simplistic appeal because they give the impression of direct user control over scheduling, they can contain several traps. If the user is completely free to assign scheduling numbers to his job, the scheduler in practice will often "degrade" to the tie-breaking rule. Users thus discover that good service is only available by specifying the most favorable value of the scheduling variable. On the other hand, if a discipline limiting the free specification of priority or deadline time is imposed on the users, the rule of this discipline is really a part of the scheduler, which may be outside of the automatic scheduling process. One naive practice is to rely on the "goodwill and cooperation" of the users to specify parameters that will ensure only the class of service they really need. Such a policy can easily fail, not only because of the human tendency to gain advantage (especially in an environment where some are always doing so), but also because it neglects the fundamental principle of good system design, i.e., that the *system, not the users*, are responsible for resolving conflicts (in this case over resource use) among the users. This must be so because individual users are rightly concerned about their own jobs and

A_i = arrival time for job i
X_i = execution (required service) time for job i
D_i = desired "due time" for job i
R_i = static priority number for job i (lowest value = highest preference for service)
P_i = service time completed for job i ($P_i \leqslant X_i$)
L_i = time job i started its last service period (quantum)

(a) Scheduling variables

Scheduler	Scheduling Variable for $\mathrm{Min}(V_i)$ i	Remarks
FCFS	A_i	First-come-first-served
SXFS	X_i	Shortest-job-first
LCFS	P_i	Least-completed-first
EDFS	D_i	Earliest-due-time-first
HSFS	R_i	Highest-static-priority-first
RR	L_i	Round robin (RR)

(b) Primitive schedulers

Fig. 4-4.1 Scheduling variables and primitive schedulers.

have neither the knowledge or incentive to worry about the system as a whole. We emphasize this point by stating the Performance Protection Principle:

A system should be so designed that it guarantees reasonably good service over a job stream, no matter what scheduling information is supplied by any single (or few) jobs.

One simple but useful test for a scheduler is to take some job in an agreed job stream and specify legal (but diabolically) determined scheduling parameters for this job in a deliberate attempt to degrade system performance. A well-designed system should show little degradation over the entire job stream, as compared to choosing favorable parameters for that same job. (This assumes that no single job's resource needs dominates the stream.)

The discussion thus far on schedulers that depend upon user-declared scheduling parameters should not, however, discourage schedulers that make use of such information, provided they take proper performance protection precautions. For example, suppose that a system requires a user estimate of job execution time and intends to use these times to schedule short jobs first. Clearly, there is a powerful temptation to all users to declare that their jobs are short, no matter what their actual length. This can be taken into account by a policy which stipulates that if a job exceeds its declared estimated time by more than some tolerance time, the job will be aborted (but still charged). Such a scheme (which is common practice) provides the needed anti-incentive to irresponsible user declarations. Note that this policy might be unfair sometimes to people who innocently underestimate time. In a positive sense, user declarations can be helpful to scheduling because the user knows some things about his job that are very useful to a scheduler and would be quite difficult to determine automatically without user cooperation. The challenge is to ensure high accuracy of this information before it is used for scheduling and to prevent abuses.

A scheduling objective that is sometimes voiced is that no job should be treated so poorly by the scheduler that it is "locked-out," i.e., suffers unfairly long delays. Of course, the key vague word here is "unfairly." We shall now try to understand what this might mean by some examples. First consider the FCFS scheduler which ensures that no early-arriving job is delayed any longer than a later arrival. Clearly, FCFS is "fair" to jobs with respect to their times of arrival, but may be considered unfair to (say) short recently arrived jobs compared to long earlier arrivals. As another example, consider the LCFS scheduler that gives very poor service to the latter parts of long-execute jobs when they are in the presence of short-execute jobs. The result is that long jobs can be delayed a very long time.

Of course, we can answer this complaint by saying to the system designer: What is your objective function? If it is not being satisfied by a particular scheduler, find another that reflects your objective of good service. But how do we arrive at an objective? This is a deep subject and will be discussed for several systems later. For the moment we simply state that scheduling objectives are complex to derive and justify, since they usually involve psychological as well as technical factors. Using an intuitive pragmatic approach, to meet some of the weaknesses of the simple schedulers, it is sometimes desirable to combine two or more of them. For example, excessive delays for long jobs in the case of the LCFS scheduler can be eliminated as follows. Monitor the L_i variable that records time-of-last-service. Thus, if

C = current clock time

and

$C - L_i$ = elapsed time since last service

then the LCFS scheduler can be modified so that it gives highest priority to any job i whose $C - L_i$ exceeds some specified value h. (This job is then served for one time quantum.) The scheduling variable may then be a function like

$$V = P - ((C - L) > h) \times 10,000 \tag{2}$$

so that when $C - L$ exceeds h, the inequality is satisfied ($= 1$) and the large value of 10,000 is then subtracted from P, thus ensuring a small V value.

One kind of service philosophy which is central to many systems that require intimate man-machine interaction is that short-execution-time jobs should receive preferential treatment over long ones, even though the execution times are not known to the scheduler. A general principle of providing good service in these circumstances is for the scheduler in effect to estimate the rankings (ordering) of execution times. An example of such an estimating process is to say that the *ranking* of execution times (X_i) is the same as the *ranking* of the execution times already completed (P_i). Thus, a job that has already run a long time is estimated to have a long time remaining relative to one that has run only a short time thus far. This strategy is clearly none else but the LCFS scheduler discussed earlier.

The round robin (RR) scheduler can also satisfy a requirement for good service to short jobs without knowledge of job execution times. It has the advantage over LCFS of not having a lock-out problem. The basic idea is to give one quantum of time successively to each pending job, and after serving the last one, to return to the first for another round. In terms of Eq. (1), the scheduling variable is L_i, the time of last quantum (without possibility of ties)

$$j = \underset{i}{\text{Min}} (L_i) \tag{3}$$

This specification of the scheduler is not complete unless we specify how an L_i value is to be assigned to a job when it arrives. One approach assigns a value just larger than the largest L value; this results in placing the new job at the end of the queue for the next quantum. An opposite approach, which we shall adopt, is to assign a low value (zero) to L_i for a new arrival, thus ensuring that it quickly receives its *first* quantum. This version of RR may be thought of as a two-queue system—a high priority queue for the new arrivals, and another queue containing all jobs that have had at least one quantum of service. The round-robin process of sweeping through every job with a quantum and then returning for successive passes will result in short jobs finishing first, even though the system has no knowledge of length of jobs or even their rankings. Equation (2) can also be understood as a "partial" RR scheduler.

For a stream of jobs arriving at the same time, the LCFS and RR schedulers produce identical results. However, these schedulers differ in the way they handle new arrivals. Both give preferential treatment to new arrivals for their *first* quantum (time slice). LCFS gives the next slices to the new arrival until it has received a service interval just larger than the job that received the least service before the new arrival. The RR scheduler switches to another job after the new one has its first time slice.

4-5 JOB PERFORMANCE MEASURES

Job or *job-stream performance* tells us about the delays that the jobs encounter after they arrive at the system. *Resource performance* (see Sec. 4-6) measures the utilization of the resources handling the job stream.

Figure 4-5.1 summarizes some measures of performance, starting with some single variables descriptive of each job and proceeding to measures that characterize the entire job stream. Since Q_i is the "wall-clock" time when job i is completed, the job's *elapsed time* from arrival to completion is $Q_i - A_i$. Of this time, X_i is the execution time, so that $(Q_i - A_i) - X_i$ is the time the job spends awaiting service. The *mean elapsed time,* sometimes called the *mean wait* or *mean response* time, is the average of the job elapsed times

$$\bar{t}_e = \left(\frac{1}{n}\right) \sum_{i=1}^{n} (Q_i - A_i) \tag{1}$$

The *thruput* of a job stream is defined as the number of jobs in the stream divided by the total elapsed time in servicing the stream. Thus, for a single-server model, with no idle time and no setup time, thruput is

$$H = \frac{n}{\displaystyle\sum_{i=1}^{n} X_i} \tag{2}$$

Per job parameters

$$Q_i = \text{job completion time}$$
$$Q_i - A_i = \text{job elapsed time} \ (= \text{response time})$$
$$(Q_i - A_i) - X_i = \text{job await time}$$
$$(Q_i - A_i)/X_i = \text{stretch factor}$$

Single number job stream parameters

$$\bar{t}_e = \frac{1}{n} \sum_{i=1}^{n} (Q_i - A_i) = \text{mean elapsed} = \text{mean response}$$

$$\bar{t}_f = \frac{1}{n} \sum_{i=1}^{n} (Q_i - D_i) = \text{mean deadline default time}$$

$$H = \frac{n}{\text{Max}(Q) - \text{Min}(A)}$$

$$F = \frac{n}{\displaystyle\sum_{i=1}^{n} (Q_i - A_i)/X_i} = \text{short-job-figure-of-merit}$$

Distribution function

Relative frequency distribution of $X_i/Q_i - A_i$

Fig. 4-5.1 Some job-stream parameters.

More generally, when setup and idle times are not both zero

$$H = \frac{n}{\text{Max}\,(Q) - \text{Min}\,(A)} \tag{2a}$$

It is worth noting that the thruput, although measured in the same units as the reciprocal of mean elapsed time (jobs per second), is *not* equal to the reciprocal mean elapsed time. For example, consider a two-job stream with both jobs 5 seconds long and arriving at the same time. The thruput is then 0.2 jobs per second, while the mean elapsed time is 7.5 seconds and its reciprocal is 0.133.

A glance at Eq. (2) indicates that the *thruput is independent* of job ordering, i.e., of the scheduler.* In sharp contrast, the mean elapsed time is highly sensitive to job order for unequal-length jobs. In particular, mean elapsed time will be a minimum for a given job stream when the ordering of service is shortest-job-first (SXFS). This can be seen by noting that any other ordering will find a long job earlier in the executed job stream and that all jobs scheduled later will be delayed by the execution of this long job.

The *short-job-figure-of-merit* is defined as

$$F = \frac{n}{\displaystyle\sum_{i=1}^{n} (Q_i - A_i)/X_i} \tag{3}$$

F is a sensitive measure of the system's ability to give good service to short-execute jobs. To see this, first consider the atomic term $(Q_i - A_i)/X_i$, which will be called the

*Zero job-switching time is assumed.

stretch factor, since it is the factor by which the minimum possible elapsed time (X_i) for job i is "stretched" into the actual elapsed time $(Q_i - A_i)$. Since the sum of stretch factors appears in the denominator of F, a small stretch factor contributes to a larger (better) F value. Also, for short jobs, the numerator of a stretch factor is sensitive to all jobs in process, while the denominator is simply the execution time of a single job. The better the system at giving preference to short jobs, the better the F value. Finally, it is easy to show that F is normalized

$$F \leqslant 1 \tag{4}$$

since each stretch factor appearing in the denominator has a minimum value of 1.

The above measures, Eqs. (1) to (3), are single numbers. More detail about performance, at least with respect to execution times, may be displayed by the relative frequency or cumulative relative-frequency distribution of the *reciprocal* stretch factor. This form of the stretch factor is convenient because its values always range between 0 and 1, and a 100-bucket distribution can be constructed for all systems. Such a distribution function can directly answer such important questions as: What percent of the number of jobs was completed with a stretch factor no larger than (say) 5?

The three job-stream performance measures given above are only examples of several that have been used. Each measures a different aspect of performance and, as we saw in one case, changing the job stream can change one or two of the measures without affecting the other. These effects occur even when there is no overhead (set-up time). For example, the reason that the RR scheduler often gives better mean response time than FCFS is due to its scheduler; this is true when overhead is zero in both cases.

If job-switching overhead time is zero, both RR and FCFS result in the same thruput. If overhead is not zero, the FCFS scheduler will show a better thruput than

	Job i Completion Time, Q_i	Mean Response Time, $\bar{t}_e$	Thruput, H
First-come-first-served	$\displaystyle\sum_{j=1}^{i} X_j$	$\displaystyle\frac{1}{n}\sum_{i=1}^{n}\sum_{j=1}^{i} X_j$	$\dfrac{n}{\displaystyle\sum_{j=1}^{n} X_j}$
Shortest job first	$\displaystyle\sum_{j=1}^{i} X_j^1$	$\displaystyle\frac{1}{n}\sum_{i=1}^{n}\sum_{j=1}^{i} X_j^1$	$\dfrac{n}{\displaystyle\sum_{j=1}^{n} X_j^1}$
Round-robin*	$\displaystyle\sum_{j=1}^{i} X_j^1 + (n-i)(X_i^1 - 1)$	$\displaystyle\frac{1}{n}\sum_{i=1}^{n}\sum_{j=1}^{i} X_j^1 + \frac{1}{n}\sum_{i=1}^{n}(n-i)(X_i^1 - 1)$	$\dfrac{n}{\displaystyle\sum_{j=1}^{n} X_j}$

Assumptions: 1. All jobs arrive at same time.
2. $X^1 = X$ in increasing order of X values.
3. *Round robin assumes X^1 (shortest-job) ordering and quantum = 1.
4. Zero setup, setdown times.

Fig. 4-5.2 Analytic comparison of three schedulers (under special conditions).

RR, since the former is nonpreemptive and has only one setup/setdown *per job*, while RR requires one setup/setdown *per quantum*. On the other hand, if long jobs occur early in the stream, FCFS may well show poor mean response time (due to unfavorable job ordering), while mean response time in the RR case will be relatively insensitive to job arrival. To summarize briefly, there is no one, all-inclusive performance measure; several measures are useful, depending on the type of service sought.

Figure 4-5.2 gives analytic formulas for some performance measures for some schedulers.

4-6   RESOURCE PERFORMANCE MEASURES: HARDWARE MONITORS
[Refs. DR, MU, PA, RO, SC]

Resource (as opposed to job) performance centers around the use of resources rather than the job stream. Thus, resource performance is of primary interest to the operators, managers, and purchasers of a system as well as to those who seek performance improvement. It is of less interest to individual system users and programmers. The major items of interest are:

1. *Utilization* of each resource is conveniently grouped into a utilization vector U. If u_i is the total time resource i is busy and T is the total time to process the stream, i.e., the time from first arrival to last completion,

$$U_i = \frac{u_i}{T} = \frac{u_i}{n} H$$

With this definition, a low utilization may be due to either poor resource use or to long interarrival times (or both).
2. *Maximum queue lengths* on each resource is a system parameter because part of the cost of the system is to provide facilities to hold enqueued jobs.
3. *Overlap* fractions giving the fraction of the time T_B when each resource and other resources are utilized concurrently.

Utilization and overlap information may be measured in an actual system by either hardware or software means. *Hardware monitors* typically take the form sketched in Fig. 4-6.1. The monitor uses a set of electronic probe leads that are

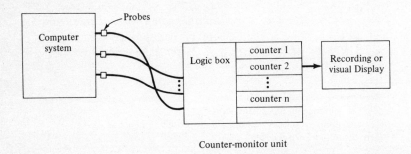

Counter-monitor unit

Fig. 4-6.1   Typical hardware counter monitor.

carefully designed so that they will not electrically disturb the computer-system circuitry. The system terminals to which the probe leads are connected are those indicating the resource states being monitored (e.g., "CPU in wait state" or "channel A busy"). The monitored signals, which are typically on/off gates, are passed through a logic box usually fitted with a "plug board" so that the probed signals may be combined according to logic functions (like AND, OR, NOT, etc.) before the result signal is sent to a counter. For example, by sensing "channel A busy" with one probe and "channel B busy" with another, these may be OR'd to count the time either A or B is busy. The monitored state is used as a gate to control entry of timing pulses to the counter so that the counter counts pulses (and hence time) only for the monitored event. Counter outputs are either displayed visually or read manually and/or sent to a recording device to make a hard-copy record.

Hardware monitors are on sale commercially and also, in the case of some systems, are on loan for limited periods from the system manufacturer, together with consulting services. Such monitors are easy to attach and require no change in the programming or operating system. The same monitor device may be used on a variety of different equipment, even those of different manufacturers. The disadvantage of hardware monitors (relative to software monitors) is that they cannot conveniently relate resource activity to particular and detailed job activity. This is because a counter is an integrator; the detailed events that were counted are not recoverable from the single-counter value. Thus, hardware monitors tell us about resource utilizations and overlaps as gross numbers. As such, they can be valuable in helping spot performance bugs like the case where one I/O channel is heavily used, while another is idle most of the time. However, further investigation is then necessary to pinpoint the job characteristics and system properties responsible.

Assuming that utilization and overlap times can be obtained with either counters or by software means, we now turn to a simple elegant way to relate these quantities. Assume as an example that each resource can be in one (and only one) of two states at any one time, that is, I = idle or B = busy. As a specific example (see Fig. 4-6.2), assume a system with a single CPU called C and two I/O channels called P and Q. Then we can set down a table that lists all eight possible state configurations. In the present case, since the states are disjoint and all together cover all possible times, the sum of the state times in the various combinations indicated allow us to express any desired utilization or overlap time (see Fig. 4-6.2b).

It is most important to realize that all of the above system and job-performance measures depend upon the *workload* as well as the system. Thus, *it is quite meaningless to quote thruput, F value, or system utilizations without specifying the workload that was used.* Lacking a real theory of performance evaluation, it is unfortunately not possible to scale performance on the same system for different workloads or to different systems for the same workload. In fact, an essential requirement for any important performance theory is that it provide such scaling rules.

In this section we have discussed measurement of resource utilization for which a hardware monitor is most appropriate. See Sec. 7-6 for a discussion of software monitoring principles in multiprogramming systems and Sec. 9-5 for techniques used in timesharing systems.

	States			State	
	C	P	Q	Time	Meaning
0	I	I	I	t_0	System Idle
1	I	I	B	t_1	Channel Q only busy (unoverlapped Q time)
2	I	B	I	t_2	Channel P only busy (unoverlapped P time)
3	I	B	B	t_3	Channel P and Q only overlap
4	B	I	I	t_4	CPU only busy (unoverlapped CPU time)
5	B	I	B	t_5	CPU and channel Q only overlap
6	B	B	I	t_6	CPU and channel P only overlap
7	B	B	B	t_7	CPU, channel P, channel Q overlap

State alphabet: I = idle, B = busy

(a) State table with timings.

Time CPU is busy:

$$T_C = t_4 + t_5 + t_6 + t_7$$

Time Channel P is busy:

$$T_P = t_2 + t_3 + t_6 + t_7$$

Time Channel Q is busy:

$$T_Q = t_1 + t_3 + t_5 + t_7$$

Time CPU overlaps with *any* channel:

$$T_{C,\text{I/O}} = t_5 + t_6 + t_7$$

Total observation time:

$$T_T = t_0 + t_1 + t_2 + t_3 + t_4 + t_5 + t_6 + t_7$$

(b) Example equations.

Fig. 4-6.2 A schema for overlap and utilization computations.

4-7 MULTIPLE-SERVER MODELS [Refs. CH,CO,HO,KA]

There are two primitive multiple-server models (see Fig. 4-7.1): (1) parallel servers and (2) pipelined servers. A primitive parallel-server system consists of m servers with identical capabilities. Each can handle an entire job, and hence there can be up to m jobs being served at one time. A primitive pipelined-server system consists of m servers, each *specialized* to only the functions necessary to one part of a job. Every job must move one step at a time through all the m servers without any backtracking. Thus we have a "bucket brigade" arrangement, and m different jobs can be in process at one time.

Unlike the parallel system, the pipelined system requires each job to sequence through the processors. Thus, even if all jobs arrive at the same time, there is a delay that may well be longer than in a single-server system before the *first* job is completed. But after this initial delay to fill the pipeline, the output flow of jobs can be comparable to a parallel-server system because of the concurrent processing of several jobs in the pipeline. Pipelining is the philosophy used in the design of some very

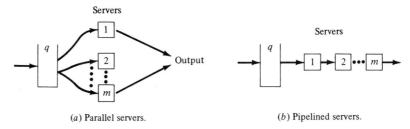

(a) Parallel servers.   (b) Pipelined servers.

Fig. 4-7.1 Two types of multiple-server systems.

high-speed computer central-processing units (CPUs) like the IBM System/360 Mod 91 and CDC-7600. In such systems, a "job" is one machine instruction; one processor typically handles instruction fetching, and another address arithmetic (indexing), another (or others) addition-subtraction, and still others multiplication-division.

A simple formula for T_n, the time for n jobs to be processed by a k-segment pipeline with segment service times t_i, is

$$T_n = \left(\sum_{i=1}^{k} t_i \right) + (n - 1) \operatorname{Max}(t_i)$$

The parallel-server system is conceptually simpler and not subject to pipeline "filling and emptying delays," but is usually more expensive because its processors must contain all functions, not just specialized ones. There may also be some loss of efficiency in a pipelined system since, if the processor times are unequal, a long time spent in an early processor in the chain can leave a later processor idle.

It is feasible and often advisable to combine pipelined and parallel processing. For example, the CDC-6600 system in its pipelined CPU uses two multiplier and two incrementer units. At a grosser level of organization, the CDC-6600 contains 10 logical peripheral-processing units, all of which can be operating in parallel for controlling input-output activity (and other tasks).

Consider an m parallel-server system with all servers identical in capability. Scheduling flexibility would appear to be highest if the servers are considered as a *pool* of resources (Fig. 4-7.2) made available to the entire workload. Because of

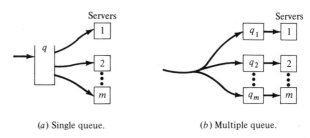

(a) Single queue.   (b) Multiple queue.

Fig. 4-7.2 Two types of queuing for a parallel-server system.

1	2	3	4	5	6	7	8	9	10	← Job
1	4	8	2	6	5	9	2	4	1	← X

(*a*) Execution time vector.

	1	2	3	4	5	
S_1	1	4	8	2	6	X
	1	5	13	15	21	Q

	6	7	8	9	10	
S_2	5	9	2	4	1	
	5	14	16	20	21	Q

Performance

Server 1
$$\bar{t}_e = 55/5 = 11; F = 120/357; U_1 = 1$$

Server 2
$$\bar{t}_e = 76/5 = 15.2; F = 45/329; U_2 = 1$$

Overall
$$\bar{t}_e = 13.1 \quad F = 0.194$$

(*b*) Separate-queue system.

1	2	3	4	5	6	7	8	9	10	
1	4	8	2	6	5	9	2	4	1	X
1	4	9	6	12	14	21	16	20	21	Q
1	2	1	2	2	1	2	1	1	1	Server

Overall
$$\bar{t}_e = \frac{124}{10} = 12.4 \qquad F = \frac{10}{47.258} = 0.212$$

(*c*) Single-queue system.

Fig. 4-7.3   Example of separate- and single-queue parallel-processing systems.

uncertainties of time requirements of individual jobs, it would seem unwise to permit the queue of jobs to be broken into definite processor assignments earlier than necessary. These characteristics are confirmed by Fig. 4-7.3, which shows tables comparing performance of two $m = 2$ processor systems on the same job stream. In one case, the waiting jobs are partitioned into two separate queues, as is the common practice at bank tellers' windows or supermarket checkout counters. The second system feeds both processors from a single queue; each job is assigned the first free processor. The performance of the second system is seen to be better on both mean elapsed time and F values. Despite the advantages of feeding multiple servers from a single queue, most practical everyday queuing situations seem to favor separate queues for each server. Among the possible reasons are:

1. Psychological factors, i.e., unless there is supervision of the queue, people tend to rush for the shortest line rather than wait in one long line.
2. A single queue requires storing the jobs/customers in one large space rather than in several small spaces.

3. Some pipelining is sometimes possible in the multiple-queue arrangement. This is evident at supermarket checkout counters where at each counter, while the clerk is checking out one customer, the next is unloading his wagon onto the counter. Of course this example only justifies a queue of 1 at each server; the rest of the workload should feed from a common queue at the last possible moment.

Another question that frequently arises in multiple-server systems is the relative merit of a single fast server compared to multiple slow servers. Aside from queuing considerations, the following are pertinent to this choice:

1. The cost of the fast server relative to slow ones.
2. The multiple-server system can achieve higher reliability due to the redundancy of servers (see Chap. 3).

If we consider the cost-speed relationship, it is often the case (at least in computer technology) that the speed of a fast processor tends to increase more rapidly than the cost, if we start with the slower processors. Eventually, however, as the current state-of-the-art limit of high-speed technology is approached, cost rises faster than increase in speed. When the ultimate limit is reached, further speed improvement is *only* possible with parallel servers, and even then may not be desirable if the speed of other resources will limit system performance.

As one specific basis of comparison, contrast the performance of a system S, consisting of a single fast processor, with system M, which has m processors, each $1/m$ of the speed of the single processor of system S. Which system is better, based on mean elapsed time? It is not difficult to see that system S will be at least as fast and usually faster than system M. We reason as follows:

1. For a job stream consisting of a single job, system S is clearly faster.
2. For a stream of k jobs of the same length, where $k < m$, system S is faster since, if system M requires t seconds, system S requires tk/m seconds.
3. For a job stream of exactly m jobs of equal length, the thruputs, i.e., the times to finish all m jobs, are the same, but system S will finish all jobs but the last sooner than system M; they will both finish the last job at the same time.
4. For a stream of any number of equal-length jobs, the above results apply by simple extension.

In the more general and practical cases of jobs of unequal execution times, the picture is not so clear. It seems intuitively plausible, however, that the advantage remains with the fast single-server system.

A further great advantage of the single fast-server system is that it automatically gives good performance on a *single long job*. For comparable speed from a multiple-server system, someone (or some thing) must express the job in a form executable by multiple processors. At present, this is not a simple task. In the future, programming languages may, through increased use of array operations and new language primitives, encourage users to express the logic of complex programs in a form that permits easy detection of parallel operations by compilers or other language translators.

Finally, we must remark on a fundamental *potential* advantage of the parallel-server system: higher system reliability. The word potential must be stressed; the reliability improvement possible with multiple servers can be realized by a system design that emphasizes "late assignment" to any member of a pool of processors. For ways to assess reliability improvement, see Chap. 3.

4-8   OUTLINE OF A SIMPLE JOB-PROCESSING SIMULATOR

Using the principles discussed in this chapter, we now consider the organization and programming for a simple simulator of a job-processing model. Two different methods of simulation are:

1. Program the simulator using a simulation language like GPSS (IBM's *G*eneral *P*urpose *S*imulation *S*ystem) or SIMSCRIPT (Refs. GO,GP).
2. Program the simulator using some general programming language like FORTRAN, APL, PL/I, etc.

The special simulation languages are easy to program, although the language itself must first be learned, which is fair enough, especially if many simulation problems are to be tackled. They have special facilities by which the user can painlessly specify (by appropriate statements) the following functions, with their tedious details done automatically:

1. Generating job-description values from user-supplied distribution functions
2. Gathering and printing workload and resource statistics
3. Permitting the user to specify system structure in an easy manner

Although these are great convenience advantages, in this section we shall outline a simulator suitable for general-purpose programming languages. This will take us closer to a *complete* simulation program, and hence give a "feel" for the entire job of simulation. It should also help us to better visualize and appreciate the inner workings of simulators and simulation languages. Some practical advantages of simulators written in general-purpose programming languages are:

1. Complete freedom in specifying the complexity of the model and formatting output reports
2. Usually greater ease in sharing data (e.g., measurement data) with programs not planned as part of the simulator
3. Better machine efficiency

These advantages are becoming less pronounced as simulation languages improve.

To describe the simulation model, we follow the categories discussed earlier in this chapter; workload description, resource (server) description, and simulator logic (including scheduling and performance measures). Figure 4-8.1 shows the general structure of the model. The details are discussed in the remainder of this section.

Each job of the workload is described by three numbers (Type II description):

1. Arrival time
2. Service (execution) time

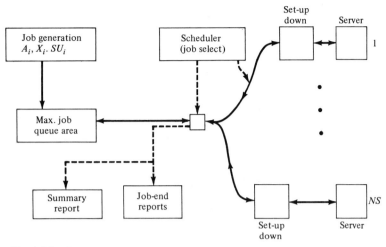

Fig. 4-8.1   General SIMJOB configuration.

3. Setup time (also considered equal to setdown time)

The user chooses one of five options, called *workload codes*, as the methods of specifying each of the above three numbers. The code options are:

1. A constant value specified by the user
2. Explicit value supplied directly by the user
3. Random value generated from an exponential distribution with a user-specified mean value
4. Random value generated from a table of cumulative probabilities supplied by the user
5. Keep the existing code from the last simulator run (useful for successive runs)

The description of the servers requires one number per server, called the *speed factor*, which is used to scale (by division) the service times of the jobs sent to the server. The user also specifies a *maximum queue length*; if exceeded, this temporarily stops the generation of further jobs. Another option is the *type of queuing*: (1) all servers feed off a single queue of waiting jobs at the moment the job is sent to the server, and (2) an incoming job is assigned, at its arrival, for all of its service to the server with the shortest effective queue. The latter is determined by taking the queue length of each server, dividing these by the respective speed factors, and then breaking any ties by selecting the server with the highest speed factor. Another major parameter supplied by the user is the *scheduler code*, which specifies that scheduling is to be any of: first-come-first-served (FCFS), shortest-job-first (SXFS), round robin (RR), etc. Several common schedulers are built into the simulator; it is extremely easy to add others, since the logic is so organized that the scheduling is done by minimizing the scheduling variable (with FCFS to break ties). Since the scheduling can be preemptive, the user must supply a *time-slice* parameter.

```
******SIMULATOR  OF  MULTIPLE  JOBS  ON  MULTIPLE  SERVERS******

          RUN   1
NO.SERV.  NO.JOBS   MAX Q    Q TYPE   QUANT.
   2.0      4.0      4.0      1.0      1.0
SCHED     W.L.CODES                  SET-UP BIAS PRNT OP.
   4.0      2.0      2.0      1.0      0.0      1.0
SERVER SPEED FACTORS
   1.000    2.000
ARRIVAL TIMES(OR MEAN OR TABLE SIZE)
   0.0      0.500    1.000    1.500
SERVICE TIMES(OR MEAN OR TABLE SIZE)
   2.000    3.000    2.000    1.000
JOB    SET-UP TIMES
   0.100    0.0      0.0      0.0
********TRACE OF SERVER START/END EVENTS********
TRACE CODES
11=SETUP START, 12=SETUP END
21=SERVICE START, 22=SERVICE END
31=SETDWN START, 32=SETDWN END, *****=JOB END
   CLOCK     JOB   SERVER CODE  SVCE.T.  COMP.T.  ARR.T.
    0.0       1       2    11    2.00     0.0      0.0
    0.10      1       2    12    2.00     0.0      0.0
    0.10      1       2    21    2.00     0.0      0.0
    0.50      2       1    11    3.00     0.0      0.50
    0.60      2       1    12    3.00     0.0      0.50
    0.60      2       1    21    3.00     0.0      0.50
    1.10      1       2    22    2.00     2.00     0.0
    1.10      1       2    31    2.00     2.00     0.0
    1.20      1      2*****    2.00     2.00     0.0
    1.20      3       2    11    2.00     0.0      1.00
    1.30      3       2    12    2.00     0.0      1.00
    1.30      3       2    21    2.00     0.0      1.00
    1.60      2       1    22    3.00     1.00     0.50
    1.60      2       1    31    3.00     1.00     0.50
    1.70      2       1    32    3.00     1.00     0.50
    1.70      4       1    11    1.00     0.0      1.50
    1.80      4       1    12    1.00     0.0      1.50
    1.80      4       1    21    1.00     0.0      1.50
    2.30      3       2    22    2.00     2.00     1.00
    2.30      3       2    31    2.00     2.00     1.00
    2.40      3      2*****    2.00     2.00     1.00
    2.40      2       2    11    3.00     0.50     0.50
    2.50      2       2    12    3.00     1.00     0.50
    2.50      2       2    21    3.00     1.00     0.50
    2.80      4       1    22    1.00     1.00     1.50
    2.80      4       1    31    1.00     1.00     1.50
    2.90      4      1*****    1.00     1.00     1.50
    3.50      2       2    22    3.00     3.00     0.50
    3.50      2       2    31    3.00     3.00     0.50
    3.60      2      2*****    3.00     3.00     0.50
********** SUMMARY   STATISTICS **********
NO. JOBS   TGT.TIME  JOBS/SEC  AVE.EXEC.  AVE.STR.FAC.
    4        3.600    1.111     2.000      0.933
AVE. ELAPSED  AVE. WAIT P.C. UT.   P.C. S.U./UT.  Q-AVE.     C OVFLO TIME
   1.775       0.650    83.333      16.667        1.972        0.0


SERVER UTILIZATIONS
SERVER SPEED F.  P.C. UTILIZED
   2  2.0000     100.0000
   1  1.0000      66.6666
       DISTRIBUTION FUNCTION OF STRETCH FACTORS
UNDER 1    1     2     3     4     5     6     7     8     9    10    11    12    13    14
    0.50 0.50 0.0   0.0   0.0   0.0   0.0   0.0   0.0   0.0   0.0   0.0   0.0   0.0   0.0
    0.50 1.00 1.00 1.00 1.00 1.00 1.00 1.00 1.00 1.00 1.00 1.00 1.00 1.00 1.00
```

Fig. 4-8.2 Example run of the SIMJOB simulator.

The simulator is of course a program, and from understanding its logic can follow good practice in program analysis. First, it is helpful to look at a sample run, as shown in Fig. 4-8.2 (from a FORTRAN version). Reading from the top, the input data for the simulator is first shown and is seen to consist of the following:

1. Number of servers
2. Number of jobs to be simulated (or else total simulated time)

3. Maximum number of jobs allowed in the queue area (MAX Q); Q type
4. Time slice
5. Scheduler code: 1=FCFS, 2=SJFS, 3=LCFS, 4=RR
6. Workload codes for arrival, service, and setup times
7. Print (trace) options: 1=full trace after change of every resource state, 2=printout after each job completion, and 3="summary only" after all jobs are completed
8. Server speed factors (second line)
9. Arrival time(s) or size of table of arrival distribution, followed by the distribution table (workload codes 4 or 5)
10. Service (execute) and setup times in the same manner as item 9

Major simulator data structures (Fig. 4-8.3) are a set of vectors describing the status of each *job* and another set giving the status of each *server*. Since brief definitions of each vector are given, we do not elaborate on these here. One vector in each set is called the *state vector* (JS for jobs and RS for servers). The heart of the simulator logic is how state values change. Figures 4-8.4 and 4-8.5 show state-transition diagrams and their tabular representations. This kind of a picture is most valuable in the planning, design, and programming of a simulator.

The logic of the simulator program is set down in rather gross flow-chart form in Fig. 4-8.6. Each numbered box on the chart may be described as follows:

1. All input parameters are accepted and variables are initialized, including the master clock CM.

1	2	3	. . .	MAX Q		Symbol	Meaning
						JB	Job numbers
						A	Arrival times
						X	Service (execution) times
						SU	Setup times (= setdown times)
						XL	Service times (completed)
						TLS	Times of last quantum (time slice)
						IP	Servers that jobs are queued on
						Q	Times jobs actually complete
						JS	Job states
						SV	Scheduling variable

(a) Job information.

1	2	3	. .	NS		Symbol	Meaning
						SF	Server speed factors
						RS	Server states
						JX	Jobs being serviced
						IQL	No. jobs in-queue on servers
						TST	Times current event started
						EJ	Times current events will end
						UT	Utilization times of servers

(b) Server information.

Fig. 4-8.3 Simulator program's vectors.

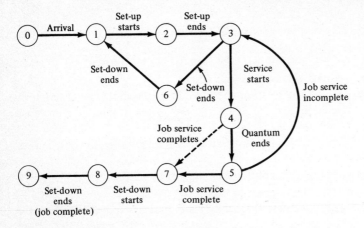

(a) Job state transitions.

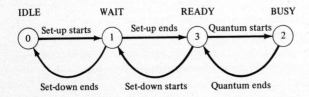

(b) Server state transitions.

Fig. 4-8.4 Job and server state diagrams.

Line	Pres. State Server	Job	Next State Server	Job	Branch	Meaning of Transition
1	1	2	3	3	1	Setup complete
2	1	6	0	1	2	Setdown ends; job not ended
*3	2	4	3	5	3	Server quantum ends
4	1	8	0	9	4	Setdown ends; job ends
*5	3	5	3	7	5	Server quantum ends; service ends
*6	3	5	3	3	5	Server quantum ends; job not ended

(a) Server-end table.

Line	Pres. State Server	Job	Next State Server	Job	Branch	Meaning of Transition
1	0	1	1	2	1	Start setup
*2	3	3	2	4	2	Start server
*3	3	3	1	6	3	Start setdown (job not ended)
4	3	7	1	8	4	Start setdown (job ended)

(b) Server-start table.

*At line 3 of server-end table, next state is cycled through the table to reach lines 5 and 6, which are resolved by a program test. Similarly, lines 2 and 3 of server-start table are resolved by a program test.

Fig. 4-8.5 Server-start and server-end tables for state diagram of Fig. 4-8.4.

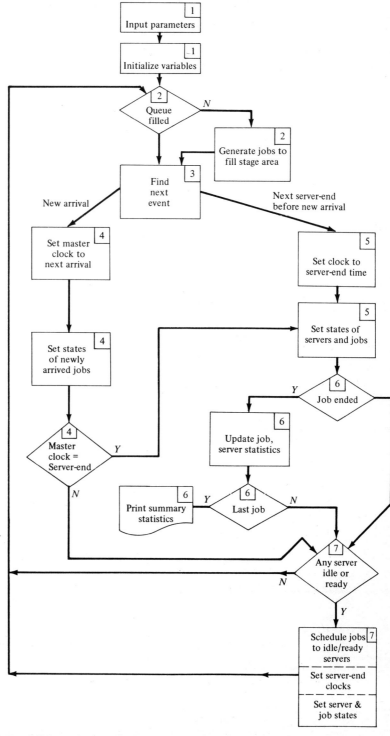

Fig. 4-8.6 Basic logic of SIMJOB.

2. If the queue is not full, generate jobs to fill it. If an arrival time of a new job is found to be earlier than the CM value, this is noted as a queue-area overflow (logic for this is not shown).

3. The next event is sought as the smaller of the next arrival time or the next server-completion time.

4. If next-arrival-time $\leqslant$ next server-end time, CM is set to next-arrival-time, then states of newly arrived jobs are set to 1. If CM is now *not* equal to next server-end time, branch to box 7; otherwise continue.

5. If the result of item 3 is a server-end time, the CM is set to this time, and job and server states are set for the server completion.

6. If the job in the server of item 5 is not completely serviced, the program branches to server-job scheduling. If the job has completed, job statistics are updated, and if this is the last job, summary statistics are computed and printed. If not, the program branches to server-job scheduling (box 7).

7. Server-job scheduling: if no servers are idle or ready, return to item 2. If a ready-server (one in the READY state) has a completed job, start setdown for that server. For each other READY or IDLE server, use the specified scheduler to determine the next job that should be served by the server. If that job is in the server, start the server. If the server is IDLE, start setup of the selected job. If the server is READY, but does not contain the job it should serve next, start setdown for its job (in anticipation of setup for the next job).

REFERENCES AND BIBLIOGRAPHY

1. [AR] Arbuckle, R. A.: Computer Analysis and Thruput Evaluation, *Computers and Automation*, January, 1966.

2. [BU1] Bucholz, W.: A Selected Bibliography on Computer System Performance Evaluation, *IEEE Computer Group News*, vol., 2 no. 8, March, 1969.

3. [BU2] Bucholz, W.: A Synthetic Job for Measuring System Performance, *IBM Systems Journal*, vol. 8, no. 4, pp. 309-318, 1969.

4. [CH] Chen, T. C.: Parallelism, Pipelining, and Computer Efficiency, *Computer Design*, January, 1971.

5. [CO] Conti, C.: System Aspect: System/360 Model 92, *AFIPS Conf. Proc.*, vol. 26, part 11 (1964 FJCC), pp. 81-95.

6. [DR] Drummond, M. E.: "Evaluation and Measurement Techniques for Digital Computer Systems," Prentice-Hall, Inc.; Englewood Cliffs, N. J., 1973.

7. [GO] Gould, R. L.: GPSS/360 An Improved General-Purpose Simulator, *IBM Systems Journal*, vol. 8, no. 1, 1969.

8. [GP] GPSS Manuals from IBM: Application Description (H20-0186); Introductory User's Manual (H20-0304); User's Manual (H20-0326). *IBM Corp.*, White Plains, N.Y.

9. [HE1] Hellerman, H.: Complementary Replacement—A Meta Scheduling Principle, *Proc. Second ACM Symp. on Operating Systems Principles*, Princeton, N.J., Oct. 20-22, 1969, pp. 43-46.

10. [HER] Herman, D. J., and F. C. Ihrer: The Use of a Computer to Evaluate Computers, *AFIPS Conf. Proc.*, vol. 25 (1964 SJCC), pp. 383-395.

11. [HO] Holland, F. C., and R. A. Merikallio: Simulation of a Multiprocessing System Using GPSS, *IEEE Trans. Syst. Sci. Cyb.*, vol. SSC-4, no. 4, pp. 395-400, November, 1968.

12. [HU] Hutchinson, G. K., and J. N. Maguire: Computer Systems Design and Analysis Through Simulation, *AFIPS Conf. Proc.*, vol. 27, part 1 (1965 FJCC), pp. 161-167.

13. [IH] Ihrer, F. C.: Computer Performance Projected Through Simulation, *Comput. Autom.*, vol. 17, no. 4, pp. 22-27, April, 1967.

14. [KA] Katz, J. H.: Simulation of a Multiprocessor Computer System, *AFIPS Conf. Proc.*, vol. 28 (1966 SJCC), pp. 127-139.

15. [KE] Keefe, D. D.: Hierarchical Control Programs for Systems Evaluation, *IBM Systems Journal*, vol. 7, no. 2, pp. 123-133, 1968.

16. [LE] Lehman, M. M., and J. L. Rosenfeld: Performance of a Simulated Multiprogramming System, *AFIPS Conf. Proc.*, vol. 33, part 11 (1968 FJCC), pp. 1431-1442.

17. [MU] Murray, R. J.: The logic and Usage Recorder, *AFIPS Conf. Proc.*, vol. 35, pp. 219-229, 1969.

18. [PA] Patrick, R. L.: Measuring Performance, *Datamation*, vol. 10, no. 7, pp. 24-27, July, 1964.

19. [RO] Roek, D. J., and W. C. Emerson: A Hardware Instrumentation Approach to Evaluation of a Large System, *ACM Proceedings of 24th National Conf.*, pp. 351-367, 1969.

20. [SC] Schulman, F. D.: Hardware Measurement Device for IBM System/360 Timesharing Evaluation, *Proc. 22nd ACM Natl. Conf.*, pp. 103-109, August, 1967.

21. [SM] Smith, E. C.: A Directly Coupled Multiprocessing System, *IBM Systems Journal*, vol. 2, no. 3, pp. 218-229, September-December, 1962.

22. [SR] Sreenivasan, K., and A. J. Kleiman: On the Construction of a Representative Synthetic Workload, *Comm. ACM*, vol. 17, no. 3, p. 127, March, 1974.

23. [WA] Walter, E. S., and V. L. Wallace: Further Analysis of a Computing Center Environment, *Comm. ACM*, vol. 10, no. 5 pp. 266-272, May, 1967.

CHAPTER **5**

Queuing Theory

The theory of queues (waiting lines or congestion) is concerned with stating and solving certain abstract models that resemble some actual systems consisting of many users that require service from a few server resources. The analytic queuing theory to be introduced in this chapter is helpful to build skills, intuition, and insights in handling congestion problems, and of course to reap the benefits of analytic solutions (precision, ease of assessing the effects of parameter changes, etc.) in those cases where the model fits reality. However, as mentioned in Chap. 4, analytic models apply to relatively few real-world systems, so that informal and simulation methods are more frequently used in practice.

Historically, queuing theory began in 1909 when the Danish engineer A. K. Erlang published a now classical paper on the mathematical analysis of congestion in telephone systems. In simple terms, the problem tackled by Erlang is the relationship between the number of connected telephone subscribers, the probability of making a call, the probability of the call requiring various lengths of time, and the number of "trunk" lines that should be installed by the telephone company.

The trunk line may be understood as follows: In the very early days of the telephone, a separate line was used to connect every subscriber to every other one. Thus, for n subscribers, $n(n-1)/2$ lines were required. As n became large, it was quickly recognized that this huge number of lines was not necessary, since not everyone calls at the same time. It should only be necessary to supply a few lines, called *trunks*, that can be reached by all subscribers (users). If k is the number of trunk lines installed, k of the n possible users (at most) can make a call at the same time. If at any given time k calls are in progress, an additional user attempting to call cannot obtain a trunk, and hence cannot complete the connection (he receives a busy signal). Qualitatively, the issues in the design of such a system are easily understood. If k is too small, the likelihood of a user not completing a call can be high, thus leading to much user dissatisfaction and reduction in revenue, since only completed calls are billed. On the other hand, if k is too large, this requires a heavy equipment investment with a strong likelihood that much of it will be idle much of the time.

It is important to have a rational basis for determining the value of k based on some realistic representation of the users' demands on the system. This kind of problem persists today (in several variations) in the design of multiuser communications and computer systems. Erlang not only gave an elegant theory of the telephone trunking problem, but in so doing made several contributions to fairly general ways of probabilistically representing user and system behavior. We study some of these in this chapter.

As discussed in Chap. 4, every model must describe its workload representation, and we begin in the next section by describing the most important model of job-arrival times, called the Poisson arrival process. We then go on to derive the important differential-difference equation of detailed balance, which plays a similar role to that played by the conservation laws in physics. The steady-state solution to this equation (or rather system of equations) is next derived and then applied to a few important special cases, including a parallel-server system and a timesharing-system model.

5-1 POISSON ARRIVAL (BIRTH) PROCESS

In this section a single aspect of queuing, the arrival of user requests, is isolated from the rest of the system. Consider a population of n users that can request service (where n is large), but completion of the service is here of no interest. More particularly, of several possible models of user arrival behavior, the one termed Poisson (or exponential arrivals) is analyzed. The Poisson arrival mechanism is singled out for two reasons: (1) it often, but not always, corresponds to actual arrival patterns, and (2) it is one of the few for which some queuing models can be solved analytically.

Since mathematical queuing theory requires several symbols to represent its variables, Fig. 5-1.1 has been prepared to serve as a convenient reference for definitions and simple relationships between variables. The reader is cautioned that notation and terminology are not uniform among authors, and it is not uncommon for two authors to use the same symbol to mean two different things.

Assume that all n users are statistically identical to all the others in the sense that in the small interval of time h, the probability of each user making a request (arriving) is ph and is the same for every user. Since the user requests are all disjoint, the probability of any (not just a particular one) of the n users making a request, i.e., arriving to the queue in the short interval h, is then $nph = \alpha h$, where α is a shorthand notation for pn. We shall also assume that in the small interval h, the probability that more than one user arrives is much smaller than αh. It now becomes necessary to make the following:

Symbol	Meaning
h	A small interval in time
j	Queue length (counting the job being served)
$\bar{j}$	Mean queue length (mean of j)
$\bar{k}$	Mean queue length not counting the one being served
n	Total number of users in system (= maximum possible j value)
ph	Probability that any particular user makes a request in time h
$P_j(t)$	Probability that the system is in state j at time t; state j means j jobs in the queue (including the one being served)
r	α/ω = traffic intensity (in Erlangs)
T	Mean "think" time
$\bar{t}_q = \bar{w}$	Mean time in queue (including time of service)
$\bar{t}_s = 1/\omega = C$	Mean service (execution) time
$\bar{t}_w$	Mean wait time (= mean time in queue, not including service time)
$\alpha_j h$	Probability that some job arrives (joins the queue) when system is in state j
λ	= pn (mean of discrete Poisson distribution)
ρ	Utilization ratio ($0 \leqslant \rho \leqslant 1$). In Poisson systems, $r = \rho$
$\omega_j h$	Probability that some job completes services (leaves the queue) when system is in state j
$\bar{\alpha}, \bar{\omega}$	Mean of $\bar{\alpha}_j, \bar{\omega}_j$ over j
σ_s	Standard deviation of service time

Fig. 5-1.1   Queuing theory notation.

DEFINITION

A system is said to be in state j if the number of users in the queue is exactly j. $P_j(t)$ is the probability of the system being in state j at time t where

$$\sum_{j=0}^{n} P_j(t) = 1 \quad \textit{(for any t)}$$

Consider now the change in the state of the system from time t to a short time later at $t + h$. In particular, state j at $t + h$ can be "reached" only as follows:

1. From state $j - 1$ at time t by one user joining the queue

   probability $= \alpha h P_{j-1}(t)$

2. From state j at time t by no users joining the queue

   probability $= (1 - \alpha h)P_j(t)$

The probability that at time $t + h$ the system is in state j is then the sum of the above two probabilities

$$P_j(t + h) = \alpha h P_{j-1}(t) + (1 - \alpha h)P_j(t) \tag{1}$$

Subtracting $P_j(t)$ from both sides, dividing by h, and passing to the limit as $h \to 0$, Eq. (1) becomes the differential equation in t and difference equation in j:

$$P_j'(t) = -\alpha P_j(t) + \alpha P_{j-1}(t) \tag{2}$$

Solving by Laplace transforms

$$sP_j - P_j(0) = -\alpha P_j + \alpha P_{j-1}$$

$$P_j(s) = \frac{P_j(0)}{s + \alpha} + \frac{\alpha P_{j-1}}{s + \alpha} \tag{3}$$

There is one such equation for each value of j. To solve this system of equations, start with $j = 0$. P_{j-1} is then zero. Equation (3) is then

$$P_0 = \frac{P_0(0)}{s + \alpha}$$

Substituting into Eq. (3)

$$\begin{aligned} P_1 &= \frac{P_1(0)}{s + \alpha} + \frac{\alpha P_0}{s + \alpha} \\ &= \frac{P_1(0)}{s + \alpha} + \frac{\alpha P_0(0)}{(s + \alpha)^2} \end{aligned}$$

In general

$$P_j(s) = \sum_{i=0}^{j} P_{j-i}(0) \frac{\alpha^i}{(s + \alpha)^{i+1}} \tag{4}$$

Taking inverse Laplace transforms

$$p_j(t) = \sum_{i=0}^{j} P_{j-i}(0) \frac{(\alpha t)^i}{i!} e^{-\alpha t} \tag{5}$$

Example: Probability of the queue having *exactly* 3 users ($j = 3$)

$$P_3(t) = P_3(0)e^{-\alpha t} + P_2(0)(\alpha t)e^{-\alpha t} + P_1(0)\frac{(\alpha t)^2}{2!} e^{-\alpha t} + P_0(0)\frac{(\alpha t)^3}{3!} e^{-\alpha t}$$

We now turn to a fundamental property of the Poisson arrival function of Eq. (5): The probability of the *growth* of the queue, by say k users, is independent of the starting size of the queue j. To demonstrate this, suppose that at time $t = 0$, the queue had j users. Then, $P_j(0) = 1$ and $P_i(0) = 0$ for $i \neq j$. At some time t after $t = 0$, the queue has grown by k users and is then of length $j + k$. From Eq. (5), using these relations,

$$P_{j+k}(t) = \sum_{i=0}^{j+k} P_{j+k-i}(0) \frac{(\alpha t)^i}{i!} e^{-\alpha t} \tag{6}$$

$$P_{j+k}(t) = \frac{(\alpha t)^k}{k!} e^{-\alpha t} \tag{7}$$

where the last equation follows from all $P_i(0) = 0$, except where $j = i$. This equation shows that the probability of the queue growing from j by k users is independent of j.

This is the reason that the Poisson process is sometimes called random (or completely random) and *memoryless*. It is a useful simplification to rewrite Eq. (7) as

$$P_k(t) = \frac{(\alpha t)^k}{k!} e^{-\alpha t} \tag{8}$$

This function shows that the probability that the queue grows by *exactly k* is small for small t, since enough time has not elapsed for the k new users to arrive. Also, $P_k(t)$ is small for large t, since there is then a high probability that the queue has grown appreciably larger than by k users. (See Fig. 5-1.2.)

In practice, the main quantity of interest is the distribution of *interarrival* times, i.e., the probability that *at least one* new member joins the queue in time t. We change notation slightly (but subtly) so that x is the running-time variable and t is some particular x value. Then

$$P_0(x \leqslant t) = \text{probability of 0 users joining the queue in the interval } t$$
$$1 - P_0(x \leqslant t) = \text{probability of at least one new user joining the queue in the interval } t$$

From Eq. (8), with $k = 0$, we then have

$$P(k \geqslant 1) = P(t) = 1 - e^{-\alpha t} \tag{9}$$

This is the *exponential distribution*, which is seen to express the interarrival-time probability of the Poisson arrival process. The mean and variance of the interarrival-time distribution is

$$\text{Mean interarrival time} = \int_0^\infty t \frac{d}{dt}(1 - e^{-\alpha t})\,dt = \int_0^\infty (\alpha t)e^{-\alpha t}\,dt$$

$$= \frac{1}{\alpha} \tag{10a}$$

$$\text{Variance of interarrival time} = \int_0^\infty t^2 e^{-\alpha t}\,dt$$

$$= \frac{1}{\alpha^2} \tag{10b}$$

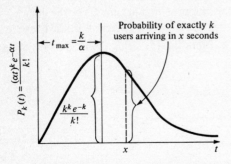

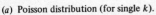

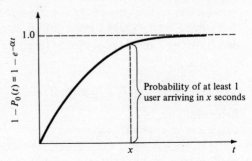

(a) Poisson distribution (for single k).   (b) Exponential distribution of interarrival times.

Fig. 5-1.2 Two descriptors of a Poisson arrival process.

The mean number in the queue at time t is

$$\bar{j}(t) = \sum_{j=0}^{n} jP_j(t) = \alpha t \tag{11}$$

Another insight into the Poisson distribution of Eq. (8) may be gained by considering discrete Bernoulli trials (see Chap. 3), i.e., a sequence of trials as represented by n tosses of a biased coin. One side of the coin is called "success," and the probability of a success in any single toss is p. The probability of j successes in n tosses was shown to be

$$P(j;n) = p^j(1-p)^{n-j}\frac{n!}{j!(n-j)!}$$

under conditions such that

$$p \ll 1$$
$$n \gg 1$$
$$\lambda = pn$$

The above binomial distribution is closely approximated by the Poisson distribution

$$P(j;\lambda) = \frac{\lambda^j}{j!}e^{-\lambda} \tag{12}$$

Equation (12) is similar in form to Eq. (8) which is reproduced here for easy reference

$$P_k(t) = \frac{(\alpha t)^k}{k!}e^{-\alpha t} \tag{8}$$

To further examine the relationship between Eq. (8) (obtained from our continuous time model) and Eq. (12) (obtained from the discrete-sequence model), assume that the time continuum t in the first model is subdivided into equal intervals h long so that

$$t_n = nh$$

Then, comparing variables in Eqs. (8) and (12) and using the above limiting conditions on p and n,

$$\lambda = pn = \alpha t = \alpha nh$$

or

$$p = \alpha h$$

The Poisson arrival process can then be thought of as arising from a sequence of Bernoulli trials, each trial taking place in the small time interval h. "Success" means that a user joined the queue.

To summarize, the Poisson arrival process leading to the exponential distribution of interarrival times is due to the following:

1. A large number of independent users that can request service (arrive).

2. In any small time interval h, the probability of any single user arriving should be small and the same as for any other user.

3. The probability of zero or one user arriving in small interval h should be much larger than the probability of more than one arriving in h.

The Poisson arrival process whose interarrival times are distributed exponentially is, of course, only one particular class of arrival processes and interarrival-time distributions. To make the general notion of interarrival time very concrete, let us describe a simple experiment for gathering data, say on arrival times of work to a batch computing center. Assume that each unit of work, called a *job*, physically consists of a deck of punched cards that is brought by someone to the "in" window of the computer center. Suppose we are the observers of this process and proceed as follows:

1. Record the time of arrival of each job to the window. Call the ordered collection of these time numbers the vector A. Suppose there are n values in A.

2. Compute D, the difference vector of A, as

$$D_1 = A_1$$
$$D_{i+1} = A_{i+1} - A_i \quad i = 1, 2, \ldots, n - 1$$

The D vector, starting at D_2, is the vector of interarrival times. Note that D could have been obtained directly by measuring each arrival time from the time of arrival of its immediate predecessor.

3. Now, using the techniques described in Chap. 2, construct a frequency distribution of the numbers D, i.e., select some time-bucket interval h and label the buckets $0, h, 2h$, etc. Then locate each element of D in a bucket by increasing the frequency count of the bucket.

4. Compute the cumulative relative frequency distribution

$$c_i = \frac{\sum_{j=1}^{i} f_j}{\sum_{j=1}^{m} f_j}$$

If the process of arrivals was Poisson, then the c_i values obtained above experimentally should closely match the formula

$$1 - e^{-t'/T}$$

where T, the *mean* interarrival time, is obtained by

$$T = \frac{\sum_{j=1}^{m} t_j' f_j}{\sum_{j=1}^{m} f_j}$$

and t' is ih.

5-2 FUNDAMENTAL DIFFERENTIAL-DIFFERENCE EQUATION [Ref. MO]

Many queuing-theory problems fit a model governed by a differential-difference system of equations. The prototype of these equations is analogous to a conservation law that is the basis for most theories in physics. We now derive such an equation; later we shall solve it, at least for the steady state. Special cases of the solution will yield the Poisson arrivals discussed previously, as well as a multiple parallel-server system and a very simple model of a timesharing system.

We start with some notation (also see Fig. 5-1.1 at beginning of this chapter).

n total number of users in the system

$P_j(t)$ probability that the system is in state j at time t. State j means that there are j users in the queue, including the one currently receiving service. Since the system must be in some state at any instant t,

$$\sum_{j=0}^{n} P_j(t) = 1$$

(Note that this sum is over all possible states for any fixed time; it is *not* a sum over time.)

h a small interval of time

$\alpha_j h$ probability that, at state j, *one* user will join the queue in the interval t to $t + h$. α_j is then the *rate* at which a new request is made, given that the system is in state j.

$\omega_j h$ probability that, at state j, one user will leave the queue in the interval t to $t + h$. ω_j is then the *rate* at which a user completes service, given that the system is in state j.

In general, α_j and ω_j are functions of j, although in many problems of interest they may be independent of j. It will be assumed that if the time interval h is sufficiently small, it will only be possible for either one or zero users to enter and/or leave the queue in h seconds, i.e., the probability of more than one user doing so is zero.

With the above assumptions, we now ask how the system can arrive at state j at time $t + h$. It is only necessary to consider transitions from states $j - 1, j,$ and $j + 1$ at time t, since only these states can result in state j by arrival/departure of zero or one user. All possibilities of such transitions are summarized in Fig. 5-2.1. Using this to supply the transition probabilities, the probability $P_j(t + h)$ is the sum

$$P_j(t + h) = \alpha_{j-1} h P_{j-1}(t) + (1 - (\alpha_j + \omega_j)h)P_j(t)$$
$$+ \omega_{j+1} h P_{j+1}(t) + h^2 f' \quad (1)$$

Here, all terms containing h^2 have been grouped as $h^2 f'$. Subtracting $P_j(t)$ from both sides, then dividing through by h, and finally passing to the limit as $h \to 0$:

$$P_j'(t) = \alpha_{j-1} P_{j-1}(t) - (\alpha_j + \omega_j)P_j(t) + \omega_{j+1}P_{j+1}(t) \quad (2)$$

where $P_j'(t)$ denotes the time derivative of $P_j(t)$. A somewhat special case is where $j = 0$. Then, $\alpha_{-1} = 0$ and $\omega_0 = 0$, since the probability of a user leaving the queue is zero when the queue is empty. Hence,

From state	To	Transitions possible	Probability expression	Expression grouped by powers of h
$j-1$	j	1 arriving and 0 leaving	$\alpha_{j-1}h(1-\omega_{j-1}h)$	$\alpha_{j-1}h - h^2 f_{j-1}$
j	j	0 arriving and 0 leaving $\Big\}$ or 1 arriving and 1 leaving $\Big\}$	$(1-\alpha_j h)(1-\omega_j h)$ $+$ $\alpha_j h \omega_j h$	$1-(\alpha_j + \omega_j)h + 2h^2 f_j$
$j+1$	j	0 arriving and 1 leaving	$(1-\alpha_{j+1}h)\omega_{j+1}h$	$\omega_{j+1}h - h^2 f_{j+1}$

Note: f denotes the product $\alpha\omega$

Fig. 5-2.1 All possible transitions to state j.

$$P_0'(t) = -\alpha_0 P_0(t) + \omega_1 P_1(t) \tag{3}$$

Equations (2) and (3) are the fundamental differential-difference equations of much of queuing theory (differential in t and difference in j). Equations (2) and (3) are really a prototype of a *system* of simultaneous equations, since there is one equation for each value of j from 0 to n. The remainder of this chapter is concerned with a general steady-state solution to these equations and their application to special cases of interest.

5-3 STEADY-STATE QUEUE BEHAVIOR   [Refs. MO,CO]

One type of queue behavior is the "steady state," defined as the time region after any startup transient of the system has died down so that there is no change of the state probabilities with time. Thus, in the steady state, $P_j'(t) = 0$ for all j and all t. Applying this condition to Eq. (3) of the last section

$$P_1 = \frac{\alpha_0}{\omega_1} P_0 \tag{1}$$

Equation (2) of the last section solved for P_{j+1} is

$$P_{j+1} = \left(\frac{\alpha_j + \omega_j}{\omega_{j+1}}\right)P_j - \left(\frac{\alpha_{j-1}}{\omega_{j+1}}\right)P_{j-1} \tag{2}$$

A few successive substitutions for values of j reveals the following solution to Eq. (2)

$$P_j = \left(\frac{\alpha_0 \alpha_1 \ldots \alpha_{j-1}}{\omega_1 \omega_2 \ldots \omega_j} \right) P_0 = \frac{\alpha_0}{\omega_j} \left(\prod_{i=1}^{j-1} \frac{\alpha_i}{\omega_i} \right) P_0 \tag{3}$$

P_0 may be obtained by summing P_j over all j; the sum of course is 1. Solve for P_0.

$$P_0 = \frac{1}{1 + \dfrac{\alpha_0}{\omega_1} + \displaystyle\sum_{j=2}^{n} \dfrac{\alpha_0}{\omega_1} \left(\prod_{i=1}^{j-1} \dfrac{\alpha_i}{\omega_i} \right)} \tag{4}$$

Equations (3) and (4) are the basic steady-state queuing equations for which we shall consider several special cases in the rest of this chapter.

The mean (or expected) queue length is obtained using Eq. (3)

$$\bar{j} = \sum_{j=0}^{n} j P_j = \left(\frac{\alpha_0}{\omega_1} + 2 \frac{\alpha_0 \alpha_1}{\omega_1 \omega_2} + 3 \frac{\alpha_0 \alpha_1 \alpha_2}{\omega_1 \omega_2 \omega_3} + \cdots \right) P_0 \tag{5}$$

As a special case of Eqs. (3) through (5), take all α_j identical to (α) and all ω_j identical to (ω). Then define the ratio of arrival to service rate

$$r = \frac{\alpha}{\omega} = \frac{\text{mean service time of a single user}}{\text{mean time between arrivals of successive users}} \tag{6}$$

This ratio is called the *traffic intensity* and its units are called *erlangs* after the pioneer in queuing theory, A. K. Erlang.

The probability of queue length j is, from Eq. (3),

$$P_j = r^j P_0 \tag{7}$$

Also

$$\sum_{j=0}^{n} P_j = 1 \tag{8}$$

Substituting Eq. (7) for P_j and using the formula for the sum of a geometric progression,

$$P_0 = \frac{1 - r}{1 - r^{n+1}} \tag{9}$$

Substituting Eq. (9) into Eq. (7),

$$P_j = r^j \frac{1 - r}{1 - r^{n+1}} \tag{10}$$

The mean queue length (including the user being served) may be obtained by substituting Eq. (10) into Eq. (5) and simplifying algebraically

$$\bar{j} = \frac{r}{1 - r^{n+1}} \frac{1 + r^n(nr - n - 1)}{1 - r} \tag{11}$$

There are three regions of interest for this equation, as derived in Ref. 2, page 18:

$$r \ll 1 : \bar{j} = r + r^2 \tag{12a}$$

$$r \to 1 : \bar{j} = \frac{n}{2} + \frac{n(n+2)(r-1)}{12} \tag{12b}$$

$$r \gg 1 : \bar{j} = n - \frac{1}{r} \tag{12c}$$

The variance of the queue length (mean-square difference from the mean) is

$$v = \sum_{j=0}^{n} (j - \bar{j})^2 P_j = \sum_{j=0}^{n} j^2 P_j - \bar{j}^2 \tag{13}$$

In the same three regions of r, this reduces to

$$r \ll 1 : v = r + 2r^2 \tag{14a}$$

$$r \to 1 : v = \frac{1}{12} n(n+2) \tag{14b}$$

$$r \gg 1 : v = \frac{1}{r} + \frac{2}{r^2} \tag{14c}$$

5-4 STEADY-STATE SOLUTION: INDEFINITE-LENGTH QUEUES

Some appreciable simplifications result if the number of users n, and hence the maximum possible queue length, can grow indefinitely large. We start with Eq. (10) of the last section, which is reproduced here as Eq. (1)

$$P_j = \frac{r^j(1-r)}{1 - r^{n+1}} \tag{1}$$

where

$$r = \frac{\alpha}{\omega}$$

Now assume that $r < 1$ and permit $n \to \infty$. Equation (1) then becomes

$$P_j = r^j(1-r) \tag{2}$$

Since P_0 is the probability that there are no users in the queue, i.e., the server facility is idle, $1 - P_0$ is the probability that the server facility is busy (utilized).

$$\rho = 1 - P_0 = 1 - (1 - r) = r = \frac{\alpha}{\omega} \tag{3}$$

Thus ρ, the utilization of the server, is found to be equal to the traffic intensity r.

The expected (mean) queue length, using Eq. (2), is

$$\bar{j} = E(j) = \sum_{j=1}^{\infty} jr^j(1-r) = (1-r) \sum_{j=1}^{\infty} jr^j \tag{4}$$

Using the general formula

$$\sum_{j=1}^{n} jr^j = \frac{r - r^{n+1}}{1 - r} \frac{1}{1 - r} - \frac{nr^{n+1}}{1 - r} \tag{5}$$

For $n \to \infty$, all r^n terms approach zero

$$\sum_{j=1}^{\infty} jr^j = \frac{r}{(1 - r)^2} \tag{6}$$

Substituting Eq. (6) into Eq. (4) and using Eq. (3), the mean queue length is

$$\bar{j} = \frac{r}{1 - r} = \frac{\rho}{1 - \rho} \tag{7}$$

To find the mean-time-in-queue ($\bar{t}_q$), we make use of the following relation, which must hold in the steady state

$$\alpha \bar{t}_q = \bar{j} \tag{8}$$

Using Eq. (7) for $\bar{j}$ and remembering that $r = \alpha/\omega$

$$\bar{t}_q = \frac{1}{\omega(1 - r)} = \frac{\bar{t}_s}{1 - r} \tag{9}$$

where $\bar{t}_s = 1/\omega$ = mean service time.

The *mean wait time* will be defined as the mean time waiting in the queue, but not counting the time being served

$$\bar{t}_w = \bar{t}_q - \bar{t}_s \tag{10}$$

Using Eq. (9) for $\bar{t}_q$

$$\bar{t}_w = \frac{\bar{t}_s}{1 - r} - \bar{t}_s = \frac{r\bar{t}_s}{1 - r} \tag{11}$$

Equations (7), (9), and (11) show that as the utilization approaches 1, mean queue length and mean wait time grow very rapidly. In other words, if the economic advantage of high utilization is pressed too far by encouraging greater service volume, the price of the near-unity utilization is a very long mean wait time.

5-5 ERLANG AND HYPEREXPONENTIAL DISTRIBUTIONS: SERIES OF STAGES [Ref. CO]

It has previously been remarked that although analytic solutions to queuing problems are usually only possible for exponential arrival and service-time distributions, in practice this type of distribution, especially of service times, is not too common. It is therefore of interest first to be able to represent other types of distribution functions, and secondly, if possible, to represent these in terms of exponentials. One scheme for doing this will now be explained; it is due to A. K. Erlang, the pioneer in queuing theory.

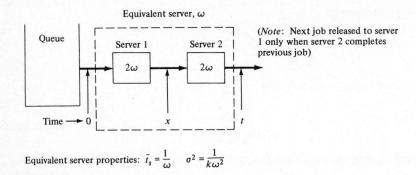

Equivalent server properties: $\bar{t}_s = \dfrac{1}{\omega}$ $\sigma^2 = \dfrac{1}{k\omega^2}$

(a) Series stages ($k = 2$) for Erlang distribution.

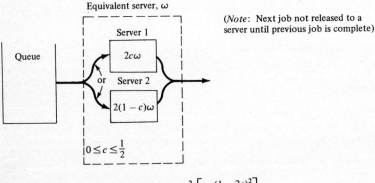

Equivalent server properties: $\bar{t}_s = \dfrac{1}{\omega}$ $\sigma^2 = \dfrac{1^2}{\omega}\left[1 + \dfrac{(1-2c)^2}{2c(1-c)}\right]$

(b) Alternative stages for hyperexponential distribution.

Fig. 5-5.1 Multistage models to visualize Erlang and hyperexponential service distributions.

Suppose that a single queue is served by k servers in *series* according to the following rule: A job selected from the queue is sent first to the first server; after being served there, it is sent to the second, etc., and finally emerges from the kth. Only then is the next job in the queue sent to the first server. Note that because the next job is not started until the previous one is completely through all k servers, the entire series arrangement of k servers can be considered to correspond to some equivalent single server. We now derive the service-time distribution of this equivalent server. Figure 5-5.1 shows the simplest case of $k = 2$ stages and how time is labelled. Time 0 is the time at the start of server 1, x is the time at completion of server 1 (and also the time at the start of server 2), and t is the time at the end of server 2. Times 0 and t are also the start and end times for the equivalent server. Now assume that both servers have identical exponential service-time distributions, each with a mean rate of 2ω (the reason for 2ω, rather than ω, will be seen later). Thus in terms of the above labelling of times, the probability of the first server completing service is

$$2\omega e^{-2\omega x}\,dx \tag{1}$$

and the probability of the second completing is

$$2\omega e^{-2\omega(t-x)}\,dt \tag{2}$$

The probability of a job completing both of the stages (equivalent server), i.e., the probability that it emerges between t and $t + dt$, is the integral of the product of Eqs. (1) and (2) over x

$$s(t)\,dt = dt\int_0^t (2\omega)^2 e^{-2\omega x}e^{-2\omega(t-x)}\,dx$$

$$= (2\omega)^2 e^{-2\omega t}\,dt\int_0^t dx \tag{3a}$$

or

$$s(t)\,dt = (2\omega)^2 te^{-2\omega t}\,dt \tag{3b}$$

Since Eq. (3b) gives the probability of a job completing the two stages between t and $t + dt$, the probability of a job completing between 0 and t is

$$\int_0^t (2\omega)^2 te^{-2\omega t}\,dt \tag{4}$$

The probability that no job was completed from time 0 to t is then

$$S_0(t) = 1 - \int_0^t 4\omega^2 te^{-2\omega t}\,dt = \int_0^\infty 4\omega^2 te^{-2\omega t}\,dt - \int_0^t 4\omega^2 te^{-2\omega t}\,dt \tag{5}$$

or

$$S_0(t) = \int_t^\infty 4\omega^2 te^{-2\omega t}\,dt = \int_{2\omega t}^\infty ye^{-y}\,dy$$

$$= (1 + 2\omega t)e^{-2\omega t} \tag{6}$$

This distribution function is *not* an exponential because of the t multiplier. The mean service time is defined as

$$\bar{t}_s = \int_0^\infty ts(t)\,dt = \frac{1}{\omega} \tag{7}$$

We now see the reason for calling the service rate of each server 2ω; the rate for the equivalent server is then ω.

In the more general case of k servers in series, each with a rate $k\omega$, it can be shown by a process similar to that above (although more complex in detail) that the following Erlang distribution function then applies to the equivalent server (Ref. 2)

$$t_s(t)\,dt = (k\omega t)^{k-1}\left(\frac{e^{-k\omega t}}{k-1!}\right)k\omega t\,dt \tag{8a}$$

from which

$$S_0(t) = e^{-k\omega t} \sum_{i=0}^{k-1} \frac{(k\omega t)^i}{i!} \tag{8b}$$

where

$$\bar{t}_s = \frac{1}{\omega} \quad \text{(mean)}$$

$$\sigma = \frac{1}{\omega\sqrt{k}} \quad \text{(standard deviation)} \tag{9}$$

For $k = 1$, the Erlang function is simply the exponential, and hence its variance equals its mean. As $k \to \infty$, the distribution approaches the constant 1 for $t \leqslant 1/\omega$ and 0 beyond; its variance is then 0. For each intermediate value of k, the Erlang distribution gives a smooth curve in t with some intermediate variance. For actual distributions (obtained approximately by measurement) where the variance is less than the mean, a proper choice of k can often give an approximate fit by an Erlang function.

It should be stressed that the series arrangement of servers in Fig. 5-5.1 used to derive the Erlang functions should *not* be taken too seriously. The physical system being modelled need not consist of several servers in series in order to use an Erlang distribution; all that is really required is that the latter supply a reasonably good fit to the actual distribution.

Another type of distribution function that results from combining exponential distributions is the *hyperexponential*. It is capable of representing a situation not expressible by the Erlang, that is, service (or arrival) distribution whose variance is *larger* than its mean. This distribution may be derived by imagining a single queue served by two *alternative* exponential servers with service rates $2c\omega$ and $2(1-c)\omega$, respectively, where c is some number (to be selected later) in the range

$$0 < c \leqslant \tfrac{1}{2}$$

As mentioned above, the two servers are fed from a single queue as follows: When both servers are idle, the next job in the queue is assigned to one server *or* the other with probability c and $1 - c$, respectively. As soon as this is done, no other assignment is made until the job is completed. Thus, the two possible servers are possible alternatives for each job, but only one server is busy at a time. This configuration can then be considered as a single equivalent server, and it is fairly easy to set down the service-time density distribution of this scheme. We take the probability density of each alternative server, multiply it by the probability of its being selected, and sum the two products

$$s(t) = c(2c\omega e^{-2c\omega t}) + (1 - c)(2(1 - c)\omega e^{-2(1-c)\omega t}) \tag{10}$$

It can be shown that the mean and variance of this distribution is

$$\bar{t}_s = \frac{1}{\omega} \tag{11}$$

$$\sigma^2 = \frac{1}{\omega^2} \left[1 + \frac{(1 - 2c)^2}{2c(1 - c)} \right]$$

The probability of no service completion in time 0 to t may be found by integration of $s(t)$

$$S_0(t) = ce^{-2c\omega t} + (1-c)e^{-2(1-c)\omega t} \tag{12}$$

5-6 THE KHINTCHINE-POLLACZEK EQUATIONS [Refs. CO,MA]

These steady-state queue results hold under the following fairly general conditions:

1. Poisson arrival times (= exponential interarrival times)
2. *Any* service time distribution
3. Any queue discipline (scheduler) *not* dependent on service time

The basic equation for mean length of queue is

$$\bar{j} = r + \frac{r^2}{2(1-r)}\left(1 + \left(\frac{\sigma_s}{\bar{t}_s}\right)^2\right) \tag{1}$$

where

$$r = \frac{\alpha}{\omega}$$

$$\frac{1}{\omega} = \bar{t}_s = \text{mean service time}$$

$$\sigma_s = \text{standard deviation of service times}$$

Several related equations may be obtained fairly easily from Eq. (1). First we list some additional notation and formulas:

$\bar{t}_q$ = mean time in queue (including being served)
$\bar{t}_w$ = mean wait time (time in queue not counting being served)
$\bar{j}$ = mean length of queue (including being served)
$\bar{k}$ = mean length of queue (not including being served)

	General	Poisson service times $\sigma_s = \bar{t}_s$	Constant service times $\sigma_s = 0$
Mean queue length	$\bar{j} = r + \dfrac{r^2}{2(1-r)}\left(1 + \left(\dfrac{\sigma_s}{\bar{t}_s}\right)^2\right)$	$\bar{j} = \dfrac{r}{1-r}$	$\bar{j} = \left(\dfrac{r}{1-r}\right)\left(1 - \dfrac{r}{2}\right)$
Mean queue time	$\bar{t}_q = \bar{t}_s\left(\dfrac{1+r}{2(1-r)}\left(1 + \left(\dfrac{\sigma_s}{\bar{t}_s}\right)^2\right)\right)$	$\bar{t}_q = \dfrac{\bar{t}_s}{1-r}$	$\bar{t}_q = \dfrac{\bar{t}_s}{1-r}\left(1 - \dfrac{r}{2}\right)$
Mean wait time	$\bar{t}_w = \dfrac{\bar{t}_s}{2(1-r)}\left(1 + \left(\dfrac{\sigma_s}{\bar{t}_s}\right)^2\right)$	$\bar{t}_w = \bar{t}_s\left(\dfrac{r}{1-r}\right)$	$\bar{t}_w = \bar{t}_s\left(\dfrac{r}{2(1-r)}\right)$

Note: For the same workload parameters, Poisson service times yield worse performance than constant service times.

Fig. 5-6.1 Comparison of general and special equations using Khintchine-Pollaczek equations.

Then

$$\bar{t}_q = \bar{t}_w + \bar{t}_s \tag{2}$$

$$\bar{k} = \alpha\bar{t}_w \tag{3}$$

$$\bar{j} = \alpha\bar{t}_q = \alpha(\bar{t}_w + \bar{t}_s) = \bar{k} + \alpha\bar{t}_s = \bar{k} + r \tag{4}$$

$$\bar{k} = \bar{j} - r \tag{5}$$

Using these, the general formulas of Fig. 5-6.1 may be derived.

5-7 PARALLEL-SERVER SYSTEMS [Ref. CO]

Until now the system has contained a single server. We now generalize the results to the case of m servers. To derive the steady-state probability of state j, consider the general solutions of Eqs. (3) and (4) of Sec. 5-3. If j (the queue length) is $\leqslant m$ (the number of servers), enough servers are available to serve the entire queue at one time, and the effective service rate is $j\omega$ (ω = service rate of a single server). If however the queue length is greater than m, the servers are saturated at an effective rate $m\omega$. In all cases it is assumed that $\alpha_j = \alpha$ independent of j. Thus

$$\alpha_j = \alpha \tag{1a}$$

$$\omega_j = j\omega \qquad 0 \leqslant j \leqslant m \tag{1b}$$

$$\omega_j = m\omega \qquad m \leqslant j \leqslant n \tag{1c}$$

Careful substitution of these equations into the general equations of Sec. 5-3 and some tedious algebraic simplification yields

$$P_j = \frac{(mr)^j}{j!}P_0 \qquad 0 \leqslant j \leqslant m \tag{2}$$

$$P_j = \frac{m^m r^j}{m!}P_0 \qquad m \leqslant j \leqslant n \tag{3}$$

where now

$$r = \frac{\alpha}{m\omega} \tag{4}$$

One use of these equations is to establish an interesting comparison between a system with a *single* high-speed server and one with several low-speed servers. To be specific, assume a single server system with service rate $m\omega$ and compare the P_j for this system with that of a system with m servers, each with average rate ω. The fast single-server queue probability is obtained directly from Eq. (10) of Sec. 5-3, where r is now $\alpha/m\omega$. The corresponding P_j for the m-server system is given by Eqs. (2) and (3). The latter is seen to be the former multiplied by $m^j/j!$, or by $m^m/m!$, both of which factors are larger than 1. It may also be shown that the P_0 in the multiserver case is always larger than the P_0 in the fast single-server case. We thus have the conclusion also obtained by simple reasoning in Chap. 4:

A single-server system will be better improved by improving the service rate by a factor of m than by providing m parallel servers at the old rate.

This result applies to this model and with this performance measure. It is *not* a general result for all possible single-server vs. parallel-server comparisons.

5-8   A TIMESHARING SYSTEM MODEL   [Ref. SC]

With appropriate interpretation of the variables appearing in the general steady-state solution of Sec. 5-3, it is possible to solve a simple model that has a useful resemblance to some timesharing systems.

Assume n signed-on users. Each may, at any given time, be in one and only one of two possible states: *thinking* or *waiting*. While in the think state, a user may request service (by typing a line in the actual system). As soon as he completes making his request, he enters the waiting state, i.e., he awaits service by the system. The time in the waiting state includes the time required to process his request, as well as the time "waiting" for his turn on the processor. During the waiting state, the user is barred from making any other request (usually because his keyboard is locked). When the system completes the processing of a request, the user leaves the wait state and reenters the think state. The following notation will be used:

$\alpha = 1/T =$ average rate at which any given *single* user requests service. Since such a request can only be made when in the think state, T may be considered an average think time.

$\alpha h = h/T =$ probability of any given single user requesting service in the small time interval h.

$\alpha_j =$ average rate at which some user (i.e., *any* one, not just a given one) requests service when the system is in state j (j requests in the queue).

$1/C =$ average rate at which the system completes service of requests.

Thus C may be considered an average processing time. Suppose a system with n users is in state j. This means that there are j in the queue and $n - j$ not in the queue; these latter are then in the think state. To use our equations, note the definition of $\alpha_j h$, from which it follows that since only the $n - j$ users not in the queue are eligible to make a request, the probability that some one of the $n - j$ users makes a request in the interval h is the sum $n - j$ times of the equally probable individual probabilities

$$\alpha_j h = \frac{(n - j)h}{T} \quad \text{or} \quad \alpha_j = \frac{n - j}{T} = (n - j)\alpha \tag{1}$$

The probability that a user leaves the queue, i.e., completes service in time interval h is

$$\omega_j h = \frac{h}{C} \quad \text{or} \quad \omega = \frac{1}{C} \tag{2}$$

It is worth noting that this model takes no account of time slicing!

With the above assumptions, we substitute Eqs. (1) and (2) for α_j and ω into Eq. (3) of Sec. 7-3.

$$P_j = P_0 \left(\frac{n\alpha}{\omega}\right)\left(\frac{(n-1)\alpha}{\omega}\right)\left(\frac{(n-2)\alpha}{\omega}\right) \ldots \left(\frac{(n-j+1)\alpha}{\omega}\right) \tag{3}$$

or

$$P_j = P_0 \frac{n! r^j}{(n-j)!} \tag{3a}$$

where

$$r = \frac{\alpha}{\omega} = \frac{C}{T} \tag{4}$$

Since the sum of all P_j is 1, Eq. (3a) summed over all j may be written

$$P_0 = \frac{1}{\displaystyle\sum_{j=0}^{n} \frac{n! r^j}{(n-j)!}} \tag{5}$$

Substituting into Eq. (3a)

$$P_j = \frac{n! r^j}{(n-j)!} \frac{1}{\displaystyle\sum_{j=0}^{n} \frac{n! r^j}{(n-j)!}} \tag{6}$$

The average queue length is by definition

$$\bar{j} = \sum_{j=0}^{n} j P_j \tag{7}$$

A general equation relating average queue length and average wait time in a steady-state queuing system is

$$\bar{\alpha} \bar{t}_q = \bar{j} \tag{8}$$

where

      $\bar{\alpha}$ = mean arrival rate to the queue
      $\bar{t}_q$ = mean time in the queue
      $\bar{j}$ = average queue length

Equation (8) has the intuitive meaning that if new members arrive at an average rate $\bar{\alpha}$ and have a mean in-queue time (including service time) of $\bar{t}_q$, the queue length will, on the average, be the product of $\bar{\alpha}$ and $\bar{t}_q$. The definition of $\bar{\alpha}$ is not to be confused with either α or α_j, but is

$$\bar{\alpha} = \sum_{j=0}^{n} \alpha_j P_j = \sum_{j=0}^{n} \frac{n-j}{T} P_j \tag{9}$$

where we have used Eq. (1) for α_j in the second sum. Simplifying Eq. (9) further, using the fact that the sum of P_j is 1,

$$\bar{\alpha} = \frac{n}{T} - \left(\frac{1}{T}\right) \sum_{j=0}^{n} j P_j = \frac{n}{T} - \frac{\bar{j}}{T} \tag{10}$$

where we have used Eq. (7) for $\bar{j}$. Substituting Eq. (10) into Eq. (8) and solving for $\bar{t}_q$

$$\bar{t}_q = \frac{\bar{j}T}{n - \bar{j}} \tag{11}$$

After some tedious algebra involving manipulation of subscripts and summation limits (see Appendix 5-A at end of chapter for details), Eq. (11) can be simplified to

$$\frac{\bar{t}_q}{C} = \frac{n}{1 - P_0} - \frac{1}{r} \tag{12}$$

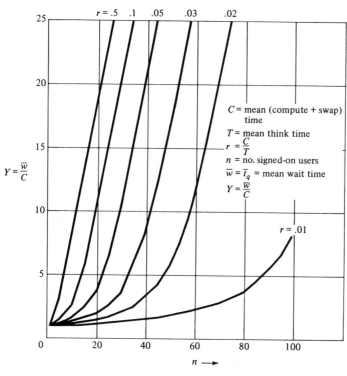

Recursion equation for Y:

$$Y(1) = 1$$
$$Y(n + 1) = (n + 1) - \frac{n}{1 + rY(n)}$$

For $n \gg \frac{1}{r}$, $Y(n) \approx n - \frac{1}{r}$

Fig. 5-8.1 Plot of normalized mean wait time for a timesharing queuing model.

Using Eq. (5) for P_0

$$\frac{\bar{t}_q}{C} = \frac{n}{1 - \dfrac{1}{\displaystyle\sum_{j=0}^{n} \dfrac{n!r^j}{(n-j)!}}} - \frac{1}{r} \tag{13}$$

Direct computation of tables of $\bar{t}_q/C$ vs. n and r is possible. However, a much simpler recursion formula for these tables (derived in Appendix 5-B at end of chapter) makes these computations far faster. These recursion equations are

$$Y(n+1) = (n+1) - \frac{n}{1 + rY(n)} \tag{14}$$

$$Y(1) = 1 \tag{15}$$

where $Y = \bar{t}_q/C$.

A plot of this formula relating mean wait, mean compute, and mean think times to the number of signed-on users (n) is shown in Fig. 5-8.1.

Finally, we should mention that the above model (in fact all of the models of this chapter) can also be analyzed by the method of Markov chains discussed in Sec. 3-17.

REFERENCES AND BIBLIOGRAPHY

1. [CO] Conway, R. W., W. L. Maxwell, and L. W. Miller: "Theory of Scheduling," Addison-Wesley Publ. Co., Reading, Mass., 1967.
2. [CO] Cox, D. R., and W. L. Smith: "Queues," Methuen & Co., London, 1961.
3. [GO] Gordon, G.: "System Simulation," Prentice-Hall, New York, 1969.
4. [MA] Martin, J.: "Design of Real-Time Computer Systems," Prentice-Hall, New York, 1967.
5. [MO] Morse, P. M.: "Queues, Inventories, and Maintenance," John Wiley and Sons, New York, 1958.
6. [RA] Rasch, P. J.: A Queuing Theory Study of Round-Robin Scheduling of Time-Sharing Systems, *J. ACM*, vol. 17, no. 1, January 1970.
7. [SC] Scherr, A. L.: "An Analysis of Time-Shared Computer Systems," MIT Press, Cambridge, Mass., 1967.

Appendix 5-A

Details of Tedious Algebra Between Eqs. (11) and (12) of Sec. 5-8

(*Note:* We shall use the shorter notation $\bar{w}$ for $\bar{t}_q$.)

$$\bar{w} = \frac{T\bar{j}}{n - \bar{j}} \tag{1}$$

$$\bar{j}(n) = \sum_{j=0}^{n} jP_j \qquad \sum_{j=0}^{n} P_j(n) = 1 \tag{2}$$

$$n - \bar{j}(n) = \left(n \sum_{j=0}^{n} P_j(n) \right) - \sum_{j=0}^{n} jP_j(n) \tag{3}$$

$$\sum_{j=0}^{n} (n - j)P_j = P_0(n) \sum_{j=0}^{n} (n - j)\frac{n!r^j}{(n-j)!} \tag{3a}$$

Since the last term of the sum $= 0$

$$n - \bar{j}(n) = P_0(n) \sum_{j=0}^{n-1} \frac{(n-j)n!r^j}{(n-j)!} = P_0(n) \sum_{j=0}^{n-1} \frac{n!r^j}{(n-j-1)!}$$

$$= nP_0(n) \sum_{j=0}^{n-1} \frac{(n-1)!r^j}{(n-1-j)!} \tag{4}$$

The sum is recognized as $1/P_0(n-1)$:

$$n - \bar{j}(n) = \frac{nP_0(n)}{P_0(n-1)} \qquad \text{or} \qquad \bar{j}(n) = n\left(1 - \frac{P_0(n)}{P_0(n-1)}\right) \tag{5}$$

Substituting into Eq. (1) and simplifying:

$$w = T\left(\frac{P_0(n-1)}{P_0(n)} - 1\right) \tag{6}$$

We now try to simplify the ratio $P(n-1)/P_0(n)$

$$P_0(n) = \frac{1}{\displaystyle\sum_{j=0}^{n} \frac{n!r^j}{(n-j)!}} \tag{7}$$

$$P_0(n-1) = \frac{1}{\displaystyle\sum_{j=0}^{n-1} \frac{(n-1)!r^j}{(n-j-1)!}} \tag{8}$$

Let $k = j + 1$ in the sum. Then $j = k - 1$ and

$$P_0(n-1) = \frac{1}{\displaystyle\sum_{k=1}^{n} \frac{(n-1)!r^{k-1}}{(n-k)!}} = \frac{1}{\displaystyle\frac{1}{rn}\sum_{k=1}^{n} \frac{n!r^k}{(n-k)!}} = \frac{rn}{\displaystyle\frac{1}{P_0(n)} - 1} \tag{9}$$

Simplifying:

$$P_0(n-1) = \frac{rn\, P_0(n)}{1 - P_0(n)} \tag{10}$$

Substituting into Eq. (6):

$$\bar{w} = T\left(\frac{rn}{1 - P_0(n)} - 1\right) = \frac{Cn}{1 - P_0(n)} - T = \frac{Cn}{1 - P_0(n)} - \frac{C}{r} \tag{11}$$

Another interesting equation for $\bar{w}(n)$ entirely equivalent to Eq. (11) is

$$\bar{w}(n) = C(1 + \bar{j}(n - 1)) \tag{12}$$

Appendix 5-B
A Recursive Formula For Average Wait Time (Sec. 5-8)

Start with Eq. (12) of Sec. 5-8

$$Y(n) = \frac{n}{1 - P_0(n)} - \frac{1}{r} \tag{1}$$

Solving for $P_0(n)$

$$P_0(n) = 1 - \frac{nr}{r + Y(n)} \tag{2}$$

From Eq. (1)

$$Y(n + 1) = \frac{n + 1}{1 - P_0(n + 1)} - \frac{1}{r} \tag{3}$$

Using the series form of P_0 of Eq. (5) of Sec. 5-8 and substituting q for $j-1$

$$\frac{1}{P_0(n + 1)} = \sum_{j=0}^{n+1} \frac{(n + 1)! r^j}{(n - j - 1)!} = r(n + 1) \sum_{q=-1}^{n} \frac{n! r^q}{(n - q)!} \tag{4}$$

Rewriting the sum on the right as the term for $q = -1$ plus the remaining sum

$$\frac{1}{P_0(n + 1)} = r(n + 1)\left(\frac{1}{r(n + 1)} + \sum_{q=0}^{n} \frac{n! r^q}{(n - q)!}\right) \tag{5}$$

Recognizing the summation as the series form of $P_0(n)$, Eq. (5) is

$$\frac{1}{P_0(n + 1)} = 1 + \frac{r(n + 1)}{P_0(n)} \tag{6}$$

Taking reciprocals of both sides and rearranging terms

$$P_0(n + 1) = \frac{P_0(n)}{P_0(n) + r(n + 1)} \tag{7}$$

Substituting Eq. (7) into Eq. (3) and simplifying

$$Y(n + 1) = (n + 1) + \frac{P_0(n)}{r} - \frac{1}{r} \tag{8}$$

Substituting Eq. (2) for $P_0(n)$ and simplifying

$$Y(n + 1) = (n + 1) - \frac{n}{1 + rY(n)} \tag{9}$$

where

$$Y(1) = 1 \tag{10}$$

Note the remarkable simplicity of this recursive form compared to the conventional form of Eq. (13) of Sec. 5-8.

CHAPTER 6

Single-Component and Single-Job Performance

In this chapter, we first consider components such as main storage and the CPU individually, and then turn to a thruput model of a system restricted to handling one job at a time, but capable of overlapping I/O and CPU operations. Even in these cases, where there are no resources shared among the jobs, there is sufficient complexity and variety of system behavior to make the performance problems nontrivial. The topics and issues discussed in this chapter will be of value for the following purposes:

1. To analyze systems that actually process one job at a time, as is the case for many small- and intermediate-size systems.
2. To understand certain performance properties, such as CPU speed, in an environment that is simple enough so that they can be defined with reasonable precision.
3. To provide some base cases that can be useful for comparison to the more difficult cases of multiprogrammed and timesharing systems.

6-1 MAIN STORAGE [Ref. HE1]

The term *main storage* usually refers to the storage that the CPU can *directly* access for instructions and data. Although this is a simple enough concept and is often a reasonably practical definition, it is not always a precise one in modern systems (see discussion at end of this section).

Main storage sizes and speeds (in the year 1972) typically lie in the range

Cycle time: 500 to 2000 nanoseconds
Size: 8k to 2M bytes = 2k–500k words = 64k–16M bits

Small main memories are typically manufactured as a single interconnected array of magnetic cores, films, or monolithic circuit elements that share a single data and address register. In such a structure, called a *module,* only one access can be in process at one time.

In most core and film memories, the physical reading from the memory is destructive of the information accessed, so that the read cycle is composed of two subcycles: access and regeneration. Much ingenuity is expended in computer design to enable the CPU to do useful work during the wasteful regeneration operation.* A single module of magnetic-core storage can be characterized by the following parameters:

1. Size (in bytes, words, or bits)
2. Width (number of bytes/words/bits per access)
3. Access time
4. Cycle time
5. Bandwidth = width ÷ cycle time

Usually, access time is about half of cycle time. Bandwidth is the most significant single number combining the effects of width and cycle time. It may be viewed as the maximum rate at which the memory can deliver/accept information in a steady stream. As larger main storage is required, the single-module organization becomes inadequate because of longer time delays and increased noise in the large array. For these reasons, main storages are often fabricated as several modules. One result is that multiple modules may be cycled at the same time, delivering more bits per access time, and thereby increasing the bandwidth of the main storage as seen from the CPU. Storage word addresses are usually *interleaved,* i.e., assigned to an N module unit in modulo N fashion so that addresses $0,1,2 \ldots N-1$ are all in different modules. This assignment achieves maximum bandwidth if successive requests for memory words are to successive locations. In the best and simplest case, the bandwidth is thus increased by a factor of N over a single module. In the worst case of successive accesses to the same module, the bandwidth is no better than for a single module. Somewhere between these extremes is another simple case, a random pattern of requests with each address occurring with the same probability as any other. In this case, B_E, the effective bandwidth of N modules, is approximately*

$$B_E \doteq B_1 \sqrt{N} \tag{1}$$

where B_1 is the bandwidth of a single module.

The bandwidth analysis given above is very simple and should serve as only a guide in evaluating main storage speeds. An added complexity is the case where there are multiple modules, but also a common single "bus path" with a fixed delay. Bus delays may be applicable both in requesting to reach the modules and in routing the output to the processor.

*See Ref. HE1, chap. 6.

In many systems, such as the IBM system/360 Mod 85 or system/370 Mod 155, 165, access to the large "main store" is for a *block* of successive words intended for a small very fast *buffer store* between the CPU and main storage. Since the main store is interleaved, this kind of access tends to use the main storage at its fastest rate. More detail on this type of system is given in Chap. 10.

6-2 CPU INSTRUCTIONS   [Refs. AP,BE,GI,RA,WH,WI]

Two major methods of characterizing CPU speed are (1) kernel, and (2) instruction mix. The first method begins with the analyst selecting or writing a *kernel,* a small program segment judged to represent high CPU activity (like the inner loop or loops of a tightly structured program). Since the selected program structure is rather simple, the analyst can follow the program logic in computing the frequency of each instruction type for the execution of the kernel. This frequency vector can then be multiplied by the vector of machine instruction times, giving a total time to execute the kernel. Such times may be determined and compared for various machines and machine features. The method is simple to apply and can get fast answers. It has several drawbacks, such as the question of how typical of system activity is the chosen kernel, and the dependence of the kernel on the programming skill and style of the person coding the kernel. Kernel analyses are used in early stages of CPU design and to obtain fast answers to CPU performance questions.

The instruction-mix method is a simple (in principle) statistical averaging technique. First, a set of programs or program segments judged to be typical are selected. Each of these is run *interpretively* by a special trace program that takes each executed instruction, determines its type, and then updates a frequency counter for that instruction type.* After the trace has been run, the instruction relative frequencies (see Fig. 6-2.1) are multiplied by the corresponding instruction execution times, and the sum of these is then the average CPU execution time (for the given program traced).

The mix method is very useful for comparing machines with the same or closely similar instruction sets, but different component speeds, since the same frequency vector (but different time vectors) may be used for both sets. The mix method using the same frequency vector is *not* suitable for comparing systems with different architectures (instruction sets, registers, etc.). A useful comparison of average instruction time is still possible, even in this case, if the same source program is used as the source of each trace. The analyst should however then be aware that subtle factors may influence the results, such as differences in object code efficiency of the compilers that produce the two traced object programs.

In Fig. 6-2.1, a complete computation using a mix is reproduced from the cited reference. Note the vague specification of the problem that generated the frequencies; such vagueness is typical in these reports. Other reports of instruction mixes confirm

---

*It is also possible to use a hardware monitor (see Sec. 4-6) to capture instruction execution statistics. Each instruction type is assigned one of the monitor's counters and is fed by a pulse emitted by the machine's circuitry when the instruction is executed. This method seems to be used much less frequently than the software interpreter described above.

Type of instruction	Relative frequency	Execution time per operation	Weighted time
Load/store	0.475	4.4	2.090
Fixed add/subtract	0.080	4.4	0.352
Increment by 1	0.030	13.0*	0.390
Fixed multiply/divide	0.003	9.3	0.028
Floating add/subtract	0.005	15.3	0.077
Floating multiply/divide	0.002	10.0	0.020
AND/OR	0.070	4.4	0.308
Branch (unconditional, register)	0.125	2.2	0.275
Branch (on index)	0.035	4.4	0.154
Test (register and storage)	0.040	4.4	0.176
Test (register and zero)	0.025	4.4	0.110
Test miscellaneous	0.005	4.4	0.022
Shifts	0.075	7.6	0.570
Miscellaneous	0.030	4.4	0.132
Mean execution time			4.704

*More than one instruction.

Machine: IBM 7090 (two arithmetic registers, three index registers)
Problem: "An application similar in nature to a command and control problem"
Reference: E. Raichelson and G. Collins: A Method For Comparing the Internal Operating Speeds of Computers, *Comm. ACM*, vol. 7, no. 5, May, 1964.

Fig. 6-2.1 Tableau showing instruction-mix computation.

the very large percentage of load/store operations, even for widely different problems. This is easily understood for a machine like the IBM 7090 with a small number of registers. Some instruction frequencies appear significantly different from problem to problem. For example, in one mix obtained from compile-only runs, floating-point operations were very infrequent, but in another mix of an object program (from a "scientific" application), floating-point operations accounted for 17 percent of the number of executed instructions (and a somewhat higher fraction of the run time).

One use of the mix method is to understand better the value of certain machine features. Figure 6-2.2 shows the results of mix analyses of three binary-fixed word machines on the same bubble-sort problem. Although all these machines have the same instruction set, they differ in number of registers and in whether indirect addressing is permitted or not.

For large machines, especially those using instruction stacks, buffer stores, and pipelining in the CPU, patterns of storage reference are as likely to be at least as important as operation-code frequencies in determining CPU performance. The mix method cannot take this factor into account.

The instruction-mix and kernel methods are useful techniques for evaluating performance of nonbuffer-store CPU organizations, but they cannot give total system performance, except in the special case where the system is heavily CPU bound.

Instruction	Time/Instr.	8 Registers, Indexing		2 Registers, No indexing*		2 Registers, No Indexing	
		Rel. freq.	Fract. time	Rel. Freq.	Fract. time	Rel. Freq.	Fract. Time
ADD	2.0	0.199	0.214	0.157	0.161	0.101	0.104
SUBTRACT	2.0	0.013	0.013	0.014	0.014	0.017	0.018
MULTIPLY	4.0	0.000	0.000	0.000	0.000	0.000	0.000
DIVIDE	6.0	0.000	0.000	0.000	0.000	0.000	0.000
SHIFTS	1.0	0.018	0.010	0.014	0.007	0.013	0.006
LOADS	2.0	0.223	0.239	0.304	0.312	0.310	0.319
STORES	2.0	0.201	0.215	0.304	0.312	0.304	0.314
COMPARE	2.0	0.120	0.129	0.090	0.094	0.046	0.047
AND,OR,EXOR	2.0	0.000	0.000	0.000	0.000	0.121	0.125
BRANCH	1.0	0.219	0.118	0.111	0.057	0.085	0.044
I/O	21.0	0.005	0.051	0.003	0.036	0.002	0.005
Ave. Instr. Time		1.854		1.936		1.938	
No. Instr. Executed		13087		17310		37717	
Run Time		24263		33512		73096	

*Indirect addressing used   *Problem:* Sort of 14 80-column cards
                                    Key field: columns 3–11
                                    Algorithm: bubble sort

Fig. 6-2.2 Instruction frequencies for simple sort.

Finally, we should mention the considerable programming effort required to write the instruction trace program essential to the mix method. This need only be done once per machine, and it is simpler if the machine has an EXECUTE type of instruction. Such an interpreter runs much slower than the program being traced (a factor of 20 to 30 is typical). Generating an instruction mix is thus expensive in machine time.

6-3 MICROPROGRAM CONTROL   [Refs. HE1,HU,RO,TU,W1]

The execution of even a single machine instruction requires a sequence of switching operations that routes information, both the instruction itself and the data it references, along various paths in the machine's internal structure. Such a sequence is called a *microprogram*. The concept is fundamental to computer design and was proposed by M.V. Wilkes in the 1950s.* However, before 1960 or so, most machine designers did not consider their task or the organization of the machine's controls as involving a type of programming. Since the mid 1960s, microprogramming has become a widely used method of designing CPU and I/O control circuitry.

In a microprogramming structure, switching-control information is organized into microinstructions that are stored in a memory device called the *control store* (CS). Typically, a CS is several times faster than the machine's main store. For economy reasons, it is often a *read-only* store (ROS), meaning that it is read at fast electronic speeds, but requires slow mechanical operations to change its contents. A simple clock circuit cycles the microinstructions one at a time from CS to the CS data register. From there, the bits of the microinstruction supply the signals to gate information on the data-flow structure, e.g., between memory address and data registers, the adder, shifter, program counter, and various machine registers. Each

*See Ref. WI.

microinstruction supplies not only the gating information mentioned above, but also bits to determine partially the location of the next microinstruction. That location is also determined by the state of selected flip-flops designating such conditions as the sign bit of a register, overflow, etc. (microprogram branching).

It is beyond the scope of this book to describe microprogramming in any detail. We shall, however, discuss some performance issues, beginning with a list of major advantages of microprogramming compared to its alternative, wired-machine controls:

1. *Design economy and ease of maintenance.* Much of microprogrammed logical design is similar to a programming discipline, with its advantages of orderly methods, including simulation and computer aids. Since control sequences are highly stylized, machine maintenance and modifications are simpler.
2. *Hardware economy.* This is most evident for complex instruction sets that amortize the cost of the control store.
3. *Emulation compatibility.* A given machine can be made to "imitate" another's complete instruction set at much higher speed than would be possible with a purely software interpreter. This is done by supplying several sets of microprograms for the CS. In this way the same machine can have a "modern" instruction set, run a modern operating system, and (with another instruction set) run the large collection of programs available from an older type machine.
4. *Special functions or customization.* Special functions, or even entire application programs, may be microprogrammed and then run much faster than the same functions if programmed on the same machine.

The second and third points above are most responsible for the present use of microprogrammed machine controls. IBM's S/360 or S/370 systems, which supply the same complex instruction set over a wide range of models, are the most conspicuous example.

The possibility of using customized microprograms for special purposes has been much proposed and discussed. The potential for performance improvement is due to the fact that the microinstructions are control "atoms" that *directly* access the actual machine resources. In contrast, ordinary instructions (built from microprogrammed sequences) are control "molecules" that provide only entire sequences of machine resource use. Since any particular function is itself a molecule of control, it is more efficient to build this molecule from the atoms, the microinstructions, rather than from other prearranged molecules. More specifically, the following are likely to be major sources of microprogram speed improvement:

1. Reduction in instruction fetching. This is replaced by microinstruction fetching, but this is from a faster store (CS not main storage) and is more specific to the particular function.
2. More efficient use of the hardware registers, fast storages, etc. for the customized purpose.

To justify microprogramming (rather than programming) a particular function, it is important to consider such factors as the expected frequency of use of the desired function and the considerable effort and skill needed to write good microprograms. One rational method of selecting functions for microprogramming is to choose one or more jobs known or estimated to be "typical" of the system workload (see Sec. 4-2) and then to run these under a trace program. The trace would record at least the operation code of every executed instruction (say on magnetic tape). The stream of instruction operations would then be analyzed for frequently occurring subsequences; these are prime candidates for microprogrammed implementation. A rough micro-program design for such functions can then be compared to the measured program sequence in the trace stream. When both timings are weighted with the occurrence of the function in the stream, a realistic assessment of the performance benefit of the microprogrammed implementation can be made. A more conservative estimate of the performance improvement would compare the microprogrammed implementation against a carefully revised "best" programmed version. To date, very little has been published about such comparisons. Intuitively, it would seem that prime candidates for microprogrammed implementations in some environments might be special mathematical functions (square root log, exponentiation, trigonometric functions, etc.), many of which are done with a polynomial that could benefit from storing the coefficients in fast registers. Another intuitive feeling is that data conversion operations (fixed-to-floating point, etc.) may also consume appreciable CPU time as programming languages become more permissive in allowing programmers to mix arithmetic modes.

Most computer manufacturers supplying systems for general-purpose use have not encouraged users to write their own microprogrammed instruction sets. If they did, it would be most difficult to supply expensive software, including sophisticated operating systems and compilers, since the costs of these must be amortized over a wide common base of users. From a performance viewpoint, two identical hardware systems with widely different instruction sets (due only to different microsequences) are completely different machines (although their hardwares are identical). Com-parisons between them are subject to all the complexities and uncertainties of comparing any two different computer systems.

6-4 AN I/O AND CPU OVERLAP MODEL*

In most modern systems, I/O devices [including auxiliary storage (AS) like tapes, disks, and drums] can be operated with a good deal of independence from the CPU and main storage (MS). This means that all of these can be operated *concurrently,* i.e., their use can be overlapped in time. There are many possibilities of such overlap. In this section, the CPU is considered as a device, and overlap of its use with those of I/O devices is investigated using a highly idealized workload and system model.

In Chap. 7, a kind of overlap called SPOOLing will be discussed whereby each device works on a different part of different jobs at the same time. Although the case now to be considered may fit this kind of overlap, it is more directly applicable where overlap is sought between parts of the same job.

Figure 6-4.1 shows a resource structure which is seen to consist of a CPU, main store, and two devices connected to main storage via (at most) two data channels. In actual systems, a data channel consists of a set of physical lines between the I/O device

*This section borrows heavily from Ref. HE2.

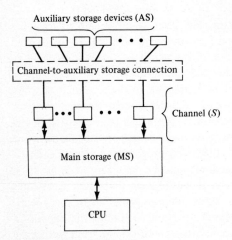

Fig. 6-4.1 Resource structure.

and main store, along with associated control and buffer logic. This enables I/O transmission or control signalling to occur independent of the CPU. Although several devices may be physically connected to one channel, a channel's single set of control-logic circuitry implies that at most one of its devices may be active at any one time. In our model, the number of channels is then the number of I/O devices that can be active at one time.

The workload will be modelled as a sequential collection of *problem records* available on one AS device. Each problem record consists of a linear string of bytes. To access and move a string of s bytes between MS and AS requires a time that may be expressed in the form

$$T = t_a + k_f s \tag{1}$$

where

$\qquad t_a =$ access time to the start of the string
$\qquad s =$ no. of bytes in the string
$\qquad k_f =$ reciprocal of the flow rate of byte transmission

Of course, Eq.(1) is a simplification of the much more complex process that exists in practice. For example, t_a is not a constant for a disk file, but instead depends on the position of the new physical record relative to the old. Also, s cannot be too large, since for a disk device, if it exceeds the cylinder size, another access is required. Equation (1) comes much closer to modelling a tape than a disk. Because t_a may be quite large, it is common practice to *block* problem records, i.e., make s fairly large by including several problem records in each transmission, thus making each t_a serve for several problem records. Blocking also conserves tape/disk storage since there are fewer record gaps. The *blocking factor n* is defined as

$$n = \lceil \frac{s}{r} \tag{2}$$

where s = no. of bytes in a block
        r = no. of bytes in a problem record
        $\ulcorner$ = "nearest equal or larger integer"

In our idealized model, each block of records is subject to three phases of processing, and the time durations of each phase is the same for all records. The times of the phases for general block i are represented by

$I = I_i$ = time to input block i (access plus flow time)
$C = C_i$ = time to compute block i
$O = O_i$ = time to output block i (access plus flow time)

The workload (job) consists of N problem records in all, where N is a large-enough number that the time to get the job started or the time for end-of-job events are negligible compared to the steady-state processing of the records. The other assumptions about the workload model may be summarized as follows:

1. Records are all of the same size (equal number of bytes).
2. For each input record, there will be an output record.
3. The number of records per block is the same for all blocks in a particular overlap case.
4. The CPU compute time for a record is the same for each record.
5. Device access and flow times are the same for all record blocks in a particular overlap case.

Four system configurations will be considered and compared for the above workload. They differ in the number of channels, and hence in the degree of overlap possible, and also in the way main storage is partitioned, but *not* in the total amount of main storage, which is M problem records in all configurations. Figure 6-4.2 shows the partitioning of main storage and the type of overlap possible for each of the four configurations. The configurations may be described briefly as follows:

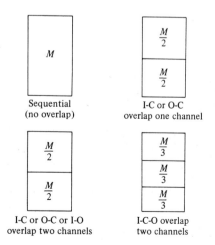

Fig. 6-4.2   Main-storage partitions.

1. S (sequential)—No overlap. Input, output, and compute occur in strict sequence; when each is active, the others are idle ($p = 1$).
2. I-C, O-C—Either input and compute or output and compute may take place at the same time ($p = 2$).
3. I-C, O-C, I-O—Two of the three phases of input, compute, and output may take place at the same time ($p = 2$).
4. I-C-O—Input, output, and compute may all take place at the same time ($p = 3$).

The p values given in each case are simply the maximum number of phases that can be in process concurrently, which by the proof of Sec. 1-3 is an upper bound on the thruput improvement factor over a sequential system. The main storage, which can hold M problem records, is partitioned into p equal areas for buffering and computation. (This does not count space for the program, supervisor, etc.) Each concurrent phase must have its own MS area.

    To help visualize the various overlap cases, Fig. 6-4.3 shows two sets of example timing sequences of all four configurations. In these particular examples,

Set 1: compute = 1 time unit; I/O = 2 time units
Set 2: compute = 5 time units; I/O = 2 time units

Set 1 corresponds to I/O bound and set 2 to compute-bound conditions.

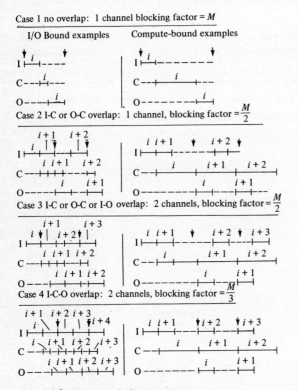

Fig. 6-4.3   Example timing sequences.

In the simplest system, where no overlap is permitted, the total time to process block i is simply the sum of the phase times

$$t_{B_i} = I_i + C_i + O_i \tag{3}$$

Consider next a potentially faster system with one data channel that permits either I-C or O-C overlap. In the first case, while the system is computing for record i, record $i + 1$ may be in its input phase, or else record $i - 1$ may be in its output phase. In this case,

$$t_{B_i} = \text{Max} \, (C_i, (O_{i-1} + I_{i+1})) \tag{4}$$

From now on we shall assume that the time for each phase is independent of i, so that $C = C_i, I = I_i, O = O_i$ for all i. Equations (1) and (2) become

$$t_B = I + C + O \quad \text{(sequential)} \tag{5}$$

$$t_B = \text{Max} \, (C, (I + O)) \quad \text{(I-C or O-C overlap)} \tag{6}$$

When a second channel is introduced, there are several more overlap possibilities. If only two phases are overlapped, computing can be overlapped with either input or output, or else input may be overlapped with output. Two subcases are possible. First, if $C \geqslant I + O$, the processing time becomes the dominant factor, since a complete input-output cycle can be done concurrently with computing. Second, if $C < I + O$, two complete cycles must be considered. In this case, the excess of $I + O$ over C can be overlapped with another input or output operation, and complete overlap can be achieved. This can be expressed as

$$t_B = \tfrac{1}{2}(C + \text{Max} \, (C, I + O)) \quad \text{(I-C, O-C, I-O overlap)} \tag{7}$$

With a two-channel configuration, up to three operations are permitted concurrently. The equation defining the processing time per block is then

$$t_B = \text{Max} \, (C, \tfrac{1}{2}(I + O)) \quad \text{(I-C-O overlap)} \tag{8}$$

These basic relationships (which the reader should verify in the example cases of Fig. 6-4.3) will now be rewritten in terms of *primary variables* more likely to be known or chosen by a user for the particular problem of interest:

t_c = the compute time for one problem record
t_a = the access time to start flow of one *block* of records
t_f = the time to flow one problem record
M = the amount of main storage, expressed as the number of *records* that is available for work space and buffering
n = the number of records per block (blocking factor)
(All times are in milliseconds.)

These variables are related to I, O, and C of Eqs. (5), (6), (7), and (8) as follows [the I/O cases use Eq. (1)]:

$$C = n t_c \tag{9}$$

$$I = t_a + n t_f \tag{10}$$

$$O = t_a + n t_f \tag{11}$$

Although the equations are in terms of primary variables, there are three secondary variables of direct user concern:

r = the record size (in bytes)
m = the total number of bytes of main storage available for buffer and work spaces
k_f = the kilobyte rate of transmission of auxiliary storage

The secondary variables and primary variables are related by

$$t_f = \frac{r}{k_f} \tag{12}$$

and

$$M = p\lfloor \frac{m}{pr} \quad \text{(to nearest equal or smaller integer)} \tag{13}$$

To simplify the comparisons of the several overlap configurations, a slightly modified version of this equation will be used:

$$M = L\lfloor \frac{m}{Lr} \tag{13a}$$

where L is the least common multiple of the p's applying to the several cases. Since $p(1) = 1, p(2) = 2, p(3) = 2$, and $p(4) = 3$, then $L = 6$.

Variable t_a is determined strictly by the equipment. If we assume a prespecified record size, t_f is determined by the physical properties of the auxiliary storage device; M is determined by the main storage size and blocking factor; and t_c is determined by both the processor speed and the problem.

Figure 6-4.4 gives equations of elapsed time per record for each configuration, the number of channels required, and the blocking factor (number of problem records moved in one access and flow operation). Available space is divided into equal parts of work (compute) space or buffering. The capacity of each area (in records) is equal to the blocking factor. Also shown are the inequality conditions for the compute and input-output-bound situations.

The elapsed time per record is a simple enough idea for sequential processing, but it is not so obvious where overlap is permitted. It is derived in all cases by writing the expression for the total time to process (i.e., compute and two-way move) all n records and by dividing by n.

Examination of the equations indicates that the improved blocking factor achievable with the sequential case is especially important when access time (t_a) is dominant. Since the greater number of records per block results in a lower penalty per record, because of the access time, the sequential case gives better performance than the two-channel I-C-O overlap configuration.

It is of interest to note that the best improvement over simple sequential processing is a factor of 3 achieved by the I-C-O configuration for

$$\frac{3t_a}{M} \leqslant t_f \tag{14}$$

$$t_c = t_f \tag{15}$$

Overlap case	No. of chan.	Req'd blocking factor	General	Elapsed time per record	
				Detailed	Normalized
1 SEQUENTIAL (NO OVERLAP)	0	M	$t_B = 1 + C + O$	$t = t_c + \dfrac{2t_a}{M} + 2t_f$	$T = 1 + 2A + 2F$
2 1-C,O-C OVERLAP	1	$\dfrac{M}{2}$	$t_B = \text{Max}(C, 1 + O)$	$t = \text{Max}\left(t_c, \dfrac{4t_a}{M} + 2t_f\right)$	$T = \text{Max}(1, 4A + 2F)$
3 1-C,O-C,I-O OVERLAP	2	$\dfrac{M}{2}$	$t_B = \frac{1}{2}(C + \text{Max}(C, 1 + O))$	$t = \dfrac{t_c}{2} + \frac{1}{2}\text{Max}\left(t_c, \dfrac{4t_a}{M} + 2t_f\right)$	$T = \frac{1}{2} + \frac{1}{2}\text{Max}(1, 4A + 2F)$
4 1-C-O OVERLAP	2	$\dfrac{M}{3}$	$t_B = \text{Max}(C, \frac{1}{2}(1 + O))$	$t = \text{Max}\left(t_c, \dfrac{3t_a}{M} + t_f\right)$	$T = \text{Max}(1, 3A + F)$

Case	Condition	Compute bound case Elapsed time/record		I/O Bound case Elapsed time/record	
		Detailed	Normalized	Detailed	Normalized
1	—	$t = t_c + \dfrac{2t_a}{M} + 2t_f$	$T = 1 + 2A + 2F$	$t = t_c + \dfrac{2t_a}{M} + 2t_f$	$T = 1 + 2A + 2F$
2	$t_c > \dfrac{4t_a}{M} + 2t_f$	$t = t_c$	$T = 1$	$t = \dfrac{4t_a}{M} + 2t_f$	$T = 4A + 2F$
3	$t_c > \dfrac{4t_a}{M} + 2t_f$	$t = t_c$	$T = 1$	$t = \frac{1}{2}\left(t_c + \dfrac{4t_a}{M} + 2t_f\right)$	$T = \frac{1}{2} + 2A + F$
4	$t_c > \dfrac{3t_a}{M} + t_f$	$t = t_c$	$T = 1$	$t = \left(\dfrac{3t_a}{M} + t_f\right)$	$T = 3A + F$

NOTATION

r = number bytes per problem record
t_c = processor time per problem record, in milliseconds
m = processor storage, in bytes, for all buffer and work space
$M = \lceil m/r \rceil = m$ expressed as number of problem records
t_a = access time of auxiliary storage to one block of problem records, in milliseconds

k_f = data rate of auxiliary storage, in kilobytes per second
$t_f = r/k_f$ = time to flow one problem record, in milliseconds
$A = t_a/Mt_c$ = normalized access time
$F = t_f/t_c$ = normalized flow time
$T = t/t_c$ = normalized total time
Blocking factor = number problem records read/written with one access $= n$

Fig. 6-4.4 Summary of equations of elapsed time per record.

Processing time limits	Time per record Shortest Longest				Remarks
$0 \leqslant t_c < \dfrac{t_a}{M} - t_f$	3	1	4	2	
$\dfrac{t_a}{M} - t_f \leqslant t_c < 2\dfrac{t_a}{M}$	3	4	1	2	If $t_c = \dfrac{t_a}{M} - t_f$ then $4 = 1$
$2\dfrac{t_a}{M} \leqslant t_c < \dfrac{4t_a}{M} + t_f$	4	3	2	1	If $t_c = \dfrac{2t_a}{M}$ then $1 = 2$ and $3 = 4$ For $t_c > \dfrac{3t_a}{M} + t_f$, 4 is compute bound
$\dfrac{4t_a}{M} + 2t_f \leqslant t_c$	4 = 3 = 2				2, 3, 4 compute bound

Relative effectiveness of idealized cases.
1 = sequential; 2 = I–C, O–C overlap; 3 = I–C, O–C, I–O overlap; 4 = I–C–O overlap.

Fig. 6-4.5 Comparison of cases.

When the record size, main storage size, and auxiliary storage are specified, the decisions of the designer cannot affect the satisfaction of Eq. (14). If it is satisfied, Eq. (15) can only be satisfied by adjusting t_c (the compute time per record). However, t_c is influenced by both the problem and the CPU speed.

Figure 6-4.5 defines the critical intervals within the processing-time spectrum and ranks the speeds of each overlap case for each interval. This figure shows that a two-channel system (configurations 3 or 4) can always be organized to give the best performance, although it may not necessarily utilize a full I-C-O overlap mode. However, if the system is heavily compute bound, a single-channel system will do as well. It also shows that a single-channel system, when highly input-output bound, will best perform as a purely sequential system because of the higher blocking factor. Figure 6-4.6 gives the critical conditions defined by the equations of Figs. 6-4.4 and

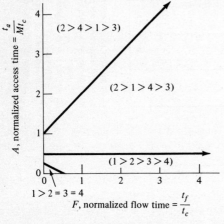

Fig. 6-4.6 Graphical comparison of cases.

6-4.5 in a graphical form. Since the sequential configuration is the easiest to program and characterize, it is convenient to use it as a "standard" of comparison for the other configurations.

In summary, a system that can run p resources concurrently can at best have p times the thruput of one system, with the same resources restricted to sequential ($p = 1$) operations. This theoretical improvement can be achieved only for certain workloads and with a careful match of configuration and problem parameters. For other workload conditions, lesser but still significant overlap (and thruput) may still be achieved by a judicious choice of equipment parameters and data-movement programming.

Equations have been developed relating the key parameters for best thruput with one class of workload. This workload is characterized by fixed-size records with regular demands for input, output, and compute resources. These equations indicate that the main-storage partitioning required for a high degree of overlap significantly affects thruput, especially when access time is of the order of one-half the compute time. Systems with two channels can always be designed for greater thruput than sequential or one-channel systems, although the maximum does not necessarily occur with maximum overlap.

6-5 EQUIPMENT PERFORMANCE SUMMARY:
IBM SYSTEM/360   [Refs. AL,GR,IN,OP,RU]

As has been shown in this chapter, the equipment of a computer system may be considered to be composed of several subsystems—the main store modules, the CPU, and auxiliary storages. There are also other items such as printers, card reader punches, terminals, and CRT display devices, etc., etc. Some of the methods of characterizing the performance of each such subsystem have been discussed, and a simple model illustrating some of the interrelations of the subsystems for the case of simple, idealized overlap conditions was presented in Sec. 6-4. Throughout, it was found that only the most rudimentary "raw" performance factors could be stated without regard to the workload. The performance of even simple combinations of system parts working together requires specification of, and is particular to, the workload. This is not surprising because of the computer's very great function generality, and also because the interconnections of system parts are quite flexible and under program control.

Figure 6-5.1 is a concise form that includes many hardware-performance factors that are reasonably workload independent. This form is not intended as a complete performance summary, but is a start in obtaining a performance picture of the hardware capabilities of a given system. The reader is encouraged to discover for himself the difficulties in obtaining actual values of the listed items in particular systems. It will soon be found that not only is some such information not published, but also that each manufacturer uses its own terminology, which is often hard to translate into the above categories. Also, seemingly minor details, which may well be quite complex, can be of major significance. For example, even fixed-point ADD time may well have several values within the same system, since some ADD instructions obtain their operands from fast registers (like the IBM System/360 RR ADD), while

Machine name_____ Model_____ Manufacturer_____

Date announced_____ Reference document_____ Date_____

Main storage size(s)_____ Cycle time_____ Bits/access_____

Interleave factor_____ Max. bandwidth_____

No. check bits/access_____

No. instructions_____ Bits/instr._____ Instr./access_____

CPU address space_____ Indirect addressing_____

No. index registers_____ No. addressable registers_____

CPU buffer store: No. bits_____ Bandwidth_____

Real time clock_____ Relocation regs._____ Protection_____

No. interrupt locations_____ Min. time for interrupt_____

No. bits in: F.P. word(s)_____ $F1$.Pt.char._____ $F1$.Pt.fraction_____

Fixed Pt. timings: ADD_____ COMPARE_____ BRANCH_____ MPY_____

Float Pt.timings: ADD_____ COMPARE_____ BRANCH_____ MPY_____

Time to move 256 bytes (storage-storage)_____

I/O subsystem:

No. devices addressable_____ No. concurrent transmissions_____

Byte format: no. information bits_____ No. check bits_____

Maximum I/O byte rate_____ % CPU interference_____

First auxiliary store device: Type_____ Capacity_____

Ave. access_____ Byte rate_____

No. bytes available in 1 access_____

Other devices, remarks:_____

_____

_____

_____

Note: Include units of times, bandwidth, and storage sizes.

Fig. 6-5.1 Machine summary form.

other ADD instructions (like the RX ADD) obtain one operand from slow main storage. Also, machines with fast instruction stacks-buffers-caches may have greatly differing ADD times, depending on whether the instruction and/or data is in the fast store or not. For these reasons, Fig. 6-5.1 should be used with more than the usual amount of caution in comparing systems. In these difficult cases, the problem of obtaining a firm performance picture seems to center on the statistical nature of the workload, especially its storage reference patterns. No good way exists at present to concisely characterize these properties.

    The IBM System/360 computer line was planned as a collection of functionally similar models, all of which could run the same machine language programs, as long as sufficient system resources, especially main storage size, were available. The models differ greatly in both speed and cost. A speed comparison is shown in Fig. 6-5.2. (This

Model	Internal relative speed	Main storage				Controls		General-purpose and floating-point registers			Adder width	Circuit delay
		Cycle	Width	Interleave	Bandwidth	Type	Cycle	Type	Width	Cycle		
30	1	2.0	1	–	500	ROS	1.0	core	1	2.0	1	0.030
40	3.5	2.5	2	–	800	ROS	0.625	core	2	1.25	1	0.030
50	10	2.0	4	–	2,000	ROS	0.5	core	4	0.5	4	0.030
65	30	0.75	8	2	14,933	ROS	0.2	circ	4	–	7	0.010
75	45	0.75	8	2-4	21,300	circ	0.195	circ	4,8	–	8	0.006
85	120	1.04	16	2-4	N.A.	circ	0.80	circ	8	–	8	0.005
91	135-420	0.75	8	8-16	N.A.	circ	0.60	circ	8	–	8	0.002

Notes:
1. All widths in bytes.
2. All cycle and delay times in microseconds (multiply by 1000 to get nanoseconds).
3. Storage bandwidths include a square-root factor for interleave.
4. ROS denotes "read-only storage"; circ denotes "logic circuitry."
5. Mod 85 includes 16- or 32-kilobyte "cache" memory (0.080-μsec access).

Fig. 6-5.2 Comparison of some IBM System/360 models.

chart appears in Ref. HE1.) The "internal relative speed" is the result of a mix analysis. It is seen that speed increases by about a factor of 3 from one model to the next; the width of main storage and interleaving account for most speed increases. Note that it is quite difficult to relate precisely speed factors of the various system components to the internal speed factors.

6-6 COMPILER PERFORMANCE   [Refs. AL,GR,IN,OP,RU]

Almost all computer users now communicate with a system by means of some symbolic language, called generically a *source language*, that must be translated into a machine or *object language*.* Three major classes of performance implications in this process are:

1. *Language performance* User convenience, which translates into "user performance," i.e., time to write and debug the program.
2. *Translation performance* The storage requirements and speed of the compiler program (or interpreter)
3. *Object-code performance* The storage requirements and speed of the object programs produced by the compiler.

These three categories are fundamental to the evaluation of languages and compilers. Each is influenced by unique parameters, but there is also interplay between the categories. In the brief summary that follows, we give some feel for the considerations and the state-of-the-art; see the references for details.

Language performance is believed by almost everyone to be a very important factor, perhaps the most important of the three categories, but it is the most difficult to quantify. There are almost no published quantitative studies of language efficiency,

---

*Strictly speaking, *source* and *object* refer to the programs that are input and output of a compiler. The object language need not be a machine language.

nor is there a methodology for obtaining such results. This should not be surprising, since computer languages, like natural languages, are intimately tied to our most fundamental thought processes which, despite great efforts by psychologists, linguists, and others, still defy precise analysis. Perhaps the simplest description, from a measurement viewpoint, is the number of characters in the source program. This and a few other descriptors could, it would seem, be included in the following kind of experiment to compare two languages: (1) select a collection of problems to be solved with data examples and (2) give the problems to a group of programmers who must code and debug them in two languages. During these efforts, measure their human time in writing and debugging the programs and the lengths of the source programs (in number of characters). A little thought will reveal the many traps in this procedure, a few of which are: (1) differences in the programmers' prior knowledge and experience in one language compared to the other, (2) differences in the programmers' prior knowledge and experience in the problems to be programmed, (3) inherent skill differences of the programmers, and (4) closeness of a problem to some built-in capability of one language, but not the other. These are only a fraction of the difficulties in comparing two languages. The first three factors have to do with the people observed in the test. The fourth is illustrated, for example, by the following situation. Suppose we are comparing COBOL and APL, and the problem is matrix inversion. APL does this problem with a single built-in operator, while COBOL (as well as most other languages) requires a program of nontrivial difficulty. To summarize, objective evaluation of language performance is presently at the frontier of computer science.

Translation performance can be characterized, at least crudely but still usefully, by two numbers: the main-storage space required by the compiler, and the compilation speed, say in statements compiled per minute measured as an average over a stated set of programs. Usually, only the speed is quoted, and we are left to trust that the statements measured were "typical" of a workload. The amount of main storage required by a compiler need not be the total storage needed by it. It is a widespread practice to "fold" a compiler so that most storage it requires is not main storage, and only pieces of it or its tables or the source program are moved as needed to main storage. Using this technique, compilers for very complex languages and excellent diagnostic features may be provided for even small computers. In the design of a compiler, at least in a nonvirtual storage environment, the amount of main storage available to the compiler is a fundamental parameter that greatly influences its performance. Like most other carefully written programs, the more main storage available, the faster the compiler program that can be designed.

We now illustrate the above discussion with a few examples from current practice. In planning the IBM System/360 Operating Systems, at least three compilers for the widely used FORTRAN IV language were implemented: FORTRAN F, G, and H. These letters denote main-storage sizes (for the compiler) of 64k, 128k, and 256k bytes. Another example is the PL/1 (F) compiler that requires only 64k bytes of main storage for translating what is probably the most complex of the widely used languages. This compiler is heavily folded and often requires over 20 passes of the source program, involving many disk accesses.

The sensitivity of compiler performance to an assumed main-storage size is likely to lessen, if not disappear, with the advent of virtual storage (see Chaps. 10 and 11). Compiler design for virtual storage systems is presently a developing art, and one which is being intensively explored.

Translation speed is only one of the major performance categories listed at the start of this section. The class closest to it is object-code performance. These two categories can be traded to some extent, as we shall now see. Intuitively, it would seem that all else being equal, the more the compiler tries to produce efficient object code, the more it must analyze the source program, and the longer the translation process will take. Conversely, it is possible to bias the compiler towards fast compilation, with a resulting relatively slow object speed. Naturally, which direction a given compiler design should take depends on the intended type of use of the compiler. Many computer manufacturers see most of their market as primarily running object programs, as is typical of industrial and commercial users, where a program (once debugged and compiled) is executed many many times on different data. It is therefore not surprising to find that many manufacturer-supplied compilers are biased to produce fast object code and are relatively slow in compilation speed.

Universities and research laboratories often find that a good deal of their total computer activity is program development, rather than production/execution of already developed programs. This is typical of students or researchers learning new languages or exploring new methods.* A few universities have taken the lead in producing fast-compile compilers. The two best known recent cases are the WATFOR FORTRAN compilers (produced by the University of Waterloo in Canada) and PL/C, a PL/1 compiler designed and coded at Cornell University. Both feature very fast compilation and excellent diagnostic aids which, somewhat surprisingly, do not degrade translator performance (compared to production-oriented compilers on the same workload and equipment). The fast compilers however have some limitations. For example, PL/C includes only a subset of the PL/1 language and omits some of the more powerful features like file accessing, based storage, and generality (the ability to use keywords as identifiers or "names"). Both PL/C and WATFOR are "in-core" compilers, i.e., the entire compiler is main-storage (in-core) resident throughout the compilation process *and* during the execution of the object program. PL/C requires approximately 100k bytes of main storage during compilation and object execution time. The in-core compilers generally depend on doing the entire translation job in a single epoch of time, and hence they do not need to produce relocatable code or an intermediate form to permit other separately compiled programs to link to the current program. For this reason, the "link-edit" and "load job-steps" (in OS/360 jargon) are eliminated; their counterparts (performed as part of the translation process) are much simpler and faster. Finally, the in-core compilers can further benefit in compilation speed by feeding them one job after another in sequence, thus eliminating the

*The distinction between industrial and university/research use is made here to help motivate the discussion. It is *not* intended as a generalization of the kinds of computer uses of each type of institution. For example, the activity of many university computer centers show most jobs being of the student type, but most system utilization is for administrative and other types of production runs.

Problem	Object-Times (seconds) Mod 65 IBM FORTRAN Compiler				Mod 50	
	G	H0	H1	H2	G	H2
Sum of 100,000 integers	1.02	1.07	0.94	0.20	3.94	0.80
Formula evaluation	0.07	0.08	0.07	0.05	0.29	0.18
Matrix multiplication ($N = 128$)	0.35	0.48	0.38	0.13	1.26	0.47
Fast Fourier transform ($N - 512$)	0.35	0.32	0.27	0.31	1.25	1.10

Fig. 6-6.1 Comparison of IBM FORTRAN compilers and Mod 50 and Mod 65 on four scientific problems.

overhead requirement to bring the compiler into main storage for each job they compile. The major disadvantage of the in-core compiler is space inefficiency during object time, since the compiler then accomplishes no useful purpose, and for a main store of given size, restricts the size of the object program.

The third category of compiler performance is the "space time" required by the object program produced by the compiler. The term *compiler optimization* is generally used to describe the tactics used to achieve this kind of efficiency. The subject has received very intensive study and development. By 1972, several coherent accounts of available techniques were published.* In the next few pages, we shall outline some of the techniques and give some feel for the extent of their power in performance improvement.

To gain some perspective of the magnitudes of object performance achievable, consider Fig. 6-6.1, which shows the object execution times of programs for four scientific-type problems written in FORTRAN. The programs were compiled by the IBM OS/360 FORTRAN G compiler and the three optimization versions of the FORTRAN H compiler. Also shown for comparison are Mod 50 execution times. The G compiler produces respectable if not outstanding code, while Fortran H2 (although written in the mid 1960s) still reflects the state of the optimization art. More important than the actual numbers, Fig. 6-6.1 illustrates some trends and anti-trends that should be carefully noted. First, the run-time ratio, say between FORTRAN G and FORTRAN H2, depends on the problem; the H2-compiled program is from 5.1 to only 1.13 times faster. Naturally, such comparisons of compiler object efficiency must be made on the same machine. Note, however, that using a good compiler can (for some problems) give improvements comparable to using a faster machine with a poorer compiler. For example, although the Mod 65 is about 3.6 times faster than the Mod 50 with the same compiler, a Mod 50 using the H2 compiler for the matrix-multiplication program compiled code was only about 1.3 times slower than the program produced by the G compiler for the Mod 65. However, for the fast Fourier transform problem, the code produced by H2 is only slightly faster than G, so that the machine/speed ratio of 3.6 is only slightly changed (to 3.1) by using the Mod 50 with H2, compared to the Mod 65 with G. In summary then, at least from the small sample of Fig. 6-6.1, speed improvement on the order of 5 to 1 is achievable for some programs by using modern compiler optimizing techniques, but some programs are

*See Refs. GR and RU, both of which contain summaries and extensive bibliographies.

improved only slightly. Also, of course, we do not exclude the possibility of factors greater than 5 to 1, depending on the source program and data.

Having briefly discussed each of the three categories of language-compiler efficiency, we now turn to examine optimization more closely. Some relationships between the categories will also be discussed. To begin, we state what should be fairly obvious: The code produced by an optimizing compiler cannot be faster than the best code produced by the most capable programmer who has complete knowledge of translation methods and machine resources. Having stated this extreme case, we note that it is (in practice) mostly irrelevant, since *most* programmers (and hence most programs) do not satisfy these conditions. The real question is: Can a compiler optimize better than most programmers working in their actual environment to produce logically sound code under deadline pressure? The answer is a resounding yes!

One class of optimization tactics is the removal of redundant computations within a statement. For example, consider the PL/1 or FORTRAN statement

$$R = A * X * X * X * X + B * X * X * X + D$$

Two multiplications can be saved by recognizing that $X*X*X$ appears twice, so that the above can be rewritten as

$$T = X * X * X$$
$$R = A * X * T + B * T + D$$

Another kind of subexpression worth identifying (but much harder to detect) is a common expression in several statements. For example, consider the familiar statements for finding the two roots of a quadratic equation

$$R1 = -B + (B*2 - 4*A*C)**0.5$$
$$R2 = -B - (B*2 - 4*A*C)**0.5$$

These may be rewritten as

$$T = (B*2 - 4*A*C)**0.5$$
$$R1 = -B + T$$
$$R2 = -B - T$$

with a saving of almost a factor of 2 in execution time.

Perhaps the most important class of optimization methods relate to program loops. The simplest technique is to identify statements within a loop that are *invariant* to loop execution, i.e., whose values do not change with passes through the loop (except for the first pass). Removing an invariant statement from a loop can clearly improve execution speed, since its one-time execution replaces its N-times execution with no damage to program logic.

A loop-compaction technique, called *jamming*, consists of coalescing two or more loops into one. Program B below shows the result of jamming on program A. Both programs do identical jobs, i.e., they set all elements of vectors X and Y to 0.

Program A	Program B
DO 10 I=1,100	DO 10 I=1,100
$X(I)$=0.0	$X(I)$=0.0
10 CONTINUE	$Y(I)$=0.0
DO 20 I=1,100	20 CONTINUE
$Y(I)$=0.0	
20 CONTINUE	

Of course, if program B was the source program in the first place, the same object code would be produced, but there would now be no improvement due to the compiler. In short, modern compiler techniques can give very significant speed improvements over "casually" (sloppily) coded source programs, but much less improvement over carefully written codes (from a performance viewpoint). The jamming (loop-fusion) technique mentioned above seeks to coalesce loops, thus eliminating redundant "index updates" and "test branches." In order for two loops to be coalesced, it is sufficient that all of the following hold: (1) If one loop is executed, so is the other; (2) computations in one loop do not depend on those in the other; and (3) both loops are executed the same number of times. Jamming not only reduces object time, it also reduces required storage.

Another compiler-optimization technique is *unrolling* loops. A little thought will show that a simple loop can be written "straight-line," i.e., with all of its executed instructions and also its written instructions. Thus, for example, consider the two FORTRAN programs

Program A Loop	Program B Straight-Line
DO 10 I=1,4	$Z(1)$=$X(1)$+$Y(1)$
$Z(I)$=$X(I)$+$Y(I)$	$Z(2)$=$X(2)$+$Y(2)$
10 CONTINUE	$Z(3)$=$X(3)$+$Y(3)$
	$Z(4)$=$X(4)$+$Y(4)$

In program A, only the second statement is essential. The DO statement translates into initialization (register load) instructions plus (with every loop traversal) an index update, a test, and a branch. Program B avoids the execution loop-control instructions at the price of more written statements. The unrolling technique seeks to recover some of the speed of the straight-line technique (and suffers some of its space expense), but yet retains much of the advantage of looping. For example, program D is the source language counterpart of a two-times unrolling of program C.

Program C	Program D
DO 10 I=1,100	DO 10 I=1,100,2
$Z(I)$=$X(I)$+$Y(I)$	$I1$=I+1
10 CONTINUE	$Z(I)$=$X(I)$+$Y(I)$
	$Z(I1)$=$X(I1)$+$Y(I1)$
	10 CONTINUE

The time advantage from unrolling by two is at most 2. In most cases, however, it will be far less (in the above example, the floating-point ADD instruction predominates and is executed the same number of times in both rolled and unrolled versions). One difficulty with unrolling arises if the index-limit quantity is a variable rather than a constant (like 100), as in the above example. Unrolling can still be used, but added statements (outside the loop) must be inserted to ensure proper execution of the loop.

We now summarize some of the techniques of object-time optimization:

1. Invariant statements removed from loops. Invariant statements are those inside a loop whose result variable does not change during loop execution.
2. Reducing redundant expressions within a single statement, or between statements.
3. Jamming or coalescing several loops into one loop, thus saving redundant loop-control executions.
4. Unrolling a loop to save loop-control executions.
5. Peephole optimization, which involves scanning the object code produced by the compiler for sequences that can be replaced with more efficient sequences or with microcoded sequences.
6. Alternative "parsing," which can be especially useful in parallel processing or pipelined machines. For example, consider

$$Z = A + B + C + D$$

parsed as follows:

$$P1:Z = (((A + B) + C) + D)$$

and

$$P2:Z = ((A + B) + (C + D))$$

Here, $P1$ must be executed sequentially, but with $P2$, the $A + B$ and the $C + D$ can be executed concurrently in a two-adder system.

We might mention in passing that the sophistication of modern optimizing compilers can sometimes lead to surprising performance results. For example, in some installations, one of the "benchmark" programs used to compare CPU speeds is a formula evaluation containing several statements inside a loop. The statements are designed to contain a known number of various types of arithmetic operations and do not contain the loop-control variable. By permitting the loop to be executed, say 100,000 times, the computer speed can be measured with a stopwatch. This method can give crude but valuable results, and the process is under the control of the user, and not of the manufacturer of the tested system. But now consider what happens when an optimizing compiler translates such a program. The timing statements, all of which are invariant, are moved outside the loop so they are only executed once! The system speed then observed will be unrealistically high, thanks to the compiler, and almost independent of the processor speed!

The compiler designer has a variety of techniques available to help him do his work, some of which are discussed briefly above. Qualitatively, one of the prices of optimization is slower compilation speed. Furthermore, one might suspect that of all the methods available, some are much more beneficial than others. The question of which are best might well depend on the program being compiled. On the other hand, some methods may well be very fruitful in most cases. These considerations all suggest a common idea: Gather data on the execution-time properties of programs and relate them to the static written program. An instrument for doing this can help identify the high-activity regions of programs. If there are patterns common to many programs, the compiler designer, by finding them, has gained vital information to improve compilers. The individual user can use the same kind of tool to help him focus attention on the most active parts of his program. He can then concentrate on improving the performance of these parts.

Dan Ingalls and Don Knuth of Stanford University have reported on results of this kind. They developed a type of software tool called an Execution-Time Profile Monitor. This program accepts as input a FORTRAN source program to be analyzed. It processes this to produce a new FORTRAN source program with additional statements that update counters of various types (e.g., one for each time a statement is executed or for each time some class of statement is executed). After execution, the information in the counters is printed as a frequency table or histogram. Ingalls cites a case (which we suspect is quite typical) where a program had 35 subroutines, but only one of them accounted for 67 percent of program execution time. This focussed attention on that program and, by a little further inspection, they discovered an invariant statement in the inner loop. By simply moving it outside of the loop, they shaved 15 minutes from a 40-minute run! Figure 6-6.2 shows the results of another study cited by Ingalls. This time the profile analyzer was used to identify the inner

Opt. level	Execution time rel. to level 4	Rel. to level 4 without in-line subroutines
0	4.6	3.7
1	3.4	2.7
2	1.9	1.5
3	1.3	1.1
4	1.0	0.8

Definitions of optimization levels

OPT = 1   Local optimization; common subexpressions eliminated. Register contents retained across statements

    = 2   Global optimization; invariant expressions removed, load-store motion, etc.

    = 3   Like level 2, but with machine-dependent optimizations for IBM S/360 (use of BXLE, LA, double indexing)

    = 4   All known compiler optimizations applied

    No. Programs in sample: "over 20"

    Source Language of Programs: FORTRAN IV

    Method: Use software trace (execution-time profile) to find high-frequency "inner loops" of programs. These loops then hand-simulated and timed for each optimization level.

Fig. 6-6.2 Summary of Stanford University study of execution-time behavior (reported by D. Ingalls [15]).

loops of several programs. Hand simulation of five compiler-optimization techniques was then done. As shown in the table, the best compiler tactics gave a factor of 4.6 improvement over the simplest type. This is reasonably close to the most favorable ratio between times due to IBM's FORTRAN G and H2 compilers, as stated in Fig. 6-6.1. It is recalled that in Fig. 6-6.1, the degree of improvement depended on the programs.

The execution-profile analyzer (EPA) is an excellent tool to improve the programmers' awareness of performance of their programs. The complexity of the programming task, coupled with the great difference between the written and executed program, means that we must develop new intuitions about program performance. The EPA can help students, professional programmers, and even managers focus on those tasks that are most fruitful for improving program speed. It should also be a great aid in identifying codes suitable for implementation as microprograms. Compilers can be designed to supply an EPA at user's option.

After our introduction to the three performance categories of language, translation, and object performance, we spent most of the discussion on the latter two topics because most is known about them. We must, in closing this brief review, take note of two other factors. First, optimization techniques depend fundamentally on extracting information from the source program about what it is doing. It seems reasonable to suppose that the higher the level of the language, the easier this may be, since the user's statements concentrate more on *what* he wants to do and leaves *how* it is to be done to the compiler. For example, using APL's powerful array operators, a user can specify matrix multiplication or inversion in a single statement, thus giving the compiler designer maximum opportunity, by a simple signal (the single operator symbol), to optimize these operations. In contrast, say in FORTRAN or PL/1, a matrix multiplication or inversion program consists of many loops and is hardly recognizable (especially the way some programmers write their code). The case of translating from a high-level array-oriented language is also very useful in compiling for a parallel-processing machine or for a microcoded machine.

Finally, we must mention that this section has been concerned only with performance considerations. Other factors, like logical clarity, reliability, and documentation, are also vitally important to the success of programs.

REFERENCES AND BIBLIOGRAPHY

1. [AL] Allen, F.E. and J. Cocke: A Catalogue of Optimizing Transformations, in "Design and Optimization of Compilers," R. Rustin, ed., Prentice-Hall, Englewood Cliffs, N.J., 1972.
2. [AN] Anacker, W. and C.P. Wang: Performance Evaluation of Computing Systems with Memory Hierarchies, *IEE Trans. Comp.*, vol. EC-16, no. 6, pp. 764-773, December, 1967.
3. [AP] Apple, C.T.: The Program Monitor, A Device for Program Performance Measurement, *Proc. ACM 20th National Conf.*, August, 1965.
4. [BA] Baldwin, F.R., W.B. Gibson, and C.B. Poland: A Multiprocessing Approach to a Large Computer System, *IBM Systems Journal*, vol. 1., no. 1, pp. 64-76, September, 1962.
5. [BE] Bell, G. and A. Newell: "Computer Structures," McGraw-Hill Book Company, New York, 1971.
6. [CA] Calingaert, P.: System Performance Evaluation: Survey and Appraisal, *Comm. ACM,* vol. 10, no. 1, January, 1967.

7. [ES] Estrin, G., D. Hopkins, B. Coggan, and S.D. Crocker: Snuper Computer: a Computer in Instrumentation Automation, *AFIPS Conf. Proc.*, vol. 30, pp. 645-656, 1967 *SJCC*.

8. [FU] Fuchi, K., H. Tanaka, Y. Manago, and T. Yuba: "A Program Simulator by Partial Interpretation," *Second ACM Symposium on Operating System Principles*, Princeton University, pp. 97-104, October 20-22, 1969.

9. [FU1] Fuller, S.H.: Minimal-Total-Processing-Time Drum and Disk Scheduling Disciplines, *Comm. ACM*, vol. 17, no. 7, July 1974.

10. [GI] Gibson, J.C.: The Gibson Mix, *IBM Technical Report TROO.2043*, June, 1970.

11. [GR] Gries, D.: "Compiler Construction for Digital Computers," John Wiley and Sons, New York, 1971.

12. [HE1] Hellerman, H.: "Digital Computer System Principles (2nd edition)," McGraw-Hill Book Company, New York, 1973.

13. [HE2] Hellerman, H. and H.J. Smith, Jr.: Thruput Analysis of Some Idealized Input, Output, and Compute Overlap Configurations, *ACM Computing Surveys*, vol. 2, no. 2, June, 1970.

14. [HU] Husson, S.S.: "Microprogramming Principles and Practice," Prentice-Hall, Inc., Englewood Cliffs, N.J., 1970.

15. [IN] Ingalls, D.: The Execution-Time Profile as a Programming Tool, in "Design and Optimization of Compilers," R. Rustin, ed., Prentice-Hall, Englewood Cliffs, N.J., 1972.

16. [KN1] Knight, K.E.: Changes in Computer Performance, *Datamation*, vol. 12, no. 9, pp. 40-54, September, 1966.

17. [KN2] Knight, K.E.: Evolving Computer Performance 1963-1967, *Datamation*, vol. 14, no. 6, pp. 31-35, January, 1968.

18. [OP] Opler, A.: Measurement of Software Characteristics, *Datamation*, vol. 10, no. 7, pp. 27-30, July, 1964.

19. [RA] Raichelson, E. and G. Collins: A Method for Comparing the Internal Operating Speeds of Computers, *Comm. ACM*, vol. 7, no. 5, pp. 309-310, May, 1964.

20. [RO] Rosin, R.F.: Contemporary Concepts of Microprogramming and Emulation, *Computing Surveys*, vol. 1, no. 4, 1969.

21. [RU] Rustin, R. (ed.): "Design and Optimization of Compilers," Prentice-Hall, Englewood Cliffs, N.J., 1972. (Consists of seven papers and bibliography.)

22. [TU] Tucker, S.G.: Microprogram Control for System/360, *IBM Systems Journal*, vol. 6, no. 4, pp. 222-241, 1967.

23. [WH] White, P.: Relative Effects of Central Processor and Input-Output Speeds Upon Throughput on the Large Computer, *Comm. ACM*, vol. 7, no. 12, pp. 711-714, December, 1964.

24. [WI] Wilkes, M.V.: Microprogramming, *Proc. Eastern Joint Computer Conference*, December, 1958.

25. [WN] Winder, R.O.: A Data Base for Computer Performance Evaluation, *Computer*, vol. 6, no. 3, pp. 25-29, March, 1973.

26. [WO] Wood, D.C., and E.H. Forman: Thruput Measurement Using a Synthetic Job Stream, *AFIPS Conf. Proc.*, vol 39, pp. 51-56, 1971.

CHAPTER 7

Operating Systems: Evolution and Fundamentals

Most general-purpose computers operate under a collection of system programs designed to achieve several general objectives, including:

1. To insulate programmers from certain detailed and tedious tasks, such as the direct naming and programming of physical I/O devices and the mechanics of storage and device allocation.
2. To reduce the efforts required of human system operators in job setup and termination.
3. To schedule jobs in a manner that provides good user service according to some criterion, for example, highest priority jobs are scheduled first.
4. To utilize hardware resources as fully as possible, such as the CPU, main storage, I/O channels, and I/O devices.
5. To permit multiple users or jobs to concurrently share system resources, such as the CPU, main storage, programs, and data-bases.

These objectives (and others) have been attained in varying degrees in most of today's operating systems. In comparison with systems of 15 to 20 years ago, current operating systems, even those on small computers, seem quite sophisticated. However, there is still room for improvement. Many main-storage management techniques result in wasted main storage, a problem called *fragmentation*. Also, too many detailed job-scheduling parameters must typically be provided by human schedulers and operators and are not determined automatically by the operating system. Information protection and privacy mechanisms are presently also rather primitive.

This chapter sketches the functional evolution of operating systems. We begin by describing computer operation with no operating system. The final system class considered has a general multiprogramming capability. This evolution will be traced in terms of objectives because performance can only be described in terms of objectives. It would be best to consider operating-system design from the viewpoint of optimizing some objective or set of objectives. Unfortunately, although objectives are often stated, operating-system theory and practice have not yet reached the point where such statements are precise enough actually to determine design parameters.

We shall discuss several key functions that have been found in various operating systems. Wherever possible, we shall show the applicability of the scheduling principles and performance measures introduced earlier in this book. General references on operating systems include [DO,FR1,HU3,SE1,ST1].

7-1 COMPUTERS WITH NO OPERATING SYSTEMS

Consider a system with no software except for compilers (including an assembler). This environment is of historical interest, but is sometimes encountered even today with small systems. It is also of interest as a conceptual starting point for understanding the nature of operating-system features.

We begin by briefly reviewing certain characteristics of programs, since they are the interface between users and any system. A computer's CPU may only fetch instructions and access data directly from a logical main storage. It follows that a running program must, at least in part, be resident in main storage. The representation of this executing program must be in machine language. Programs are, however, not written in machine language, but rather in some symbolic source language. A source program in any source language may be considered to reference a symbolic *name space* specifying logical data or instructions. During compilation, the compiler translates names into addresses, i.e., the name space is transformed into an address space. A program's address space contains machine instructions and places for all data items and instructions that might be referenced during execution. A program's address space produced by a compiler will be called an *object module* (this is also IBM terminology). How a program's object module is further translated and eventually moved into main storage for execution will be discussed for each step in the functional evolution from "no operating system" to a general multiprogramming one.

In the case of no operating system, users' jobs are executed one-at-a-time so that each job, when it is running, has the computer system all to itself. In the scheme called *open-shop* operation, the system is physically turned over to each user to run his own job. In contrast, in *closed-shop* operation, all jobs are run by a person, called the *operator*, who usually is constrained to follow operating guidelines specified by the *installation*, i.e., the people fiscally and organizationally responsible for the system. In any case, since the entire computer system is a single scheduled resource, once the next job is selected, it is considered to occupy the system fully until the job ends.

Assuming closed-shop operation, the only scheduling decision required of the operator is to select what job should next be serviced. To start a job, the operator initiates *loading* an object module from an input medium, such as punched cards or magnetic tape, into main storage so that actual execution of the job's program may begin. This process starts with IPL (initial program load), which is physically initiated by pressing a special machine button (and setting dials). This activates a built-in machine sequence that moves a small amount of information from (say) a card reader into main storage, starting at location 0. Program sequencing then starts at location 0. This program is typically a "bootstrap" loader that first reads the rest of itself into main storage from a stored copy on cards or auxiliary storage (disk). Upon completing its own entry, the loader then turns to its main task, reading our job's object module into main storage. In the simplest type of system, called *absolute loading*, there is no further modification of the addresses of the object module. This means that the addresses produced by the compiler are also the physical machine addresses. We then say that a program's address space is *bound* to main storage at compile time. Such programs are sometimes called *absolute* programs, in contrast to *relocatable* programs that will be discussed later. Following entry of the object module, the loader branches to it, and the job itself starts to execute.

In addition to instructions and data directly named in a program and assumed to be in main storage, many programs also reference data obtained from and delivered to I/O devices during execution. With no operating system, names of I/O devices are usually bound to physical I/O devices at compile time. To change a device assignment first requires a change in the source program and then a new compilation. For these and similar functions related to the logical binding of symbolic names to physical names, the services of an operating system assume an essential role. We shall explore this fundamental subject in the next section.

From the viewpoint of resource sharing, the machine with no operating system is totally deficient, since there is no sharing; each job has all machine resources to itself when it is running. There is then a strong incentive for each job to specify as much resources as it can possibly use. Note, however, that even if a given job uses all of the resources at some time or other during its run, many resources, such as parts of main storage or I/O devices, are idle during much of the execution time. As technology has developed to the point where faster operations with larger main storages become economically feasible, most single programs cannot productively use most of the resources most of the time. Incentives then increase to share the computer's resources concurrently among several "ready" programs, i.e., among several kept in main storage at once. This is the rationale of multiprogrammed operating systems to be discussed later in this and the following chapters.

7-2 MONOPROGRAMMED OPERATING SYSTEMS [Ref. HU1]

There are many functions that can enhance the operation and usefulness of a computer, even if it processes only one job at a time. A control program can provide functions such as

1. The ability to link two or more object modules to form a new executable module without reprogramming or recompilation.

2. Utility programs to perform common tasks such as listing a file of tape records on a printer or sorting a file of records.
3. Easy transition from job to job with minimal operator intervention.
4. The ability to store user programs or system programs in libraries within the system, for example, on a direct-access storage device.
5. The ability to assign I/O devices to a job just before execution, not during compilation. This late binding can save compilation runs and be responsive to actual device availability.
6. Accounting for the time each job uses each system resource.

Objectives such as these directly result in the class of *monoprogrammed operating systems. Monoprogrammed* means that whatever services are supplied, jobs are still executed only one by one, each to completion before the next is started.

Consider the situation shown in Fig. 7-2.1. Depicted is a set of jobs shown as punched-card decks (the job-input stream), the system resources used to process the jobs (shown as main storage and direct-access devices), and the printed output of the jobs (the job-output stream). To describe how the above functions can be implemented, we now trace the flow of a job through the system.

Legend:
⬜⬜→ Unused main storage

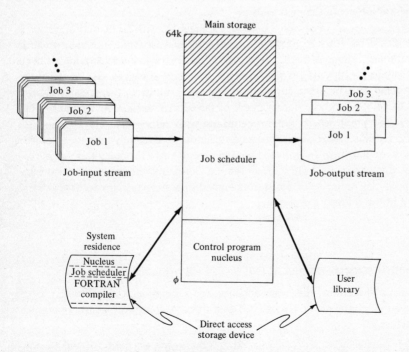

Fig. 7-2.1 A monoprogrammed operating system.

The *job-input stream* is a set of jobs to be processed, with each job uniquely identified by a name. *Job* is the term used to identify a unit of work that is logically independent of all other jobs. A job may consist of one or more *job steps*. A job step is simply a logical subdivision of a job. For example, consider a job that requires first translation (compilation) and then execution of a program. The first job step is then compilation, and the second job step is the execution of the compiled program (often called the GO step).

As shown in Fig. 7-2.2, the job-input stream is contained on punched cards. The first card is of the *job-control* type that identifies the job by name, and possibly gives other information like a billing account number. A similar (but not identical) card must identify each job step by at least naming the program used by the job step, followed by one or more cards to specify any required I/O devices or prestored data-sets used by each job step. This sequence of specifications is defined according to the rules of the *job-control language* (JCL) used by the operating system. Statements in the job-control language (simply called JCL statements) are seen to identify a job and to specify its requirements for system resources. A job step that requires punched-card input data would have the data in the job stream following the JCL for the job step. Figure 7-2.2 shows how the sequence of job-control cards might look for a job that we call JOB SIM. Each job in the job-input stream would have a similar set of job-control cards. (See Sec. 8-1 for discussion of IBM OS/360 job-control cards.)

As described, the job-input stream (i.e., the job queue) is physically present in the system card reader. The job selection rule is then first-come-first-served (FCFS), at least among the job decks in the reader. (The operator can, of course, have used various rules to determine the sequence of jobs to be placed in the card reader.)

We now turn to the function of job scheduling in a typical monoprogrammed operating system. This function is performed by a system program that we call the *job scheduler*, as shown in Fig. 7-2.1. The job scheduler program is always stored on the system residence device (usually a direct-access device like a disk), but it need not always be present in main storage. Typically, to save expensive main-storage space, only a *nucleus* of the scheduler is held there, and at the end of each job step, the nucleus moves a copy of the scheduler from system residence into main storage to

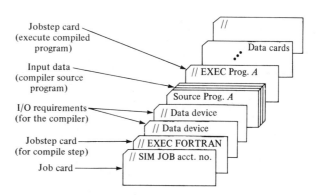

Fig. 7-2.2 Sketch of job-control language (JCL) functions in job-input stream.

schedule the next step. Job selection is a simple matter in this system, since the FCFS rule is used and the scheduler simply reads the next job from the card reader. The job scheduler reads the parts of a job into the system, one job step at a time. While reading the JCL for a job step (see Fig. 7-2.2), the job scheduler interprets the JCL statements and identifies the program that will be used by the job step and any I/O devices that the job step will use. The job scheduler will then request the service of the *control program nucleus* to assign I/O devices to the job step (unless specific devices are identified in the job step's JCL statements) and to load the program requested by the job step. Program loading is performed by the control program. This assumes that the object module (or address space) of the program to be loaded is contained in a user library on a direct-access device (as shown in Fig. 7-2.1). An object module could also be in punched cards within the job stream. In either case, after loading, it will overlay the job scheduler and be bound to the assigned I/O devices. If any operator action is required (for example, to mount a tape), the control program would notify the operator with appropriate messages. The job step can then begin execution. Figure 7-2.3 shows the structure of main storage at this time. While the job step executes, no other jobs or job steps may use the system. During execution, any system messages or job-step output will be printed on the system printer. When the job step ends, the control program is notified. The control program will then load a copy of the job scheduler into main storage (from system residence), overlaying the job step, and the job scheduler will then schedule the next job or job step (following the same procedure just described).

There are many advantages to such a system over one with no operating system.

1. User programs may be stored in a user library and called from the library by a JCL statement, thus eliminating the need to store many user object modules in punched-card decks.

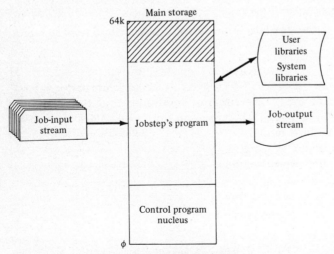

Fig. 7-2.3 Main storage during job-step execution.

2. There is less reliance on the operator, and hence on slow and error-prone human operations, because the job-control language performs many detailed functions such as calling prestored system programs from a library on disk.
3. There is less dependence on the operator for smooth job-to-job and job-step-to-job-step transition because the jobs can now constitute a stream, each with JCL statements that specify much of its own setup.
4. I/O devices are not bound to a program at compile time, but rather at program load time.

It is also possible for the control program to monitor (record) the CPU time, wall-clock time (time of day), the main storage, and I/O devices used by a job and/or job step. This information can be used for job accounting and billing. The CPU hardware required for these functions includes a real-time clock or interval timer (see Sec. 7-4).

Because the job-control language *is* a language, it is possible to store commonly used JCL statement sequences (JCL subroutines) in a JCL procedure library on a direct-access device; the statement sequence may be called by a single statement when a job's JCL is being read into the system. Any commonly used utility programs can also be stored in a system or user library and called for execution through JCL. JCL also permits late binding of program names to prestored data.

Thus far, we have examined monoprogrammed operating systems by following a job through the system. In doing so, we have described functions performed by many of the required software resources such as the control program nucleus and the job scheduler. Another way to view the system is through its software resources.

System residence is established on a direct-access device as shown in Fig. 7-2.1. This system residence pack contains a copy of the control program nucleus, the job scheduler, system software resources (like compilers, sorts, and utilities), and a bootstrap loader program. All are in executable format (object modules).

We now consider how the operating system is "started" (assuming, however, that the system residence pack exists and that it was generated previously or on another system). If machine power has just been turned on, the first job of the human operator is to "IPL" the operating system. In effect, since at this moment the machine has no active operating system, the same process of IPL (described in the previous section) as used with a no-operating system is followed. Typically, the operator, by pressing buttons or turning dials on the console, specifies the system residence device and then presses the IPL button that initiates movement of information from that device into main storage, followed by a branch to the information read in. This is simply a bootstrap loader that in turn reads in the operating-system nucleus. It, in turn, typically requests the operator to supply information such as time-of-day and date used for job accounting. Following this, the loading program branches to the part of the nucleus that we shall simply term the *control program*, which links to various operating-system programs as needed. We shall use the term nucleus as roughly synonymous with control program.

After the IPL procedure, the nucleus will load a copy of the job scheduler into main storage. Job scheduling could then proceed as described earlier. Any required software resources like compilers and utilities can be specified by JCL and loaded when needed from the system residence pack. In a like manner, an installation can store application programs in a user library and they can be requested with JCL statements. This reduces the requirement to supply commonly used programs with every user job.

From the program-processing viewpoint, a monoprogrammed operating system appears as follows: A program is first coded in some source language. The program is then compiled using the compiler stored on the system residence pack. The programmer calls the compiler with an appropriate JCL statement. The output of compilation is an object module, the program's address space. We here assume that the origin of every address space begins at zero. Since the control program nucleus resides in main storage, starting at location zero, object modules require additional translation before they can be loaded for execution. A system program called a *linkage editor* is often used for address translation. It does two types of things.

1. It combines two or more object modules, i.e., already compiled programs, to produce a single address space called a *load module*.
2. It can do the necessary modifications of certain information in the object modules so that the resulting load module can be placed at any location in main storage specified at link-edit time.

Linkage editing is only possible if compilers are designed to produce object modules that conform to certain conventions. These center around special identification of external names, i.e., all the names used in a procedure (program) that refer to programs or data outside of that procedure. They are usually placed in a table called the *external symbol dictionary*, where the linkage editor can identify these names in order to link the various object modules together into a single address space. A very similar specification is needed to identify the address constants and instructions, whose values depend upon (and hence must be changed with) different locations of the module in main storage. The process of changing these items is sometimes called *relocation*, or in this type of case, *static relocation*.

The binding of logical program addresses to physical main-storage locations may then be done at link-edit time. In a monoprogrammed operating system, where it is usually reasonable to assume that all programs are loaded starting at the same origin, linkage editing (including static relocation) is sufficient for address binding. In multiprogramming systems, final binding of addresses to main storage at link-edit time results in considerable inflexibility in main-storage allocation (as will be discussed later). Nevertheless, even in this case, link-editing is an important intermediate type of binding.

For the number of new functions provided, the monoprogrammed operating system does not require too many resources, either hardware or software. The hardware resources include part of main storage and some direct-access storage. The control program nucleus resides in main storage during system operation. The job scheduler is a transient system resource that uses main storage between jobs and job steps. Direct-access storage is used for system residence, system libraries, and user libraries. The software resources include the special programs described in this section: the control program nucleus, the job scheduler, the IPL program, the linkage editor, compilers, and special-purpose utility programs (like sort programs). The structure and interaction of these resources are basic to monoprogrammed and multiprogrammed operating systems.

The simplest monoprogrammed operating system does its work serially. The job queue is in the card reader. When a job or job step is selected from the card reader, it controls the entire system: card input is first obtained directly from the card reader; processing then occurs in main storage; and printed output is transmitted directly to the printer. Although input, computation, and output could be overlapped within a single program, as described in Sec. 6-3, this is possible only in certain programs and requires special programmer effort. More typically, monoprogramming results in frequent idle time for the card reader, the printer, and the CPU. If good thruput (the work done over a given period of time) is a major system objective, a productive technique to reduce these idle times would tend to meet this objective. This is possible in a system that *overlaps* system input, job processing, and system output. This type of overlap is called SPOOLing (Simultaneous Peripheral Operation On Line). The SPOOLing technique will be described in the next section.

7-3 MULTIPROGRAMMING: SPOOLing-ONLY SYSTEMS

The primary objective of SPOOLing is to improve a system's thruput. This is accomplished by overlapping system input, job processing, and system output. By system input we mean the job-input stream that was described in the previous section. System output here refers to punched-card and printed output, including JCL listings, system messages, and user job output printed by the high-speed printer. We still assume that user jobs execute one at a time. SPOOLing requires two special kinds of system programs to be resident in main storage (see Fig. 7-3.1). The first will be called the *system reader* (or simply reader). Its function is to move the job-input stream from the card reader to direct-access storage (phases 1*a* and 1*b*). The second program is called the *system writer* (or simply writer). Its function is to write (or print) system output from direct-access storage (phases 4*a* and 4*b*). Although a SPOOLing system in effect removes the slow devices like card equipment and printers (and sometimes tapes) from direct user control, this is a fact of implementation, *not* logical structure, i.e., each source program logically "reads cards" and "prints output" in the same manner as would be done with no SPOOLing.

The overlap (and multiprogramming) achieved in a SPOOLing system is possible because of *input-output channels*. A channel is a hardware device that is functionally similar to a small special-purpose computer designed to move input from I/O devices to main storage and output from main storage to I/O devices. A CPU instruction is usually required to initiate a channel operation, but once started, the slow transmission and buffer operations themselves are done by a channel independently of CPU instruction execution. The independence of most CPU and channel operations means that they can be done concurrently, i.e., overlapped in time.

The key function of SPOOLing is then to buffer system input and output through an intermediate level of direct-access storage. The buffering is controlled by the reader and writer system programs that attempt to keep the card reader(s) and printer(s) operating concurrently, as much as possible, by applying them to different

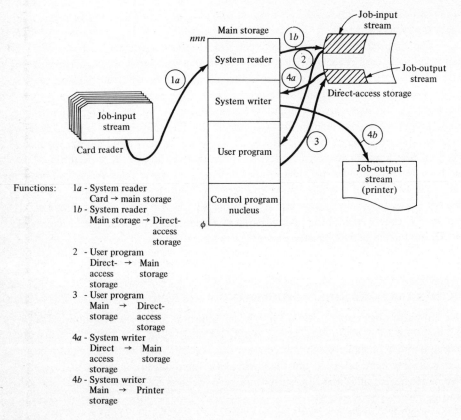

Functions: 1a - System reader
            Card → main storage
            1b - System reader
            Main storage → Direct-
                              access
                              storage
            2 - User program
            Direct- → Main
            access   storage
            storage
            3 - User program
            Main → Direct-
            storage access
                     storage
            4a - System writer
            Direct → Main
            access   storage
            storage
            4b - System writer
            Main → Printer
            storage

Fig. 7-3.1   The system reader and writer functions.

jobs at the same time. Since these system programs share main storage with a user program, SPOOLing is a primitive form of multiprogramming.

SPOOLing features automatic movement of system I/O between devices and direct-access storage (via main storage). It is logically independent of any user-program activity that may request transmission between main storage and direct-access storage (e.g., update of files).

Since SPOOLing moves the job-input stream to direct-access storage, the job queue in effect is now on direct-access storage. To schedule a job, the job scheduler will search the job queue for the next best candidate; "best" is defined by the scheduling algorithm. Direct-access devices, unlike card readers, are not serial devices. The job scheduler, therefore, is not limited to the use of the FCFS scheduling rule. For example, a type of highest-static-priority-first-served (HSFS) scheduling rule could be (and often is) used.

A typical job-scheduling process is shown in Fig. 7-3.2. The job scheduler selects the next job for execution. The program used by the first job step is loaded into main storage, overlaying the copy of the job scheduler. During execution, any punched-card input is actually read from direct-access storage, where the card images were stored by

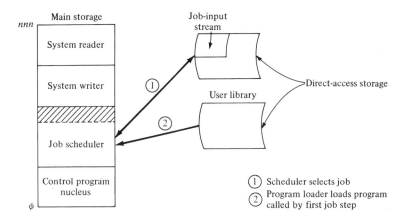

Fig. 7-3.2 Job scheduling in a SPOOLing system.

the reader (this corresponds to phase 2 of Fig. 7-3.1). All printed output is also stored on a direct-access device in a separate area (phase 3).

During certain times, job output may accumulate faster on direct-access storage than it can be printed. The excess information is held in storage until the printer(s) can accept it. Naturally, if the accumulation rate is higher than the print rate for too long a period, the processing that is causing the accumulation must be suspended. The writer controls printing the output from jobs. Assuming that the writer uses the FCFS rule to select the next job for printing (although a different rule could be used), the system writer can operate concurrently with both the user program and the system reader, in the sense that the card reader, printer, and CPU are active at one time. Once a job is selected by the writer, the writer moves the records (images of printed lines) from the output job stream to the high-speed printer (phases 4a and 4b of Fig. 7-3.1).

Thus far, we have seen how the separate hardware devices of input, output, and CPU processing can operate concurrently over the appreciable time periods involving slow I/O operations. However, it was noted that even the channels that control the devices require some CPU attention (e.g., to start them). Hence a technique is needed to schedule the CPU among the reader, writer, and user-program demands. This kind of CPU scheduling is often called *dispatching*. In a SPOOLing system, dispatching is done by the control program nucleus. The technique used is typically a static priority rule with preemption. Sharing of CPU time is controlled by a preemption and interrupt scheme. For the moment, we assume that interrupts are caused by two kinds of events: (1) a request for I/O, and (2) by the channel at the end of an I/O operation.

The reader and the writer are by nature I/O processing programs. Because the devices they control are slow, keeping them running continuously is essential for good thruput. Since they only occasionally need the CPU for short bursts of time to initiate new device operations, they are assigned higher priorities than the user program. Priorities are typically assigned in this order: (1) system reader (highest), (2) system writer, and (3) user program (lowest). Hence, the reader always has first chance at the CPU. If it has work to do, it will retain control of the CPU until it requests I/O, thus causing an interrupt. Then the nucleus, through a privileged *START I/O* instruction will start the channel for the reader. This starts the card-reading process and the nucleus then passes control of the CPU to the writer (assuming it is ready to execute). After the writer starts I/O for the printer, control of the CPU is then passed to the problem program (assuming that it is ready to execute). Otherwise, the CPU would go into a WAIT state. When the reader's I/O operation ends (the second type of interrupt), control of the CPU returns to the reader through the nucleus.

This type of dispatching is *event driven*. The dispatching events are interrupts. It is preemptive, since whenever the reader program needs the CPU it gets it (even if the CPU is busy on another program), and it uses a static priority scheme. Since the reader and the writer tend to be I/O bound, there is usually plenty of opportunity for the user program to execute. SPOOLing-only systems are a primitive but very important example of multiprogramming. However, they suffer from a fundamental defect: only one *user* program, ready for CPU execution, is kept in main storage at one time. If that program reaches a point where it must wait for I/O, the CPU will then be idle (except for the relatively rare SPOOLing demands on the CPU). This CPU idleness can be avoided by keeping one or more other user jobs in main storage concurrently. This strategy results in a more general multiprogramming system. It is especially appropriate as CPU speeds and main-storage sizes increase, as they have tended to do with the advance of computer technology.

7-4 MULTIPROGRAMMING: HARDWARE FEATURES

In a SPOOLing system, space and time are shared by the system reader, the system writer, and a user job. The space being shared is main storage and some disk space for system I/O buffering; the time is CPU time. A more general type of multiprogramming system is one that can share all of a system's resources—the CPU, main storage, I/O channels, I/O devices, and software resources—among two or more user jobs that concurrently reside in main storage. If the system reader and the system writer are considered "jobs," then SPOOLing is a form of multiprogramming. However, a general multiprogramming system allows two or more *user jobs* to share system resources concurrently, in addition to system programs (like readers and writers). We will first describe the requirements for special hardware in a multiprogramming system. Specific examples are taken from the IBM System/360 and System/370, but these features are also found (with some variations) in many other systems.

Four hardware functions considered in modern practice as essential to implement a multiprogramming system are:

1. Storage protection (main storage)
2. Privileged instructions
3. Interruption scheme
4. Interval timer or real-time clock

The first item, *storage protection*, ensures that no user program can store information in a storage area occupied by another user program or the control program. In addition to this "write protection," some systems also provide "read protection," which prevents user jobs from reading beyond the area of main storage assigned to them.

Storage protection requires a check for authorized access each time storage is referenced. The high speed of main storage requires that this check be done by hardware, or system speed would suffer intolerably.

One technique used to implement storage protection is a key-lock mechanism. Part (*a*) of Fig. 7-4.1 shows a schematic representation of such a mechanism as used in the IBM System/360. To be specific, consider 64k bytes of main storage divided into 2k blocks, each containing a lock. Part (*b*) of the figure shows each lock's structure, which is seen to consist of 4 bits. All 4-bit locks are held in a special lock-store storage unit. The 4-bit locks mean that there are $2^4 = 16$ possible locks, and it is then possible to protect up to 16 distinct storage areas concurrently in main storage.

Before a user program is allocated main storage, it is assigned a storage "key value" by the control program, which then sets the locks of all main storage assigned to the program to one of the unused key values. Before starting or resuming execution of any given program, the operating system places the key value of the program into the 4-bit protect-key field of a CPU register, which is called the *program-status word* (PSW). Whenever the program tries to store data into main storage, the key in the PSW is compared to the stored lock bits of the referenced storage block. If the lock and key values are not equal, the store operation is not executed and a *protection interrupt* occurs, which calls the control program. The control program will then take some action, such as terminating the program and giving the user an error message. The PSW key of 0 is a special case; when set to this value, the program can reference or alter all of main storage. In a multiprogramming system, the control program is assigned the key of zero. Thus, the control program can reference or change any location in main storage. User programs can only alter locations in their assigned main-storage areas. Also, only the control program has the privilege of changing the contents of the storage containing the locks and the PSW-key register.

If a multiprogramming system allows multiple-user programs to share system resources, its control program must control the allocation and use of certain major system resources. For example, only the control program should be capable of

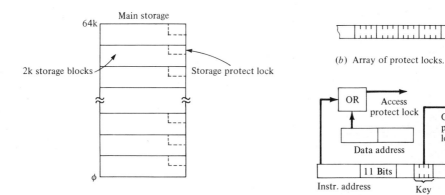

(*a*) One protect lock per 2k-byte storage block.

(*b*) Array of protect locks.

(*c*) Program status word showing key.

Fig. 7-4.1 Storage protection; key-lock scheme.

executing the instructions to set a lock or key. All I/O allocations must similarly be managed only by the control program. In IBM's System/360 and System/370, this is accomplished through a set of *privileged instructions*. The CPU's PSW register contains one bit, called the *monitor bit*, that designates whether the current CPU program may execute privileged instructions. This bit is ON when the CPU is executing the control program. The bit is turned ON early in the response events to most interrupts, and it is turned OFF by the control program before it turns over control of the CPU to another program. If the monitor bit is OFF, indicating the control program is not executing, any attempt to execute a privileged instruction is aborted and an interrupt is generated to the control program.

One example of a privileged instruction is "SET STORAGE KEY" for some storage-protect block. Another is "START I/O," which allows the CPU to activate channel operations. Only the control program may then control all I/O operations and respond to requests from multiple users for a device (for example, a data channel). If a channel were assigned to a single-user program for the duration of the job, all of the I/O devices attached to that channel would then be dedicated to that single user. To summarize, privileged instructions can ensure that only the control program can allocate system resources to user work.

A control program is really a collection of system programs linked together by references to each other and "stimulated" to execution by interruption signals. The *interrupt system* is the mechanism by which this signalling takes place. The interrupt scheme on the IBM System/360 and System/370 has five "levels" with the following priority ordering:

1. *Machine interrupts* that are caused by a hardware malfunction. When a machine check occurs, an operating system usually may not continue operation.
2. *Program interrupts* that are caused when a program malfunctions, for example, division by zero is attempted.
3. *Supervisor call (SVC) interrupts* that allow a user program to request the service of the system's control program, for example, to start an I/O operation.
4. *External interrupts* that are caused by special system devices. As one example, an external interrupt request is generated when the interval timer reaches zero at the end of a programmable time interval.
5. *I/O interrupts* that are generated when an I/O operation ends or when an I/O device, such as a card reader, is made ready.

I/O and SVC interrupts are predominantly involved in CPU dispatching (or scheduling) when event-driven static-priority dispatching is used by a control program. This is the usual dispatching technique in multiprogramming systems like IBM's OS/MVT. If a time quantum is used in CPU dispatching, as in timesharing systems, then an *interval timer* or *real-time clock* is required (see Chap. 9). As we continue our description of general multiprogramming systems, we will refer to the use of the hardware features just described.

7-5 MULTIPROGRAMMING: TIME AND SPACE SHARING [Refs. CA,DE,FR]

For any storage device, it is possible to share space only, time only, or both space and time. Main storage is a vital storage resource in a multiprogramming system. Part (*a*) of Fig. 7-5.1 shows *space sharing only* for main storage, i.e., the same storage cells are used to hold the same information over all time. Such a situation is not uncommon in certain continuously on-line process control systems. Note that although the main store is not timeshared, CPU time is shared among the resident tasks.

Time sharing only of main storage is shown in Part (*b*) of Fig. 7-5.1. This is the situation that was described for computers with no operating system, where main storage is dedicated to one user or one program at a time. Part (*c*) of the figure represents what should be achievable with general multiprogramming. Multiple user jobs may occupy main storage concurrently, and new user jobs will be loaded into main storage as old ones complete. This suggests that a measure of job *j*'s use of main storage is its *space-time product*, that is, S_j, the space in bytes reserved for job *j* times the time this space remains so reserved

$$P_j = T_j S_j$$

The concept of a program's address space, or object module produced by a compiler, was discussed earlier. With no operating system, the address space is usually

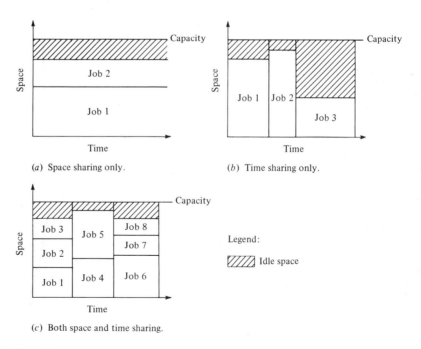

(*a*) Space sharing only.

(*b*) Time sharing only.

(*c*) Both space and time sharing.

Fig. 7-5.1 A computer's main-storage device: time-space sharing.

bound to main-storage locations at compile time. In monoprogrammed operating systems, a technique is often used where a program's address space is bound to main-storage locations at the later linkage-edit time. We assumed the same technique to be used in a SPOOLing system. All three examples, in effect, use programs that are bound to main storage in advance of program loading or execution. Although this is satisfactory in monoprogramming, it results in poor main-storage utilization in a multiprogramming system. The reason is that the actual occupancy of main storage at execution time is not predictable at compile time. For example, if four jobs were in the job queue and each job were bound to overlapping main-storage areas, only one job at a time could be loaded into main storage for execution. This would be true even though enough contiguous space were available to load several of the waiting jobs. The result would be idle main storage.

A much more effective technique for multiprogramming is one where a program's address space is not assigned a contiguous area of main storage until program load time, when the control program knows the actual state of available main storage. This technique is called *static* or *load-time relocation*. The idea is illustrated in Fig. 7-5.2. The same program's address space may be assigned a different area of main storage each time the program is run.

With static relocation, the loader program must translate the addresses in a program's address space to their physical main-storage locations. With this function, we call the loader a *relocating loader* (as indicated in Fig. 7-5.2). Because addresses are translated or relocated *only* at load time, a program once started is bound to its main-storage locations during its entire execution. Even if the program's execution were interrupted and the program moved from main storage to direct-access storage, to resume execution, the program would have to be returned to the same area of main storage.

Figure 7-5.3 illustrates the technique of static relocation for main-storage management using a short example job stream. In this example, each job has one job step that calls one program. The time and space requirements for the program are specified under the job name. It is assumed that main storage is assigned to jobs from the top down and that jobs are scheduled by the FCFS rule. Main-storage size is assumed to be 128k bytes, the first 28k being used for the control program nucleus. The first three jobs can be scheduled immediately [Part (a)]. However, when JOB 2

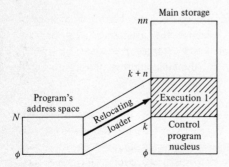

Fig. 7-5.2 Static (load-time) relocation.

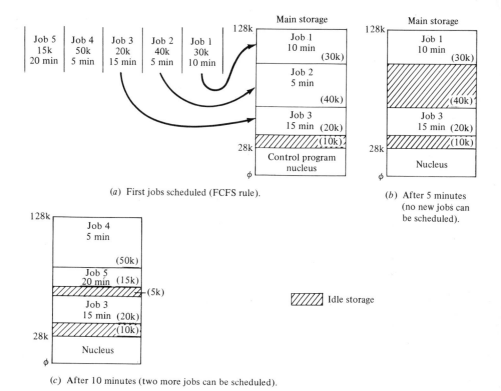

(a) First jobs scheduled (FCFS rule).

(b) After 5 minutes (no new jobs can be scheduled).

(c) After 10 minutes (two more jobs can be scheduled).

Fig. 7-5.3 Main-storage management with static relocation.

ends, main storage is badly *fragmented* [Part (b)]. That is, there is plenty of unused space, but it is noncontiguous (in fragments). Because JOB 1 and JOB 3 are bound to their main-storage locations, they cannot be moved to schedule space for another job. After say 10 minutes of operation [Part (c)], JOB 1 terminates and two more jobs may be scheduled. Figure 7-5.3 thus shows three snapshots of main storage sharing time and space. The efficiency of the static-relocation technique is affected by main-storage fragmentation. In a *dynamic relocation* system, even of the simplest type, fragmentation can be reduced.

With dynamic relocation, a program's address space is not bound in advance to its physical main-storage locations. This is because the program's addresses are translated throughout program execution at *every storage reference* by special hardware in the CPU. We now describe a type of dynamic address translation called *single-base relocation.*

With single-base relocation, a program's address space (after compilation and/or link editing) is still relative to a zero origin. At load time, before execution, the program's address space is simply loaded into any sufficiently large contiguous area of main storage (with no additional translation). Addresses in the address space are, therefore, still relative to a zero origin. Also at loading, the control program sets a special *relocation register* to the origin of the storage area for the program. This

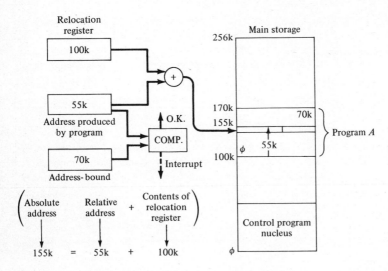

Fig. 7-5.4   Address translation using the relocation register.

process is indicated in the example of Fig. 7-5.4. Program A has been loaded into main storage, starting at location 100k, and none of its addresses have been relocated by this loader. When program A starts to run, it generates references to its address space in the range 0 to 70k, even though it has been placed in main storage at 100 to 170k. If the CPU directly used such a logical address like 55k, it would reference main storage between 0 and 70k, which is not in the physical area now occupied by the program. Clearly then, program A's logical addresses must be translated for every storage reference by the CPU. This is done by the hardware as shown, which adds the logical address and the origin address in the relocation register to obtain the final location in main storage.

In systems that is multiprogramming, the relocation register contains the main-storage origin of the program that is currently executing. Just prior to passing control to another program, the control program loads the relocation register with the main-storage origin of the program about to begin execution. Since only the control program can be permitted to modify the relocation register, the instruction type that loads this register is a privileged machine instruction.

In systems that use single-register relocation, a simple technique of storage protection is usually used. A second special-purpose register, called the *address-bound register*, is set by the control program at program-load time to the highest relative address of the loaded program. In the example in Fig. 7-5.4, this would be the value 70k. Before each address translation (or sometimes concurrently with it), the logical address is compared to the contents of the address-bound register. If the former value is greater, a protection interruption occurs, since the executing program has tried to reference an address beyond its address space size.

Using the single-register relocation scheme, programs are not bound in advance to their main-storage locations. An operating system has more opportunities to utilize main storage better by reducing fragmentation. Consider the situation that was shown in Part (*b*) of Fig. 7-5.3. In a system with a relocation register, JOB 3's program could be moved in main storage under JOB 1. Besides physically moving JOB 3's program, the control program would only have to note the program's new origin in main storage and post this value in a table of origin values. When JOB 3 is again executed, its new main-storage origin would be loaded into the relocation register. If JOB 3 is moved, it is possible to begin execution of JOB 4 five minutes earlier than with the static-relocation technique used in Fig. 7-5.3.

Single-register relocation is one type of *dynamic relocation*; it is so named because address translation is continually being done. Some operating systems expand the relocation-register approach and use more sophisticated techniques. Perhaps the simplest such generalization permits several pairs of relocation and address-bound registers, say one for program and another for data relocation. Although this seems simple enough, the effects on the sophistication of the control program can be very great. Segmentation and paging systems may be considered as two classes of examples, but we defer discussion of these to Chap. 10.

To schedule a job in a multiprogramming system, the control program must allocate enough main storage to hold the job's program(s), and it must also allocate to the job all I/O devices and data-sets that the job requests (if any). A multiprogramming system then must have a rule (or a set of rules) for job scheduling, that is, some algorithm to select the next job for loading and execution. Scheduling rules might be based on parameters like the amount of main storage *requested* by a job and/or a job classification assigned to the job by the installation. In modern multiprogramming systems, the job queue is usually kept on a direct-access device (such as a disk). A variety of scheduling algorithms are then practical, since the job queue (or its descriptors) can be searched rather rapidly. Some specific schemes for job scheduling will be discussed in Chap. 8 for the IBM OS operating system.

Whatever the algorithm, job scheduling in our terminology results in moving a job's program into main storage, where it contends with other programs there for CPU processing. This last notion introduces a second major scheduling function in a multiprogramming system, called *dispatching*: Of all the programs resident in main storage, which should next be allocated the CPU? In a SPOOLing-only system, the reader, the writer, and one user program all must be dispatched. A more general multiprogramming system may have several user programs and the system programs concurrently residing in main storage contending for the CPU. To perform its dispatching function, the control program must have a list (or queue) of all system and user programs that currently reside in main storage. There is one entry in the queue to identify each program. We will call these entries *task control blocks*. For the purpose of this discussion, a task is synonymous with a program.

Various dispatching rules can be used to decide which resident program will get the CPU next. For example, round robin (see Chap. 4) could be the dispatching rule. Whether system programs like the input reader or the output writer are controlled by the same dispatching rule as user programs is usually a system design choice. Typically, systems programs receive a higher dispatching priority. Most IBM multiprogramming systems use a *highest-static-priority-first-served* (HSFS) dispatching algorithm. It is *preemptive*, which means that higher-priority programs can interrupt lower-priority programs and gain control of the CPU. Dispatching priorities for many system programs are bound and can be changed only at system generation time. Dispatching priorities for user programs (or jobs) are assigned by the "user," who may be a programmer, a special operator with scheduling responsibilities, or someone assigned this task in an installation. The assigned dispatching priority is communicated to the control program through a JCL card, either the job card or the job-step card. This amounts to HSFS dispatching, so that once a job is in the system job queue, its dispatching priority is bound (although the operator is usually able to change it). Once a job is loaded for execution, its dispatching priority is bound throughout execution, unless the dispatching algorithm includes a feature that can dynamically modify priorities.

The HSFS scheduling and dispatching philosophy makes the user and operator responsible for achieving high utilization of the CPU, I/O channels, and devices. This responsibility is exercised by the way the user assigns dispatching priorities. This can be done with good results for a good mix of I/O-bound and CPU-bound jobs. For example, I/O-bound jobs usually require relatively little CPU time in order to keep the I/O devices active. Such jobs should be assigned high dispatching priority relative to CPU-bound jobs. This assignment scheme would then tend to keep all system components active, and hence improve utilization and thruput.

7-6 SOFTWARE MONITORS   [Refs. AR,BE,CA,CM,CHE,KO,ST1]

The monitoring of the behavior of a system is a data-gathering task the computer is especially well suited to do, since the data is generated by its own activities. Before discussing specific techniques, it may be well to characterize some of the purposes of performance monitoring/measurement:

1. To help develop or improve a system in its design and debug phases [Refs. AR,CA].
2. To help make decisions on rental/purchase of new equipment or services.
3. To help "tune" a system, i.e., to select various options for the operating system, such as which system programs and tables are to be main-storage resident, dispatching intervals, etc.
4. To help build a science and technology of system design and performance evaluation.

In Chap. 4 we discussed the hardware monitor. It was found to be a useful tool to determine equipment resource use, and also had the great advantage of *portability*, i.e., the same monitor hardware could be attached to almost any system without requiring any modification to the system. However, the hardware monitor has a major defect, that is, it cannot conveniently provide detailed information about *where* in the system and problem *programs* and the *data sets* the various activities are concentrated. Just this information, which is essential to the use of the monitored information to improve many aspects of performance, is available from a software monitor. The output of a software monitor typically consists of a listing of frequency of references (or an actual reference stream) to such items as I/O devices, storage areas, etc. This information can be analyzed as follows:

1. By visual inspection (not too practical)
2. By statistical program reduction
3. By feeding the monitored data into a system simulator

At present, method 2 is the usual technique, but several reports on method 3 have also appeared in the literature (such as IBM's AMAP technique and the simulators fed by monitor information available from some consulting firms). The great advantage of the simulator is that the analyst can experiment with various parameters of the system (model) under realistic workload conditions. See Chap. 9 for an example of this technique on a timesharing system.

The feasibility of the software monitor follows from the architecture of the hardware aids to operating systems for detecting conditions that affect resource assignment and use. These include the privileged mode and the interrupt structure. Such signalling mechanisms are typically relatively few in number (the IBM System/360 has only five interrupt locations), so that it is not too difficult in principle for a monitor program to be written to intercept all interrupts and capture certain information about what triggers them. Unlike the hardware monitor, this requires considerable detailed knowledge of each system's operating-system structure; software monitors are *not* portable from one type of system to another.

The maximum rate at which interrupts are generated may be quite high in a fast machine. This has the following implications on software monitoring:

1. The processing by the monitor to capture the interrupt events can be an appreciable overhead.
2. Since during the monitoring instants, interrupts may be disabled, this may make the system response sluggish or generate timing problems, especially in "real-time" systems.
3. Space must be provided in main storage to hold the monitored information; this space must be larger the faster the interrupt rate.

The first two difficulties can be overcome to a considerable extent by doing only the minimum possible immediate processing of monitored information, i.e., simply recording it (possibly with a time stamp). These records are then written on disk (or tape) and this "stream" is processed later by another program that runs as an ordinary job on the system. However, some main-storage space must be provided at monitor time to buffer the records to the disk or tape. Reasonable-size buffer areas can ensure that in most cases, peak interrupt activity can be recorded without loss of information.

Depending on the interrupt rate, the machine speed, main storage available for monitor activity, etc., the monitoring process itself may or may not significantly affect system speed. Also, the most detailed monitoring may yield much more information than is needed or than can be conveniently used for certain purposes. These disadvantages may be overcome through the use of a *sampling* technique of monitoring. Typically, this means invoking the monitoring function only at regular time intervals by causing the machine to be interrupted by the interval timer for the monitoring task. At these times, the monitor program inspects the contents of certain tables that contain records of resource, program, and data-set reference activity and writes a monitor record or updates monitor activity tables. Note that some information on response use is still being recorded more frequently than at the monitor sample times. However, these recordings themselves do not require time-space-consuming interrupts. With care in the design of the operating system, the recordings can be made simply and quickly. The time-consuming monitor records are then only written at the relatively infrequent sampling intervals. The length of the sampling interval may easily be made a parameter specified by system programmers or operators. Most of the time, the interval may be set to a large value, with resultant small monitoring overhead and crude (but still useful) performance information delivered. The interval may be shortened for the conduct of a more detailed study.

Cantrell and Ellison [Ref. CA] report on results typical of those obtained with sampling software monitors. Their context was improving performance during the development of a large operating system for a GE-635 computer (approximately one million instructions per second). One of their monitors sampled CPU status at 1-millisecond intervals. It slowed the CPU by about 30 percent and was useful in finding several performance bugs, including one in the FORTRAN compiler that had degraded its performance by 27 percent. Their second monitor sampled gross resource and job states at (typically) 2-second intervals and recorded such information as channel and CPU utilizations, program start-end times, etc. It required 4k words of main storage and cost about 10 percent in system overhead.

For a discussion of some of the monitoring facilities provided in the IBM OS/360 system, see Sec. 8-5.

7-7 COOPERATING SEQUENTIAL PROCESSES: DEAD-LOCK THEORY   [Refs. COF,DI,HAB,HO]

A shared-resource system that also permits concurrent operations is open to a "logical disease" called *deadlock*. Deadlock occurs when a pattern of resource requests are so related that some jobs will never be completed. In this section, we discuss the general principles of this subject using mostly simple contrived examples to highlight the various classes of deadlock. In Sec. 6 of the next chapter, provisions for handling deadlock in a particular operating system, IBM OS/360 MVT, will be discussed.

Our general concept of a system in operation is a collection of jobs, all logically independent of each other, with each job requiring various resources from time to time. Any particular job may be thought of as a written sequence of requests for allocation and release of resources. We shall call such a sequence a *process*. A process is like a written program in that it consists of a sequence of statements, but each process statement results in a change in state of the job through the assignment or release of a resource. (Resources include the CPU, channels, disk and tape drives, areas of main and auxiliary storage, and common programs.) Because we are here concerned only with resource management, a process may omit any program statements that manipulate data in the usual sense.

Most of a computer's resources are shared among its users, at least at different times. Clearly, if a situation arises (either by intent or accident) that causes a job to seize sole control of a resource for an indefinitely long time period, this denies the resource to other jobs and may well delay them indefinitely. Such a "lockout" phenomenon can occur under a variety of circumstances, some easy to avoid, others quite subtle and due to fundamental decisions in system architecture and design.

An example of a lockout situation that has no theoretical solution, but a rather satisfactory practical one, is the "endless-loop" problem. The theory of computability tells us that if we consider the class of all programs that will end in a finite time, a program that can tell us if *any* program is a member of this class is itself not a member of the class. In simpler terms, this means that it is impossible to devise any precise procedure to detect an endless loop in all programs in which it may occur, and hence we have no precise general way to tell whether a long-running program is legitimately long and will eventually complete, or whether it is pathological and will never end. But we should not despair at not obtaining a precise solution from theory, since there is a very reasonable practical answer to the problem of monopolizing the CPU. This is the method (used in most systems) that requires the user to declare an estimate of "run time" of each job (say on a job card). If the CPU time the job actually uses exceeds this estimate, the job is terminated by the system. The user is induced to estimate job time reasonably well because of the following reward-penalty scheme: If the estimate is too long, the job will often suffer longer scheduling delays, since many schedulers give lower priority to long jobs (see Chap. 4). If on the other hand the estimate is too short, the estimated time will be exceeded and the job will be terminated (but the time still billed). Also, in the latter case, there will be a delay to submit a new run. Thus, the overall strategy to prevent CPU hogging is a mixture of user-supplied information and automatic response. It depends on the fact that the CPU resource is *interruptible*, and hence jobs using this resource may be preempted.

One situation that arises in many systems capable of concurrent processing is the enforcement of an *exclusive-use rule* for a resource or process. For example, consider an airline seat-reservation system in which two CPU's have access to common data, called FILE, that records all seat reservations. Suppose now that two agents, at about the same time, request a seat on the same flight, but there is only one available. If exclusive (one-at-a-time) access is not enforced, it is possible for both agents to be assigned seats. We shall now assume in this example that each agent is serviced by a program in a different CPU, so that both requests can be processed concurrently. Figure 7-7.1 shows what appears at first glance to be a scheme to ensure exclusive access to FILE. It will indeed work in some cases, but cannot *guarantee* exclusive access, since the figure shows a case in which it fails to do so. The logic of the access control uses control variable X as a program switch; X can have one of two values, BUSY or IDLE. The two processes, $P1$ and $P2$, that can access FILE each start with a preamble that accesses X and tests it for BUSY. If X is found at BUSY, it is seen that the process branches back to test again and continues to do so until X is set to IDLE (by whatever process is currently using FILE). A case where the control fails is illustrated in the figure. Basically, the failure is due to a second process, $P2$, that starts the control preamble before the previous one has finished the preamble. Thus, while $P1$ is testing X, but before it has changed it to BUSY, $P2$ finds X still set at IDLE, and hence proceeds also. Both $P1$ and $P2$ are, therefore, accessing FILE concurrently, thus violating the at-most-one-use rule. A cure for this problem is to *force exclusive use* of at least some control portion of a process. For example, if during steps (1) through (4) only one process could access control variable X, the problem would be solved.

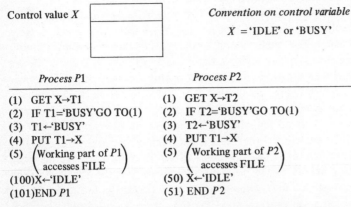

Control value X

Convention on control variable

X = 'IDLE' or 'BUSY'

Process $P1$	Process $P2$
(1) GET X→T1	(1) GET X→T2
(2) IF T1='BUSY'GO TO(1)	(2) IF T2='BUSY'GO TO(1)
(3) T1←'BUSY'	(3) T2←'BUSY'
(4) PUT T1→X	(4) PUT T1→X
(5) (Working part of $P1$ accesses FILE)	(5) (Working part of $P2$ accesses FILE)
(100)X←'IDLE'	(50) X←'IDLE'
(101)END $P1$	(51) END $P2$

Conditions: At most, one process may (in its working part) access FILE at the same time. There are two processors (CPUs); one can execute $P1$ at the same time the other can execute $P2$. All statements require the same time to execute.

Example timing sequence

Time →	1	2	3	4	5	6	7	
$P1$ step	(1)	(2)	(3)	(4)	(5)	(6)	(7)	etc. →
$P2$ step	–	(1)	(2)	(3)	(4)	(5)	(6)	

Conclusion: Both processes $P1$ and $P2$ are accessing FILE in their working parts at the same time.

Fig. 7-7.1 Illustrating failure of exclusive control.

Precisely this kind of situation arises in a multiprocessor system accessing common main storage. In the IBM System/360/370, a special instruction called TEST-AND-SET is provided that is executed as follows: The instruction specifies the address of any byte X, which is then tested, and the CPU condition code is set as follows

0 if the leftmost bit of X is 0
1 if the leftmost bit of X is 1

The byte X is then set to all 1's; during this entire process, no other accesses to byte X are permitted. The TEST-AND-SET instruction is a hardware feature essential to ensure exclusive-access control to an area of main storage in the access environment found in most computer systems.

Consider next a logical situation whereby two processes may block each other indefinitely, as shown in Fig. 7-7.2. It is assumed that if one process calls another, the calling process remains stalled at the point-of-call until the called process reaches its END. Also, once called, a process must reach its END before another call on it may begin execution. The latter exclusive-use rule may be enforced by a mechanism like TEST-AND-SET described earlier. An analysis of Fig. 7-7.2 starts with processes $P1$ and $P2$ both initially idle when some other process (not shown) calls $P1$. As seen, eventually $P1$ calls $P2$, at which point $P1$ stalls awaiting $P2$ to reach its END. $P2$ then

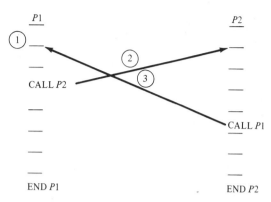

(Note: Circled numbers show relative times)

Fig. 7-7.2 A simple deadlock situation.

starts sequencing until it reaches the point where it calls $P1$. $P2$ stalls there until $P1$ reaches its END. However, as easily seen, this wait is futile, since the call on $P1$ by $P2$ cannot even begin. $P1$ is already in execution and will never complete, since it must await END of $P2$. In other words, processes $P1$ and $P2$ are in a "deadly embrace," each blocked and doomed to infinite waiting.

In many systems, resources are *serially reusable*, which simply means that once a resource is allocated to a process, no other process may use it until the current one has released it. This is just another term for exclusive use as we have used that term above. In the following discussion, we assume only serially reusable resources (unless otherwise stated).

The above example of deadlock involved processes that call each other. Deadlocks are, however, possible even if they do not. Figure 7-7.3 shows a case of two processes that do not call each other, but do access common resources ($R1$ and $R2$). Note that both $P1$ and $P2$ allocate (request) both resources, but in opposite order. In this example, assume that timing is such that $R1$ is first allocated by $P1$, then $R2$ by $P2$. Then $P1$ attempts to allocate $R2$ which, since it is already in use, stalls $P1$. Sometime later, $P2$ attempts its allocation of $R1$, which is in use by $P1$. At this point, both $P1$ and $P2$ are stalled awaiting release of resources which, as seen, will never occur, since both processes cannot sequence further to their RELEASE statements. We then have another instance of a deadlock.

To understand what follows better, we now introduce the term *task*. In the context of our deadlock discussion, a task is the executed form of a process. In other words, a task is to a process what an executed program is to a written program. We may think of a task as a recording of the executed steps of a process. With these basic definitions, we now present a more formal view of deadlock theory.

Much theoretical work has been done recently on characterizing deadlock problems and how to handle them. For example, Coffman, Elphick, and Shoshani [Ref. COF] have summarized that if all of the following conditions occur, a deadlock results:

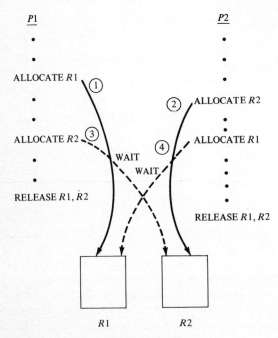

Note: Circled numbers denote relative times

Fig. 7-7.3   Deadlock on common resources.

1. *Mutual exclusion* Tasks claim exclusive control of resources they require.
2. *Wait-for* Tasks hold resources already allocated to them while awaiting additional resources.
3. *No preemption* Resources cannot be removed from a task unless the task releases them.
4. *Circular-wait* Each task holds one or more resources that are requested by the next task in the chain.

A formal model useful in deadlock problems may be stated as follows: Given a set of tasks $\{T_1, T_2, \ldots, T_n\}$ in some arbitrary state of execution. Consider a set of distinct resources $\{R_1, R_2, \ldots, R_m\}$ and assume only one resource of each type. At any instant in this model, the system state may be represented by a graph (as shown in Fig. 7-7.4). The nodes represent the resources and an edge (line) from R_i to R_j if, at the instant under consideration, some task possesses R_i and is requesting R_j. It may be shown that if the first three conditions stated above hold, then the circular-wait condition will exist if, and only if, the graph has a closed loop, i.e., if a path can be found from any node back to that node by following the arrows.

Three types of strategy have been identified for dealing with deadlock problems:

1. Detection
2. Prevention
3. Avoidance

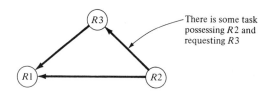

Fig. 7-7.4 A graph model at any instant.

Detection of deadlock can be done by algorithms (i.e., system programs) that periodically examine the state of resource allocations and unsatisfied requests to detect if a deadlock situation exists. If it does, the system preempts some resources involved in the deadlock, thus abnormally terminating some of the processes requesting the resources. Detection has the disadvantage of overhead in the detection process, since most of the detection processing finds no deadlocks. Also, even if a deadlock exists, any time from when the deadlock starts until it is detected is wasted. Finally, a detection strategy depends on the ability to preempt processes after detection. This is difficult in the case of some devices (like tape drives).

The deadlock *prevention* strategy depends on controlling the structure of the processes through certain ordering rules. If followed, deadlocks can never occur. A prevention strategy may be based on the four conditions stated earlier, which must all be present for a deadlock to occur. Hence, if it can be guaranteed that even one never occurs, deadlocks will not occur. Suppose, for example, that the system architecture permits the first three conditions, but avoids the circular-wait condition by insisting that two processes that request the same resources must request them in the same order. (As seen earlier, opposite ordering is conducive to circular waits.) Since circular wait is now impossible, so is deadlock, and this is done without preemptive or detection mechanisms. This strategy was followed in the design of the IBM OS system (see Sec. 8-6 for a description).

A system model and accompanying algorithms for a deadlock *avoidance* strategy has been described by Habermann. Our version will use the following notation:

MR = vector of numbers of resources of each type installed in the system
    Example:
        MR = 5,2,1,2,1 means that the system has 5 tape drives 2 disk drives,
        1 CPU, 2 printers, and 1 card reader
NR = number of resource types (= dimension of MR)
NT = number of currently active tasks (those started but not completed)
MC = matrix of *maximum claims* of each task on each resource type
        MC [I;J] = element I,J of MC is the maximum number of resources of
        type J that task I can require
CC = matrix of *current claims* of each task on each resource type
RR = vector of numbers of resources of each type currently available, i.e., not
        allocated to any task

The values for RR elements are easily seen to be given by

$$RR[J] = MR[J] - \sum_{I=1}^{NT} CC[I;J] \qquad J = 1, 2, \ldots NR$$

A major feature of the model is that each task, when it starts, must declare its *maximum possible claims* for each type of resource, which are then posted as a row of the *MC* matrix. However, this maximum does *not* result in these resources being immediately reserved for the task, which would lead to wasteful resource allocations. Instead, each task is permitted to request resources as it needs them. Of course, its totals may never exceed its declared maxima of each type and also, before granting a request, the control program must ensure that in giving the requesting task its resources, there will still be enough remaining so that all of the tasks can complete in some order or another. This assurance is the heart of the avoidance problem, and we now turn to see how this can be done.

We first define two related terms. By the *state* of the system, we shall mean a specific collection of values for the arrays *MR, MC, CC*, and *RR*. A *safe state* is defined as a state such that there is some sequence in which every active task can acquire its maximum declared needs for resources, and hence can complete. As a trivial but important example, at the instant after all tasks have declared their maximum needs (but none have made any requests), the system state is certainly safe, since the tasks may be run in strict sequence, each to completion before another starts, and hence all will complete. More generally, to test whether a state is safe, we first ask whether *RR* has large enough values to permit any active task to acquire all of its maximum declared resources so that it can surely complete. Formally, this may be done by testing whether there is any task *K* such that

$$RR[J] \geqslant MC[K;J] - CC[K;J] \qquad \text{for} \qquad J = 1, 2, \ldots NR$$

If no such *K* can be found, then we clearly have a potential deadlock. If, however, there is at least one task *K* satisfying this relation, then we note that this task can complete. When it does, it releases the resources it holds. These resources revise the tentative *RR* vector favorably, thus perhaps permitting other tasks to complete. The tests then continue with this new tentative *RR* vector. In principle (but not in practice, as will be seen shortly) every possible sequence of task completions can be explored to see if there is some sequence that results in *all* tasks completing, in which case, the original state is safe (otherwise it is not).

It can be shown that to guarantee avoidance of a deadlock, the system states must always be safe states. We now sketch the algorithm for ensuring safe states. Assuming that the system is in a safe state, suppose task *I* then requests resources as a vector *R*, in addition to those it is currently using. If the request were granted, this would put the system in a new state that we call the *trial state*. The central question is now: Is the trial state a safe state? The answer could be found by the test method described above.

A more efficient algorithm is as follows: Starting with the available resources of the trial state $(RR - R)$, test to see whether the requesting task *I* can complete. If so, the trial state is a safe state, the test ends, and *I*'s request can be granted. If not, see whether some other task can complete. If no other task can complete, the test ends and the request cannot be granted. If some other task can complete, add the resources that it would release to the RR pool, then again test whether task I can complete. If so, the trial state is safe, if not, continue the testing process. Note that the safety of the trial state is assured as soon as it is shown that the requesting task I can complete. To see why, recall that since the state before the trial state was safe, all tasks could then complete. It is therefore only necessary to show that after the current request is granted, task I can complete. When it does, it releases all of its resources, thus leaving RR in at least as favorable a condition as the safe state before the trial state.

Consider as an example the following system state:

Total resources: $MR = 5,5,5,5$
No. of tasks: $NT = 3$
Maximum claim: MC *Current claims:* CC

Task 1	2	2	3	3		1	1	2	1
2	1	1	0	1		1	1	0	1
3	3	1	2	2		2	1	2	2

The remaining resources are then

$RR = 1,2,1,1$

Suppose task 1 now makes a new request for resources

$R = 1,1,1,1$

To see if it can be granted, first compute what the CC and RR arrays would be (the trial state) if the request was granted:

	2	2	3	2
CCT	1	1	0	1
	2	1	2	2

$RRT = 0,1,0,0$

From this we compare the vector sum (RRT + row 1 of CCT) with row 1 of MC and find that the former is sufficient for all resource types but the fourth. There are then insufficient resources to guarantee the completion of task 1 directly. However, we do not despair (yet). We go on to make a similar comparison for task 2. Now we find that the result is favorable, ensuring that task 2 can complete. Assuming it does, row 2 of the MC matrix tells us that it will release resources in the amounts 1,1,0,1, which then increases RRT by these values. A new test is then made to see if our requesting task 1 can complete with the new values for RRT, and this time we find that it can. Hence, the trial state is safe and task 1's request for resources may be granted.

We have now discussed the detection and prevention strategies briefly and an avoidance strategy in some detail. Mixtures of the strategies have also been suggested at various levels of the logical hierarchy that constitutes an operating system (see Ref. HOW).

REFERENCES AND BIBLIOGRAPHY

1. [AR] Arden, B. and D. Boettner: Measurement and Performance of a Multiprogramming System, *Second ACM Symposium on Operating System Principles*, Princeton Univ., 1969.
2. [BE] Bemer, R.W. and A.L. Ellison: Software Instrumentation Systems for Optimum Performance, *Proc. IFIP Congress 68*, pp. C39-C42, August, 1968.
3. [CM] Campbell, D.J. and W.J. Hefner: Measurement and Analysis of Large Operating Systems During System Development, *AFIPS Proc.*, vol. 33, part 1, 1968 FJCC.
4. [CA] Cantrell, H.N. and A.L. Ellison: Multiprogramming System Performance Measurement and Analysis, *AFIPS Conf. Proc.*, vol 30, pp. 213-221, 1968 SJCC.
5. [CHE] Cheng, P.S.: Trace-Driven System Modelling, *IBM Systems Journal*, vol. 8, no. 4, p. 280, 1969.
6. [COF] Coffman, E.G., M.S. Elphick, and A. Shoshani: System Deadlocks, *Computing Surveys*, vol. 3, no. 2, June, 1972.
7. [DE] Denning, P.J.: Third Generation Operating Systems, *ACM Computing Surveys*, vol. 4, no. 1, 1971.
8. [DI] Dijkstra, E.W.: The Structure of the "THE" Multiprogramming System, *Comm. ACM*, vol. 11, no. 5, pp. 341-346, May, 1968.
9. [DO] Donovan, J.J.: "Systems Programming," McGraw-Hill Book Company, New York, 1972.
10. [FR] Freeman, D.N. and R.R. Pearson: Efficiency vs. Responsiveness in a Computer Utility, *AFIPS Proc. SJCC*, 1968.
11. [GO] Gosden, J.A. and R.L. Sisson: Standardized Comparisons of Computer Performance, *Information Processing 1962 Proc. IFIP Congress 62*, North-Holland Publishing Company, Amsterdam, 1962.
12. [HAB] Habermann, A.N.: Prevention of System Deadlocks, *Comm. ACM*, vol. 12, no. 7, pp. 373-377, 385, July, 1969.
13. [HO] Holt, R.C.: Some Deadlock Properties of Computer Systems, *ACM Computing Surveys*, vol. 4, no. 3, September, 1972.
14. [HOW] Howard, J.H., Jr.: Mixed Solutions to the Deadlock Problem, *Comm. ACM*, vol. 6, no. 3, pp. 427-430, July, 1973.
15. [HU1] Hume, J.N.P. and C.B. Rolphson: Scheduling for Fast Turnaround in Job-at-a-time Processing, *Proc. IFIP Congress*, 1968.
16. [HU2] Huseman, L.R. and R.P. Goldberg: Evaluating Computer Systems Through Simulation, *Computer J.*, vol 10, no. 2, pp. 150-156, August, 1967.
17. [HU3] Hutchinson, G.K.: A Computer Simulation Project, *Comm. ACM*, vol. 8, no. 9, pp. 559-568, September, 1965.
18. [KO] Kolence, K.W.: A Software View of Measurement Tools, *Datamation*, January, 1971.
19. [LA] Lampson, B.W.: Dynamic Protection Structures, *AFIPS Proc.*, 1969 FJCC.
20. [PR] Presser, L. and J.R. White: Linkers and Loaders, *ACM Computing Surveys*, vol. 4, no. 3, September, 1972.
21. [SAY] Sayers, P. (ed): "Operating Systems Survey," Auerbach Publ., 1971.
22. [SE1] Seaman, P.H. and R.C. Soucy: Simulating Operating Systems, *IBM Systems Journal*, vol. 8, no. 4, pp. 264-279, 1969.
23. [SED] Sedgewick, R., R. Stone, and J.W. McDonald: SPY-A Program to Monitor OS/360, *AFIPS Conference Proc.*, vol. 37, pp. 119-128, 1970.
24. [ST1] Stanley, W.I.: Measurement of System Operational Statistics, *IBM Systems Journal*, vol. 8, no. 4, pp. 299-308.
25. [TS] Tsujigado, M.: Multiprogramming, Swapping and Program Residence Priority in the FACOM 230-60, *AFIPS Proc.*, vol. 32, pp. 223-228, 1968.

CHAPTER 8

The IBM OS/360 Operating System

In 1964 the IBM Corporation announced the System/360, a line of six computer-system models ranging from small to intermediate-large and covering an internal (CPU) speed range of about 50 to 1. A major objective of these systems was *program compatibility*, meaning that all would be capable of running the same machine language programs. To begin to make this possible, a uniform machine *architecture* was used for all models, i.e., they have the same data representations, instruction-sets, addressing characteristics, and input-output logic. Although uniformity in these characteristics is necessary, it is not sufficient to ensure program compatibility. What is additionally required is that all models have logical access to the same amount of various system resources, especially main storage. This condition was not satisfied in System/360, and for this reason several versions of many system software programs were supplied, such as the FORTRAN F,G,H compilers, each for a different main-storage size. User programs were not guaranteed movable from System/360 system A to system B unless B's resources were at least as plentiful as A's. These restrictions on program compatibility, at least due to main-storage size, were largely removed in the System/370 virtual-storage systems announced in mid 1972 and described in Chap. 11.

Despite the above-mentioned restrictions, the System/360 did provide a practical degree of program compatibility over a performance range wider than ever attempted before. A single operating system called OS/360 was designed to serve all System/360 models and all classes of system operation and user service. Development of OS/360 was a long expensive process, due primarily to lack of previous experience with such a large programming project with such diverse objectives and applications. Eventually, three versions emerged with the same logical characteristics for individual jobs, including a common job control language (JCL), but differing in job scheduling and resource-management functions.

In this chapter, we describe aspects of OS/360 that influence system performance. The emphasis is on scheduling algorithms and their expected space-time performance benefits and weaknesses. The two multiprogramming versions of OS (MFT and MVT) will be covered, but we shall not discuss here the OS timesharing option (TSO), which is described in Chap. 9.

8-1 OVERVIEW   [Refs. BR,CL,IB1,IB2,IB3,IB10,IB11,ME,W1]

There are three versions of OS:

1. The primary control program (PCP)
2. Multiprogramming with a fixed number of tasks (MFT)
3. Multiprogramming with a variable number of tasks (MVT)

PCP is a monoprogrammed operating system that does not even do any SPOOLing. It is very similar to the operating system discussed in Sec. 7-2, and for this reason it will not be considered further.

The MFT and MVT versions have much in common with PCP and with each other, but differ in multiprogramming management of main storage and CPU allocation. These differences will be highlighted in later sections. For now, we concentrate on the general logical structure of OS/360 and some of the terminology used to describe it.

All three OS/360 options (PCP, MFT, and MVT) have a common user-system interface in the job control language. JCL is a programming language, and hence is capable of expressing a rich variety of user desires. It is beyond the scope of the present discussion to describe in any detail the complex syntax and semantics of JCL. Yet we can summarize some salient features by introducing the three major kinds of JCL statements, briefly describing each, and giving an example.

1. A JOB statement always starts a *job* and specifies the names of the job and user, the account number to be charged, and optionally such parameters as main-storage and CPU time needed by the job and scheduling parameters such as job class and priority (we shall discuss these later).
2. An EXEC statement always starts a *job step* and specifies the program to be run, or else names a prestored *cataloged procedure* of JCL statements. A cataloged procedure is a JCL subroutine that can contain any number of JCL statements. This is a very great convenience to users, since now they need not replicate JCL sequences in detail for every job; instead each job's EXEC statements can simply reference a cataloged procedure that will be copied automatically into the JCL sequence for the run of the job. Some parameters of the JOB statement (such as

CPU time limit) can be also given in an EXEC statement, in which case it applies only to a job step, rather than to the entire job.

3. A DATA DEFINITION (DD) statement specifies a data object used by a job-step program. Since a step's program often references several such objects, there are usually several DD statements following each EXEC statement. A primary function of a DD statement is to *bind* two types of names to each other. The first name on a DD card is called a DD name used in the program. This is also called a *file* name. The second type of name on a DD card is known to the operating system and is termed a *data-set* name. The two types of names provide a subtle but very important convenience to programmers. They can change the data referenced by a program by changing only the data-set name on a DD card, thus changing the binding of the program's file name to a new data-set. A DD statement, which is by far the most complex of the JCL statements, can specify many more things than the two names to be bound. These include names of disk or tape volumes, device characteristics, buffering techniques, etc., etc.

To understand something of how JCL works in a specific case, suppose we want to set up a JCL catalog procedure for a common kind of job: compile, link edit, and execute a PL/1 source program. Since three separate programs are to be run, this job will consist of three job steps that we can name in any way we choose. Our names for the steps will be

PL1L   Job step to compile the source program using the OS/360 PL/1(F) compiler. The result is an object module.

LKED   Job step to linkage-edit the object module produced by the compiler and certain PL/1 subroutines specified by the compiler. The result is a load module.

GO   Job step to execute the load module. Data input is to come from punched cards and output is to be sent to the printer.

To proceed further, we must realize that two of the job steps (PL1L and LKED) use already existing OS system programs that reference data-sets by file names known in those programs. We must next determine the names of these system programs and the particular file names they use. This information can be found in IBM Programmer's Guide Manuals.* Figure 8-1.1 lists these program and file names and some associated data-set names used in our job steps. To proceed further in the precise description of how to write a cataloged procedure for our job would involve far more detail than is justified in this book. However, we can appreciate and even understand the results. In Fig. 8-1.2(a) is shown an actual JCL cataloged procedure for our three-step job. The reader should be able to verify the various file-to-data-set bindings with the help of Fig. 8-1.2(b), which shows the composition of a complete job deck that starts with a JOB statement and is then followed by an EXEC statement specifying the name of our cataloged procedure. The remaining cards are other JCL statements, the source program, and the data cards for the program. Note that the two uses of the file name SYSIN apply to cards in the job itself. The DD statements required to bind file SYSIN

* The example shown is from Ref. IB11, p. 96.

Job step	File name	Program or data-set name	Purpose/Remarks
PL1L	---	IEMAA	Execute the PL/1(F) compiler program stored in the system library under name IEMAA
	SYSIN	*	Source program card input to compiler
	SYSPRINT		Printed listings and messages from compiler
	SYSLIN	&&LOADSET	Object module produced by compiler (&& means this data-set is temporary for this job)
	SYSUT1 SYSUT3		SYSUT1 and SYSUT3 are names of files used for intermediate storage by the compiler (IEMAA)
LKED	---	IEWL	Execute the linkage-editor program stored in the system library under name IEWL
	SYSLIN	&&LOADSET	Input to linkage editor (object module)
	SYSLIB	SYS1.PL1LIB	Library of subroutines specified by the compiler
	SYSPRINT		Printed output of the linkage editor
	SYSLMOD	&&GOSET(GO)	GO is a partition of the temporary data-set &&GOSET that receives the linkage-editor output (a load module)
	SYSUT1		Name of file used for intermediate storage by the linkage editor
GO	---	*.LKED.SYSLMOD	Execute the program stored in the data-set specified by the file name SYSLMOD in the job step named LKED of the current job (*)
	SYSIN	*	Data input is the deck that follows
	SYSPRINT		Result (output) of program is to file to be printed

Fig. 8-1.1 Conceptual layout of program, file, and data-set names for a 3-step OS/360 job.

to the data cards of the job deck are included in the job as shown. The file name SYSIN is qualified by the job-step name (like GO.SYSIN) to designate to which step the data applies.

Figure 8-1.3 shows the major classes of OS functions in a highly schematic manner. They include:

1. Job management
2. Task management
3. Data management

Also important in understanding OS (or any other system for that matter) are the provisions for system-operator communications, the system residence device, and the job control language just described with a brief example.

Job management controls the movement of jobs within OS from the time that they enter the system (usually from a card reader or tape device) until they complete (usually with printout). Some major functions of job management are:

1. Reading jobs into the system and placing them on the job input queue.
2. Scheduling jobs in the input queue by allocating data-sets, main-storage space, and I/O devices needed by each job during execution.

//PL1L	EXEC	PGM=IEMAA, PARM='LOAD,NODECK' REGION=52K
//SYSPRINT	DD	SYSOUT=A
//SYSLIN	DD	DSNAME=&&LOADSET, DISP=(MOD,PASS), UNIT=SYSSQ, SPACE=(80, (250,100))
//SYSUT3	DD	UNIT=SYSSQ, SPACE=(80, (250,250)), SEP=SYSPRINT
//SYSUT1	DD	UNIT=SYSDA, SPACE=(1024, (60,60), CONTIG), SEP=(SYSUT3,SYSPRINT, SYSLIN)
//LKED	EXEC	PGM=IEWL, PARM='XREF,LIST', COND=(9,LT,PL1L), REGION=96K
//SYSLIB	DD	DSNAME=SYS1.PL1LIB, DISP=SHR
//SYSLMOD	DD	DSNAME=&&GOSET(GO), DISP=(MOD,PASS), UNIT=SYSDA, SPACE=(1024,(50,20,1), RLSE)
//SYSUT1	DD	UNIT=SYSDA, SEP=(SYSLMOD,SYSLIB), SPACE=(1024,(200,20))
//SYSPRINT	DD	SYSOUT=A
//SYSLIN	DD	DSNAME=&&LOADSET, DISP=(OLD,DELETE)
//	DD	DDNAME=SYSIN
//GO	EXEC	PGM=*.LKED.SYSLMOD, COND=((9,LT,LKED), (9,LT,PL1L))
//SYSPRINT	DD	SYSOUT=A

(a) Cataloged procedure.

Fig. 8-1.2 A cataloged procedure and a job calling it.

```
//MYJOB  JOB '800,SMITH', REGION=100K,
//        CLASS=C, PRTY=2
//        EXEC  PL1LFCLG
//PL1L.SYSIN DD  *
           (Source program cards)
//GO. SYSIN DD*
           (Data cards)
//
```

(b) Job deck.

Notes: 1. PL1LFCLG is the name of a partitioned data-set holding the cataloged procedure of (a).

2. Note qualified file name for SYSIN that specifies job step to which it applies (like GO.SYSIN).

3. When an * is used as a data-set name, it means "the records that follow until a // delimiter."

4. COND = (9,LT, PL1L) means current step is bypassed if 9 is less then return code produced by step PL1L.

5. SEP = specifies data-sets to be accessed by separate data channels.

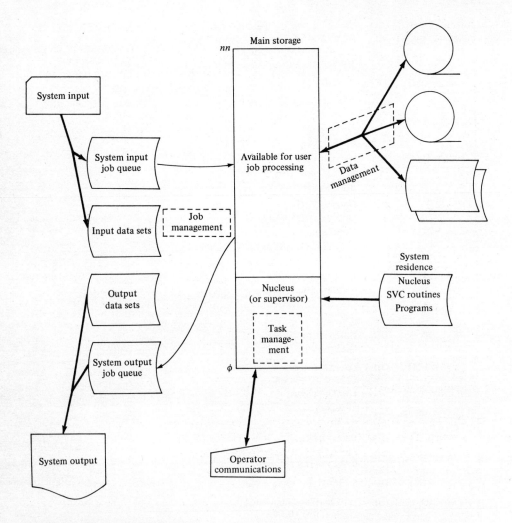

Fig. 8-1.3 Primary OS functions.

3. Storing the unit record (e.g., print output) for jobs on direct-access storage and later transferring this output to a unit-record device.

Task management is the system programming function that *dispatches* tasks. Dispatching in OS/360 means determining which task among those in main storage should next receive CPU service. The term *task* is closely related to "job step" in OS terminology as follows: a job (which always starts with a JOB JCL statement) may be composed of several job steps (each beginning with an EXEC JCL statement). When a job step is scheduled for execution and hence brought into main storage, OS creates a small record called a *task control block* (TCB) that will be used by task management to record status and dispatch the job step's program. At the point the TCB is created, the job step becomes a task. The program(s) loaded for the job step are associated with the one user task. In a special option of MFT and in MVT, user tasks may create subtasks that have their own TCB's for dispatching. Our description of OS will consider only one user task per job step. As indicated in Fig. 8-1.3, the task-management functions are contained in the OS nucleus. Task management controls dispatching for both user tasks and system tasks.

The OS nucleus shown in Fig. 8-1.3 is the heart of the operating system. It controls essential system functions and remains permanently resident in main storage during OS operation. The nucleus contains certain *system tasks* that, through their interaction with user jobs and with each other, control system operation. Another component of the nucleus is the task-management function discussed above. The input-output supervisor (IOS) that controls all I/O and channel activity is also included in the nucleus.

System programs less vital than the nucleus may or may not be made resident in main storage at the discretion of the installation. Supervisor-call (SVC) programs are one example. These are invoked when a user program requests a service from the nucleus, for example, START-I/O. If the system program that responds to an SVC is resident in main storage, control can be passed to it immediately. However, if it is not resident, the nucleus must move the SVC response program from disk into a *transient area* (an area within the nucleus) before the user request can be serviced. Because access to disk is slow (from a purely speed viewpoint), it is advantageous to make frequently referenced SVC's resident in the nucleus. However, the cost is increased nucleus size with less main storage remaining for user programs. Other examples of system programs for which main-storage residence is an option will be discussed later. Deciding on which system programs and tables are to be made permanently resident in main storage is a very important user-installation responsibility in OS/360 that can have a very great impact on system performance, as will be discussed more fully later.

Data management is the third major system function performed by OS. Data management controls all I/O operations and provides services that permit an installation to create, maintain, and access both system and user data-sets. System data-sets are libraries that contain system programs, such as SVC's and user programs that are stored in either executable (load-module) format or in source-program format. These libraries are typically held on direct-access storage devices (like disks). User data-sets are generally used to store records that are particular to one or more jobs, such as payroll master file. Such data-sets are also stored on direct-access or tape devices. Since the major service provided by data management is not essential in describing how OS implements multiprogramming, this topic is not discussed further in this chapter.

System residence in OS is an area (or areas) on direct-access storage containing copies of all system programs, as well as user programs, that have been placed in a system library. In Fig. 8-1.3 we show the nucleus and SVC routines as examples of system programs that are stored on the system residence device. The system residence area(s) serves three major functions:

1. System operation is started when the IPL program loads a copy of the nucleus from system residence into main storage; control is then transferred to the nucleus.

2. Transient system programs (like many SVC's) need not be resident in main storage all the time, since copies can be moved as needed from system residence to main storage under control of the nucleus.

3. User programs may be stored in a library on the system residence pack and may be moved to main storage at execution time, thus eliminating the need to load frequently used programs from punched card decks.

A person called an *operator* is required to run OS. His duties include:

1. Starting the system through the IPL procedure.

2. Feeding input jobs in the form of punched card decks or tapes and routing final output (such as printed listings) to user stations.

3. Starting and stopping certain system programs such as the reader-interpreter (which reads jobs into the system from a card reader or tape drive) and the initiator-terminator (which selects jobs for processing by moving their programs to main storage).

4. Mounting tape reels or disk packs as they are required during job processing (as directed by console messages).

5. Attempting recovery procedures in case of system failure.

To operate OS then requires a certain amount of communication between the operator and OS itself, as indicated in Fig. 8-1.3. This *operator-system communication* is controlled by an OS program called the *master scheduler*. The master scheduler is always resident in the main-storage nucleus during OS operation. It routes all *system messages* to the operator; they are usually printed on a typewriter or CRT display called the system console. The master scheduler also includes a program that interprets and executes all *commands* submitted by the operator through the system console.

The scheduling functions experienced by a single job may be concisely summarized with the aid of Fig. 8-1.4, which shows the states of a job as it is processed through the system. Each state may also be identified with a storage of some type that currently holds the job or task. The lines between states denote state transitions that are labelled with the names of the system programs that cause the transitions.

The purpose of this brief overview has been to sketch some of the major functions of OS/360. Both MFT and MVT versions have these same major functions. The differences between MFT and MVT are only understood with a more detailed description of how they manage multiprogramming.

8-2 OS/MFT [Ref. IB4]

Figure 8-2.1 shows how main storage is structured in an MFT system. The nucleus resides at the low end of main storage. The remainder of main storage is divided into partitions of which there are two types: *system partitions* and *problem-program partitions* (i.e., user partitions). System partitions are used for certain system programs such as a reader that SPOOLs card input to disk and a writer that SPOOLs output to a printer, tape, or card punch. An installation may specify up to 52 partitions (including

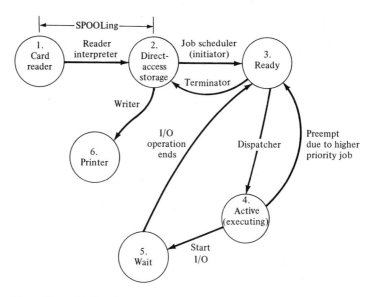

(Note: User task is in main storage for states 3, 4 and 5)

Fig. 8-1.4 State diagram for each OS job showing system programs responsible for state transitions.

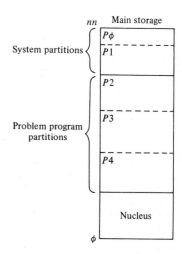

Fig. 8-2.1 MFT main-storage structure.

system and problem-program partitions), although from one to five system partitions is probably typical of most MFT installations.

Job scheduling consists of assigning jobs to problem-program partitions (PP). Once a job is assigned to a PP partition, all of its job steps will execute in that partition. Since no more than 15 PP partitions may be specified in an MFT system, 15 is the maximum number of user jobs that can be multiprogrammed. This limit is due to MFT's use of the System/360 and System/370 storage protect scheme that was described in Chap. 7. Its 4-bit key lock provides 16 distinct key values. The key of zero is used for all system programs, i.e., the nucleus and all programs that execute in system partitions. Each remaining key can be assigned to a PP partition. System programs then can reference main storage within the boundaries of their PP partition.

Every OS system starts its life by being "born" in a process called *system generation*. Here, a master copy of the operating system is fed options and then produces a version of the operating system that is appropriate to the resources and options of the particular installation.

An MFT installation specifies the number of partitions, both system and PP partitions, at system-generation time. The number of partitions cannot be increased without a new system generation (which is a long process). Another consideration on the number of partitions selected is that each partition requires some storage space in the nucleus for control blocks. The size of each partition is also defined, in multiples of 2k, during system generation. However, partition sizes may be *redefined* manually by the operator during operation. For example, two adjacent partitions can be merged to form a larger single partition.

Partitions are identified by the names $P0, P1, \ldots, Pn$. The integers in these names determine the task-dispatching priority of the jobs occupying the partitions (as will be discussed later). For the moment, we note that dispatching priority of the partitions is tied to the ordering of their labels from the top of main storage down, with lower partition numbers having higher dispatching priority.

We have said that *job scheduling* simply involves assigning user jobs to PP partitions. MFT job scheduling is a part of its job-management function, which was described earlier in a general way. Figure 8-2.2 gives a more detailed picture of MFT's job-management functions, identifying the system programs used. It is an expanded version of Fig. 8-1.3. The circled numbers indicate the flow of user jobs through these functions. User jobs enter MFT on punched cards or magnetic tape. Each job includes JCL statements that identify the job, its job steps, and required data-sets and devices. The stream of input jobs is called *system input*. MFT SPOOLs system input. The *reader-interpreter* system program (called the Reader) moves the job stream into the system while performing the following functions:

1. It inserts any JCL cataloged procedures called by the job's JCL into the job stream.
2. It *interprets* the JCL statements creating the control blocks required by MFT to schedule a job. If there are any JCL errors in a job, the job is cancelled (with appropriate error messages).
3. It places jobs and their related control blocks on the *system (input) job queue* stored on direct-access storage. Later, the jobs will be scheduled from there.

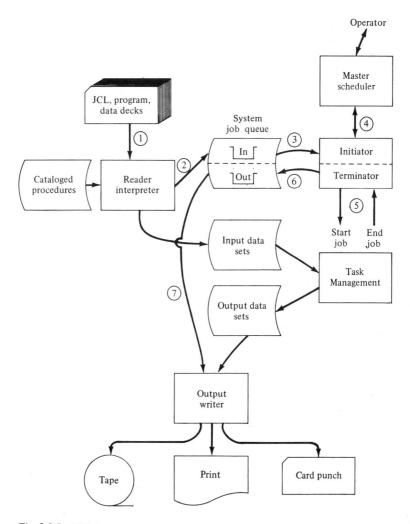

Fig. 8-2.2 OS job management.

4. It labels and stores the jobs' input data on direct-access storage. During job execution, its input is read from direct-access storage.

Since MFT's system input is SPOOLed, the reader program is multiprogrammed with user jobs. In other words, while the reader is preparing jobs, other jobs may be in main storage and in various states of CPU execution and I/O activity.

Once jobs are stored in the system job queue, they can be scheduled for execution. As shown in Fig. 8-2.2, job scheduling is performed by an *initiator-terminator* system program. To activate a PP partition, the operator (through the master scheduler program) issues a command to start an initiator in the partition. The initiator can then begin to schedule jobs, usually for that partition only. Thus, the operator controls the number of active partitions in the system. Each PP partition with an initiator started may be thought of as a logical machine with its own job scheduler.

During operation, job scheduling begins when a job ends in a PP partition. Then a copy of the initiator program is loaded, overlaying the program of the job that just completed. The terminator function of the initiator places the completed job on the *system (output) job queue*. From there, its *system output* will be scheduled to a printer card or tape device. The terminator also releases any I/O device(s) assigned to the completed job, returning them to the control of MFT. The initiator may then schedule a new job (or job step) into the PP partition. Using the MFT job scheduling algorithm (which will be explained in detail later), the initiator selects the "best" candidate from the system-input job queue. The initiator must then allocate the data-sets and I/O devices requested (in the job's JCL statements). Often, a user simply requests the type of device, say a disk or tape, without identifying any specific device. (Messages to the operator to mount specified "volumes," i.e., tape reels or disk packs, are issued by OS from JCL information.) Thus, a job is bound very late to specific I/O devices, thereby increasing scheduling adaptability to actually available resources. After all I/O devices are allocated, the initiator may start the job's first job step by passing control to the relocating loader program in MFT's nucleus. MFT, like other OS/360 versions uses load-time (static) relocation. Its loader will process the addresses of the job step's load module, relocating them to the origin of the PP partition. The program is then moved to the partition. Then control is passed to it and the user task may begin to execute. From this point on, its access to the CPU is under the control of MFT's task-management function, as indicated in Fig. 8-2.2. At job-end time, as described earlier, the initiator-terminator is loaded into the PP partition, the terminator terminates the job, and the initiator schedules another job from the input job queue. Because MFT has a relocating loader, programs are not bound to their main-storage locations until program load time and jobs can be scheduled in different partitions for different runs (without changing their programs or their JCL). However, because there is no dynamic relocation, once a program begins execution, it must complete in the same area of main storage. And in MFT, once a job is scheduled for a PP partition, all of its job steps must execute in that partition.

With MFT's job management now in perspective, we next examine how MFT schedules jobs from the system job queue. What scheduling rule does an MFT initiator use to select the next job from the queue? Figure 8-2.3 gives a specific example to help see how this is done. $P\emptyset$ and $P1$ are system partitions that hold a writer and a reader-interpreter. There are also three PP partitions, $P2$ through $P4$. Assume that $P2$ and $P4$ have been scheduled with say JOB 7 and JOB 8 and that $P3$ is now ready for another job. A copy of the initiator is then currently residing in $P3$. Job scheduling is done with a *job-classification* scheduling scheme. Job classes, represented by letters A thru O, are assigned to *both* PP partitions (at SYSGEN time or by the operator) and to user jobs (by users). The initiator will schedule the "best" candidate of all jobs in the job queue that have been assigned a class value that has also been assigned to the partition. We now examine some details of this scheduling process.

The job's class is punched by the user on the JOB JCL card with the CLASS = parameter, as shown in the picture of a JOB card in Fig. 8-2.3. The assignments of job

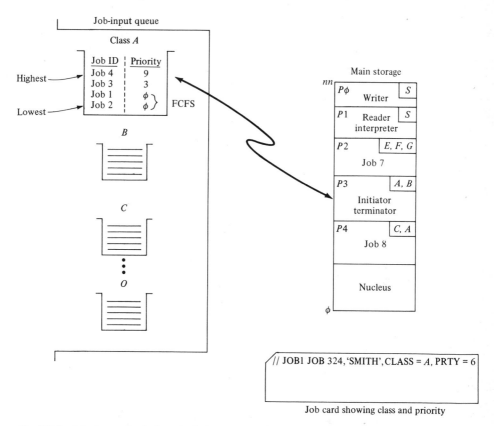

Fig. 8-2.3   Job class and priority scheduling.

classes to jobs can be considered to divide the input queue into several subqueues, one for each class, as indicated. Since several jobs may have the same class, a tie-breaking scheme is needed. The first tie-breaking provision permits users also to supply, on the JOB card, a *priority* value (PRTY=) ranging from 0 (lowest priority) through 13. If, using the PRTY values, the initiator still does not have a unique job, the remaining ties are broken by the order in which the jobs entered each queue (i.e., FCFS within priority and class).

From *one to three* of the 15 possible *A-0* job classes may be assigned to *each* PP partition by the operator. Jobs for a partition may be scheduled only from queues whose class(es) corresponds to the class(es) assigned to the partition. The first job class assigned to a partition is given highest priority for job scheduling in that partition; if there is a second, it would be second highest, a third would be lowest. Figure 8-2.3 shows a particular scheduling problem with job-class queues and classes assigned to partitions. Partition classes are indicated in the upper right-hand corner of each partition; class priority is indicated from left to right. Notice that we have assigned an *S class* to the system partitions. From this example, several characteristics may be observed about class scheduling in MFT. The initiator in $P3$ may schedule jobs from either job-class queue A or job-class queue B. All jobs in queue A will be scheduled first, since A is the first entry in $P3$'s assigned class list and therefore has a higher priority for $P3$ than queue B. Assuming that queue A has several jobs, the initiator then will schedule the "best" candidate from queue A. Jobs in queues E, F, and G may only be scheduled in $P2$. Notice also in Fig. 8-2.3 that the same job class may be assigned to different partitions. For example, $P3$ and $P4$ may both schedule class-A jobs, although in $P3$, class-A jobs have a higher scheduling priority. MFT will maintain 15 job-class queues, even though only 6 job classes have been assigned to the PP partitions, as in our example. If, for example, a job that is assigned class G enters the system, it will be placed in the class-G job queue. This job cannot be scheduled until the operator assigns class G to one of the PP partitions. Just as an operator can redefine partition size during system operation, he can also redefine partition class assignments.

The user assigns classes to jobs. The system operator or installation assigns classes to partitions. Therefore, the operational meaning that is associated with a class is determined at least in part by each user. Installations advise users how to assign class labels to jobs. For example, the installation may designate that a specific class, or set of classes, be assigned to I/O-oriented jobs. Likewise, a set of classes could be reserved for CPU-oriented jobs. Job class could also be related to job size. For example, all jobs with a size requirement from 80k to 100k can be assigned to a 100k PP partition using a specific class or set of classes.

Since MFT partition sizes are *statically* allocated, that is, the operator defines partition sizes when the partitions involved are idle, the MFT user must be careful (when assigning class values to jobs) to ensure that the class can be handled by a partition large enough to run the job. Once a job is assigned to a partition, all of its job steps must execute in that partition. Job size (main-storage requirement) then can be considered as the size of a job's largest job step. Thus, if a job has three steps, 70k, 90k, and 80k in size, it must be scheduled in a 90k partition. If the job is scheduled in say a 200k partition, 130k, 110k, and 120k, respectively, are wasted during the execution of the job's three job steps. Even a 90k partition results in 20k of idle space during the first step and 10k during the third step. This wasted main storage is an example of internal *fragmentation*, a problem that was described earlier for static-relocation systems in general. The degree of fragmentation in MFT depends on how cleverly the partitions are formed by the installation operator and how well a user assigns a job size to a partition. This "fitting" problem must be balanced with the objective of assigning I/O-bound jobs to high-priority partitions and CPU-bound jobs to lower-priority partitions, thus achieving a good overall use of system resources. This latter consideration will be discussed further a bit later. Class scheduling has the advantage of permitting the MFT user and installation to assign meaning to job classes, but the disadvantage of making these people, not the system, responsible for good utilization of all system resources.

The class and priority assigned to a job in MFT in no way directly affects the *dispatching priority* that the job receives. Class and priority are used as job scheduling parameters only. However, since job class determines the partition (or partitions) in which a job may be scheduled, it indirectly affects dispatching priority. This is because as mentioned earlier, the partition number-label determines dispatching priority, as will be shown later in the description of MFT task management.

To summarize the MFT job-management functions, we will follow the flow of a specific job through the system. As an example, we use a PL/I compilation (a one-step job). Figure 8-2.4 shows the system input for the job. The job card identifies the job, its scheduling class (*F*), and scheduling priority (12). The execute (EXEC) card identifies the job step (in this case indirectly by naming a JCL-cataloged procedure called PLIFC). In effect, this specifies that a copy of a PL/I compiler is to be loaded from a system library into the assigned PP partition at job scheduling time. The *data definition card(s)* (DD) specifies the input and output data-sets required by the job step, in this case the PF/I F compiler. These data-sets are mostly specified by DD statements in the procedure named PLIFC (not shown). The DD * statement specifies by the * that the PL/I source program cards that follow is the data-set for the job step (the PL/IF compiler). The source program is followed by a // delimiter card to specify the end of system input for this job.

Figure 8-2.5 schematically depicts the flow of this PL/I job through MFT. We assume a resident reader that places the job in the class-*F* queue and SPOOLs the source-program input data to direct-access storage. *P4* is the only class-*F* PP partition; therefore, our PL/I job must be scheduled in *P4*. After this job is initiated, it will read the source program input from direct-access storage during execution. Also during execution, all printed output will be placed on an output data-set in direct-access storage. When the job completes execution, the initiator-terminator is called and it places results on the system-output job queue. Using an FCFS scheduling rule, the system writer program SPOOLs the PL/I job's output by moving it from direct-access storage to the system printer via a SPOOL buffer area in main storage. Other observations can be made from the main storage map in Fig. 8-2.5. Nucleus size is shown as 70k bytes. Minimum nucleus size for MFT is about 38k, although selection of options such as multiple partitions and resident SVC's expand the nucleus size (resulting in certain benefits). Obtaining a good balance between MFT functions, their resulting benefits, and their required resources is the primary objective when "tuning" an MFT system. Also notice in Fig. 8-2.5 that the reader and writer functions are main-storage resident. In an MFT system with a small main storage, the operator may have to "schedule" main storage between these SPOOLing functions and a user

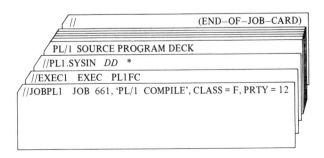

Fig. 8-2.4   Sample job stream.

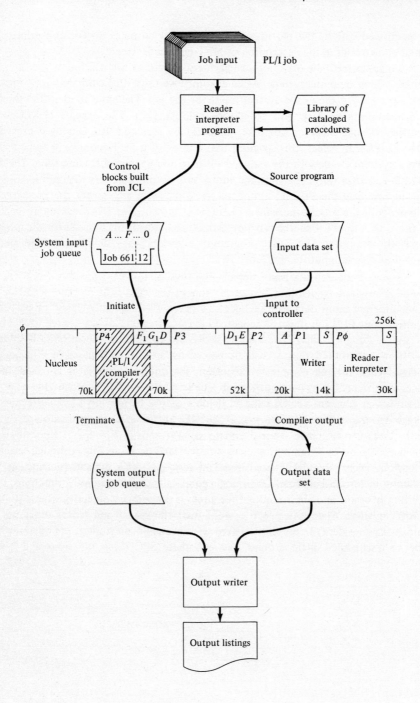

Fig. 8-2.5   Flow of sample job in MFT.

partition. Partition $P1$ in Fig. 8-2.5 is only 20k in size. $P1$ is a "dependent" partition because minimum initiator size in MFT is about 30k. $P1$ must then be scheduled by an initiator in another partition. This may result in scheduling delays for $P1$, but it will also avoid internal fragmentation of main storage if an installation has many small jobs (20k or less).

Job scheduling in MFT determines what jobs (user tasks) are moved into PP partitions and allocated I/O resources. The I/O supervisor in the MFT nucleus (a part of MFT's data-management function) schedules I/O operations, and thus the system's channels, on a *first-come-first-served* (FCFS) basis. The *task dispatcher* (a part of MFT's task-management function) schedules the CPU among the active tasks that are resident in MFT's nucleus and its main-storage partitions. In the remaining discussion of MFT, we will describe this *task dispatching* (also called, simply, dispatching).

MFT uses a *highest-static-priority-first-served* (HSFS) dispatching technique (with preemption) similar to the technique described in Chap. 7. *System tasks* reside in MFT's nucleus and system partitions. System tasks within the nucleus, such as the master scheduler, are assigned the highest of the priorities during system generation. *User tasks* execute from PP partitions. It is recalled that MFT's design fixes the dispatching priorities to the labelling of partitions, $P\emptyset$ being highest, $P1$ next highest, and so forth. An MFT user cannot change these partition priorities. As was stated earlier, a user may only indirectly influence actual dispatching priority. This is because his primary constraint is that he must assign a job class to the job that has been assigned to a partition large enough to run the job. In the event that only one partition has been assigned this class, his job must execute in that partition, and the job's dispatching priority is then completely determined by the partition number. If, however, the job is assigned a class that can be serviced by more than one partition, then the job will encounter a different dispatching priority, depending on the partition in which it runs.

Figure 8-2.6 schematically represents the *dispatching queue* in MFT's nucleus that is used by the task dispatcher. The priority sequence is indicated by the levels in the queue. Queue entries are called *task control blocks*. MFT will first dispatch any ready system tasks. If no system tasks need the CPU to execute, the task in $P\emptyset$, whether a system or user task, is dispatched, assuming that it is ready to execute. $P\emptyset$'s task will continue to execute until one of two events occur:

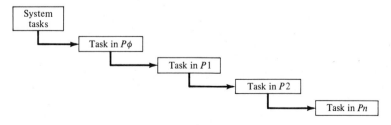

$n \to$ the lowest priority (task) partition generated in MFT

Fig. 8-2.6   MFT dispatching queue.

1. It goes into the wait state, for example, for an I/O operation.
2. A task with a higher priority, i.e., in a lower-numbered partition requires the CPU, say by completing an I/O operation (signalled by an interrupt).

The maximum number of entries in the dispatching queue is determined by the number of tasks in the nucleus and the number of partitions in the system.

Job scheduling in MFT can result in "poor" or "good" use of the system's CPU and I/O resources because of the HSFS dispatching rule. Poor dispatching results when a CPU-bound job has been scheduled into the highest priority PP partition. CPU-bound jobs rarely go into the wait state, and I/O-bound jobs in lower priority partitions will have little opportunity to execute. With a similar job mix, "good" dispatching can be achieved if I/O-bound jobs are scheduled in higher-priority partitions. They will frequently go into the wait state (while processing I/O) and allow time for lower-priority CPU-bound jobs to execute. More system activity, and thus a higher thruput, will result than with the previous "poor" job-scheduling arrangement.

Through job scheduling, the MFT user tries to accomplish two major objectives in a batch-oriented multiprogramming environment: (1) good CPU dispatching, and thus improved system thruput, and (2) good use of the main-storage resource with little main-storage fragmentation.

With statically allocated partition sizes and only indirect control of job-dispatching priorities in MFT, it is difficult to accomplish both objectives. Most of the burden is placed on the user and installation with little help from MFT toward accomplishing these objectives. The OS/MVT system makes job scheduling easier through its main-storage allocation technique and its dispatching-priority assignment.

8-3 OS/MVT   [Refs. IB5,IB6]

OS/MVT is similar in many ways to the MFT version of OS, and much of the preceding MFT description applies to MVT as well. In this section we will describe the two major functional differences of OS/MVT relative to MFT: (1) its main storage management technique, and (2) its task management function.

Each job step enters MVT with a user-assigned JCL parameter (REGION = nnn) indicating its main storage requirement (nnn kbytes). When a job step is scheduled, it is assigned the amount of main storage requested. This will tend to be more efficient than MFT, which must assign an entire job to a partition of prespecified size. Thus we see the first great improvement in flexibility; MVT, unlike MFT, can respond to different main-storage requirements for the job steps of a single job.

Figure 8-3.1 shows a simple main-storage layout of OS/MVT. The MVT *nucleus* is loaded at the low end of main storage. In function, the nucleus is similar to MFT's; it contains task management and the I/O supervisor. At the high end of main storage is the MVT *link pack area* (LPA). The basic routines in LPA are used primarily for main-storage management and job scheduling in conjunction with the MVT initiator-terminator (initiator) program. These routines are always resident in main storage during MVT operation. With only these routines, LPA size is about 6k bytes. However, an MVT installation may (and usually does) load reentrant system, user routines, and the directories of system libraries into LPA. Their presence can greatly improve system

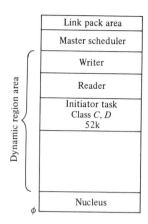

Fig. 8-3.1   MVT after an initiator is started.

performance, since if not there, disk accesses are necessary to fetch them. For example, frequently used access methods may be made resident in the LPA. A user job that requires a resident access method can then be simply "linked" to the copy in LPA. Multiple user jobs may then concurrently share the same copy of the access method, thus saving main storage space. Frequently referenced SVC's can also be made resident in LPA. Also, the directory to the SVC library on direct-access storage (and other system libraries) can be placed in LPA, which significantly reduces the amount of disk access time. The list of items to be made resident in LPA is specified by the MVT operator at IPL time. It may only be changed with a new IPL.

The MVT master scheduler is similar in function to MFT's. It is the main communication link between the operator and the MVT system. If the operator starts an initiator, his command to do so would be read, interpreted, and executed by the *communications task* of the master scheduler. Likewise, an operator can start readers and writers through the master scheduler.

The main storage used by the nucleus, the link pack area, and the master scheduler is called the *fixed area* because its contents are main-storage resident throughout operation. The remainder of main storage is called the *dynamic region area*, as shown in Fig. 8-3.1. In MVT, a *region* is a contiguous block of main storage that is assigned from the dynamic region area to a system task or a user job step in multiples of 2k. Unlike MFT's partitions, region size is dynamically allocated based on the main storage requirements of a system task or a user job step. Regions are assigned from within the dynamic region area from the top down.

System tasks that reside in the dynamic region area are primarily reader(s), writer(s), and initiator(s). Each system task resides in its own region. The MVT reader-interpreter and writer perform SPOOL functions identical to those in MFT. Also, as in MFT, multiple readers and writers may be resident in MVT. The only difference in the two systems is this: in MFT, writers (and sometimes readers) reside in system partitions; in MVT, Readers and Writers reside in regions that are dynamically allocated when the operator starts these system tasks.

MVT's initiator task schedules user jobs into main storage using the same job-classification scheme described for MFT. One of 15 possible job classes is assigned by the user (programmer) to each job. When a job enters the system, it is placed in a queue according to its job class.

The job class letters A through O themselves have no inherent ordering implications. An initiator schedules a job in the same way as in MFT. It selects the "best" candidate from its highest-priority class queue that has waiting jobs. The "best" candidate is determined by using the user-assigned job priority (and a FCFS tie breaker) from the PRTY parameter punched in the JCL EXEC or JOB card. As in MFT, a job's scheduling priority may be assigned from $\emptyset$ to 13, with 13 the highest scheduling priority within job class. Since PRTY may be specified separately on each EXEC card, different job steps of the same job may be assigned different priority.

The job selection process in MFT and MVT is the same, but this is where the similarity ends. The MVT initiator resides in a region. When it schedules a job step, the initiator allocates a region for the job step. Main storage is allocated dynamically to *job steps* (and not necessarily to entire jobs) from the dynamic region area. To illustrate these differences, we now trace the main-storage (region) allocation process, first using as an example an MVT configuration with one active initiator, and later showing multiple initiators.

Figure 8-3.1 shows main storage after the operator has started a reader task, a writer task, and an initiator. The reader and writer have been allocated regions in the dynamic region area as shown. The initiator was started by an operator command, START INIT, that specified job classes C and D (in that order) and a region size of 52k bytes. An initiator capable of scheduling jobs of class C or D is then loaded into a 52k byte region as shown. It will start to schedule a job from the class C queue, using the job-priority parameter to break ties. After all the class C jobs have been completed, the initiator will start to schedule class D jobs. Assume that the first job selected is named JOB2. The first resources allocated for it are its data-sets, and then a region of size equal or larger than the job-specified REGION parameter (Fig. 8-3.2) is allocated. In this example, JOB2 requires a 90k region to process all of its job steps (assuming regions for job steps are not individually specified in EXEC JCL statements).

To allocate the region, the initiator first releases its own region. An initiator routine that is in the link pack area requests a 90k region from the nucleus. The nucleus controls main-storage allocation, and it has a record of current main storage assignments in the dynamic region area. The first 90k of available contiguous main storage will be assigned to a region for JOB2 in our example. This is shown in Part (*a*) of Fig. 8-3.3. If 90k of contiguous main storage is not available, the initiator goes into the

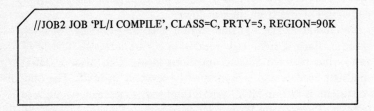

//JOB2 JOB 'PL/I COMPILE', CLASS=C, PRTY=5, REGION=90K

Fig. 8-3.2   Region parameter in MVT job statement.

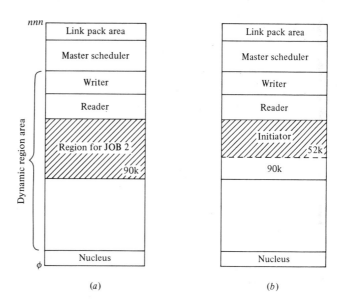

Fig. 8-3.3 Region allocation in MVT.

wait state. Job initiation is postponed until 90k of contiguous main storage becomes available.

After the region is allocated for JOB2, the initiator is loaded into it, as shown in Part (*b*) of Fig. 8-3.3. The initiator will next allocate the I/O devices for the first job step in JOB2. When all devices are allocated, an initiator routine in the LPA will attach the first job step in JOB2 as a user task in the allocated region. The program(s) required by this user task is loaded, and the user task may begin execution. When the first job step completes, its 90k region is released, a new region (52k) is allocated for the initiator, the initiator is loaded, and it begins the termination process for the first job step. All I/O devices for the first step are released and the initiator will schedule the next job step in JOB2, first allocating a new 90k region, then I/O devices, and so forth.

Some unnecessary activity may seem to be involved in region allocation when showing an example with only one active initiator. In a moment, an example with multiple active initiators will demonstrate the region-allocation technique in MVT. First, however, consider some additional characteristics of MVT's main-storage management methods.

In the previous example, a user programmer specified region size in the JCL job statement. In the case of a job with three job steps, requiring 60k, 90k, and 70k, respectively, a single region size would have to be at least 90k. This would result in fragments (i.e., unused main storage within a region) of 30k and 20k while STEP 1 and STEP 3 execute. To avoid this wasted storage, MVT allows users to specify region size for *each job step* in the JCL EXEC statement. Fragmentation within regions can then be avoided to the extent that a user knows the size requirements of his job steps.

Minimum region size in MVT is determined by the size of the initiator. Standard is 52k, as shown in our earlier example. Therefore, if a job requests (say) a 40k region, the nucleus will allocate a 52k region to load the initiator for job-step scheduling, resulting in a 12k waste during job-step execution. Many of the initiator routines, especially the termination routines, are *reentrant*. These routines, therefore, can be shared by multiple initiators if placed in the link pack area. If this technique is used, minimum region size can be reduced to as small as 12k. An installation with numerous jobs smaller than 52k can benefit in main-storage utilization by placing reentrant-initiator routines in LPA.

An initiator may only schedule jobs for the class(es) that it is assigned. In the earlier example, the initiator was assigned classes C and D. If no jobs are in the class C and class D input queues, this initiator has no work and will go into the wait state. However, it will not remain in its region wasting main storage. When an initiator goes into a wait state because it has no jobs to schedule, it releases its region. All initiators are linked to a reentrant routine in LPA that will reactivate an initiator when a new job enters one of its class queues.

Multiprogramming is achieved in MVT when multiple initiators are started, each scheduling jobs for the job class(es) assigned to it. To illustrate MVT's dynamic allocation of main storage, we take a simplified example:

1. Three initiators are active.
2. Each initiator is scheduling jobs for a single different job class: the first initiator for class A, the second for class D, and the third for class G.
3. Region size for each job is assigned on a job-step basis.
4. The dynamic region area in main storage has 400k available for job scheduling.
5. Initiator size, and therefore minimum region size, is 52k.
6. The system currently has three job steps executing, as shown in Part (*a*) of Fig. 8-3.4.

The three regions shown in Part (*a*) of Fig. 8-3.4 show job name, step name, and (in parenthesis) job class. The shaded areas represent unused main storage. Parts (*b*), (*c*), and (*d*) show three changes that will occur in main storage when new job steps are scheduled for the three jobs.

Part (*b*) assumes that JOB 4, STEP 2 has completed and that JOB 4, STEP 3, which needs 120k, was scheduled by the class-*A* initiator. When STEP 2 completes, MVT releases its 70k region and allocates a 52k region (at the top of the dynamic region area) for the class-*A* initiator. The initiator-terminator routines release any I/O devices used by STEP 2. The initiator will then schedule the next job step (STEP 3) of JOB 4. If JOB 4 had no more steps, the initiator selects the next "best" job in the class-*A* queue. When STEP 3 is scheduled, the class-*A* initiator first checks the step region size (REGION = *nnn*). In the example in Part (*b*), STEP 3 needs 120k. The initiator releases its region and allocates the 120k region shown in Part (*b*) (MVT searches from the top down, but in this case the only contiguous area large enough is at the bottom of the dynamic region area).

Part (*c*) assumes that JOB 9, STEP 1 has terminated and that JOB 9, STEP 2 was scheduled by the class-*D* initiator. Its 80k region is allocated at the top of the

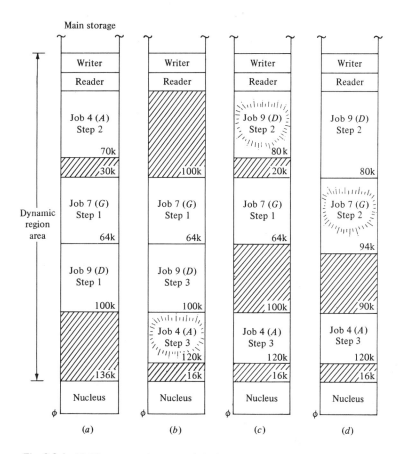

Main storage

Fig. 8-3.4   Multiprogramming example in MVT.

dynamic region area where a large block of unused main storage existed. Part (d) shows another transition in the system when a new step in JOB 7 is scheduled.

In all these examples, there are fragments in main storage, but the fragments keep changing as MVT allocates new regions. There are never more than three regions allocated because only three initiators are active. The size of the fragments indicates that another initiator can probably be started to increase the level of multi-programming. Up to 15 initiators may be started in MVT, each being assigned a separate storage protect key.

MVT has an option that makes its main-storage management technique even more dynamic. The option is called *rollout-rollin*. With rollout-rollin, a region can dynamically increase in size during job-step execution. An MVT installation must specify what job steps can rollout other job steps and which job steps may be rolled-out. A "privileged" job step can increase its region size, "adding on" to itself during execution, by requesting more main storage from the dynamic region area. If free space is available that satisfies the job step's request and that is contiguous with the job step's region, it will be attached to the region until released by the job step. If a region adjoins the "privileged" job step, and it can be rolled-out, the region's job step will be interrupted and stored on direct-access storage, and the "privileged" region may expand in size. When the rolled-out job step's region again becomes available, the job step will be rolled-in to resume execution. The job step must return to the same area of main storage because MVT is a static relocation system. Rollout-rollin is a nice feature for job steps that have temporary needs for increased main storage, like teleprocessing jobs at peak load time.

MVT's job-management techniques determine what job steps (user tasks) are resident in main storage. Task management (dispatching) determines which system or user task (of all those resident in main storage) gains control of the CPU. CPU dispatching in MVT is controlled by the task dispatcher in the system's nucleus. Like MFT, the standard dispatching rule is HSFS. However, unlike MFT partitions, MVT regions have no inherent (by system design) dispatching priority. In MVT, the user (usually with advice from the installation) specifies the dispatching priority for each job step that enters the system.

Dispatching priority is assigned with a JCL parameter (PRTY=). When all job steps in a job are to have the same dispatching priority, the *PRTY parameter* in the JOB statement may be used. However, the PRTY parameter can be specified separately for each job step on the EXEC cards. Note the dual use of the PRTY value: (1) for breaking ties on jobs of the same class for job scheduling, and (2) as the priority for CPU dispatching.

There is a distinct advantage in allowing the user to specify dispatching priority to a job when compared to MFT's technique. A user may explicitly assign high dispatching priorities to I/O-bound jobs and lower priorities to CPU-bound jobs to achieve high usage of all system resources. This presumes, of course, that a user knows his job characteristics. If, however, the PRTY parameter were only permitted in the JOB statement, this could result in two problems:

1. Since the PRTY parameter is used for both job scheduling priority and dispatching priority, an installation may have a job that requires high job-scheduling priority and low dispatching priority, for example, a high-priority (to be scheduled) CPU-bound job.
2. An installation usually has jobs with some job steps that require a high dispatching priority and others that should be assigned a lower priority.

For these reasons, MVT allows dispatching priority on a job-step basis with the DPRTY parameter in the JCL EXEC statement. When multiple job steps are concurrently executing with the same dispatching priority, a FCFS rule is used as a tie breaker.

Because an MVT user assigns dispatching priorities to jobs (or job steps), and because the MVT user is not concerned about "fitting" jobs to partition sizes, MVT is easier to operate than MFT. With MVT's dynamic control of main storage, there is less need for the MVT operator to redefine main-storage allocation than in MFT. The problem of fitting a job to a partition with the appropriate dispatching priority, as in MFT, is eliminated in MVT, since the MVT user assigns dispatching priority.

In addition to the HSFS dispatching rule, which is incorporated into MVT's design, an MVT installation may also use the *time-slice option.* All executing user tasks with a selected dispatching priority (that has been specified by the installation) are handled according to a round-robin scheduling rule (see Chap. 4). All user tasks above and below the time-sliced priority level would be scheduled using HSFS. When CPU time is available for time-sliced tasks, each ready task will be given a fixed time quantum of CPU time in a round-robin manner until interrupted by a higher-priority task, or until all time-sliced tasks go into the wait state. In the latter case, the dispatcher (using the HSFS rule) would select a lower-priority task. The time-slice option is also available in OS/MFT. As discussed in Chap. 4, round-robin scheduling using time slicing can significantly improve response time for short CPU-bound jobs.

Unlike the standard version of MFT, which allows only one user task per partition, user tasks in MVT may *attach* subtasks to their region. This function is performed by the "ATTACH macro." When a subtask is created, the user task must specify its main-storage requirement and its dispatching priority (which cannot be greater than that of the main user task). Main storage must be allocated for the subtask from within the region. A task control block (TCB) is created for the subtask for dispatching, and programs can then be loaded into the subtask's main-storage pool. Once active, a subtask functions independently within the region, although communication may be established and data passed between the user task and the subtask. A user task may attach multiple subtasks, providing it has the main storage required for each subtask within its region. Within a region then, a job step may create several concurrent functions. This is especially useful for a teleprocessing control program where concurrency can be achieved between line control and message processing. Multitasking may only be invoked in a job step if a programmer uses the assembler language or PL/I.

In the introduction to Chap. 7, we said that today's operating systems seem complex and sophisticated, yet some of their functions are still rather primitive. MFT and MVT both have job-scheduling and CPU-dispatching functions, but the user is, in effect, required to make many scheduling judgments requiring some understanding of job characteristics other than those of his own job. This is summarized in Fig. 8-3.5. These systems cannot dynamically adjust priorities during job-step execution as the characteristics of a job step change. For example, a job step in early processing may tend to be I/O bound, and then later become CPU bound. Requirements such as this have resulted in some "user-developed," (rather than OS system-developed) functions to enhance OS. One example of such a function is the *H*ouston *A*utomatic *SPOOL*ing system (*HASP*).

8-4 THE HASP SCHEME [Ref. RY]

HASP was developed within IBM, but by a "user group" in Houston, not through the normal system-development process. HASP enhances MFT and MVT with two major functions:

1. It SPOOLS system input and system output better than standard OS/360.

Type	Purpose	Priority rules
Job scheduling	Select a job from job queue and move it to main storage	*PCP:* No job classes or priority. Jobs serviced in same order as entered.
		MFT: 1. User assigns to each job (on job card) CLASS = {*A* thru 0} priority-order meaning of the letters is fixed by the order in which they are typed by the system operator in starting initiator PRTY = {0 thru 13} 13 = highest priority, 0 lowest 2. Each main store partition assigned up to three classes at SYSGEN time or by operator 3. Job initiator for a partition selects highest CLASS job. Ties within class broken by PRTY. Ties within PRTY broken by FCFS
		MVT: 1. Job CLASS, PRTY assigned by user as in MFT 2. Job initiator (started by operator) specifies classes it can service 3. Initiator breaks ties on class by PRTY. Ties on PRTY broken by FCFS
Dispatching	Select a job for CPU execute among jobs in main storage	*PCP:* No dispatching (at most one job in main store) *MFT:* Partition numbered $P0$ has highest priority, $P2$ next, etc. *MVT:* PRTY only is used for dispatching among regions

Notes: 1. Job scheduling is *not* preemptive (new job never replaces an uncompleted job).
2. Dispatching is event-driven (initiated when an interrupt occurs) except for time-slice option. Dispatching priority may be specified for each job step by DPRTY on EXEC card.

Fig. 8-3.5 Summary of OS/360 job scheduling and dispatching rules.

2. It has a dispatching option (also available in the OS/VS system) that monitors I/O and CPU activity and dynamically adjusts dispatching priorities currently observed, thus giving I/O-bound job steps higher priority than those that are currently CPU bound.

When used with MFT or MVT, HASP executes as a high-priority system task. The HASP SPOOLing function operates more efficiently than OS readers and writers for two basic reasons: (1) HASP readers do not interpret JCL when reading system input, and (2) HASP does its I/O and manages buffer space for input and output data-sets more efficiently than standard OS techniques.

HASP operates as an interface to OS, processing all system input and output. HASP schedules and then releases one job at a time to the OS job queue. At that time, the job's JCL is interpreted and scheduled for execution. Deferred JCL interpretation enhances HASP's system input speed. Its disadvantage is a delay in user notification of a JCL error.

HASP has a dispatching option, called *heuristic dispatching*, that attempts to improve utilization of hardware resources by giving high priority to I/O-bound tasks. When used, a HASP installation must specify which job steps will be controlled by the heuristic dispatcher. This is done by dispatching priority assignment in MVT or partition assignment in MFT. During execution, these job steps are placed in a *heuristic-dispatching group*. When the OS task dispatcher passes control to this group, HASP controls which job step will be dispatched.

Heuristic dispatching is based on the assumption that an operating system should be able to monitor certain characteristics of a job step during its execution. In particular, the heuristic dispatcher detects whether a job is currently I/O bound or CPU bound. When a ready task in the dispatching group is dispatched, it is given a time quantum of CPU time. If the task uses this entire time slice, it is assumed to be CPU bound and is placed in the CPU subgroup. If, however, a task goes into the wait state for an I/O operation before time-sliced end, it is placed in the I/O subgroup. The heuristic dispatcher schedules the I/O subgroup first and, if all I/O tasks are in the wait state, then dispatches the CPU subgroup. Any task in the I/O subgroup can preempt a CPU task. What results is an algorithm that starts as much I/O as possible and then dispatches any remaining CPU time among CPU-bound tasks in a round-robin fashion. As tasks change in characteristic, from CPU bound to I/O bound, or vice versa, HASP changes their subgroup. For example, if a task from the I/O subgroup uses its entire time slice, it is placed at the top of the CPU subgroup. These changes occur dynamically during job-step execution.

Besides monitoring executing tasks, the heuristic dispatcher also monitors the effectiveness of the time slice being used. At installation-specified intervals (much longer than the time slice itself), the dispatcher compares the ratio of I/O tasks (and all tasks being controlled) to a desired mix ratio of I/O and CPU tasks that is also installation specified. If not enough I/O tasks are being identified, the time slice is increased. To increase the number of CPU tasks being identified, the time slice is decreased. Time-slice adjustments are made within an upper and lower bound. The HASP heuristic dispatcher is most effective in an environment where the actual workload contains a mix of I/O- and CPU-type jobs. The primary objective of the heuristic dispatching function is to improve system thruput.

HASP is one example of an operating system enhancement that resulted from a user's needs. There have been many others for numerous operating systems. The trend is to make operating systems more automatic in detailed scheduling, controlling resources, and balancing resource availability against workload requirements. This leaves users to concentrate on the important (but less detailed) job of setting system objectives and policies and monitoring system performance.

8-5 SOFTWARE MONITORING [Refs. CA1,IB7,IB8,IB9]

OS/360 provides software monitoring (see Sec. 7-6) at two basic levels of activity resolution. They correspond to the two monitoring programs: (1) the system management facility (SMF), and (2) the generalized trace facility (GTF). Both tools are optional. When used, they require some main and direct-access storage. SMF collects data at the job and job-step level. Thus, data such as CPU time, elapsed time, and gross measures of I/O activity in terms of number of I/O operations, can be recorded. SMF data can be used for job accounting and, through statistical reduction, for workload analysis; the data can also be used to examine the workload for content, function, and the frequency of job steps, such as use of various compilers. When used with OS/360, the SMF programs are incorporated into the system nucleus during system generation, thus increasing nucleus size. Two direct-access data-sets are required for data collection. Aside from data collection, SMF also allows an installation to insert its own routines at specified locations in the OS control process.

GTF records system events at a more detailed level of activity resolution—at the interrupt level in System/360/370. An installation can selectively record one or more interrupt types, or all interrupt-associated events during a trace session, and store the trace records in an internal table (in main storage) or in auxiliary storage on tape or disk. GTF then can be directed to operate on this data for: (1) program or system error debugging, and (2) program or system fine tuning of performance. Tracing the events that precede a system or program error can provide significant assistance in detecting the cause of the error. In *internal trace mode*, GTF records all of the most recent interrupt-associated events in a table in main storage. Table size determines the number of events recorded, and a wrap-around technique is used to retain the most recent events. If system failure (or user program failure) occurs, the table can then be examined to reconstruct the preceding system activity.

Of more interest for performance measurement studies is GTF operation in *external trace mode*. Trace records are stored in I/O buffers and transferred to tape or direct-access storage when buffers are filled. As mentioned earlier, buffer sizes (and the number of buffers used) must be large enough to avoid losing trace information. With care, a judicious balance can be achieved between buffer space and lost information. Selective tracing can be performed, for example, for all events associated with I/O interrupts, and selections can be made within an interrupt class such as: trace only events associated with specific SVC's, ignoring all other SVC types. It is possible, then, to perform selective studies such as:

1. Identifying the most frequently referenced SVC's to determine which should be main-storage resident
2. Measuring data-set or device utilization
3. Measuring the distribution of I/O activity across channels

If all interrupt-type events are collected in a GTF trace, the data could be used as input to drive an OS simulator. A tool such as GTF provides opportunities to study many aspects of an OS system in operation. When used, GTF requires its own partition or region and a small percent of CPU time. Data produced by GTF can then be analyzed by writing the programs appropriate to produce the type of analysis required.

8-6 DEADLOCK AVOIDANCE IN OS/360 [Refs. HAV, IB3]

In this section we illustrate some of the general principles discussed in Sec. 7-6 for the case of the IBM OS/360 MVT operating system.

To prevent CPU lock-out by, for example, a program in an endless loop, OS/360 provides an optional key-word parameter like

TIME = (5,20)

that can be specified for each job step, i.e., in an EXEC job-control statement (or for the job as a whole, in the JOB statement). The above specific example states that if the current job step (or job) uses more than 5 minutes, and 20 seconds of CPU time, the entire job of which this step is a part is to be terminated. The maximum time that can be specified in this way is just under 1440 minutes (24 hours). In addition to a CPU time limit, OS automatically monitors for any job that is in the WAIT state for longer than 30 consecutive minutes, in which case the system automatically cancels the job. Because it is conceivable (although very rare) that either the CPU time or WAIT time limits may be legitimately exceeded by a very long job, the user may specify TIME = 1440, which declares that all limits on both CPU time and WAIT time are ignored. Finally, if the user omits the TIME parameter entirely, default limits are supplied automatically by a parameter list in the input reader (specified by the system programmers at the installation).

Note that if the CPU time limit is specified for each job step, and any such limit is exceeded, the entire job is canceled.

The major provisions for handling deadlocks in IBM OS systems has been described by J.W. Havender [Ref. HAV]. He also unfolds the reasoning behind many of the design decisions. The following discussion closely follows Havender's treatment.

In OS/360/370 terminology, a program called a *job-initiator* (or sometimes just an initiator) starts each job step. Once started, the step is called a *task*. The initiator acquires certain resources for the step before starting it. Other resources are acquired at the start of an entire job, and still others may be acquired during a job step, as will be discussed later. For the moment, consider only the job-initiator's function. Since several copies of the initiator may be active concurrently, i.e., started but not completed, OS is a multitasking system. The resources required by jobs and job steps may be classified as:

1. Devices: tapes, card-reader, printer, etc.
2. Data-sets: named regions of direct-access storage within the naming context of the job-control language (JCL)
3. Main storage space

A serially reusable resource can be used by at most one task until it releases the resource. These are requested and released by OS's ENQ and DEQ macroinstructions, which enforce "exclusive use" and maintain queues on resources.

Devices are considered to be nonpreemptible, serially reusable resources due to their physical nature. Allowing job steps to dynamically allocate devices could result in deadlock. Hence, OS requires each job step to declare its needs for all devices, and the step is not started until they are all obtained. This treatment of devices is then seen to follow the deadlock-avoidance strategy. While the initiator is actually allocating devices, the operating system locks out any other initiator from doing likewise, since devices are exclusive-use resources. At the end of each job step, all devices allocated to it are released.

The acquisition of data-set resources presents a somewhat different problem from devices. Data-sets could, by their physical nature, be accessed concurrently by several job steps. (This possibility may be declared by the user with the SHR option on the DD JCL statement.) However, most data-sets are not so used. It is most desirable to permit data-sets to be global between job steps of the same job and yet to prevent access to a data-set from steps due to other jobs during this time. If data-sets were allocated on a job-step basis with interlocks to enforce exclusive use, deadlock could occur. For example, suppose the first step of Job 1 allocates data-set A and the second step allocates B; Job 2 then allocates B in its first step and A in its second. The two jobs are seen to request the data-sets in reverse order, making deadlock possible. To permit a job to retain exclusive use of data throughout all of its job steps, and yet avoid deadlock, OS acquires all data-sets needed for a job before starting the job (unlike devices, which are acquired and released on a job-step basis). This is done by scanning all of the job-control statements of a job and compiling a list of all non-SHR data-sets declared for the job (from information on the DD cards). The job is not started until all of the data-sets are acquired. This strategy would seem to avoid deadlock on data-sets. Unfortunately, avoidance is not airtight because OS also permits data-sets to be acquired dynamically, not only by the job initiator. This can result in deadlocks.

The third class of resource is main-storage space for a job step which is called a REGION. As described earlier, the size of a region may be declared separately for each job step (in the EXEC statement of JCL), or else all region sizes for a job may default to the region size specified in the JOB statement. The fact that regions can be assigned on a job-step basis rather than to entire jobs adds considerably to the flexibility of assignment of the precious main-storage resource, since some steps require more space than others.

Consider next some of the detail of how a job step gets started. We first set the stage by considering *where* various things will take place and then proceed to consider the events in time-order. The initiator program does the allocations and de-allocations of resources needed to start a job step. Since the initiator is itself a program, it requires space. OS avoids space overhead for this function through the use of an overlay technique whereby most of the initiator is executed in the same space as a region. However, a small but critical "seed" module of the initiator always resides in the supervisory link pack area of main storage. Having thus set the stage, let us now consider what happens when a job step ends. This calls a terminator routine (part of the initiator) that overlays the task that has just been completed. The terminator releases devices and then invokes the initiator to start the next job step. This must allocate both a region and devices to the new job step. Does it matter in which order this is done? It might appear that devices should be allocated first, since if some are not available, the new unallocated region (i.e., main-storage space) would not then be tied up. This suggests the allocation ordering

DEV→REG

Assume that this is done for Job 1, Task 1. When it completes, the terminator is executed in the same region, and the next job step should then begin with device allocation (using our hypothesized ordering). Since the allocation of devices may require appreciable main-storage space, to avoid space overhead, OS would use this same region for allocation of devices for Job 1, Task 2. If this is successful, the initiator would then release the region, exit to its link-pack module and then allocate the region for Task 2. But suppose now that during device allocation, Task 2 attempts to allocate (say) a tape unit that is found to be already allocated. Suppose further that the job holding this tape has just finished device allocation and is attempting region allocation, and to satisfy this, space must be used from the region of Job 1, Task 2. Although this is planned for release, it is tied up awaiting allocation of the tape. Clearly, this is a deadlock, and its cause is effective opposite-order allocation.

> Job 1, Task 2: REG→DEV
> Job 2, Task 1: DEV→REG

It might seem that Task 2 is violating the assumed ordering, but as seen above the REG is needed to do the DEV. For these reasons, OS actually does its device and region allocation in the order

> REG→DEV

As mentioned earlier, data-sets are allocated earliest at the start of the entire job, so that the final ordering is

> DS→REG→DEV

Although deadlock is thereby avoided, acquiring the region before the devices in a step can result in appreciable idle time of main storage as a step awaits the availability of devices.

REFERENCES AND BIBLIOGRAPHY

1. [BR] Brown, G.D.: "System/360 Job Control Language," John Wiley and Sons, New York, 1970.
2. [CA1] Campbell, D.J. and W.J. Heffner: Measurement and Analysis of Large Operating Systems During System Development, *AFIPS Conf. Proc.*, vol. 33, part 1, pp. 903-914, 1968 FJCC.
3. [CL] Clark, W.A.: The Functional Structure of OS/360 Part III Data Management, *IBM Systems Journal*, vol. 5, no. 1, pp. 30-51, 1965.
4. [FRE] Freeman, D.N.: A Storage Hierarchy System for Batch Processing, *AFIPS Proc.*, vol. 32, pp. 229-244, 1968.
5. [HAV] Havender, J.W.: Avoiding Deadlock in Multitasking Systems, *IBM Systems Journal*, vol. 7, no. 2, pp. 74-84, 1968.
6. [IB1] IBM Corp: "IBM System/360 Operating System Introduction," No. GC28-6534, IBM Corp. Data Processing Division, White Plains, N.Y. 10604.
7. [IB2] IBM Corp: "IBM System/360 Operating Systems Feature Guide," No. GC28-6716, IBM Corp. Data Processing Division, White Plains, N.Y. 10604.
8. [IB3] IBM Corp: "OS/360 Job Control Language Users Guide," No. GC28-6703, IBM Corp. Data Processing Division, White Plains, N.Y. 10604.
9. [IB4] IBM Corp: "IBM System/360 Operating System: MFT Guide," No. GC27-6939, IBM Corp. Data Processing Division, White Plains, N.Y. 10604.
10. [IB5] IBM Corp: "IBM System/360 Operating System MVT Guide," No. GC28-6720, IBM Corp. Data Processing Division, White Plains, N.Y. 10604.
11. [IB6] IBM Corp: "IBM System/360 Operating System Planning for Rollout/Rollin," No. GC27-6935, IBM Corp. Data Processing Division, White Plains, N.Y. 10604.

12. [IB7] IBM Corp: "IBM System/360 Operating System Management Facilities Reference Manual," No. GC28-6712, IBM Corp. Data Processing Division, White Plains, N.Y. 10604.
13. [IB8] IBM Corp: "OS/VS Service Aids Manual," No. GC28-0633, IBM Corp. Data Processing Division, White Plains, N.Y. 10604.
14. [IB9] IBM Corp: "AMAP (Advanced Multiprogramming Analysis Procedure Service Description Manual," No. GH20-0725, IBM Corp. Data Processing Division, White Plains, N.Y. 10604.
15. [IB10] IBM Corp.: "OS/360 Job Control Language Reference," No. GC28-6704, IBM Corp. Data Processing Division, White Plains, N.Y. 10604.
16. [IB11] IBM Corp: "IBM System/360 Operating System PL/I [F] Programmers Guide," No. GC28-6595, IBM Corp. Data Processing Division, White Plains, N.Y. 10604.
17. [ME] Mealy, G.H.: The Functional Structure of OS/360 Part I Introductory Survey, *IBM Systems Journal*, vol. 5, no. 1, pp. 3-11, 1965.
18. [RY] Ryder, K.D.: A Heuristic Approach to Task Dispatching, *IBM Systems Journal*, vol. 9, no. 3, pp. 189-198, 1970.
19. [WI] Witt, B.I.: The Functional Structure of OS/360 Part II Job and Task Management, *IBM Systems Journal*, vol. 5, no. 1, pp. 12-29, 1965.

CHAPTER 9

Timesharing Systems

The timesharing type of computer system first appeared in its present form in the early 1960s. Although related in some ways to earlier military "command and control" and airline reservation systems, the term *timesharing* now usually denotes a multiuser system in which each user has the ability to define and run his own programs on what he perceives as his own private general-purpose computer, with the added proviso that the system must respond to certain of his requests quickly enough to be comfortable for man-machine interaction. Compared to the more common "batch system," timesharing is then a different way for *people* to interact with a computer. Since it is a much more intimate way, activities such as problem solving, engineering design, and all types of program construction and debugging are very convenient. This major enhancement of the creative environment not only results in economies arising from more productive uses of human resources, but also presents us with an open-ended challenge to enhance human creativity.

In addition to user-oriented justifications, resource efficiencies (at least potential ones) tend to favor timesharing. One of these is the hope that the high demand rate of the many users connected to the system together with a batch workload will improve CPU utilization, which typically runs as low as 30 to 40 percent in many batch systems. However, this potential may be offset at least in part by swapping "overhead" (see below).

The "timesharing" of the central processor from which the system derives its generic name is only one of several increased opportunities for *sharing*. Others include the sharing of main storage and other *devices*, as well as the sharing of *programs*, especially translator programs (interpreters and compilers), libraries of subroutines, and users' programs. This accessibility, available at human reaction times, means that a timesharing system becomes a vast communication medium whereby people can quickly access the experience of others.

Having introduced the key motivations for timesharing, we now turn to some characteristic features of the implementation of such systems. One issue, which has been resolved in a surprisingly simple manner, is that the equipment of a modern medium-large computer system requires relatively little in the way of additional *types* of devices or features to run many timesharing systems. Three essential CPU features: an *interrupt scheme, real-time clock*, and a *storage protection mechanism* were already common in most computers emerging in the 1960s, since they are also needed to run modern multiprogrammed-batch operating systems efficiently.* The one type of device essential and somewhat unique to the timesharing environment is the *terminal*, which today typically consists of a typewriter-like device such as a teletype or IBM "golf-ball" typewriter with appropriate electronics to connect the device to a telephone line. Terminals of this kind are relatively cheap, and users can then connect to any timesharing system that expects the given type of terminal (provided, of course, that prior billing arrangements are made). It is thus quite feasible for a single terminal to connect (*dial up*) through the usual telephone facilities to several different remotely located central-processing facilities at various times to accommodate different needs for computer languages and other conveniences and facilities. The common very extensive telephone system is then often a part of a timesharing system. At the computer site, the signals on each of the incoming lines are changed electrically by a modem (modulator-demodulator), then usually multiplexed into a single register, and thence distributed to the buffer areas of main storage where system programs process their messages. This multiplexing function requires a device that is typically called a *transmission control unit*.

A timesharing system must recover its costs by servicing a fairly large number of users concurrently. A typical medium-sized computer services on the order of 50 users. A large number is essential for economic viability and is also technically feasible, since each individual user is likely to be a light load on the system. This is because even during long sessions at the terminal, much time is usually spent in thinking and keying. Of course one major objective of timesharing is fast response to certain critical human demands like editing a program; these usually require relatively little processing from a reasonably fast computer (more on this important point later).

The many connected users (in aggregate) require considerable storage to hold their current programs and data. This storage is usually well beyond the economical

---

*Circuitry to permit dynamic relocation of programs can improve efficiency but is not essential. In the IBM S/360 computers, only Mod 67 had this feature. Most CDC, Burroughs, GE, and other systems had relocation hardware (see Sec. 10-11).

sizes of high-speed main storage. Only a few (sometimes only one) users' required storage space can be held in main storage at a time and the rest must be kept on a cheaper, slower, but higher capacity auxiliary store like a drum or disk. When the system decides to work on a particular job, if it is not in main storage (as will often be the case), it must first move a current resident job out of main storage to the (say) drum (so that its state is thereby saved for later resumption of processing). The desired job is then sent from the drum to the just-vacated part of main storage. This process is called *swapping* and is characteristic of most timeshared systems. Swapping is done automatically by the operating system program. Decisions on order-of-servicing jobs, which determines what and when to swap, can follow scheduling principles of the type discussed in Chap. 4. Many other rules have been developed also; we shall examine some of them in the rest of this chapter. All such rules must satisfy one key requirement: fast response to those requests that are essential to man-machine interaction.

A word is in order about terminology. In discussing communication-computer systems, the work required for one interaction between the user and the system will be called a *tract*, which is an abbreviated form of *transaction*. A tract is somewhat similar to what we have previously called a *job*, but to the individual user, a "job" (like getting some program to work) usually takes many interactions and hence many tracts.

Some timesharing systems provide their terminal users with only a single programming language, in which case the system is sometimes said to be *dedicated*. Examples of dedicated systems include IBM's QUIKTRAN and some APL and BASIC systems. Some analysts use the term *dedicated* to mean that timesharing users may be given more than one language, but a background (batch) workload cannot run concurrently. Since programs in a batch mode can often require greater machine resources, a desirable feature is that the languages and compilers used at the terminals be *compatible* with those used in the batch system. If compatibility is not available, this can cause much frustration, especially if a job evolves from the small-scale algorithm-development stage to handling large volumes of data. The trend is definitely towards multilanguage (i.e., nondedicated) timesharing systems with batch-compatible languages.

To summarize some essential points made above, the timesharing system's primary objective is effective, economical, and comfortable man-machine interaction. The sharing of common resources, including hardware, programs, and data on the time scale of human reaction times, requires certain fairly unique equipment at each user location (terminals and communication devices). It can make good use of existing telephone equipment for communications and requires a major reorientation of the system's internal management of its own resources, i.e., a different operating system from the usual batch type. A considerable number of timesharing systems include many features that are also used or would be useful in a batch system, such as *multiprogramming* and *virtual storage*, which are considered elsewhere in this book. Since these are not unique or essential to the timesharing system per se, they will *not* be discussed in this chapter.

9-1 THE USER VIEWPOINT AND SOME CONSEQUENCES
[Refs. BRY,GO,SA1,SA2,SC3,SM]

In our introduction, some major user benefits of timesharing were stated. We now turn to one study that gives at least some organized evidence that supports such claims. Evidence of this type is quite difficult to obtain and analyze, since it involves the work habits of *people*, which is a most difficult subject from which to draw any general conclusions. One study done at MIT [Refs. SA1,SA2] involved 66 students in a management class that used a simulation model of the construction industry inplemented by DYNAMO, a simulation language. Each student was given certain information about the industry and market conditions and was to use the model (on a computer) to optimize his return. The class was divided into two groups. Both used the same model, but to one group the computer was available as a timeshared system, while to the other as a batch system. Data on the student's performance and attitudes was obtained by questionnaires, by instructor's analysis of problem solutions, and by the usual computer accounting of the use of its resources. The major outcomes of this experiment may be summarized as follows:

1. Total cost (system plus user's worktime) for both groups did not differ appreciably. The costs were, however, distributed quite differently. The timeshared group had a lower man-effort cost, but a higher computer cost.
2. The timesharing users achieved a significantly better solution to the assigned problem.
3. More than twice as many people in the batch processing group did *not* obtain a useful answer to the assigned problem.
4. More people liked the timesharing system.

The experiment indicates the importance of including the benefit of a better solution to the problem and user attitudes, as well as the easy-to-measure direct costs. Other similar studies point to another important conclusion: *there was more variability of user performance within each group than between groups.* This suggests that differences between people's skills are probably more significant than the type of system used.

One important aspect of the individual user's viewpoint must include the costs for the equipment and services he directly uses. Figure 9-1.1 gives a listing which is primarily of interest because of the categories of costs rather than the specific values (which will undoubtedly change with time). Terminal rental, telephone data-set, and telephone line costs need no further elaboration. The *CPU rate* is applied only to the time the system works for the individual user. The connected rate is applied to each hour the user is "signed on" to the system, whether he uses it or not, and is justified by the need to tie up some central computer resources, such as main-storage areas for terminal buffering, and a subchannel for communication line control. Figure 9-1.1 gives rates for the various categories of charge; costs will depend on times also. For typical times, most of the cost may well be for the communications part of the system rather than CPU use. This is often the justification for using a device, called a *telephone-line concentrator*, that can combine the signals of several terminals in the same locality in order that they can more economically share an expensive leased line

Category	Typical Rate	Assumed Usage	Cost/month
Terminal rental (IBM2741)	$100/month	1	$100
Telephone data-set	28	1	28
Telephone leased line*	3/mile/month	50 mile	150
CPU charge*	5/minute	20	100
Connect charge*	12/hour	40	480
File charge	1/7k byte/month	70k byte	10

*Connect charge typically includes:
   1 minute CPU time/hour of connect time
   Prorated share of leased telephone line

Fig. 9-1.1   Typical rates (year 1971).

to the central system. This becomes more important as distances (hence costs) between clusters of terminals and the computer become longer.

In order to understand the performance issues in timesharing systems, we now consider how the user would like the system to appear to him. It is relatively easy to make a long "laundry list" of desirable features, most of which are also common to any other kind of general-purpose computing system, but this will shed little light on the special concerns of the timesharing user. We rather ask the question: What system properties are unique or at least most important to the user of a timesharing system? We may begin an answer by concisely restating some of the considerations discussed in the introduction to this chapter: *The primary objective of a timesharing system is to provide fast, convenient, and economical man-machine interaction.* To make this statement as clear as possible and to illustrate it by several examples is the major objective of this section.

We first examine the context of only *one person* interacting with his "private" computer through his terminal; we shall momentarily set aside those performance issues that are due to the many users who share resources (see later sections).

Most timesharing systems are often said to be *conversational* because the user-machine interaction may be considered to take the form of a "polite" conversation whereby each transmits messages to the other in strict alternation. This is usually imposed by the system locking the keyboard after receipt of a user's typed line of transmission until it finally responds either with results, a message of its own, or sometimes simply a keyboard unlock.

The major types of functions needed by the user are listed in Fig. 9-1.2. They are provided by system-supplied programs that interpret the *commands* by which the user may make various kinds of requests for service. To help sharpen our understanding of these facilities, we shall be comparing them to the needs of a user of a batch system. Likewise, we shall initially assume that the language translator that converts the user's programs to machine-executable form is of the compiler type commonly found in batch systems.

Most of the items of Fig. 9-1.2 imply the requirement that user programs and data must be stored within the system from session to session. Items 1 and 4 are

1. *Program and Data Objects*
      (*a*) List current names & descriptions
      (*b*) Assign & delete names
      (*c*) Reference objects by name

2. *Program Editing (statements and entire programs) By Line Number and Context*
      (*a*) *Display*
      (*b*) *Modify*
      (*c*) *Delete*
      (*d*) *Insert*
      (*Note:* Modify can be done by: *Delete,* then *Insert.*)

3. *Data Editing on*
      (*a*) Input to program
      (*b*) Computed data

4. *Composition*
      Combine named objects (programs, files) into new named objects

5. *Sequence Control*
      (*a*) Sign on & off (Log-on & off)
      (*b*) Start a program
      (*c*) Interrupt a program
      (*d*) Resume an interrupted program

6. *Detection of User Errors*
      (*a*) Line by line at entry
      (*b*) After program entry
      (*c*) During execution

Fig. 9-1.2 Checklist of desirable user facilities.

usually supplied to the named objects by a naming scheme implemented by a collection of directories. To prevent confusion between identically named objects of different users, most systems keep a hierarchy of directories. In effect, each user's objects automatically and implicitly have his name (or identifier) included as part of their names.

Program and data editing are usually supplied in the form of a program that appears to the user as a set of "edit commands" corresponding to the operations mentioned in item 2. The editing of source *data* intended for entry under control of the user's program can be handled by much the same facilities as for program editing.

The major difficulties in satisfying the listed requirements center on item 5—the interruptibility of programs. (Remember, we are here talking only about the interruptibility required by one user, *not* by the system for its swapping functions.) We may begin by asking whether this is really essential. If so, what is the minimal facility to satisfy the fundamental need? The ability to interrupt a program is indeed essential because the theory of computation tells us that there is no way to tell in advance whether programs will end. Thus, a long-running program may be executing properly or be in an endless loop. For this reason, batch systems always provide *some* means to abort a program in order to prevent it from unduly monopolizing system resources. Usually, this is done by the machine operator, who receives a message from the operating system if a program runs longer than some user-estimated time specified on a job card. The same type of scheme could be used in a timesharing system.

However, having *only* this would not be appropriate. The reason is the immediate physical presence of the user, who can often (but not always) recognize that a program is running too long and is probably in error. Also, he may well come to this conclusion by observing the printout of intermediate results (which no one sees during running of a batch system).

Although the user must be permitted to interrupt a program, say by using an "attention" button on his terminal, the facilities he then requires to respond are not so clear. The simplest requires him to restart the translation and run of the program (usually after he has modified the source statements or input data). This needs no special capabilities of the compiler. With this convention, a timesharing system may use a compiler taken from an existing batch system with little change (at least to respond to the interrupt requirement), since after every interruption, there is a new complete compilation. To reduce compile time (often at the expense of object speed), a fast-compile compiler like the highly successful WATFOR for FORTRAN IV, developed at the University of Waterloo, is desirable. If the system *must* permit the user to resume an interrupted program at a later time without a recompile, then additional facilities must be provided. To see what is needed and how these may be provided, let us consider what a user might want to do following his requested interrupt. First, he probably will want to "see" some data values (like a loop-control variable). Of course, he should only need to refer to this by its name used in his program. To translate this name to the address (location) in memory of the data value requires the symbol table (and possibly other tables, like a relocation table) that has usually been discarded after compilation. Thus, to satisfy this requirement, the system must retain the symbol table produced by the compiler. Also, the requested data must be displayed to the user in source-language form, which requires at least some of the usual compiler's facilities. To summarize, the ability to display and modify *computed values* in response to on-demand user requests requires features not necessary, and hence not usually available, in compilers written for the batch environment.

The problem of responding to the user's syntactical errors (item 6 of Fig. 9-1.2) is essential to any programming system, timesharing or batch. Whether the timesharing system has unique requirements here is somewhat controversial. Some people believe (strongly) that every line of program should be syntactically checked upon entry and any errors sent to the user as fast as possible. Others feel (strongly) that a concise report listing all errors after the entire program has been entered is sufficient, and even preferable. It is possible that this issue can never be resolved once and for all, since it may depend on the work habits of individual people. At this writing (1975) some of the most successful timesharing systems, like IBM's APL and CMS systems, do not syntactically check line-by-line, while others do. To provide the line-by-line syntax-check feature is not too difficult if the compiler is being written from the beginning; it requires nontrivial changes to modify a compiler to have this feature.

We may summarize the above discussion by saying that it is possible to supply adequate interaction facilities for many purposes by using a fast-compile compiler, even one designed for a batch system, together with a good human-engineered file-edit and handling subsystem. However, such a system will not supply certain facilities

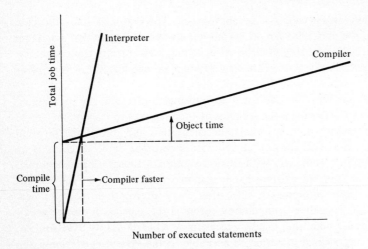

Fig. 9-1.3 Sketch of compiler vs. interpreter performance considerations.

desirable (if not essential) for debugging, especially the ability to modify computed data (referenced in source form) and to resume the interrupted program.

All of the above desirable functions (and some others) may be supplied most conveniently to both the user and the translator programmer if the translator program is an *interpreter* rather than a *compiler*. It is recalled that an interpreter translates each statement of the source program each time the statement is *executed*, while a compiler translates the entire user program once to a machine (object) program in a distinct translation phase, and only then executes the resulting object code. Interpreters usually spend most of their time on the *repetitive translation* of statements rather than on productive execution. The relative performance properties of compilers vs. interpreters is sketched in Fig. 9-1.3. It is seen that the interpreter may be faster for very short-running programs (especially one with no loops, due to the initialization of the compiler), but that the compiler is better for almost any looping program. However, the interpreter, since it translates each statement as it executes the statement, can easily permit *changes* in the program without the need to recompile. It can also permit the language to be somewhat more convenient, since it depends on "last-moment" information about storage allocation and resource use, while the compiler must know by user declaration or rules about these things *before* the program is run (when it is translated). To put it another way, an interpreter requires the latest possible *binding time* of user-oriented names and parameters to machine resources. Actually, the distinction between compiler and interpreter need not be as strict as it might seem from the above discussion, which for exposition purposes emphasizes the differences. Nevertheless, the more a compiler uses interpreter techniques, the better the convenience for the user, but the poorer the running time.

It cannot be too strongly emphasized that the essential man-machine interaction facilities, which include editing of program and data operations, are usually very frequent, but usually require very little computation time. For this reason, they will be called *trivial tracts*. In a sense, this is an unfortunate term, since they rank highest in the importance of being serviced quickly. In other words, fast responses to trivial requests are not only possible, but essential.

The requirement of fast response to trivial tracts may be viewed as a special case of a more general principle of man-machine psychology:

A RESPONSE DESIGN PRINCIPLE

The system should be designed to give fastest response to those requests that the human user expects to be quickly processed, provided that each such request, when run alone, can be processed in a short time.

This principle may seem at first glance to be rather obvious, but if accepted, it can give a very useful guide to the design of resource schedulers. Thus, beyond giving highest priority to the trivial tracts of program editing and display, other short-time tracts should also be given higher priority than longer runs. Since run times are often not known in advance, a scheduler like round robin (see Chap. 4) can complete short tracts quickly, even when it cannot identify them. It is also worth noting that the user may well expect the time required to service a tract to be much less than the system's processing time for the tract. In this case, the response will *necessarily* be unsatisfactory. The above principle insists however that where this conflict is not present, the system should respond so as to meet human expectations.

Knowledge of expected "length of run" (and storage required in some systems) can be a very valuable aid to the scheduler. Although the round-robin scheduler does not make use of such knowledge, this scheduler in its simple form can require appreciable swapping delays, which tends to undo some of its scheduling advantages. The question of prior knowledge of tract processing times is a profound one. In dedicated systems with only one (or a very few) specific language and file-edit processors, the designers and the scheduler can easily get information about the resource needs of important classes of tracts. For example, the IBM RAX system, which used one compiler of the FORTRAN language, reduced swap overhead by being designed to do a complete compilation without swapping, since most compile times were judged to be short enough so as not unduly to affect trivial responses. RAX did however "time slice" (and swap) object program executions, since their run times were unpredictable.

The more general the system in terms of variety of language translators, file-edit facilities, etc., the more difficult it will be to make use of prior knowledge of use of resources. Thus, general systems must depend increasingly on their own observations and measurements of resource use for resource scheduling.

9-2 CHOICE OF TIME SLICE   [Refs. BE,COR,LA,IB2]

The fundamental purpose of time slicing is to force the operating system to reconsider its resource-scheduling decisions. This is essential to most measures of good response performance because the scheduling variables (see Chap. 4), and hence priorities, often change their values as time progresses. Since computation of these variables and their relative ranks requires use of the same central computer that services users, it is essential to interrupt the CPU from time to time (time-slice intervals) to do these computations and make resource allocation decisions based on them.

From the most simplistic view, which neglects overhead in scheduling variable updating and job switching, the time slice should be very short in order to ensure very fast response to changes in state of the scheduling variables. More realistically, however, a switch of the CPU from one tract to another really involves two switches: (1) current user program to operating system (scheduler), and (2) operating system to user program. In most systems, the first step is fairly fast. The second step can also be fast if the return is to the program mentioned in step 1. However, if a new program is involved in step 2, and if this program must be swapped into main storage from slow storage, and if this must be preceded by swap out of a program already in main storage, the process of job switching can be quite time consuming. The job switching overhead then should influence the lower limit of feasible time-slice values. However, in many systems there are two sets of jobs to which the system can switch—those currently resident in main storage and those currently not resident. Since switching overhead is much lower for the first class than for the second, this suggests using *two time slices*. Some systems have variable time slices, but in such cases, if the maximum time slice is long (say several seconds), the CPU is interruptible to new tracts, since they may well be in the critical trivial-response category.

To summarize, too large a time-slice value tends to make a system sluggish in response, and too small a value tends to increase CPU task-switching overhead. To reduce swapping, another major source of inefficiency, and yet seek to retain as much response sensitivity as possible, separate time-slice intervals are often chosen for (1) the time a tract is to remain in main storage before swap out, and (2) the time the CPU is allocated to one tract before being switched to another tract in main storage. The length of the time slice(s) may be fixed at system-design time, it may be specified as a parameter to be supplied by system programmers/operators, or it may be automatically computed by the operating system based on its own observations of job and system activity. Examples will be given later for specific cases.

9-3 THE MIT CTSS SYSTEM   [Refs. COR,SC1]

The *C*ompatible *T*ime-*S*haring *S*ystem (CTSS) developed at MIT in the early 1960s is among the first reported in detail in the literature. As its name suggests, the system was designed so that *any* program that ran on a conventional IBM 7090 computer would run without change (compatibly) on the timeshared system. This requirement (which is desirable but not essential to timesharing systems per se) has the advantage that users may construct, debug, and modify programs on the timesharing system and be sure that these will run as production jobs in the more machine-efficient batch system. This also means that all of the resources, especially all of main storage, that are available to the batch user are also available under timesharing.

A sketch of the CTSS equipment configuration is shown in Fig. 9-3.1. It is seen to consist of a single IBM 7094 central processing unit with two 32k-word, 2-microsecond core-storage boxes. One of these was used only for one problem

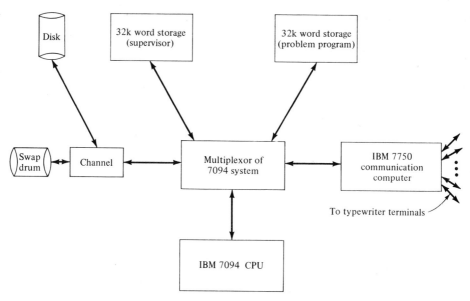

Fig. 9-3.1 MIT CTSS system configuration (partial).

program at a time, and hence satisfied the compatibility requirement, since the standard 7094 system had only 32k words of storage. The other 32k-word core box was used for CTSS's system programs. Like most other IBM 7090/7094 systems, this one also used the special-purpose IBM 7750 computer for line multiplexing and control. A high-speed channel controlled transmission between the main core boxes and a drum and disk. The drum was the major "swap" device.

The compatibility feature, which ensures the greatest possible storage space available to the user, eliminated many of the scheduling and control problems that occur in systems that manage resources in a more flexible manner. Thus, since CTSS kept only one user program at a time in core storage, there was no space sharing or need for dynamic program relocation. The IBM 7090 computer originally used by CTSS had these as specially designed features; they were not used. Another consequence of keeping only one program in main storage at a time is the impossibility of "overlap swap" of one user's job with CPU work on another (see Sec. 9-6 for a discussion of overlap swapping). As is true of most systems, to reduce swap time, CTSS only swapped the used portion of the maximum space of 32k words.

Although many scheduling problems common to later timesharing systems were not present in CTSS, the system did its one major scheduling function, i.e., deciding which tract should next receive service and for how long, in an elegant and interesting manner. Figure 9-3.2 summarizes CTSS's "exponential" scheduling algorithm, which may be briefly described as follows. The scheduler gives a *new* incoming request high priority, since it may well be a short interactive one for which fast response is most critical. In that case the tract will be serviced quickly. As a tract proves to require longer and longer processing time, its priority is set lower and lower. However, as the

1. *9 priority levels; several jobs can be in each level*

Highest	0	
priority	1	
	2	New jobs: space < 4095 words
	3	New jobs: space ≥ 4095 words
	4	
	5	
	6	
	7	
Lowest	8	
priority		

2. *Job scheduling algorithm*

    (*a*) Tract for next CPU service from highest priority nonempty level.

    (*b*) A tract not selected for 60 seconds is moved to next higher priority level.

    (*c*) A tract in level q, once selected for service, is run until first occurrence of an I/O request, job completion or 0.5×2^q seconds. Longest possible burst time = 128 seconds.

    (*d*) If a tract does not complete by end of the burst, it is moved down one priority level.

    (*e*) A tract currently in execution (burst) is preempted (swapped out) in favor of a new arrival to level q if the current job has run at least 0.5×2^q seconds. A preempted job is returned to the queue level just before its current burst started.

Fig. 9-3.2 CTSS exponential scheduler.

priority of a tract drops, meaning it is less likely to be selected for service, its service period (time slice) once selected is longer than for high-priority tracts. This latter feature is intended to reduce swapping (during which the CPU is idle) for jobs that require long CPU times, thus improving thruput. To summarize, CTSS assumed a new job was short and gave it good service at first. As a job lingered, thus proving itself to be long, it slipped into the "background" where it was treated more like a batch job. One refinement of the above principles was a crude attempt at estimating the probable rank of job lengths for incoming jobs by presuming a correlation between space required and the (unknown) time to run. Thus jobs requiring more than 4095 words were initially set one priority level lower than the jobs requiring less space.

9-4 THE APL SYSTEM   [Refs. AN,BRE,HE1,HE3,IV]

The APL system is named for K.E. Iverson's book (*A Programming Language*) in which a powerful and elegant programming language was described and applied to a wide variety of algorithms [Ref. IV]. The language was intensively used "on paper" by a small but dedicated collection of people for at least six years before the first machine translation appeared. Thus, unlike most other programming languages, this one enjoyed a long period of careful conceptual development before being frozen by an implementation and its inevitable pressures for expediency and compatibility.

    Although not designed explicitly for timesharing, the Iverson language is ideally suited to the man-machine environment, due to its philosophy, which permits and even encourages the user to specify much processing with a minimum of symbols and hence keystrokes. The following language features will help make this clear:

1. A name can denote an array, i.e., a vector, matrix, or multidimensional structure that is permitted to shrink or expand in size without specific attention by the user.
2. A wide variety of operators, each denoted by its own special symbol (or simple symbol combination), are applicable to entire arrays, as well as to the usual single values or indexed variables. These include profound generalizations of the operators of matrix algebra, as well as many others.
3. Three data types (number, bit, and character) are provided with automatic translation between bit and number types (and also between integer and floating-point numbers) without any explicit act from the user.

The value of many of these properties to man-machine interaction was demonstrated in 1964 by a "pilot" system that used many of APL's language ideas [Ref. HE1].

The language evolved through the preimplementation years and was improved even further during the implementation, where for example, the strict right-to-left rule for scanning statements was finally refined, and the extension to multidimensional arrays was completed. The implementation of APL was done under the overall supervision of K.E. Iverson and A.D. Falkoff at IBM's Watson Research Center in Yorktown, N.Y.

The translator for the IBM System/360 is an *interpreter* (as opposed to a compiler) and is mainly the work of two people, L. Breed and R. Lathwell, over a period of less than a year. This pair of young wizards, with the help of R. Moore of I.M. Sharp Associates (Toronto, Canada), also built the software for terminal handling and swapping, as well as a simple command language to permit the user to access a limited amount of disk space. The early APL system ran under DOS, the major IBM operating system used on small and intermediate-sized System/360s in the mid 1960s. Later (about 1968), APL was available under the more comprehensive OS/360 operating system. Although many Mod 40 and Mod 50 systems with as little as 250k bytes of main storage serviced about 50 connected APL users, the system more typically included a Mod 50 (or faster CPU) with at least 500k bytes. These were able to run an OS batch workload, as well as say 50 or more APL terminals with response times to APL trivial requests usually well within the comfortable range of 3 seconds.

From a performance viewpoint, APL may be considered from two aspects. First there is the language and its translator. These can be analyzed neglecting the timesharing environment. The second aspect is concerned with the multiuser resource-allocation problems such as swapping.

It was decided to use an *interpreter* translator to help ensure that the elegance and user convenience of the language would be compromised as little as possible. It is almost certain that any compiler implementation of the language would require declarations and possibly other user annoyances. However, the price of the interpreter in execution time is considerable, since it must translate every statement every time it is executed (instead of only once per program, as for a compiler). This great inefficiency of the interpreter is, however, somewhat softened (compared to other languages) because the APL language tends to result in much execution per statement, owing to the powerful array operators. Yet performance tends to be poor in programs that loop appreciably. The *space efficiency* of the interpreter method of translation for APL would seem to be better than that of a compiler. APL uses a single resident copy of the interpreter shared by all users. This requires space comparable to the storage that would be taken for a resident compiler designed for fast response. The real saving in space is, however, due to the fact that the language permits concise programs of what in other languages are extensive programs. The interpreter only requires intermediate scratch storage for one statement at a time; a compiler requires storage of the larger object program.

There is an interesting interplay between APL's time and space use. Many of the operations that make best use of arrays and result in very compact statements, which themselves require little storage and are fast to translate, unfortunately require quite a bit of storage space. As an extremely simple example, to sum the first N integers in the simplest and fastest APL fashion, the statement is

$$+/\iota N$$

However, this statement requires APL to store N numbers, far more (for large N) than would be required if the same calculation was programmed with a loop. However, the loop is more inconvenient to program and would run much slower (in APL).

These considerations can easily be used to "prove" all sorts of things (both favorable and otherwise) about APL's translator performance. A fair statement would appear to be that with the interpreter translator, the user pays a considerable time price for the conveniences of the language, and this price can be lessened by the often lavish use of space that results from many of the array operators. Of course, space efficiency is only really important when one's space is exhausted. Until then, and this applies to small problems, the most concise program (with as little looping as possible) is most convenient and reasonably fast.

One interesting and important performance feature of APL is the set of "I-beam" operators (so called because the operator invoking them is a composite of two symbols that give the appearance of the cross section of a steel beam). A partial listing of these operators that can be used at any terminal and *can be included in any program* is given in Fig. 9-4.1. Certain of the I-beams can be of great value to the individual programmer in assessing and improving the performance of his programs. These include I22, which gives the amount of storage remaining in his workspace, and I21, which gives the reading on his particular CPU clock. Using the latter, the CPU time to execute any portion of a program can be obtained as an APL variable. Note that CPU time for a program depends only on the performance of the timed program, and not on the sharing of the system by many users. Other I-beams (numbered 14 and lower) refer to vectors of frequency distributions of various types of system activity. These I-beams may be restricted to only "privileged" terminals in order to conserve valuable core-memory space. In all, the I-beams give any user access to valuable aspects of individual user and system performance. (For more examples of these in a system performance study, see Sec. 9-6.)

We now turn to the second aspect of APL performance, that is, the handling of multiple users. Figure 9-4.2 shows a sketch of main storage. A small storage area (about 600 bytes) is reserved in main storage for *each* signed-on user to buffer terminal

X	*Definition of IX:*
19	Accumulated keying time (total time of keyboard-unlock) during this session[1]
20	The time of day
21	The CPU time used in this session
22	The no. of bytes remaining in the workspace
23	The no. of terminals currently signed on
24	Time at the start of the session
25	The date[2]
26	The first element of $I27$
27	Vector of statement numbers in the state vector

Notes: 1. All times are in $1 \div 60$ of second.
      2. The date is represented by a 6-digit integer; the pairs give month, day, and year.

Fig. 9-4.1 Some APL I beams.

messages. Since transmission between this space and the terminal is controlled by the machine's multiplexor channel, which can operate independently of the CPU, many such transmissions can occur concurrently with each other and with CPU processing. This means that the user can be entering a program or data or receiving output, at least for a limited time, even when his workspace has been swapped out. The system is also designed so that the overlap between CPU time and terminal transmission is possible even for the same program (as well as between programs). Thus, a program that repeats the sequence: compute-a-line/type-a-line, appears at the terminal to run at printout speed, provided the computation part is not excessive and the number of demands for CPU service is not too high.

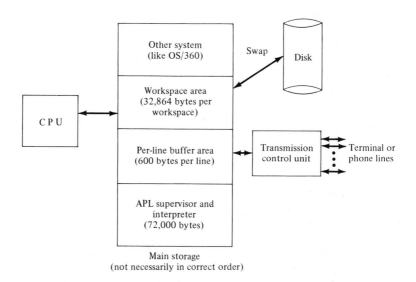

Main storage
(not necessarily in correct order)

Fig. 9-4.2 Typical APL resources.

A single copy of the APL translator in main memory is shared by all users. The Installation may specify that two or more workspaces (each 32k bytes) be held in main storage concurrently. Swapping is between these areas and a disk (IBM 2311 or 2314/3330). Because more than one workspace may be held in main storage concurrently, overlap is possible between input and output swapping and computation (on different APL jobs). Some quantitative idea of the performance benefit of this potential will be discussed later (see Sec. 9-6). One limitation of IBM-supplied APL systems (as of 1972) is the restriction of the user to fixed-size workspaces (usually 32k bytes). Only one can be "active," i.e., accessible to his program at one time. A manually executed command is required to access a nonactive workspace. This serious practical restriction was removed by at least one APL system (provided by the Scientific Time-sharing Co.). The SV (shared variable) version of APL announced in 1973 for System/370 machines can also provide file accessibility. It is worth noting that APL runs on *any* standard IBM S/360 or S/370 with the requisite configuration. No special (nonstandard) equipment of any kind is necessary.

Unusually high reliability was evident even in the first days of APL operation. In part this is due to the use of the system by the designers and implementers during development and debug. An APL system typically runs "unattended" (no machine-room operator) for several days over holidays.

9-5 PERFORMANCE MEASUREMENT   [Refs. AN,BA,DO,HE3,MA,SC1,SH]

Some properties of performance-measurement techniques have been discussed in Chap. 4 for hardware monitors and in Sec. 7-9 for software-measurement tools. In this section we confine attention to methods applicable to the timesharing environment, i.e., a computing system servicing many terminals manned by human beings. Such a system may of course (and often does) also run a batch workload. There are two basic classes of measurement technique, internal and external, each leading to a quite different type of measuring experiment with greatly different implications to the required knowledge and skills of those conducting the measurements.

With the *internal* method, those interested in measurement must have access to, and may even have to modify, the operating system program (although many measurement facilities are now included in most modern operating systems). Timesharing systems, like batch systems, often have interrupt-interpreter programs that intercept all interrupts and store a record for each, thus giving a time stamp and description of the event for later data reduction. A timesharing system will, in addition, need to capture in some way the activities of each of its terminal users. Since this data is usually much more voluminous than for a batch system, greater care must be taken to prevent the mechanics of measurement from significantly degrading performance. Many, if not most timesharing systems reported in the literature describe some internal measurement scheme. Note, however, that *any* internal software measurement instrument is almost sure to be particular to a *single* operating system. Although it is a valuable, if not indispensable, tool in the development phase and can also be of great value to those installing a system, users of internal measurements must usually be quite knowledgeable about internal system structure. This need not be inherent in internal methods; with care, performance data obtained this way could be displayed in a form not requiring knowledge of the internals of a system. But at present at least, this is a statement more of hope than fact.

The *external* method of measurement treats the system as a kind of "black box" with only the usual user terminals available for conducting all measurements. Unlike internal methods, the external scheme depends critically on control of the workload and how the system appears to the user, but needs no knowledge of the details of internal system behavior and no access to the internals of the operating system.

As was discussed in Chap. 4, the performance of any system, including a timesharing system, depends on three kinds of factors:

1. The workload
2. The system structure (hardware and software)
3. The performance measures

Since we are now considering *measurement* of performance, an actual system must of course be presented to us. The system structure is then completely determined; there remains the task of including a careful description of it in the report. Item 3, performance measures, also need not be a formidable problem. In particular, the following criteria are representative:

1. *Response times:*
    (*a*) Mean, median, standard deviation
    (*b*) Frequency distribution (in execution-time ranges)
2. *Central system utilizations:*
    A vector of percent busy time of each component, such as CPU, channel swap devices, etc., while running the workload

The remaining item, the *workload*, is the most difficult one to fix for measurements; this is the reason that most of this section centers on this problem. The reason is easy enough to understand. Since the workload on a timesharing system is applied by *people* personally interacting with the system, their behavior at the terminal must be part of the workload specification. One immediate consequence is a disturbing one for a physical scientist, although not unfamiliar to behavioral scientists; it will be most difficult to obtain *reproducible* results if one insists on using live user activity. However, with care, the results may be *statistically* reproducible. For example, if measurements are made on the same system at the same time of day for successive workdays, although the details of each user's activity will almost certainly be different, the frequency distributions of their collective activity may well be similar. Needless to say, this is not a statement of fact, but rather of plausibility, and should itself be checked by measurement. The monitoring of actual system activity is readily possible with an internal-measurement instrument. It is much more difficult using the external-measurement technique, although some performance information can be obtained externally by the use of a *snooper terminal*. A snooper terminal (or terminals) consists of an ordinary user terminal at which the measurement user requests a known and measurable quantity of work, like a sequence of interactive requests for service or selected compile-and-run jobs. During this time, other users are behaving in their usual manner. The snooper measures the system's responsiveness to his requests and records how this varies with (say) time of day and the nature of the snooper request. He may also wish to compare these times to those of another system on which he snoops (preferably with the same snooper workload).

The most basic concept of workload characterization for a timesharing system is the *script*. A script consists of a collection of records of the interactions of real or imagined users with the system, with the time stamps for each item on each record. To visualize a script for a single user, imagine a session at the terminal with the terminal printout annotated so that each line is stamped with the time at which the line appeared as output or input. The script for a measurement experiment consists of a collection of such individual user scripts. After such a collection is obtained and concurrence is achieved on its suitability, it is then possible to reproduce the response of the system to *that* script. The same script may be used as a workload description to investigate changes in configuration or the operating system. The script is then the input data to a simulator of the system.

Selecting a script is a similar problem to choosing any benchmark (see Sec. 4-2). We shall *not* discuss this problem now, but simply assume a script is available. Although the script idea is simple enough in principle, even when an acceptable script exists, the mechanics of representing and applying it can be formidable. Since the information volume of a script can be large and the time sequencing crucial, manual input of any but the simplest script is not feasible. We shall presently consider machine representations of scripts. However, it is worth digressing briefly to suggest that it *is* possible, economical, and feasible to apply *very simple* scripts *manually* to a system as follows:

1. *Pretest preparation:*
    (*a*) Choose and debug some test programs and store them in several test users' files. A script will typically be one of *j* people calling for a test program (see below).
    (*b*) Arrange for time to "take over" the system for testing.
    (*c*) Arrange for a team of people who will physically enter the scripts at test time. They should have some familiarity (as users) with the system under test.
2. *Measurement tests* (*some typical ones*):
    (*a*) Trivial-response test: Have *j* users *concurrently* make trivial requests as fast as they can and measure the response times by stop watch. First make *j* = 1 then 2, 3, etc.
    (*b*) Run-response tests: Have *j* users synchronously call the same program and record response times. Repeat the test for *j* = 1,2,3,etc.
    (*c*) A mixture of trivial-response and run-response tests.

Although the above kind of test is simple in principle, actual execution of it requires considerable human coordination. However, it requires no special equipment or tampering with the system itself. By judicious choice of the test programs, this method can quickly uncover many performance properties and difficulties.

It is necessary and feasible to represent complex scripts in machine-readable form so that a computer can supply them to the system under test. The procedure for translating script information into requests for service and recording the system responses may be implemented as a *program* to which the script is input data. It is even possible for the system under test to run *this* program, in which case, the system resources are not only shared by the tested scripts, but also by the mechanics of the test itself! There are some obvious problems here, such as

1. The system under test has its resources (especially main storage) diminished by the test.
2. The test procedures require tested-system time.
3. The terminals to which the script outputs should be applied may not be available.
4. Some software interface will be necessary so that the computer is shared between the test generator-recorder program and the tested system.

The first two and the last points are obvious. The third point is worth some comment. In the actual system, the user's requests typically arrive over telephone lines to the transmission-control multiplexor device connected to the computer. In most systems, it is *not* possible for the same computer to generate inputs to these terminals! Such a feature is, incidentally, valuable in system tests as well as performance measurements, but many systems do not as yet have it. Of course, the measurements can still be made using self-generated tests, but now the generated requests must be supplied to some internal system region, like the terminal buffer areas of main storage, in a form suitable for these areas.

A much purer scheme that surmounts the self-test difficulties at the expense of more hardware is to use a *separate computer* to supply the tests and to receive and record the results. A sketch of such a system is shown in Fig. 9-5.1. The test-generator computer is first loaded with its program to translate scripts to machine form and receive and record the tested system response. The scripts themselves (say in card or

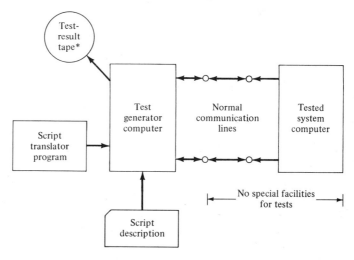

*Test-result tape processed later (so test generator computer can respond as quickly as possible during script)

Fig. 9-5.1 Using one computer to test another.

tape form) are then sent to the test-generator computer. The tested system is started up in the usual manner, and care should be taken that no human users are permitted to "sign on." Since the scripts all start with sign on, as soon as the test-generator system sends out its first messages, the tested system will start to respond. Note that a hypothetical observer at the tested system would have no way of knowing that there are not real people at the other end of the telephone lines (rather than the test-generator computer)!

9-6   A TIMESHARING SYSTEM SIMULATOR   [Refs. HE2,HE3,NI1,SH,STR]

A simple simulation model of the swapped-workspace kind of timesharing system will now be described and used to provide a concrete mechanism for investigating certain performance issues. The model is essentially a variant of the general job-processing model of Chap. 4, with the addition of certain characteristic features of computer timesharing systems like swapping.

Figure 9-6.1 shows a sketch of the resources modelled by the simulator and lists the parameters that the user must supply to the model. It is seen that up to MXM tracts may be resident in main storage (MS) concurrently. A one-way swap of a workspace between MS and AS requires ST seconds, and a CPU overhead time of PSV seconds is required to initiate a swap. Overlapped swapping is (or is not) specified ($V = 1$ or 0), and any of six schedulers is specified by SC, which may or may not be time sliced, as specified by the variable STS ($= 1$ or 0). The time slice is specified by H.

A Type I workload of the direct class (see Chap. 4) describes each tract with its time of arrival and execution time. Figure 9-6.2 shows a state diagram with the definitions of states and state transitions. Figure 9-6.3 gives some idea of the data structures used inside the simulator which, together with the state diagram of Fig. 9-6.2, can help us begin to visualize how the simulator logic is organized.

The scheduling decision selecting the tract to next receive a time slice or to be swapped into or out of MS is done at the end of each time slice or at the end of a tract. Scheduling is considered in two parts with a simple, interesting duality relationship between them. The first part, called *admission rule*, decides which tract *should* receive the next time slice. This is done by finding among the tracts eligible for service the one that has the smallest value of the scheduling variable (we assume also some suitable tie-breaking rule). When the tract has been identified, there are two major cases: (1) the tract is in MS, and (2) the tract is not in MS (being therefore in AS). In the first case, the tract is given the next time slice. In the second case, if there is an empty workspace in MS, "swap in" of the selected tract starts to that space. During swap in, if the overlapped swapping option is specified, the scheduler will apply the admission rule to those tracts in MS and select the best one for a time slice during swap in.

In the event that there is no empty space in MS, the scheduler first seeks a completed tract in MS as the tract to be swapped out. If such a tract is found, it is swapped out, and again a tract in MS may be given a time slice during this period. If there is no completed tract in MS, then the system invokes the *complementary replacement rule* to select the tract that should be swapped out from MS to AS to

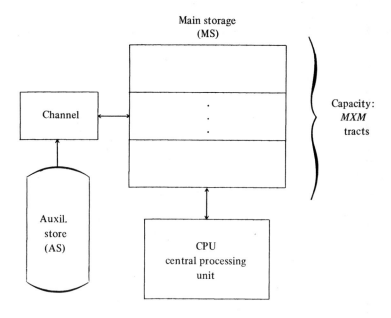

Resource Parameters

MXM = Max. no. of tracts resident in MS concurrently
ST = One-way swap time
H = Time slice
PSV = Per swap CPU overhead time
V = 0 – No overlap of swap with compute
       1 – overlap
STS = 0 – No time slicing
       1 – Time slicing
SC = Scheduler code
RB = Bias value for jobs not in MS

Workload Parameters

For each tract (I)
$A[I]$ = Time-of-tract request
$X[I]$ = Execution time

Fig. 9-6.1 Simulation model.

make room for the selected tract. This rule works as follows: The admission rule is applied to those tracts already in MS and the *poorest ranking* tract is the one selected to be swapped out (replaced). During swap out, another tract in MS may be given a time slice. Once swap out is completed, there is in effect an empty workspace in MS, and the admission rule described above is then applicable. The complementary replacement rule is not simply a single scheduling algorithm, but rather a statement *about* scheduling replacement rules. More specifically, it tells how to derive a replacement rule from a given admission rule.

Figure 9-6.4 is a flow chart of the logic of the simulator. The simulator as described thus far is a useful educational device for learning about the interrelationship

Tract states:

1. Not arrived
2. Arrived: in AS
3. In channel: AS to MS (swap in)
4. Arrived: in MS (CPU not executing)
5. CPU executing (in MS)
6. In channel: MS to AS (swap out)
7. Tract complete: in MS
8. Tract complete: in AS

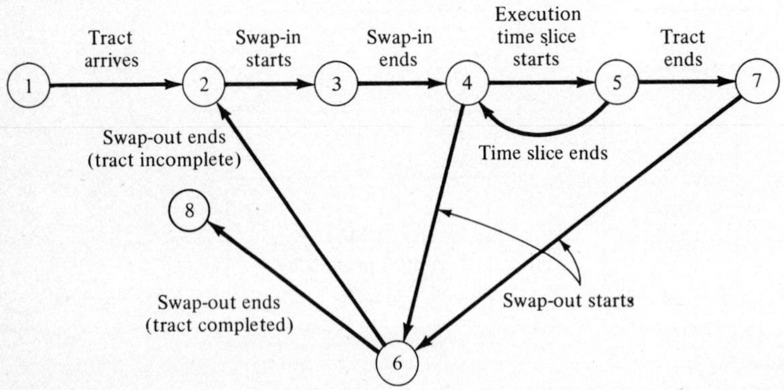

Fig. 9-6.2 State definitions and transition diagram for a tract.

Tract →

		1	2	3	4	etc.
Arrival times	*A*					
Execution times	*X*					
State vector	*S*					
Execution times complete	*P*					
Times of last slice	*L*					
Completion times	*Q*					

(*a*) Tract variables.

		Alu. 1	Chan. 2
Times of completion	*CV*		
Tracts in service	*ID*		
Utilization times	*U*		
Required execution times	*XT*		

(*b*) Resource variables.

Fig. 9-6.3 Some internal simulator variables.

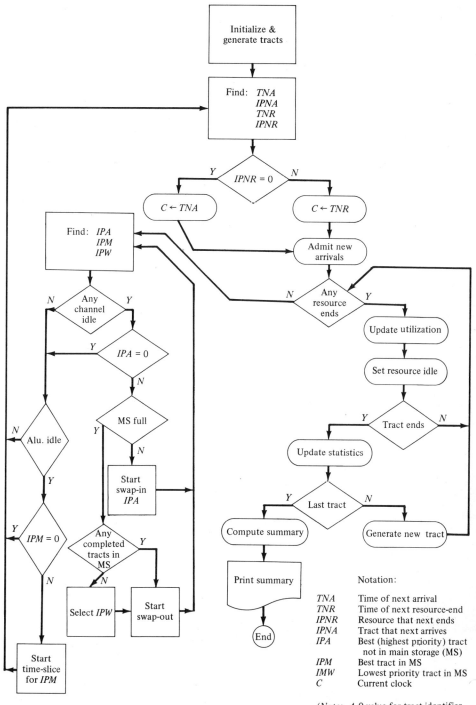

Fig. 9-6.4 Sketch of basic simulator logic.

Notation:

TNA	Time of next arrival
TNR	Time of next resource-end
IPNR	Resource that next ends
IPNA	Tract that next arrives
IPA	Best (highest priority) tract not in main storage (MS)
IPM	Best tract in MS
IMW	Lowest priority tract in MS
C	Current clock

(*Note*: *A* 0 value for tract identifier signifies no tract satisfies condition) of various system parameters. The workload description can be a stream of number pairs, each pair being an arrival time and execution time for each tract. By synthesizing a few such streams with very few tracts in each (say ten), a user can get a good feel for the effects of different scheduling algorithms, more than one workspace in MS at a time, swap times, etc.

We have now completed our description of the logic of a simulator which, through parameter selection, can simulate a class of timesharing systems. How can this simulator be used? We turn now to this important question by identifying two classes of activity that must be addressed by the designers of any simulation model:

1. Obtaining data about the workload to drive the simulator
2. Establishing confidence that the simulator gives correct and useful results

Since the simulator described earlier can, by parameter selection, be made to approximate the logic of APL's management of resources (see Sec. 9-4), this system will be used as the example in what follows.

Any practical evaluation tool, including a simulator, must be driven by some realistic representation of the workload the system actually encounters. An ideal source of such data is a software monitor (see Sec. 8-5). Our simulator requires arrival and execution times. The APL system includes a software monitor that supplies *histograms*, i.e., frequency distributions of the occurrences of various events. One of these is the cumulative frequency distribution of *think* times, i.e., interarrival times between user requests (tracts). One measured distribution is plotted in Fig. 9-6.5 together with the exponential distribution (see Chap. 5), which has the same mean value. The two functions are seen to agree quite closely.

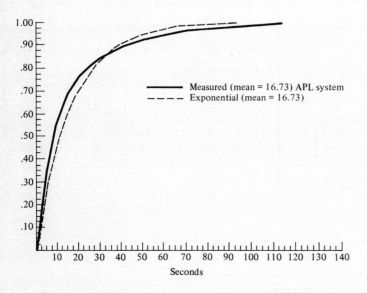

Fig. 9-6.5 Think-time cumulative relative-frequency distribution.

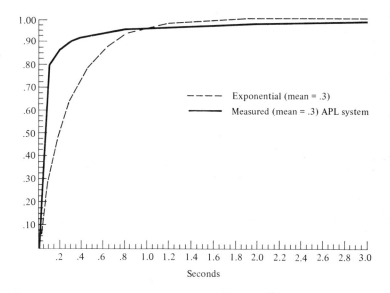

Fig. 9-6.6 Execution-time cumulative relative-frequency distribution.

Figure 9-6.6 shows a similar plot of the measured histogram of *execution times*, again with an exponential plot, but which is seen to be in poor agreement with the measured distribution. This is due to the "long tail" of the measured execution-time distribution, which indicates that execution times that are several multiples of the mean are much more common in the measured data than is predicted by the exponential law. Thus, for example, the exponential law predicts that less than 1 percent of the executions are longer than 1.8 seconds (6 times the mean). Measured data shows however that about 3 percent of the executions are in this category. Although the tail of the distribution of course represents only a small fraction of the total *number* of tracts, it often represents an appreciable fraction of the total execution *time* required by the tracts. For this reason, it is of great significance in resource use. Although as seen in Fig. 9-6.6, the measured distribution does not match a single exponential with the same mean, it has been found that a close fit is possible to a hyperexponential with about four terms.

The think- and execution-time distribution functions of Figs. 9-6.5 and 9-6.6 can be used (as described in Chap. 2) with a programmed random-number generator to supply the arrival and execution times for each simulated tract.

Having at hand the data to drive the simulator, we now turn to the second point made earlier, i.e., establishing confidence in the logic of the simulator. One way to do this is to verify that it gives the same results as obtained by mathematical analysis. This kind of test is, of course, a necessary but *not* a sufficient test of the simulator logic, since it usually involves model degeneration, that is, using a highly simplified case of the model for which an analytic solution exists (Sec. 5-8). Figure 9-6.7 shows the results of use of the simulator in this way. Two schedulers, RR and FIFO, were used with exponential arrival- and execution-time distributions. The analytic and simulated results are seen to be very close.

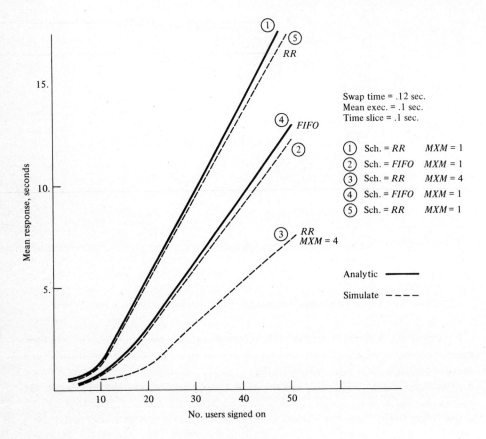

Fig. 9-6.7 Comparison of simulated and analytic results.

Another and more important way to establish confidence in a simulator is to compare its results with *measured* results. One of the first choices to be made here is the set of variable values to be compared. For example, it is possible to select a variable that is rather *insensitive* (or as the statisticians say, *robust*) to many of the system parameters that determine performance. It is then relatively easy to obtain good agreement between measurement and simulation. Conversely, it is possible to choose variables for comparison that are quite sensitive to many system parameters. Excellent agreement will now be difficult because small differences between the model and the system will produce large differences in the selected variable values. In what follows, we have chosen variables that are (1) most-significant indicators of performance (given the objectives of a timesharing system), and (2) available as measured values from the APL system. These variables are quite sensitive to system parameters, so that appreciable differences between measured and simulated results are to be expected and are observed. Perhaps more important than actual agreement between values are closeness of function shape and tracking of trends, all of which are quite good, as will now be seen. The measurements were taken on an IBM S/360 Mod 50 running only APL with 55 signed-on users.

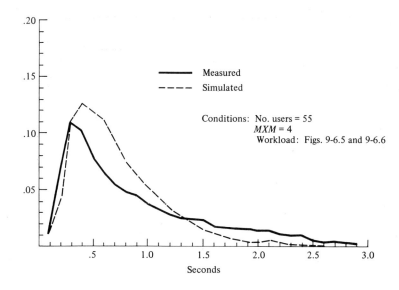

Fig. 9-6.8   Reaction-time relative frequency distribution.

Figure 9-6.8 shows measured and simulated reaction-time distributions. *Reaction time* is defined as the time between tract arrival and first time slice. Figure 9-6.9 shows the cumulative relative distributions of execute/elapsed times, i.e., the reciprocal of the "stretch factors." Thus, for example, the point on solid curve (10%, .7) means that "70 percent of the (measured) tracts had execute/elapsed time ratios of .1 or less." In other words, 70 percent of the tracts had stretch factors of 10 or more times.

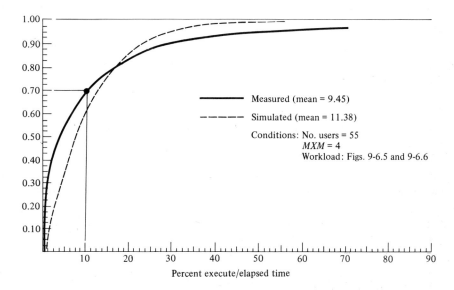

Fig. 9-6.9   Percent execute/elapsed times cumulative relative-frequency distribution.

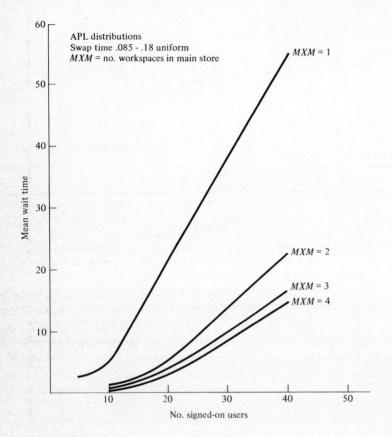

Fig. 9-6.10 Simulated APL performance with various numbers of workspaces in main store.

Both Figs. 9-6.8 and 9-6.9 give performance measures for all tracts together. It is recalled from our earlier discussions that the success of a timesharing system depends most critically on its ability to service trivial tracts (and other short ones) quickly. How well does APL do this? We can begin to get some idea by noticing from Fig. 9-6.6 that about 80 percent of the tracts are in the trivial category that requires one time slice (.1 second in this system) or less of execution time. Figure 9-6.8 indicates that most requests receive their *first* time slice (the only one the trivial tracts require) in less than 1 second. These facts strongly indicate that APL is very responsive to trivial requests. It can be shown that this characteristic degrades only very slowly with the number of signed-on users (unlike the response to long nontrivial tracts). All these observations are qualitatively confirmed by the experience of APL users.

Figure 9-6.10 shows the results of a simulator study to determine the effects of keeping more workspaces in main storage concurrently (but with only two swapping channels). It is seen that for the same number of signed-on users, performance improves greatly from one to two resident workspaces, but the improvements beyond that (say for *MXM* from 3 to 4) are marginal.

No. Signed-on users	30	30	50	50	30	30	50	50
CPU Speed factor	4	4	4	4	1	1	1	1
MXM (Max. no. in MS)	2	3	2	3	2	3	2	3
Mean think time	16.75	16.75	16.75	16.75	16.75	16.75	16.75	16.75
Mean execute time	0.08	0.08	0.07	0.08	0.28	0.29	0.21	0.25
Mean wait time	0.44	0.34	1.30	0.73	1.37	0.80	5.69	2.44
Mean queue length	0.85	0.66	0.82	2.2	2.86	1.82	15.35	7.48
Mean new queue length	0.5	0.5	2.0	1.9	0.7	0.6	1.3	1.7
Fig. of merit	0.41	0.43	0.18	0.21	0.37	0.42	0.17	0.20
Thruput	2.99	3.28	2.96	3.40	1.95	2.28	2.05	2.58
% CPU utilization	17	17	27	28	52	55	58	79
% channel utilization	50	46	84	77	63	54	88	89
% overlap	9	9	17	20	33	34	45	69

Conditions for all runs in this table:

No. tracts/run = 2000
Workload = APL distributions (see Figs. 9-6.5 and 9-6.6)
Time slice = 0.1 second
Swap times = 0.025 to 0.25 second
Per-swap CPU overhead = 0.01 second
Channel interference = 0.15

Fig. 9-6.11 Representative simulation results.

Figure 9-6.11 gives a summary table showing the effects of selected variations in

1. Number of signed-on users
2. CPU speed factors
3. Number of resident workspaces

on mean wait time, queue length, new queue length (new arrivals), figure-of-merit (short job), thruput, resource utilization, and overlap. It shows the type of summary display that is useful in making judgments about major system-design parameters.

9-7 IBM TIMESHARING OPTION (TSO) FOR SYSTEM/360/370
[Refs. IB1,IB2,IB3,LE,MA,SC2]

The main idea of this system, first released in 1971, is to provide the extensive facilities of IBM's general-purpose Operating System (OS/360) in a timesharing mode. TSO also gives its interactive users access to certain language facilities designed especially for the timesharing environment and not provided in the batch system. However, the user may choose to develop programs completely compatible with OS batch. Batch runs may be initiated from a terminal, and the system can run a batch workload concurrently with servicing the timesharing (foreground) jobs.

We shall now briefly describe TSO in two contexts. The first considers facilities available to each individual user, and the second covers the resource-management and sharing-scheduling aspects.

Single-user facilities

Each user sees TSO first via a *command language* that performs the same functions as the job control language in the batch system, but which is extended and "humanized" for the timesharing environment. The command language includes:

1. EDIT commands for conveniently entering, storing, displaying, and modifying stored information called *data-sets*. Edit facilities include both context-search and line-number referencing.
2. Commands to associate data-set names and names used in programs (file names) to achieve late binding of stored objects and devices to program names.
3. Execution of programs.

A significant feature is the ability to *store sequences of commands* as *command procedures* (i.e., subroutines in the command language). These are the counterparts of OS JCL-cataloged procedures (see Chap. 8). Each such sequence is given a name and may be supplied parameters that are much the same as in the usual subroutine-linking or macro-call manner. In fact, the syntax of the TSO command language closely resembles the OS Assembler Macro Language. A command procedure may process both positional and key-word (self-identifying) parameters. The latter may be assigned "standard" (i.e., default) values. For example, consider the following *header* of a stored command procedure called (say) PLICLGO (this name is not included in the procedure itself)

PROC 1,&X, SYS1 (*), SYS2 (*)

The writer of this procedure has specified by the "1" that there is one positional parameter; its name is *X* (the first name following the number). The SYS1 and SYS2 are key-word parameter names, their default values are *, which is the symbol for the terminal as a device. Thus, a user may call this procedure (named PLICLGO) by statements like

PLICLGO STAT SYS1 (DATA)

or

PLICLGO STAT

In the first case, the procedure is invoked, the name STAT will replace X everywhere it appears in the procedure, and the name DATA will be used wherever SYS1 appears in the procedure. Note that since no mention of SYS2 was made in the call, each time it appears in the procedure, its default value * (meaning the terminal) will be used. To summarize, the first above version calls the command procedure named PLICLGO which, with the above PROC header, can result in (say) compilation then execution of the program stored in the data-set named STAT. This program expects input data from the data-set named DATA and gives its output at the terminal. The second above version of the call is similar, but because SYS1 is also omitted, input data as well as output data devices are both defaulted to the terminal.

The idea of stored command procedures is very important. It not only relieves tedium in repeating commonly used sequences, but it also permits language subsystems to be built and supplied to application-oriented users who have little interest and knowledge of internal system operations. Such subsystems may be programmed by IBM or, more commonly, by installation system programmers. Even ordinary users may, if they desire, construct their own command procedures.

At this writing (1975), experience with TSO's command language indicates its great potential, which is presently somewhat marred by certain oversights in its architecture. TSO provides, at optional charge, three language versions intended for interactive use: ITF/BASIC, ITF/PL/I, and code-and-go FORTRAN. All feature line-by-line syntax checking at entry time and other debugging facilities.

The standard OS/360 compilers for FORTRAN, COBOL, PL/I, ALGOL, and Assembler are also available. OS sequential-access methods (BSAM and QSAM) may be directed to the terminal. Some of the processors are offered in somewhat modified versions for the timesharing environment. A TEST command permits START/STOP and trace of running programs from the terminal. Unfortunately, this tool does *not* offer source-language debugging. Since outputs are in machine language, the user must eventually translate TEST outputs to symbolic outputs using a symbol table.

Resource management in TSO*

To begin to understand resource management in TSO, consider Fig. 9-7.1, which shows the major objects as they appear in a logical hierarchy. The central resource scheduler is called the *driver*. It communicates with all other major control functions through its *timesharing interface program*. The driver receives reports about both task and resource states and, together with certain parameters specified by the installation, decides on which job should be swapped into and out of storage and how much CPU time each should receive (more on this later). The driver also is a major control over the batch (background) component of the workload.

The flow of system control may be roughly traced using Fig. 9-7.1. Consider the system just after the system operator has started MVT, but before he has started TSO. He starts TSO by giving a command that initiates a system program called the *time sharing control task* (TSC), which can further communicate with him (to accept parameters) and can also initiate a *region control task* (RCT) for *each* foreground region. Each RCT in turn can call a copy of the LOGON scheduler in response to a LOGON command entered from a terminal. The LOGON scheduler accepts the information in the user's LOGON message and also has access to a data-set called the *user attribute data set* (UADS) that contains prestored information about each authorized user (account number, LOGON passwords, etc.). Included in the UADS is the name of an OS JCL (job control language) cataloged procedure called the LOGON procedure. A LOGON procedure specifies a single OS job step, and for this reason each TSO session from LOGON to LOGOFF at any single terminal is considered as a single-step OS job. It may be recalled from Chap. 8 that a job step is specified in JCL by one EXEC statement followed by several DD statements. The EXEC statement specifies a program to be executed. In the case of a LOGON procedure (Fig. 9-7.2), the program thus called is one for interpreting all terminal

---

* For more details on this topic, see Ref. IB3, pp. 37-52.

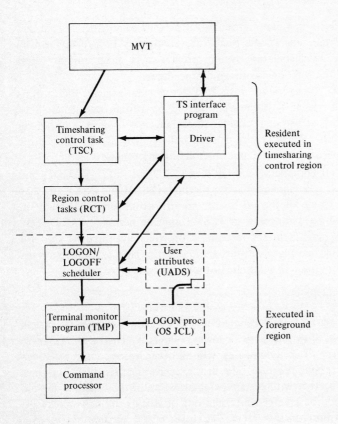

Fig. 9-7.1 Logical hierarchy of control in TSO.

```
//NFSPROC     EXEC     PGM=IKJEFTO1,ROLL=(NO,NO)
//SYSUDUMP    DD       SYSOUT=R
//SYSHELP     DD       DSN=SYS1.HELP,DISP=SHR
//SYSEDIT     DD       DSN=&EDIT,UNIT=SYSDA,SPACE=(1688,(50,20))
//SYSPROC     DD       DSN=SYS1.CMDPROC,DISP=SHR
//DD1         DD       DYNAM
//DD2         DD       DYNAM
//DD3         DD       DYNAM
//DD4         DD       DYNAM
//DD5         DD       DYNAM
//DD6         DD       DYNAM
//DD7         DD       DYNAM
//DD8         DD       DYNAM
//DD9         DD       DYNAM
//DD10        DD       DYNAM
```

Fig. 9-7.2 A typical LOGON procedure.

commands that the user will enter during the session. Although this interpreter program may be written by the user for his specific purposes, we shall assume (as is often the case) that the program called is the one supplied by IBM, called the *terminal monitor program* (TMP). The TMP may be thought of as a "local supervisor," since it interprets user commands (it may call a command interpreter for syntax analysis) and starts the process of calling whatever programs are needed to satisfy the commands. In addition to the EXEC statement, the LOGON-cataloged procedure specifies several DD statements (for reserving disk space and binding data-sets to names) that will be needed during the user session. Each user may have several LOGON procedures in his catalog; their names are stored in his UADS and he specifies which one he wishes in his LOGON message (or one is supplied by default). All of these events connected with LOGON may be thought of as a way to get each user's "private" logical machine specified and started.

Figure 9-7.3 gives a summary of each of the logical objects. Figure 9-7.4 shows the layout of main storage in a typical TSO system with one foreground and one background region. Note that most of the areas are those required by OS MVT. The new ones include the timesharing control region holding most of the permanently resident TSO system programs and, of course, the foreground region. Note that the latter is divided into two parts; one is assigned from the top down and the other from the bottom up. The second of these is called the *local system queue area* and is reserved for storing control-block information connected with the current activity in the region; this will be swapped out (and later swapped back in) along with the other valid information in the region. (Only that part of the region that contains valid information is swapped.)

One major performance issue can be discussed using Fig. 9-7.4. The *extended link-pack area* in the timesharing control region holds copies of commonly used system programs needed by TSO users. As in any conventional (nonvirtual storage) OS system, each installation must specify how much space is to be used for this purpose and which routines and data are to be made resident there. Since any routines not resident here will have to be fetched from disk (or drum) for each use, the selection of high-activity modules is essential for good performance. The manufacturer supplies some suggestions to help an installation get started. However, good performance requires use of a software monitor to identify the best collection of modules to make resident. This is perhaps the primary performance issue in an OS-like system that features highly modularized and complex data and program structures. Unless residences are chosen very judiciously, I/O activity for OS data management (still very much a part of TSO) may play a greater role in device contention than swapping.

We now turn to another important performance issue, i.e., the scheduling of terminal jobs into main storage (called *major time slicing* or servicing) and the scheduling of the CPU among the jobs already in main storage (including background jobs). TSO's control programs (driver and TSC) schedule movement of information between the foreground region(s) and a swap device. Only the actually used part of a region, called the *swap load,* is actually swapped, and *swap out is started only after any ongoing nonterminal I/O involving the region is completed,* a process called *quiescing.* Buffer space for each terminal is kept permanently resident in main storage

Object	Abbr.	Type	Number	Active residence	Major functions
Driver	–	System program	One per system	T.S. control region	Master resource allocator for TSO and batch
Timesharing control task	TSC	System program	One per system	T.S. control region	1. Starts RCT's 2. Communicates with TSO system operator 3. Controls swapping
Region control task	RCT	System program	One per foreground region	T.S. control region	1. Quiescing control 2. Starts LOGON/LOGOFF procedures
Terminal monitor program	TMP	System or user program	One per signed-on user	Foreground region	Interprets commands directly from terminal, calls command processor
User attribute data-set	UADS	Partition of data-set	One per authorized user	Disk	1. Names of LOGON procedures 2. Account number, LOGON passwords 3. User profile
LOGON procedure	–	OS JCL cataloged procedure	One or more per user	Disk	Starts TMP, specifies data-sets needed in terminal session (including procedures)
Command procedure	–	Partition of data-set	Any	Disk	Stored subroutine of commands that: 1. Calls system and user programs to execution 2. Reserves space 3. Binds data-sets (names of physical space) to files (program names)

Fig. 9-7.3 Important system objects in TSO.

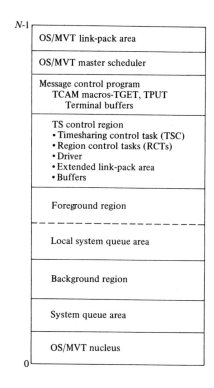

Fig. 9-7.4 Main-storage layout for typical
TSO system.

(as is done in APL) so that terminal messages may proceed even when a user's region is swapped out. Thus, there is no need for quiescing terminal I/O.

Scheduling of the vital resources of CPU and a main-storage region center on two scheduling time intervals. The first is called a job's *major time slice*, which is defined as the time the job gets to remain in main storage between its swap in and its next swap out. The second, called its *minor time slice* is the maximum contiguous time the CPU is allocated to a currently resident job. Both types of time slice depend on several parameters, some of which are supplied by the Installation (system programmers) and others of which are measured by the system itself. A collection of specific parameter values will be called a *logical queue*. A collection of user jobs with a common logical queue constitute a queue of jobs to be serviced. In TSO, "servicing a job" refers only to swapping it into a main-storage region. A logical queue is, therefore, a collection of scheduling parameters that determine the major time slice of every job that belongs to the queue. Note that there may be several queues on a single main-storage region. The jobs awaiting service on any single queue are serviced in round-robin order. However, TSO may maintain several queues so that jobs may be assigned different classes of service. We shall shortly discuss in some detail the scheduling parameters that determine a logical queue, how a job gets assigned to a queue, and how it may be moved among queues. Before doing so, we must mention that the scheduling of minor slices (i.e., CPU time slices) to those jobs currently in main storage (and ready to run) also depends on certain scheduling parameters, as will be described later.

As indicated above, each main-storage region may have several queues of jobs. Any given queue is managed by reference to fixed values assigned by the Installation to the following parameters that can only be changed manually:

$A_{R,Q}$ = average service time for jobs in the queue
$M_{R,Q}$ = minimum major time slice
$SL_{R,Q}$ = swap-load limit
$IL_{R,Q}$ = interaction time limit
$SC_{R,Q}$ = number of service cycles before advance to the next queue

An additional parameter $(N_{R,Q})$ is determined by the system from time to time. It denotes the number of ready jobs in the queue. $A_{R,Q}$ is the time interval between two successive swap ins of any given job in the queue. The purpose of $M_{R,Q}$ is to ensure that jobs on the queue remain in main storage long enough so that some productive work is done on each. $SL_{R,Q}$ measures the maximum amount of main storage that jobs on this queue may require. $IL_{R,Q}$ is the maximum total time in main storage permitted since the user's last request for service. Any specific set of these four values describes the nature of a class of jobs' scheduling properties. From the above parameters for a queue, the scheduler computes the major time slice for each job on the queue as follows:

$$T_{R,Q} = \text{Max}\left(M_{R,Q}, \frac{A_{R,Q}}{N_{R,Q}}\right)$$

Each job is then kept in main storage for the time $T_{R,Q}$; all jobs in the queue are serviced in this way in round-robin order. After $SC_{R,Q}$ cycles on the current queue, the next queue is serviced.

The limit parameters SL_R and $IL_{R,Q}$, if exceeded by a job, cause the system to seek a new queue for the job that can contain that job's parameters. The new queue must be on the same region, since the lack of dynamic relocation in System/360 does not permit a program to be moved to a new region once its execution starts. Such a new queue will, however, in general specify different values for the other parameters. For example, consider two queues as follows:

	Q1	Q2
A	1	10
M	.2	1
SL	100k	100k
IL	.1	5

Here, Q1 with its small IL and A values is clearly intended for rapid swapping to service highly interactive requests, while Q2 is intended for jobs already found to be fairly long. Note that the large A value will tend to retain Q2 jobs in main storage longer, thus giving them a better chance for productive CPU work between swap ins.

Of the jobs occupying the TSO regions of main storage at a given time that are ready to execute (i.e., not waiting on I/O) one is selected (*dispatched*) for a CPU interval called a *minor time slice*. TSO permits the systems people running the system to specify some guaranteed percentage of total CPU time for the batch workload. The remaining CPU time is called *foreground time*, and it is the subdivision of this time into minor time slices that will now be described.

The time available for foreground CPU time may be allocated into minor time slices according to any one of three schemes (selected by system programmers):

1. *Simple dispatching:* The minor time slice is set equal to the foreground time; this time is given to the highest priority job (i.e., the job swapped in the longest time ago). *Simple* dispatching is always used whenever only one foreground region is used in the system.
2. *Even dispatching:* The minor time slice is the foreground time divided by the number of ready foreground jobs in main storage.
3. *Weighted dispatching:* The system computes an estimated wait-time percentage for each job based on its past behavior with respect to I/O wait (not counting terminal I/O, which does not require swap in). The longer the estimated I/O wait time, the longer the minor slice that is computed. This compensates for the parts of a time slice that I/O-bound jobs will lose to CPU-bound jobs due to I/O wait.

9-8 THE G.E. INFORMATION SERVICE NETWORK [Ref. GE]

Until now we have discussed timesharing of a single CPU system to which several users may be connected via telephone lines. Such systems are in common use to service a single organization's needs, where the same equipment is often shared with a batch workload. A somewhat different type of marketing scheme is the case where a company offers timesharing services on a subscription basis to anyone having access to a terminal.

The General Electric Company's *information services network* is a subscription service composed of an equipment and software configuration designed to service many remote users; subsets of these may or may not belong to the same organization and may or may not share common information (like user files). Furthermore, the system resources (as well as the users) may be widely dispersed geographically and may change in time with minimum disruption to subscribers. Such a system is sometimes called an *information utility* because in many ways it resembles other utilities like those that supply electric power, telephone communications, etc. Each user, considered as a subscriber, only pays for the facilities he uses (including his share of space time of central facilities), but he is shielded from the burden and responsibility of heavy investment, development, and management of system resources. The organization supplying these earns its revenue by providing acceptable user services.

Figure 9-8.1 shows a fragment of the network to illustrate some principles of the communication configuration. Starting at the user end, terminals (not shown) connect to a small computer (GE 235) in the locality by dialing an appropriate telephone number. Once connected, all communication (from a hardware viewpoint) is directly with the GE 235, which can service several terminals in the locality (like Chicago,

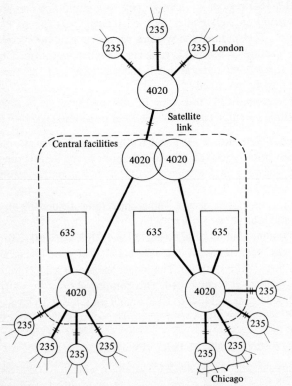

Fig. 9-8.1 Sketch of a fragment of G.E. information services network (c1972).

Illinois). The local computer serves as a *concentrator* of messages. It accumulates (buffers) incoming (and outgoing) messages from several local lines and eventually transmits the messages to a single long-distance *leased* telephone line that reaches the site of the central computer (say in Cleveland, Ohio). At the central-computer location, another computer (4020) deconcentrates the messages, performs error checking (and requests retransmit if errors are found), and forwards the messages to a G.E. 635 central-computer system. This description has been in terms of messages inbound from terminals to the computer; a similar process is done in the outbound direction. As mentioned in the introduction to this chapter, the line concentrator can substantially reduce telephone charges by efficiently sharing a single leased line. Each user directly pays only local telephone charges (a share of the leased line is included in his subscription rate).

Some other features of the network evident from Fig. 9-8.1 are worth noting. Subscribers in the same city may reach any of several concentrator computers, each with direct access to a specific central facility; this is seen on the diagram in the case of two concentrators in Chicago. Each central concentrator computer (4020) is connected to others in such a way that each computer-processing facility can communicate with every other one, and each user's terminal can in principle reach any of the several central computers.

One of the potentially great advantages of a network is the ability to pool resources so that they may be partitioned in different ways as the actual demands develop. There are several possible ways that this may conceivably be done; we now mention some of these for the G.E. network. As of this writing (mid 1972), each subscriber's account number is associated with file storage at a particular G.E. 635 system location. This association is done automatically by the system so that services for a given subscriber number are *not* moved between systems automatically. However, in making the assignments, an attempt is made to load balance the system by assigning the subscriber number to a 635 whose load is relatively light. Another useful load-balance factor is the time difference between various geographic locations (i.e., New York is 3 hours later than Los Angeles) so that business days, and hence activities, are staggered.

Thus far we have discussed only the communications aspects of the G.E. network. A brief description will now be given of the facilities available to individual users, with emphasis on those features not found in the APL or TSO systems discussed previously.

The system presently supplies three languages: BASIC, FORTRAN, and REMAPT (a previous version also provided ALGOL). BASIC is a FORTRAN-like language originally designed at Dartmouth College and since greatly expanded to include file handling and character-string manipulation operators (among other types). Both BASIC and FORTRAN use compiler translators. REMAPT is a language for conveniently describing parts; the descriptions are translated into programs for numerically controlled machine tools. A central program library is available to all users and includes statistical programs, scientific computation programs, management games, etc. A convenient *text editor* facility is available for easily creating, displaying, and modifying source programs and data. Rather extensive files may be kept on disk (the user pays for what he uses by the kilobyte per month). The *file system*, holding both programs and data, is notable for its careful attention to security and privacy features. For example, when a file is deleted by a user, its contents are overwritten to prevent the new user assigned this space from inadvertently reading the file. It is relatively easy to design a secure file system as long as shared access is not also required. The G.E. system provides *both* sharing *and* security. First, some security is provided by the usual password scheme. A password may be assigned by the user to a file; access requires the password as well as the file name. Second, user X may give *permission* to selected other users (or exclude them) to access X's files. Four types of access may be specified by a PERMIT command

EXECUTE
READ (implies EXECUTE)

WRITE (implies APPEND)

APPEND

The PERMIT status may be changed only by the X user.

There has been no published description of the G.E. network. Informally at this writing, it is said to contain twelve G.E. 635 computers. Each of these has a memory-cycle time of 1 microsecond (36 bits) and a fixed-point ADD/SUBTRACT/ COMPARE time of 1.9 microseconds. A 635 machine has an interrupt system, privileged mode, and a single address register for relocation (and protection). Drums are among the devices that can be attached; each drum has 4.7 million bytes, an average access of 18 microseconds, and a 370 kbyte/second transmission rate. Fixed-head and removable disks may also be attached. Some of these devices are undoubtedly included in the system.

No system configuration or performance information has been published. Informally, it has been learned that the network presently serves about 1000 users concurrently with "comfortable" response times.

REFERENCES AND BIBLIOGRAPHY

1. [AN] Anderson, H.A., and R.G. Sargent: A Statistical Evaluation of the Scheduler of an Experimental Interactive Computing System, in "Statistical Computer Performance Evaluation," W. Freiberger, ed., Academic Press, New York, 1972.
2. [BA] Bard, Y.: Performance Criteria and Measurement for a Time-Sharing System, *IBM Systems Journal*, vol. 10, no. 3, 1971.
3. [BE] Bernstein, A.J. and J.C. Sharp: A Policy-Driven Scheduler for a Time-Sharing System, *Comm. ACM*, vol. 14, no. 2, February, 1971.
4. [BL] Blatny, J., S.R. Clark, and T.A. Rourke: On The Optimization of Performance of Time-Sharing Systems by Simulation, *Comm. ACM*, vol. 15, no. 6, June, 1972.
5. [BRE] Breed, L.M. and R.H. Lathwell: APL/360, IBM Contributed Program Library Document 360D-03.3.007, 1968.
6. [BRY] Bryan, G.E.: JOSS 20,000 Hours at a Console: A Statistical Survey, *AFIPS Conf. Proc.*, *FJCC*, vol. 31, pp. 769-778, 1967.
7. [CO1] Coffman, E.G. and L. Kleinrock: Computer Scheduling Methods and Their Countermeasures, *AFIPS Proc.*, *SJCC*, vol. 32, 1968.
8. [COR] Corbato, F.J. et al.: An Experimental Time-Sharing System, *AFIPS Conf. Proc.*, *SJCC*, vol. 21, pp. 335-344, 1962.
9. [DO] Doherty, W.J.: Scheduling TSS/360 for Responsiveness, *AFIPS Conf. Proc.*, vol. 37, pp. 97-111, 1970.
10. [GE] General Electric Co.: Mark II Command System Reference Manual, No. 711223E, General Electric Co. Information Services Dept., 7735 Old Georgetown Rd., Bethesda, Maryland 20014.
11. [GO] Gold, M.M.: Time-Sharing and Batch Processing: An Experimental Comparison of Their Values in a Problem Solving Situation, *Comm. ACM*, vol. 12, no. 5, May, 1969.
12. [HE1] Hellerman, H.: A Personalized Array Translator System, *Comm. ACM*, vol. 7, no. 7, July, 1964.
13. [HE2] Hellerman, H.: Some Principles of Time-Sharing Scheduler Strategies, *IBM Systems Journal*, vol. 8, no. 2, 1969.
14. [HE3] Hellerman, H., and Y. Ron: A Time-Sharing System Simulation and Its Validation, *IBM Tech. Report 320-2984*, *IBM New York Scientific Center*, April, 1970.

15. [HE4] Hellerman, H.: Complementary Replacement—A Meta Scheduling Principle, *Second ACM Symposium on Operating System Principles,* Princeton University, 43-46, October 20-22, 1969.

16. [IB1] IBM Corp: "IBM System/360 Operating System: Time-Sharing Option: Command Language," No. GC28-6732, IBM Corp. Data Processing Division, White Plains, N.Y. 10604.

17. [IB2] IBM Corp: "IBM System/360 Operating System: Time-Sharing Option: Terminal User's Guide," No. GC28-6763, IBM Corp. Data Processing Division, White Plains, N.Y. 10604.

18. [IB3] IBM Corp: "IBM System/360 Operating System Time-Sharing Option Planning for TSO," No. GC28-6698, IBM Corp. Data Processing Division, White Plains, N.Y. 10604.

19. [IV] Iverson, K.E.: "A Programming Language," John Wiley and Sons, New York, 1963.

20. [LA] Lampson, B.W.: A Scheduling Philosophy for Multiprocessing Systems, *Comm. ACM,* vo. II, no. 5, May, 1968.

21. [LE] Levy, D., A. Kellerman, H. Hellerman, and J. Kaufman: MIN/TSO Primer, State University of New York at Binghamton, 1972.

22. [MA] Maranzano, B.J., and B.J. DiMarisco: TSO Performance Analysis Routines User Guide, SHARE Document No. 360D04.4.012.

23. [MA1] Martin, J.: "Design of Real-Time Computer Systems," Prentice-Hall, New York, 1967.

24. [NI1] Nielson, N.R.: The Simulation of Time-Sharing Systems, *Comm. ACM,* vol. 10, no. 7, pp. 397-412, 1967.

25. [NI2] Nielson, N.R.: Computer Simulation of Computer System Performance, *Proc. ACM,* 22nd Natl. Conf., pp. 581-590, August, 1967.

26. [OP] Oppenheimer, G., and N. Weizer: Resource Management for a Medium Scale Time-Sharing System," *Comm. of the ACM 11,* no. 5, pp. 313-322, May, 1968.

27. [PI] Pinkerton, T.B.: Performance Monitoring In a Time-Shared System, *Comm. ACM,* vol. 12, no. 11, November, 1969.

28. [SA1] Sackman, H.: Time-Sharing vs. Batch Processing: The Experimental Evidence, *AFIPS Conf. Proc., SJCC,* vol. 32, pp. 1-10, 1968.

29. [SA2] Sackman, H.: "Man-Computer Problem Solving; Experimental Evaluation of Time-Sharing and Batch Processing," Auerbach Publishing Co., New York, 1970.

30. [SC1] Scherr, A.L.: "An Analysis of Time-Shared Computer Systems," MIT Press, Cambridge, Mass., 1967.

31. [SC2] Scherr, A.L. and D.C. Larkin: Time-Sharing for OS, *AFIPS Proc., FJCC,* vol. 34, 1970.

32. [SC3] Schatzoff, M., R. Tsao, and R. Wiig: An Experimental Comparison of Time-Sharing and Batch Processing, *Comm. ACM,* vol. 10, no. 5, pp. 261-265, May, 1967.

33. [SH] Shemer, J.E. and D.W. Heying: Performance Modelling and Empirical Measurement in a System Designed for Batch and Time-Sharing Users, *AFIPS Conf. Proc.,* vol. 35, pp. 17-26, 1969.

34. [SM] Smith, L.B.: A Comparison of Batch Processing and Instant Turnaround, *Comm. ACM,* vol. 10, no. 8, August, 1967.

35. [ST1] Stimler, S. and K.A. Brons: A Methodology for Calculating and Optimizing Real-Time System Performance, *Comm. ACM,* vol, 11, no. 7, pp. 509-516, July, 1968.

36. [ST2] Stimler, S.: Some Criteria for Time-Sharing System Performance, *Comm. ACM,* vol. 12, no. 1, January, 1969.

37. [STR] Strauss, J.C.: A Simple Thruput and Response Model of EXEC 8 under Swapping Saturation, *AFIPS Conf. Proc.,* vol. 39, pp. 29-49, 1971.

38. [TO] Totaro, J.B.: Real-Time Processing Power: A Standardized Evaluation, *Comput. Autom.,* vol. 17, no. 4, pp. 16-19, April, 1967.

39. [WA] Watson, R.W.: "Time-Sharing System Design Concepts," McGraw-Hill Book Company, New York, 1970.

CHAPTER 10

Virtual-Storage Principles

The equipment of every computer system includes several types of storage devices that differ in speed and cost per unit of stored information. This variety is the result of a persistent fact of technology—cheap storage is slow and fast storage is relatively expensive. For this reason, most computer systems are composed of a *storage hierarchy* consisting of a small fast store, a larger, slower and cheaper store, and a still greater capacity and cheaper-type storage, etc. A simple familiar example is the two-level configuration of main storage and auxiliary storage. The faster-member main storage presently has access times in the microsecond range and is typically built with all-electronic technology, such as magnetic cores or solid-state integrated circuitry. The slower member is typically an electronic-mechanical configuration, such as a magnetic drum or disk with access times in milliseconds. The main store is so called because instructions and the data they reference must, at the moment of execution, be in main storage. The total logical storage required by a program and its data may well exceed the space available in main storage. The total storage needed by a program is provided on auxiliary storage, and copies of pieces of this totality are moved from auxiliary to main storage prior to execution of each such piece. The processed pieces are moved in the opposite direction to save results and to permit other pieces of the total problem to have their turn for processing. The strategy of selecting the pieces (and related operations) has aptly been called *folding* and is a common operation done one way or another in every computer system. From a speed and performance viewpoint, folding operations should be governed by the principle that the most-frequently accessed instruction and data bytes should occupy main storage most of the time.

In conventional (nonvirtual) storage systems, folding has been the responsibility of each individual problem programmer. As discussed in Chaps. 7 and 8, system programs like I/O macros and the compilers for high-level languages shield the problem programmer from many of the details of I/O operations, which is a major technique used to fold programs. However, the problem programmer must still plan and write his program, assuming some definite size of main storage that must be no larger than the physical main store, and he must specify when and where in the program (if not how) information is to be moved between main and auxiliary storage. Examples of folding operations performed by programmers in conventional systems include:

1. Dividing a large program into *multiple job steps* that are processed sequentially, with no step larger than available main-storage space.
2. Creating an *overlay structure* for a program (i.e., a procedure) that is too large for available main storage. Overlays are specified by the programmer who divides the large program into parts and preplans what parts must concurrently reside in main storage. This structure is then declared to the compiler or linkage editor in appropriate control statements.
3. Using "spill" files or work files for data, such as large tables, that won't fit into main storage.
4. Creating intermediate data files to pass data from one job step to another.

A common class of program that often requires extensive folding is a compiler, especially one for modern, complex high-level languages. The logical functions performed by a compiler, together with its algorithm for optimizing the object code, can result in a very large program (say 500k bytes or more). To make such a large program fit into a reasonable size of main storage, the compiler is divided into phases. During compilation, only a single phase (or possibly a few) resides in main storage at a time to process the source program. The phase structuring of compilers is a type of overlay technique.

The programmer's time and effort required to fold programs manually is considerable (for estimates see *Sayre* [Ref. SA] and is an ample incentive to develop a class of resource-management functions called a *virtual system* that *automatically folds* data and programs between two or more levels of storage. There are also other advantages to automatic folding that will be discussed in the next section.

ATLAS, the first practical virtual-storage system, was a joint venture of Britain's Manchester University and the Ferranti Company in the early 1960s. Several other firms, including Burroughs, Xerox (then Scientific Data Systems), IBM, RCA, and G.E. (in affiliation with MIT), introduced virtual-storage systems in the mid 1960s. The larger Burroughs systems during this period used the concept intensively. In 1965, IBM announced the System/360 Mod 67, a Mod 65 with special hardware for virtual storage. The original virtual-storage operating system for the Model 67 was called TSS (Time Sharing System). As its name implies, TSS was designed for timesharing as well as virtual storage, although as mentioned in Chap. 1, timesharing and virtual storage are independent properties. In about the same time period, MIT, in conjunction with

G.E., announced the development of Multics (Multiplexed Information and Computing System). Multics is an operating system that provides virtual storage on a G.E.
(now Honeywell) 645, a specially modified version of the G.E. 635. Another IBM
effort, the M44 system, was built using a specially modified 7044 computer. It served
as a research tool at the IBM Research Lab in Yorktown, N.Y. from 1966 to 1969.
This project, conducted by R. A. Nelson, R. W. O'Neill, D. Sayre, F. Gustavson,
B. Brawn, L. A. Belady, and others, explored the virtual-storage (automatic folding)
concept in a fairly systematic manner without commercial development pressures.
Many of the M44 concepts were used in CP-67, developed at the IBM Cambridge,
Mass. Scientific Center. This virtual machine-operating system has gained several Mod
67 users. It is a direct ancestor of IBM's VM/370 system announced in 1972. Another
Mod 67 virtual system that achieved some success was the University of Michigan's
MTS system.

The experience gained with virtual-storage systems during the 1960s established
the practicality and value of the concept. This has led to the development of an even
greater variety of virtual-storage systems during the 1970s.

10-1   RATIONALE FOR VIRTUAL-STORAGE ORGANIZATION
[Refs. BA2,BE3,FO,HE,KA,RA1,SA,SI]

Let us begin by playing devil's advocate to the virtual-storage idea. Certainly,
user-specified folding of programs has at least a potential efficiency advantage over an
automatic folding scheme; the user presumably knows in advance many of the
storage-access characteristics of his problem and should, therefore, be able to specify
efficient foldings. However, programmer-specified folding can require excessive
programming and debugging time and may not always accurately reflect actual
data-dependent storage-access patterns. It has long been a vision of some computer
system architects to do most folding automatically rather than in response to specific
user requests. A *virtual-storage* system consists of a storage hierarchy, usually between
two levels of storage, where folding is done automatically by the system, and hence
requires no special user planning and programming. Instead, by responding to actual
executed storage requests, machine logic and system programs identify the time and
nature of folding operations. The objective of a virtual-storage method of resource
management is to free programs from dependence on preplanned, physical main-
storage sizes, thus ensuring the following advantages:

1. The programmer is relieved of the difficult task of manually specified folding.
2. Programs will execute correctly even if main-storage size is reduced or the program
   is carried to a smaller system. However, execution speed with a small main store
   may well be slow. Conversely, if storage is increased, the program will often
   execute faster, without reprogramming.
3. In a multiprogramming environment, the operating system has far greater flexibility
   when allocating the precious fast-storage resource among programs, since it need
   not supply every program with a fixed amount of storage. To the operating
   system, main storage can more nearly be a *pool* of space to be allocated, rather
   than a fixed size into which various problem sizes must be fitted.

4. A virtual-storage system allocates its fast storage in accordance with *actually observed* demands for space, rather than worst-case user estimates made prior to any program execution.

This last point is worthy of particular emphasis. A written program and its data represent a collection of "possible" storage references described in Chap. 7 as the program's address space. Many locations within the address space will not be referenced or will be referenced infrequently during any one execution of a program. This is due in part to data-dependent branches that bypass certain program parts. For example, many programs consist of three parts: initialization routines, a main-line routine, and exception routines. Initialization routines might be referenced only once per run. Some exception routines may never be referenced for certain collections of data. Even the storage locations actually referenced are not referenced with uniform frequency. The time distribution of the references to the same area of storage may also vary widely. Typically, program references tend to dwell in relatively small areas over fairly long time periods, a property called *locality of reference*. The simplest example is the storage references for instructions in a program loop. A well-designed virtual-storage system effectively identifies high locality and maintains only such areas in high-speed storage. As the program's activity shifts to various regions of address space, these are automatically moved into main storage.

We have now outlined some of the motivation for virtual storage and are ready to proceed with some definitions, logical facilities, and some of the methods of storage-reference research that form the underlying theory of virtual-storage management. Some example systems will be considered. These examples will be found to belong to two classes of context: (1) a main-store/auxiliary-store hierarchy or *system-design context*, and (2) a buffer-store/backing-store hierarchy or *CPU-design context*.

The system-design context was the one used in discussing the rationale of virtual storage. The primary incentive for the system-design context is to provide a large address space for each executing user. It is implemented through a combination of hardware and software techniques.

The CPU-design context is concerned with the design of a fast central-processing unit. The small fast member of the hierarchy (called a *buffer store*) is interposed between the processing unit and the larger main store (also called the *backing* store) that is the slower member of this type of hierarchy. In many ways, the buffer now plays the role of the main store in a conventional system, i.e., it is the direct source of data and instructions for the processing unit. However, there is one important difference, the running program is presumed to be referencing main storage (not the buffer), and hence all folding operations between the main store and the buffer are done automatically by hardware circuits and are completely invisible to the programmer. The first CPU-design context system was the IBM S/360 Model 85. Similar principles are used in the later IBM S/370 models 155, 165, 158, and 168 (the latter two machines also implement the systems-design context).

An important practical distinction between the two contexts of virtual storage is the speed ratios of the physical stores. Typically, in a system-design context, the ratio is on the order of 5000:1, while in a CPU-design context, it is closer to 5:1. As may be expected, this results in quite different details of implementation. In a system-design context, the most frequent processes for automatic folding are done by hardware circuits, while the remainder are done by an operating-system program. In the CPU-design context, high-speed requirements dictate an all-hardware implementation.

In the following sections, we will focus attention on the processes (algorithms) used to implement virtual storage. To help visualize the principles in a concrete way, we will use the system-design context as the primary one, unless otherwise stated.

10-2   ADDRESS SPACE AND MAPPING: PAGED SYSTEMS
[Refs. DE2,KU2,LI1]

The logical-storage space supplied to a program is called its address space (AS), the concept that was introduced in Chap. 7. To help visualize address space, we may think of it as a contiguous area of a large auxiliary-storage device (although, as will be seen later, this is not physically the case). In a nonvirtual-storage system, a problem's address space is restricted to being no larger than the computer's main-storage size. This restriction is removed in a virtual-storage system. Let

n = the number of words of AS
m = the number of words of main storage (MS)

Then it is permitted that

$n > m$

Thus, as indicated in Fig. 10-2.1, only a small portion of address space can fit into main storage at one time.

Now imagine a program written for some address space. While it is executing, it may well happen that its locality is good, but that the frequently accessed instructions and data, although requiring only a small amount of space, are not contiguous; that is,

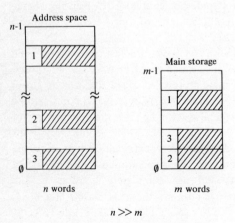

$n \gg m$

Cross-hatching shows currently active reference areas.

Fig. 10-2.1   Address space and main storage.

they are located in a few (but scattered) *patches* in AS. For example, for several thousand instruction executions, fetching may dwell in one area and data referencing in another. This suggests that it is advantageous for several *noncontiguous* parts of address space to be able to occupy main storage at the same time. However, this aspect of automatic folding, like all other aspects, must be transparent to the user. Two fundamental processes are involved in virtual storage:

1. *Selecting* the pieces of AS that are to be in main storage during each execution period
2. *Mapping* or translating each address generated by the program, which is an address to AS, into a physical address to main storage

The mapping function will now be discussed in some detail. Figure 10-2.2 shows the simplest conceptual mapping scheme (although not the most economical). We shall

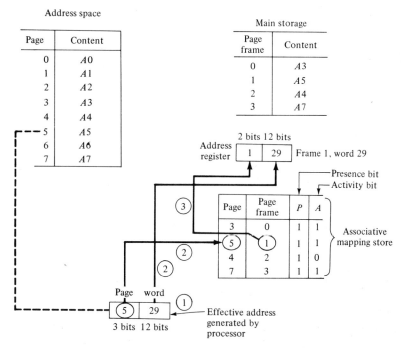

Summary of operation:

① Processor effective address specifies a location in address space (virtual storage)

② Effective address parts:
    Page part: used to search mapping store (left column)
            Match found: second column sent to address register
            No match: Page fault; interrupt to page supervisor program
    Word part: send to address register

Fig. 10-2.2 Mapping with associative store.

call the scheme *associative mapping*. An address space of 2^{15} = 32k words, and hence requiring 15 bits to address it, is depicted in the figure. This AS is structured as eight pages of 4096 words per page. An address to it, shown labelled "effective address," is then considered as composed of a 3-bit page address and a 12-bit word address. Main storage in this example has 2^{14} = 16k words considered as structured into 4 blocks (each of 4096 words) called *page frames*. (This terminology avoids confusion between AS pages and main-store pages, since the latter are termed page frames.) The values like $A0, A1$, etc., in Fig. 10-2.2 may be considered as a snapshot of the state-of-the-system at some instant after it has been running for a while, so the values are the result of prior activity. At the moment, pages $A3, A5, A4$, and $A7$ are seen to be resident in the main-storage page frames.

The 15-bit effective address to AS references a word we hope is present in main storage. Where is this word? More precisely, how can the hardware locate this word? In the example shown, we see that it is the word at address 29 of page 5 in AS. We now presume that the system program that implements our virtual storage has already placed AS page 5 in page frame 1 in main storage. Furthermore, it has recorded the *correspondence* between these two page addresses ($5 \rightarrow 1$) in a word of a special-storage device called a *mapping store*, as shown in Fig. 10-2.2. In fact, the mapping device holds a *table* of correspondences of AS $\rightarrow$ page frame addresses. With this understood, it should not be difficult to understand the mapping process described in Fig. 10-2.2.

The mapping device shown must have as many words as there are page frames. Each mapping entry holds three kinds of information:

1. Address-space page address
2. Main-storage address of the page (page frame address)
3. Control bits, such as the map-presence-bit (P) specifying whether the cell contains actual mapping data (or garbage from previous activity), and one or more bits giving some measure of page activity in the recent past

The actual mapping process consists of using the 3-bit page-address part of the effective address as a search argument to the leftmost column of the map, and, at the same time, checking for a 1 in the presence-bit of the map entry. If a match is found, the bits in the main-storage-address part of the mapping entry is the address of the page frame in main storage. The address of the word within the page is taken directly from the low-order bits of the effective address. If the search into the mapping device produces no match, the processor is attempting to reference a page that is not currently in main storage. This is called a *page fault*. Since mapping operations are very frequent (they are required for every storage reference), mapping must be a fast implemented function or the process would slow the system very significantly. Page faults, on the other hand, can be expected to be relatively rare, and the response to them is rather complex. Their response is therefore handled by an operating-system program called by a program interrupt that is generated automatically when there is a page fault. This program must then decide where the referenced page is to be placed in the main store (probably replacing some existing page that may first be saved for later referencing). The operating system must move the page and update the contents of the mapping device—the mapping directory—to delete the old and include the new page address. This entire process is called *page replacement* or *page turning*, and there are several algorithms for doing this, some of which shall be discussed later.

It has been assumed that mapping is done by using the high-order bits of the effective address to search the mapping directory. How is this search to be accomplished? Linear searching of even a fast-mapping store is intolerably slow. A binary search is not practical because it requires an ordered list, and this ordering requires significant processing time (and even then, several accesses per search). A hardware solution is indicated for fast mapping. If the mapping device is to use the minimum number of cells shown in Fig. 10-2.2, it is usually an *associative storage*, that is, one capable of fast *parallel search*. This means that it has the internal-logic circuitry which enables a search to be made between some given argument and *all* of its words at one time (in parallel). One consideration in the selection of page size is the resulting size of the mapping storage, which if implemented as an associative store, is significantly more expensive per bit stored than an ordinary storage. In particular, for a given main-store size, the smaller the page, the more page frames, and the larger the required size of the mapping storage. To say it the opposite way, large page size results in economical mapping hardware. It also tends to be economical, in time per moved word, to transfer large rather than small blocks between auxiliary and main storage. These advantages are at least partly offset by the fact that the larger the page size, the fewer the number of pages (and hence noncontiguous areas) that can be kept in main storage at the same time. The best compromise between these conflicting requirements depends on many factors of the particular system and is usually resolved by simulation studies during system development.

Figure 10-2.3 shows another type of mapping scheme that will be called *mapping by addressing*. Its mapping device uses a standard storage organization and requires as many cells as pages in AS. The effective page address is simply used as an address into the mapping directory, and if the map-presence bit in that word is found to be 1, the mapping cell holds (among other information) the desired main-storage location of the page being referenced. The economy of a conventionally organized (nonassociative) type of storage for mapping can more than offset the extravagance that requires the mapping directory to have as many entries as there are pages in AS. This is usually far more entries than the number of page frames. (Only the latter number of entries is required in the associative scheme described earlier.) For relatively small address spaces and simple systems requiring only a small amount of mapping information per mapping cell, mapping by addressing is quite feasible.

Control of the contents of the mapping directory implies control of main storage, a vital shared resource in a multiprogrammed or timeshared system. For this reason, changes in the mapping directory are made only by the operating system, never by a problem program. Typically, the operating system must change the contents of the directory (or one or more pointers to a directory) whenever: (1) a page is entered or replaced in main storage (in this case, directory entries must be changed), and (2) the processor switches from one program to another (in this case, the pointer to a directory is usually changed).

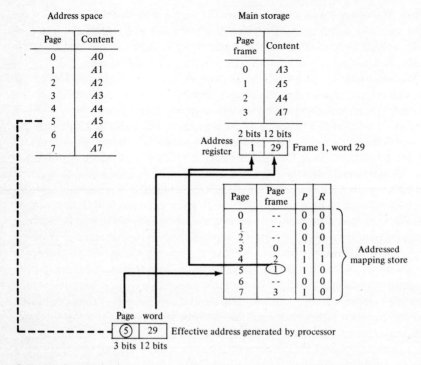

Summary of operations:

> Similar to Fig. 10-2.2, except the page part of effective address is used as an address to the mapping store

Fig 10-2.3 Mapping with addressed-storage mapping device.

10-3 SEGMENTATION [Refs. BA1,BU,DE4,GR,KE2,RA2]

Modern programming systems usually impose a logical-block structure on programs for at least the following reasons:

1. Program modularity. Each module is given a name and the module implies a scope for names within the module. Each module may be compiled separately.
2. Data structures, for example, arrays or lists.
3. Protection against unauthorized access.
4. Sharing. Program A may want to borrow module 5 from B, even though 5 has been bound to addresses in B that A is already using for other purposes.

A segmented address space considers the total address space as partitioned into several segments, each a contiguous area. Some virtual-storage systems like the Burroughs Corp. B5500 have only segments and no paging structure. Other systems like the IBM Mod 67, 158, and 168 have segments that consist of an integer number of pages. In either case, a module or data structure can be assigned to a segment, thus satisfying the first and second properties. By associating protection information with segments, the third property is satisfied. By placing a shared module in a unique segment in each user's address space, a single physical copy may be shared (the fourth property).

The term *logical segment* denotes a programmer or compiler-named contiguous area of storage like a program module or data structure. A complete program and its data is, therefore, a linked collection of logical segments. Thus, an address space is partitioned into logical segments. This natural sectioning of programs and data is the basis of a type of virtual-storage system that is quite distinct from the paged systems described previously. The Burroughs Corp. B5000, B5500, and B6500 computers are examples. Our discussion relates specifically to the B5500. Its program addresses directly reference an area of main storage called the Program Reference Table (or PRT), as indicated in Fig. 10-3.1. Each PRT entry is a 48-bit word, called a *descriptor*, of which there are four types (a particular type is specified by bits in the descriptor word itself). One descriptor type is simply data. Another type describes a segment by supplying in effect the entry in the translation map for a particular segment. It specifies the main-storage address of the segment, its segment size, and a presence bit denoting whether or not it is in main storage.

If an address outside of a segment is attempted, the monitoring circuitry detects a size violation, and there is a program interrupt to the operating system. If the

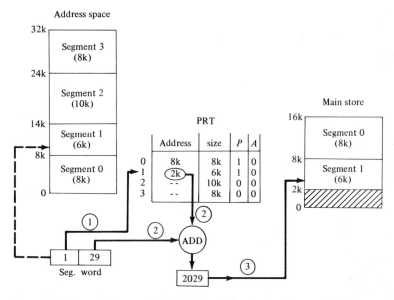

Notes: 1. Program Reference Table (PRT) maps segment to main store address; protects segment from out-of-bounds references (size field).
2. Each program has its own PRT.
3. PRT held in main storage, but small associative store may also be used for fast mapping of most-active references.

Fig. 10-3.1 Address translation in a segmented address space.

attempted reference passes the size test, but the segment is not currently in main storage, this is discovered by failure of the test on the presence bit. The attempt at reference then results in a segment-fault interrupt. This initiates a program in the operating system that requests a move of the segment into main storage.

Each program has its own PRT. Storage protection against access by one program into another's space is ensured in part by permitting only the operating system (privileged-mode instructions) to set the register pointing to the PRT origin of the currently executing program. Similarly, only the operating system can modify the address and size fields of descriptors. Although the PRT's are logically held in main storage, a few fast registers, or a small fast memory, is used in some models to hold the currently most-active descriptors; this speeds the mapping process significantly.

It is of interest to contrast segmented and paged virtual-storage properties. In both, the logical address space is larger than main storage. In paged systems, address space is usually divided into equal-sized pages that are transparent to the problem programmer. In segmented systems, address space is divided into variable-length segments; each often has problem significance as a named program module or a data array. However, operating system programs may, as in the Burroughs systems, automatically divide an object like a matrix into several parts and create a segment for each part. Each segment tends to use storage efficiently, since its size usually corresponds to a functional-problem storage unit. Pages, being of fixed size, will often be found to have unused portions, a phenomenon called *internal fragmentation.* On the other hand, efficient allocation of storage is much simpler for paged address spaces, since uniform-sized units are always allocated and replaced. In segmented systems, variable-sized blocks of storage must be allocated; this process tends to leave "holes" of unused space which, unless closed up, cannot be used to satisfy demands for large single segments. This is called *external fragmentation.* One cure is to move the segments every so often and to close up holes; thus making all unused space contiguous. This can incur a significant overhead penalty. Besides the simple hole-closing approach of moving the information, a variety of other placement and storage-management schemes have been suggested (see Refs. DE2 and KN). In general, the problem is very similar to "garbage collection" in list-processing systems. The mapping process for a segmented address space tends to be efficient, since the mapped objects are functionally identifiable problem or data segments. These are usually fewer than the number of pages that would be required, especially in large programs.

In many respects, paged and segmented schemes have complementary advantages and defects. It is therefore natural to seek to combine the advantages of both. Figure 10-3.2 shows the mapping process for a particular segmented and paged system that is very similar to the one used in the IBM Mod 67 computer. The AS structure is indicated by the way the effective address is partitioned:

4 bits for one of 16 segments
8 bits for one of 256 pages per segment
12 bits for one of 4096 (= 4k) bytes per page

The 24-bit address therefore permits an address space of 2^{24} = 16 megabytes (this is also called the virtual-storage size). The mapping facilities and processes are shown in

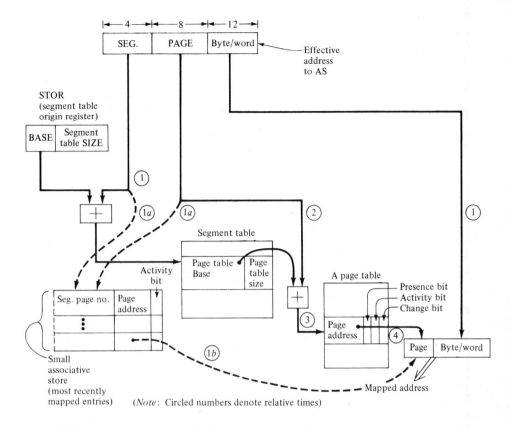

Fig. 10-3.2 Mapping for segmented-page virtual-storage system.

Fig. 10-3.2. The transformation of the effective address to AS (generated by the processing unit) into the mapped physical address to main storage is done by means of two tables held in main storage and some registers. It is assumed that all registers and tables have preassigned values (by the operating-system program or automatic hardware means). The reader is urged to trace the word description by referring to the diagram (circled numbers indicate the time sequence of events). For the moment, ignore the dashed lines, which are a speed enhancement technique that will be described later. The mapping process starts with the 4-bit SEG part of the effective address that is added to the BASE portion of the Segment Table Origin Register (STOR). Since the register points to the start of a segment mapping table, the sum points to an entry in the segment table. The major entry in the segment table is a pointer to the base (i.e., the start) of a page-mapping table describing that segment. The page table base is then added to the PAGE bits of the effective address, the sum being a pointer to a page table. The value found there is the mapped page address (designating the page frame), which is combined by concatenation with the 12-bit byte part of the effective address to produce the final physical mapped address.

The above is a concise description of the highlights of the mapping process. We now consider some important details that have been omitted. Note the control bits in each page table entry.

PRESENCE BIT	Specifies whether or not the page is present in main storage
ACTIVITY BIT(s)	Gives some measure of the recent reference activity to the page
CHANGE BIT	Specifies whether or not any modification has been made in the page's contents since it was last moved into main storage

The PRESENCE bit is tested for 1 at every reference, and when found not to be 1, it means that the page has not been entered in main storage. A *page-fault* interrupt is then generated. The ACTIVITY bit(s) are the most complex to explain; for now we note that their purpose is to help the operating system make a good choice of a page to be replaced (when main storage is filled and a page fault occurs) by selecting a page that has been relatively inactive, at least in the recent past (more about this later). The CHANGE bit is valuable to reduce the number of page transmissions during replacement operations; it is not necessary to save a copy of an unchanged page that is being replaced. A current copy already exists on disk or drum.

Another feature worth noting in Fig. 10-3.2 are the SIZE entries in the STOR and segment table entries. They specify the number of entries in the tables being referenced. This permits safe use of tables that are not full (a common case), without necessitating main storage to hold the full tables. If implemented, this feature considerably reduces the amount of main storage needed for the mapping tables.

The tables used for mapping in a segmented and paged system usually are in main storage. Thus, each program storage reference would seem to require three main-storage references: one for the segment table, one for the page table, and finally one for the data. This would slow most virtual-storage references very significantly when compared to a conventional system that requires only one reference. To avoid this speed penalty, a fast associative store is used together with mapping by addressing. A small, very fast associative store (8 cells in the IBM Mod 67) is provided to hold the most recently referenced table entries. Thus, the mapping process is first attempted by associative search, as indicated by dashed lines in Fig. 10-3.2; if it succeeds, there is hardly any mapping delay. If it does not, then the slower table-accessing process described above is followed, and the result replaces an entry in the associative store. Which entry is replaced? A commonly used algorithm is as follows: Each entry in the associative mapping store has an activity bit. All these activity bits are initially set to zero. Each time a cell is referenced, its activity bit is set to 1. When *all* activity bits become 1, they are all set to 0 (since the system cannot then distinguish relative activity any longer). When replacement of a cell in the associative store is required, the first cell with a 0 activity bit is the one replaced.

Storage protection in a segmented and paged system is achieved by having *only* the operating system (and never the problem programs) modify the STOR register and page-segment tables. Segments may be shared between programs by having each such program's segment table reference the same page table.

As described in the introduction, the large address space or virtual storage is *automatically* folded into the small fast storage. Our examples thus far have described folding in a system-design context of virtual storage, that is, between auxiliary and main storage. We have concentrated on the mapping (or translation) and main-storage management requirements of the folding process. In a later section we will describe the auxiliary-storage management requirements for implementation of a virtual-storage system. However, in the next sections, we focus on a method used to determine a program's locality-of-reference—the theoretical basis for the practicality of virtual storage.

10-4   CAPTURING AN ADDRESS STREAM

The success of virtual storage hinges on the nature of patterns of references to logical storage (i.e., address space) during execution of programs. The understanding of these patterns is vital to the rational design of a virtual-storage system. It is obtained by actually executing several sample programs representative of a workload (using a large physical store) and monitoring such programs by recording *every* storage reference. The resulting executed sequence of storage addresses is called an *address stream* (or address trace) and is usually stored on magnetic tape. We shall shortly discuss ways of characterizing address-stream information. However, some observations are first in order about how address streams are obtained and about their general nature.

Although it is easy to envision a hardware monitoring device that captures the addresses as they appear at the main-storage address registers, in practice this is not usually the method used. First, as we shall soon see, the rate of address generation in even a medium-sized computer is so high that there is no reasonably large and economical storage device that can accept the information at its natural generation rate. Also, it is usually desirable to record other information for each reference, as well as the address, like its source (program or data) and type (fetch or store). For these reasons, it is common practice to capture the address stream by executing the desired program interpretively. An interpreter program is therefore designed that simulates at least the address-determination part of the computer. The sample program(s) executes under the interpreter. The interpreter computes each effective address and then records it in the stream before permitting the CPU to use it for storage referencing. As is well known, an interpreter slows program execution appreciably (a factor of 10 to 100 is not uncommon). Thus, to obtain an address stream is expensive in time. The time cost is reduced as much as possible by recording only the addresses and closely related information; data reduction and simulation with the stream is done in separate computer runs.

A simple calculation should help give us a healthy respect for the volume of information in an address stream. Consider a medium-sized computer that has an instruction rate of say 1 million instructions per second. Most instructions generate two addresses (one for the instruction, one for data). Since a record of an address and associated information requires say 5 bytes of information, in one second of real problem-run time, the machine is producing 10 million bytes of address-stream data. In only a few seconds, a reel of magnetic tape is filled! This clearly indicates the importance of carefully selecting not only the program to be traced, but of also identifying in advance the high-activity portions of the program. It also emphasizes the need for efficiency in the simulators that will be fed the voluminous address-stream data. Once an address stream is captured, it can be analyzed in many ways. For example, it is possible to determine which of its instructions and data are most frequently referenced and what proportion of a program's size they represent. It is also possible to determine what parts of a program must co-reside in main storage at any particular time during execution in order to minimize the number of page faults that occur. One can study the effects of different page replacement algorithms (see Sec. 10-6) with respect to the number of page faults generated and the execution speed of the program. A final example is the use of an address stream to study the effect of page size on a program's execution speed, main-storage requirements, number of page transfers, and so forth. In the next section, we describe how to represent an address stream so that studies of this nature may be conducted.

In closing this brief account of the nature of address-stream data gathering, we should remark that although the subject is fundamental to computer science and to the practical design of certain hardware and software structures, the user or designer of application programs or systems need not actually conduct the expensive address-stream experiments. Instead, they can benefit from the published results of several studies (see Refs. BA1, BE1, CO1, CON, FI, GI, KE2, LE) and summaries like ours. These have produced guidelines of programming style that, once understood and used in programming practice, can result in good virtual-system performance.

10-5 CHARACTERIZING ADDRESS STREAMS: LOCALITY
AND WORKING SET   [Refs. BE2,DE1,LE,ST]

An address stream may be represented as a vector A that contains N integer values. If the address has n bits, each address in the stream is a member of the alphabet of 2^n possible values. If a page size of 2^s words is selected, the address space contains $P_n = 2^{n-s}$ pages. In an earlier example, effective address size (n) was 24 bits long. This resulted in an address space of 2^{24}, or 16,777,216 locations. Page size (2^s) was 2^{12}, or 4096 words, and the address space contained $P_n = 2^{24-12}$, or $P_n = 4096$ pages. The address stream A of word addresses may easily be converted to a *page-address stream* X by the relation,

$$X = \lfloor A \div 2^s$$

That is, each page address is obtained by dividing the word address by the page size and rounding down to the nearest equal/lower integer. For example, for a page size of 8 words, $s = 3$, and for the given stream A, the following X stream is obtained using the above formula

A	36	180	38	184	40	188	44	192
X	4	22	4	23	5	23	5	24

For the most part in what follows, we shall be interested in the page-address stream rather than the address stream (at least once the page size has been selected).

We now come to a fundamental question. From the previous discussion, we have identified the intuitive idea of *locality* and stated the empirical fact that many programs are found to exhibit strong or "good" locality by dwelling in small parts of address space for rather long sequences of addresses. We now seek some precise quantitative measure of locality that can be obtained from address streams so that we can then compare, for example, the locality of two programs for the same problem, with each program using a different algorithm. One conceivable measure is the frequency distribution of page references. It might be thought that high locality will show up as very high relative frequency in a small number of pages. However, it is easy to show that this is not an adequate measure. For example, consider two page-address streams

$$
\begin{array}{llllllllll}
A & 8 & 8 & 8 & 8 & 8 & 15 & 15 & 15 & 15 & 15 \\
B & 8 & 15 & 8 & 15 & 8 & 15 & 8 & 15 & 8 & 15
\end{array}
$$

Both of these streams have identical frequency distributions, but stream A requires access to only one page most of the time, while stream B requires two pages to accommodate the rapid alternation between pages 8 and 15. Clearly, stream B has poorer locality than A, even though they have identical frequency distributions. That the frequency distribution alone is not an adequate measure of locality should not be surprising, since locality depends on the *fine-ordering* structure of the stream; frequency distributions completely ignore the ordering in the data they describe.

A good descriptor of locality is one that identifies what parts (or pages) of a program are being referenced during a relatively long time period of program execution. One such measure is called a program's *working set*. Working-set size indicates how many *distinct* pages are being referenced during the time period. As a program executes, its working set will change. For example, the parts of a program referenced during initialization will be different than parts referenced during main-line execution. A program has good locality if it has small working sets, or if its average working-set size is small. We will now consider a technique to measure the working set.

The working set of a program's execution stream at the ith reference, that is, at the value X_i in the page-address stream vector, may be expressed in set notation

$$
W(i,h) = \{X_j | j \epsilon ((i - h) + \iota h)\}
$$

where ιh is the vector of successive integers from 1 to h. In words, the working set $W(i,h)$ is the *set* of all *distinct* pages appearing in the "window" h pages long, looking back in the stream from the page in position i. The working-set measurement is, therefore, a function of both the selected window size h and the reference point i in the stream. The size of the working set will be designated $\rho W(i,h)$, and the size of page-address stream is ρX. The expected or *mean size* of the working set is obtained by summing over all working-set sizes with a common window size. Thus

$$
w(h) = \frac{1}{\rho X} \sum_{i=1}^{\rho X} \rho W(i,h)
$$

The mean working-set size for a given stream is seen to be a function of the window size h. See Fig. 10-5.1 for a sample computation. It may be shown that the mean working-set size satisfies the following relationships:

Index →	1	2	3	4	5	6	7	8	9	10
$X \to$	4	22	4	22	4	23	5	23	5	24

(a) Stream.

	$h = 2$		$h = 5$		$h = 10$	
i	$W(i,2)$	$\rho W(i,2)$	$W(i,5)$	$\rho W(i,5)$	$W(i,10)$	$\rho W(i,10)$
1	4	1	4	1	4	1
2	4,22	2	4,22	2	4,22	2
3	4,22	2	4,22	2	4,22	2
4	4,22	2	4,22	2	4,22	2
5	4,22	2	4,22	2	4,22	2
6	4,23	2	4,22,23	3	4,22,23	3
7	5,23	2	4,5, 22,23	4	4,5 22,23	4
8	5,23	2	4,5 22,23	4	4,5 22,23	4
9	5,23	2	4,5,23	3	4,5, 22,23	4
10	5,24	2	5,23,24	3	4,5,22 23,24	5

(b) Computation table for $h = 2,5,10$.

$w(2) = 19/10 = 1.9$
$w(5) = 26/10 = 2.6$
$w(10) = 29/10 = 2.9$

(c) Computed means.

Fig. 10-5.1   Computation of mean working-set size.

1. $1 < w(h) < \min(h, 2^{n-s})$
2. $w(h) \leqslant w(h+1)$
3. $w(h+1) + w(h-1) < 2w(h)$ (concave down)

In words, these relationships state that the mean working set for a window size h cannot be less than 1 and cannot be greater than the smaller of h or 2^{n-s}, the number of distinct pages in the address space. The combination of mean working sets for window sizes $(h-1)$ and $(h+1)$ cannot be greater than twice the mean working set for window size h. These properties yield the general shape of the curve shown in Fig. 10-5.2.

A common technique to represent the locality property of programs in a paging system is some variation of the curve shown in Fig. 10-5.3. This type of curve, which is often found empirically to have the shape shown, indicates that most programs have good locality and require less main storage for execution than total program size; a

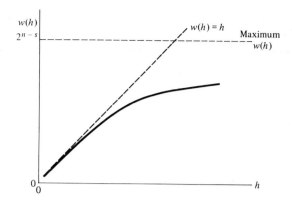

Fig. 10-5.2 General shape of curve of mean working-set size.

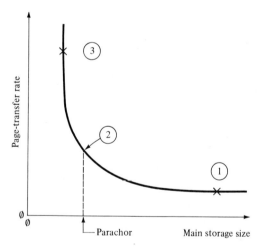

1. This point on the curve represents program execution where all of the storage declared for the program is available as main storage. The page-transfer rate is negligible.

2. This point on the curve is indicative of a program's average working-set requirement. Although significantly less main storage is available than declared, the page-transfer rate is still reasonable.

3. This point is in the thrashing region and represents a very high page-transfer rate.

Fig. 10-5.3 Locality-of-reference curve.

relatively low page-transfer rate is also required between the two levels of storage. The main-storage size at the sharp bend in the curve is sometimes called the program's *parachor* and reflects its efficient working-set size. If main storage is reduced much below this point, the page-transfer rate is seen to become very high. This means that a large number of active pages are competing for the relatively small number of main-storage page frames, a condition called *thrashing*. We will further discuss thrashing in Secs. 10-6 and 11-5.

It is possible to construct a curve plot with the axis shown in Fig. 10-5.3 for any particular program. The data for the plot requires successive executions of the program, each with a different amount of main storage, and measurement of the page-transfer rate for each execution. Although simple in concept, the experiment is costly in machine resources and time required. In Sec. 10-7 on program style and program behavior, we will describe some examples of such experiments.

In the virtual-storage literature, the terms *parachor* and *optimum storage* are sometimes used in place of *working set*. However, working set seems to be most common. Measurements of working sets formed the experimental basis for justifying and initially designing virtual-storage systems.

10-6 PAGE-REPLACEMENT ALGORITHMS [Refs. AH,HE,BE1,KI2,MA2]

Until now, the concepts presented have been related to the system-design context of virtual storage. This follows the historical practice in the literature. The description of replacement algorithms will be done using the two-level hierarchy and terminology of the CPU-design context. Later, we will also describe some of the replacement "mechanics" for a system-design context.

Figure 10-6.1 shows the two-level hierarchy and terminology to be used. As stated earlier, the small fast store is called the *buffer*, and the larger is called the *backing* store, which may be identified with the address space. As a program is

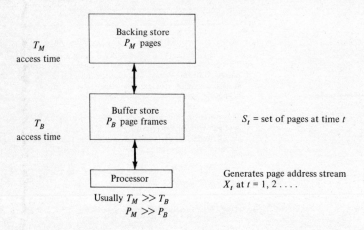

Fig. 10-6.1   Two-level hierarchy.

executed, various portions of address space become active, while others previously active become dormant. During periods of good locality, most references are to pages already in buffer storage. During these periods, the access speed of the system is the fast access speed of the buffer store. However, when a page fault occurs, the new page must be moved into the buffer from backing storage before the program can proceed. If the buffer is full, a *page-replacement algorithm* must be used to decide which page currently in the buffer store should be replaced.

"Page-in" of referenced data is, of course, an essential operation. Page movement in the opposite direction involves a somewhat greater variety of possibilities. It need not be done at all if the page involved has not been changed since its last page-in, since in this case, the original copy on the slower store is still valid. If the page has been changed, the copy in the slower store must be modified to reflect the new contents. There are two basic ways in which this is presently done. In the first, as has already been described in connection with Fig. 10-3.2, the hardware mapping or storage-access mechanism maintains a CHANGE bit as a signal that a change has been made in a page. When a page is to be replaced, the bit is checked: if ON, the page is copied back into the slow store (disk); otherwise, this copy operation is not done. This method is commonly used in system-context virtual storage. The other method, used in CPU-design contexts, is to store the changed information of a page in the slower store every time a change is made. This means that "page-outs" of entire pages are never necessary. Each method is appropriate in the speed range of the context in which it is used (as will be discussed later).

Page-replacement operations are usually the most wasteful overhead penalties in a virtual-storage system. For this reason, the performance index by which page-replacement algorithms are judged is the number of page replacements they require. Naturally, comparisons of algorithms should only be done for the same equipment and workload.

The following notation will be used:

$$C = \text{buffer capacity (no. of page frames)}$$
$$t = \text{index in the page-address stream, here called } X$$
$$S_t(C) = \text{set of pages in the buffer at reference } t \text{ in } X \ (X_t)$$
$$\rho S_t(C) = \text{no. of pages in } S_t(C)$$
$$\Gamma_t = \text{the set of } distinct \text{ pages in } X_1, X_2, \ldots, X_t$$
$$\gamma_t = \rho \Gamma_t = \text{no. of distinct pages in } X_1, X_2, \ldots, X_t$$
$$A(S) = \text{the page selected for replacement by replacement algorithm } A$$
$$\text{operating on } S$$
$$T_M = \text{access speed of the backing store}$$
$$T_B = \text{access speed of the buffer store}$$
$$P_M = \text{capacity (pages) of the backing store}$$
$$P_B = \text{capacity (page frames) of the buffer}$$

We shall be concerned here only with *demand paging*, that is, pages are brought into the buffer only on demand—when a nonresident page is referenced. With a good replacement algorithm, pages never referenced during execution will never occupy buffer space, pages seldom referenced will occupy the buffer for only short time periods, and pages heavily referenced (therefore, working-set pages) will tend to remain in the buffer.

Consider now a page-address stream X. The demand-paging process may be concisely described by the following set-notation statements (one for each case). The term *current page* refers to the page just referenced.

1. If $X_t \in S_{t-1}(C)$, then $S_t \leftarrow S_{t-1}$

    If the current page is in the buffer, the new buffer set is unchanged. Access time is T_B.

2. If $X_t \notin S_{t-1}(C)$ and $\rho S_{t-1}(C) < C$, then $S_t(C) \leftarrow S_{t-1}(C) \cup \{X_t\}$

    If the current page is not in the buffer and the buffer is not full, the current page is sent into the buffer. Access time is $T_B + T_M$.

3. If $X_t \notin S_{t-1}(C)$ and $\rho S_{t-1}(C) = C$, then $S_t(C) \leftarrow (S_{t-1}(C) \sim A(S_{t-1}(C))) \cup \{X_t\}$

    If the current page is not in the buffer and the buffer is full, the algorithm named A determines the page to be deleted: then X_t is sent into the buffer. Access time is $T_B + T_M$ or $T_B + 2T_M$, as the replaced page has or has not been changed while in the buffer.

A successful page-replacement algorithm results in as few page movements as possible. Before discussing particular replacement algorithms, it is valuable to define a measure of success for the algorithm:

Let P = probability (= relative frequency) that a page request is found in the buffer. This is sometimes called the success or *hit* function.

$1-P$ = probability that the desired page is not in the buffer, and hence requires access to the backing store.

Then mean access time, obtained by multiplying the buffer and backing-store access times by their probabilities and adding, is

$$\bar{T} = PT_B + (1 - P)T_M \tag{1}$$

The access speed of the system relative to the maximum possible access speed (if all storage was of buffer speed) is

$$S = \left(\frac{1}{\bar{T}}\right)T_B = \frac{\bar{S}}{S_B} \tag{2}$$

Dividing Eq. (1) by $\bar{T}$, substituting Eq. (2), and solving for P

$$P = \frac{1 - ST_M/T_B}{S(1 - T_M/T_B)}$$

Figure 10-6.2 shows a plot of P vs. S for various values of T_M/T_B, that is, given the speed ratio of the two stores, the curve shows the required success probability for a desired avarage-speed ratio S for several speed ratios T_M/T_B.

We begin the study of actual replacement algorithms with one called "MIN" because it is the *best* algorithm with respect to the number of page replacements. MIN

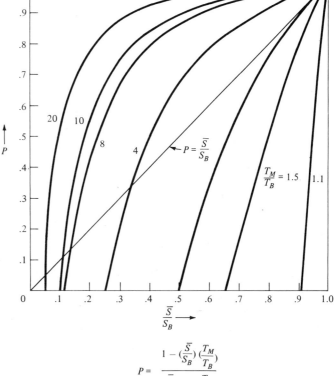

$$T_B = \text{buffer access time}$$
$$T_M = \text{main-store access time}$$
$$P = \text{required ``hit'' probability}$$
$$\bar{S} = \text{mean speed of access (overall)}$$
$$S_B = 1/T_B = \text{speed of buffer}$$

$$P = \frac{1 - (\frac{\bar{S}}{S_B})(\frac{T_M}{T_B})}{(\frac{\bar{S}}{S_B})(1 - \frac{T_M}{T_B})}$$

Fig. 10-6.2 Required "hit" probability for various speed ratios.

is best, but impractical, because it requires foreknowledge of future references in the page stream. When replacement is required, MIN considers each page in the buffer with respect to its next appearance in the page-address stream X. MIN selects for replacement that page in the buffer whose next reference in X is furthest in the future. Described in symbolic notation, let:

$\tau_t(i)$ = the distance (in number of pages) from page i in the buffer to its next appearance t in the page-address stream.

j = that page in the buffer to be replaced (selected by the MIN algorithm).

Because MIN selects that page in S_t whose next reference in X is furthest in the future (see Fig. 10-6.3), this can be represented symbolically by

$$j \leftarrow \underset{i}{\mathrm{Max}}\ \tau_t(i \in S_t)$$

X_j is the page in S_t to be replaced. In the APL language, S *and* X may be considered as vectors, and T is the index to the current reference in stream X

$$I \leftarrow T + \lceil /(T \downarrow X) \iota S \tag{3}$$

Equation (3) gives the index I in X of the last first-reference to the pages in S. Then

$$J \leftarrow S \iota X[I] \quad \text{if } I \leqslant \rho X \tag{4a}$$

$$J \leftarrow 1 \uparrow ((\rho X) < T + (T \downarrow X) \iota S) / \iota \rho S \quad \text{if } I > \rho X \tag{4b}$$

where the second case occurs if there is no match of some element of S anywhere in X forward of $X[T]$.

The MIN algorithm, although optimum with respect to number of page replacements, is *not* practical because it requires foreknowledge of the page-address stream. Although available in simulation-design studies, such knowledge is not available during program execution. Also, the MIN algorithm may not be optimal if pages not modified are not swapped out. However, in experiment and design, the MIN algorithm gives a useful comparison for replacement algorithms being considered. Figure 10-6.3 demonstrates the working of the MIN algorithm for a short address stream and a buffer with a capacity P_B of three page frames.

Index →	1	2	3	4	5	6	7	8	9	10	11	12	13	14	15	16	
Stream→	5	4	2	8	4	1	4	3	1	5	4	2	4	5	3	8	4 replacement
	5	5	5	5	5	5	5	5	5	5	5	5	5	5			operations
Buffer	–	4	4	4	4	4	4	3*	3	3	3	2*	2	2			
	–	–	2	8*	8	1	1	1	1	1	4*	4	4	4			

(a) MIN algorithm.

Index →	1	2	3	4	5	6	7	8	9	10	11	12	13	14	15	16	
Stream→	5	4	2	8	4	1	4	3	1	5	4	2	4	5	3	8	8 replacement
	5	5	5	8*	8	8	8	3*	3	3	4*	4	4	4	4	8*	operations
Buffer	–	4	4	4	4	4	4	4	4	5*	5	5	5	5	5	5	
	–	–	2	2	2	1*	1	1	1	1	1	2*	2	2	3*	3	

* The page just placed in the buffer.

(b) LRU algorithm.

Fig. 10-6.3 Two replacement algorithms.

The LRU (for Least Recently Used) replacement algorithm is a practical one that is conceptually related to MIN. In fact, it is identical to MIN, except that distances are measured to the left (past) rather than into the future (right) of the page-address stream. Thus, LRU replaces that page in S whose last reference was longest ago, i.e., the page least recently used (see Fig. 10-6.3). The fact that LRU depends only on past references makes it a good basis for a practical algorithm. See Fig. 10-6.4 for an implementation scheme for LRU.

Very often when simulating a particular page-replacement algorithm, it is desirable to obtain results for different buffer capacities. *Stack* replacement algorithms are a class characterized by an inclusion property that permits several systems differing in buffer size to be simulated with a single pass of the address stream.

Let $S_t(C)$ equal the set of pages in a buffer of capacity C at time t. Then the LRU algorithm, which always forces the buffer to contain the C most recently used pages, satisfies

$$S_t(1) \subset S_t(2) \subset \cdots S_t(Y) = S_t(Y_t + 1) = \cdots \tag{5}$$

Recall that γ_t equals the number of distinct pages in $X_1, X_2, \ldots, X_t$. Also

$$\rho S_t(C) = C \quad \text{for } 1 \leqslant C \leqslant \gamma_t$$

and

$$\rho S_t(C) = \gamma_t \quad \text{for } C \geqslant \gamma_t$$

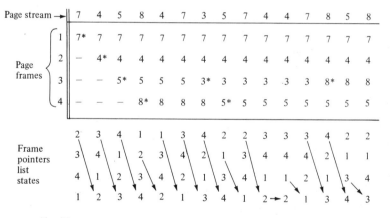

Algorithm:

Compare next page reference in stream with all pages in frames

Case I no match

Place page in frame whose position is given at top of pointer list, then rotate pointer list up one position

Case II match

Suppose matching frame is at position j. Find j in pointer list, move it to bottom of list, then rotate all pointers below it up one position

Fig. 10-6.4 Implementing an LRU algorithm with rotating pointers.

$t \rightarrow$	1	2	3	4	5	6	7	8	9	10	11	12	13	
$X \rightarrow$	a	h	e	d	e	g	h	h	h	g	d	h	g	
$-\infty$	$a\,0^*$	$a\,1$	$a\,2$	$d\,0^*$	$d\,1$	$d\,2$	$h\,0^*$	$h\,0$	$h\,0$	$h\,1$	$h\,2$	$h\,0$	$h\,1$	$S_t(3)$
$-\infty$	$-\infty$	$h\,0^*$	$h\,1$	$h\,2$	$h\,3$	$g\,0^*$	$g\,1$	$g\,2$	$g\,3$	$g\,0$	$g\,1$	$g\,2$	$g\,0$	sets
$-\infty$	$-\infty$	-0	$e\,0^*$	$e\,1$	$e\,0$	$e\,1$	$e\,2$	$e\,3$	$e\,4$	$e\,5$	$d\,0^*$	$d\,1$	$d\,2$	

(*a*)   c ≡ 3   No. replacements ≡ 7

$X \rightarrow$	a	h	e	d	e	g	h	h	h	g	d	h	g	
$-\infty$	$a\,0^*$	$a\,1$	$e\,0^*$	$e\,1$	$e\,0$	$e\,1$	$h\,0^*$	$h\,0$	$h\,0$	$h\,1$	$d\,0^*$	$d\,1$	$g\,0^*$	$S_t(2)$
$-\infty$	$-\infty$	$h\,0^*$	$h\,1$	$d\,0^*$	$d\,1$	$g\,0^*$	$g\,1$	$g\,2$	$g\,3$	$g\,0$	$g\,1$	$h\,0^*$	$h\,1$	sets

(*b*)   c ≡ 2   No. replacements ≡ 9

Notes: 1. State of buffer $S_t(c)$ is a vertical column below the double line at each page reference in stream. For each element in $S_t(c)$, its relative distance back in stream is also shown. Replacements are indicated by *.
       2. Inclusion property shown by $S_t(2) \subset S_t(3)$ for every t.

Fig. 10-6.5   Illustrating inclusion property for LRU algorithm (a stack algorithm).

These equations state that a stack algorithm applied to a buffer with a capacity of C pages will encounter, at any point t in the stream, a set of pages that includes the set that would be in the buffer if its capacity were fewer than C pages. It follows that any single stack algorithm may be simulated for capacities $1, 2, \ldots, C$ pages within a single pass of the page stream. This efficiency in simulation is of no small importance, since streams are very large data collections.

     Examples of stack algorithms include MIN and LRU. Some algorithms that are *not* of the stack class are: first-in-first-out and random replacement. Figure 10-6.5 shows how LRU exhibits the stack-algorithm inclusion property for buffer capacities of two and three page frames.

     Many variations of approximations of the LRU algorithm have been implemented in existing virtual-storage systems. In all cases, LRU's major objective is to minimize the number of page replacements. This objective in its simplest implementation gives no consideration to changed pages during the replacement selection. In a CPU-design context, this usually poses no problem. It is reasonable here to design hardware that *stores through*, i.e., updating the page in backing store at the same time as changing the page in the buffer. In such a design, when a changed page is replaced, no page-out operation is required. Store-through is not feasible in the system-design context; replacing a changed page requires a very slow I/O operation (page-out) between main storage and the backing auxiliary store. Some system-design context replacement algorithms weight the selection process to favor changed pages, thus attempting to reduce the page out I/O activity.

     The characteristics of demand paging in a system-design context are exactly as described earlier for the CPU context. In the terminology of the system-design context:

1. Data or instructions referenced in a page that already resides in main storage are processed with little delay (after translation occurs through the mapping device).
2. When a page is referenced that is not currently in main storage and a page frame is available, the page is moved from auxiliary to main store and processing resumes.
3. When a page is referenced that is not in main storage and no page frames are available, a resident page must be selected for replacement and moved to auxiliary storage if its contents have changed since last page-in; the referenced page can then be moved to main storage and processed.

To do these functions, a virtual-storage system must sense whether a page is present in main storage, identify the locations of pages in auxiliary storage, identify what main-storage page frames are available (if any), identify whether the contents of a page have been changed since last page-in, and move pages between main and auxiliary storage via I/O operations. To implement an LRU replacement algorithm requires a mechanism that indicates how recently the pages in main storage have been referenced. These functions are typically performed by a special *program* within the virtual-storage operating system with some hardware assistance.

In a segmented and paged system, the presence of a page in main storage is indicated in each page-table entry by what is called the *presence* (or "invalid") bit. This idea was introduced in Sec. 10-3. During address translation, if the referenced page is not in main storage, the presence bit has a zero value and a *page fault* results. The page fault is a hardware signal (in the form of a *program interrupt*) that activates the special operating-system program that will move the missing page to main storage (a page-in operation). We shall call this special system program a *paging supervisor.* When a page fault occurs, the paging supervisor must locate the missing page in auxiliary storage and identify an available page frame (if there are any) in main storage. One common technique used to locate pages in auxiliary storage is through a set of tables, often called *external page tables.* For each page-table entry there is a corresponding external page-table entry that gives the address of the page in auxiliary storage. When a page fault occurs, the paging supervisor refers to the appropriate external page-table entry to start the page-in process. An example of external page tables is depicted in Fig. 10-6.6.

To manage and allocate main storage, it is necessary to identify each page frame's status. Is it being used or is it available? This information can be identified in another special table that we shall call the *page-frame table*, which must be built and maintained by the paging supervisor. This table has an entry to identify each page frame of main storage. In the event of a page fault, when there is an unoccupied page frame, the paging supervisor initiates the page-in operation, updates the page-frame table and the appropriate page table, and sets the presence bit ON. Execution of the program may resume when the page-in is completed. In the event of a page fault and no unused page frames, the paging supervisor will select a page to be replaced, initiate a page-out operation (if this page has changed since last page-in), then initiate a page-in for the currently referenced page (when the freed page frame is available) and update all of the affected page-table, external page-table, and page-frame table entries. Figure 10-6.6 represents the demand-paging page-replacement process just described. This brings us to the last two details for implementing demand paging in a segmented and

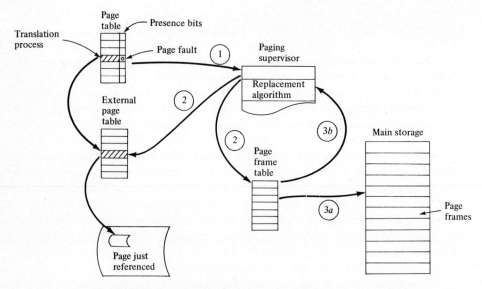

1. When a page fault occurs, the paging supervisor is activated.

2. The referenced page is located in auxiliary storage through the external page table;
   the page frame table is referenced to see if there are any free page frames.

3a. A free page frame is available. The page-in operation can be started.

3b. No free page frames are available. A replacement operation is required.

Fig. 10-6.6 Demand paging and page replacement mechanics in a system-design context.

paged system: (1) how to identify changed pages, and (2) how to implement a
replacement algorithm, particularly the commonly used LRU algorithm.

The contents of a page can only be changed by a store operation. If a hardware
mechanism associated with each page frame is triggered by a store operation, the
paging supervisor need only examine the status of this mechanism to decide if a page-
out is required. In many virtual-storage systems, this hardware assistance is called a
change bit, and it is associated with each page frame either in the memory of the frame
or in the page-table entry. Any time the contents of a page is changed, the associated
change bit is automatically turned ON (set to 1) by hardware. Change bits may only be
examined and turned off by a program that executes in privileged mode. Thus, the
paging supervisor can examine the appropriate change bit in making the replacement
decision and turn off the change bit after page-in operations.

Another hardware feature to help the paging-supervisor program is the reference
bit included in each page-table entry (or main-storage page frame). The reference bit is
turned ON any time a storage reference is made to the page. When all reference bits are
ON, they are turned OFF. Only a privileged program can selectively turn off reference
bits. The paging-supervisor program can use them to implement a rough approximation
to the LRU replacement algorithm, i.e., at page replacement times, only pages with
reference bits OFF are selected for replacement.

10-7 PROGRAMMING STYLE AND PROGRAM BEHAVIOR
[Refs. BR1,BR2,CO1,CO2,FI2,FR,GU,HA1,JO3, MC2, NE,VE]

It has already been emphasized that a primary objective of virtual storage is to give each programmer a large address space that is automatically and dynamically folded into a fast store which, in the systems-design context, is the main store. The expected improvement in ease of programming should be accompanied by reasonably good performance because of the principle of locality of reference. Experiments have shown that even representative existing programs not written with virtual storage in mind have reasonably good locality. Also, certain simple programming techniques have been identified that can improve locality. There is experimental evidence that virtual-storage performance is sensitive to programming style, more sensitive in fact to this factor than to the page-replacement algorithm. For this reason, we now turn to some common ways that programming style affects a program's storage reference pattern.

The storage-address stream produced by a running program depends on the following factors:

1. The problem given the programmer
2. The algorithm and the source language used
3. The program translator (compiler)
4. The particular data being processed

Since most programs are written in high-level languages, the language translator programs (e.g., compilers) can play an important role in how storage is referenced. For example, if the same constants are referenced in different pages of a program, it might be beneficial (although costly in storage) to store copies of the constants in each page that references them, since otherwise the page containing the constants will be required with other pages that reference them. Some fairly simple beneficial measures can be taken immediately in compilers designed for virtual-storage environments. More sophisticated steps have also been suggested, such as care in linking programs expected to be used together.

Most programmers must use an available language and compiler so that their only type of performance control is the organization of the problem for good locality. To cite a specific case for discussion, consider Fig. 10-7.1, which shows two FORTRAN programs (omitting input-output) that produce the same result: the vector RMIN giving the row minima of matrix A. In discussing these programs, it is important to remember that FORTRAN stores its matrices in *column order*. Program (a) marches across each row and replaces the current row minimum RMIN(I) by the matrix element $A(I,J)$ only if the latter is smaller. If matrix A is large, the locality of this program may be quite poor, since successive elements of A are stored down the columns but the program is marching across rows. There is then a good chance that successive references in the same row of the A matrix may be to different pages—this is poor locality. Program (b) also finds the minima of the rows, but it does so by marching down columns. The program begins by moving column 1 of A into RMIN. Element I of column 2 is compared with RMIN(I), and the smaller replaces RMIN(I). After column 2 has been so treated, the program proceeds to column 3, and so forth.

```
    DIMENSION A(100,100), RMIN(100)
    DO 1 I = 1, 100
    RMIN(I) = A(I,1)
    DO 2 J = 2, 100
    IF (A(I,J) – RMIN(I)) 4,2,2
 4  RMIN(I) = A(I,J)
 2  CONTINUE
 1  CONTINUE
    END
```

(a) Program that marches across rows.

```
    DIMENSION A(100,100), RMIN(100)
    DO 1 J = 1, 100
 1  RMIN(J) = A(1,J)
    DO 2 J = 2, 100
    DO 3 I = 1, 100
    IF (A(I,J) – RMIN(I)) 4, 3, 3
 4  RMIN(I) = A(I,J)
 3  CONTINUE
 2  CONTINUE
    END
```

(b) Program that marches down columns.

Fig. 10-7.1 Two programs that find the minima of the rows of a matrix.

Note that although this program also finds the row minima, successive accesses to matrix *A* are to successive *column* elements—the same order in which the matrix is stored. Hence, the locality is much better than the locality of program (a).

The example just described demonstrates how a language characteristic, in this case how FORTRAN stores its matrix elements, can affect a generated program's locality. To achieve good locality for this problem, a programmer must know how FORTRAN stores matrices. Likewise, other languages such as COBOL or PL/I have characteristics that affect a program's locality, and thus its performance in a virtual-storage system.

Some programming techniques used to obtain good locality include:

1. Placing data near the instructions that reference it whenever possible
2. Placing frequently called subroutines (for example, a square-root routine) in line rather than calling them
3. Separating unusual-situation routines, such as error routines, from the main section of a program, preferably as separate modules

Many programming techniques obtain good locality at the expense of address space (virtual storage). In general, modular programming results in good locality. However, module content should be problem oriented, not function oriented. For example, placing all I/O functions in a separate single module will probably not result, in itself, in good locality.

In addition to coding techniques, program structure can also affect locality. One aspect of structure has already been stated, i.e., the idea of separating unusual-situation procedures, such as initialization and error routines, from the main-line program.

Another good structure tactic is to place modules that reference one another close together, if possible in the same page of AS. Many compilers generate object-code modules (called CSECTS in IBM systems) that are linked together when loaded into the address space. If it is possible to identify module and intermodule activity, it may be possible to separate a frequently referenced code from an infrequently referenced code and to pack certain modules into the same page in an attempt to improve locality and reduce working-set size. Of course, this assumes that a programmer has advance knowledge of module activity and intermodule relationships. This information cannot usually be obtained without considerable effort; it may however be obtained with a software monitor (see Chap. 6). A segmentation system, with compiler-generated segments, lends itself more naturally to this type of structuring.

Having said so much about programming techniques (and having only scratched the surface), an important question arises: How much effort should a programmer devote to special programming techniques when using a virtual-storage system? The answer is simply: it depends! If a program is used once, then discarded, or only once in a great while, special laborious effort may be unjustified to measure or improve its locality. Frequently used programs may require some attention if their paging activity seems excessive. A program whose average working-set size is say 150k bytes would probably have no bad effects in a multiprogramming environment with 2048k bytes of main storage available; it may however warrant attention for revision in the same environment with only 384k of main storage. Empirical data from locality studies demonstrates that most programs, including those written ignoring the paging environment, exhibit adequate and in many cases good locality. By observing a few new considerations, as discussed above, a programmer can with relatively little effort usually obtain good locality and yet enjoy most of the conveniences and advantages of programming for a large address space.

To understand better some of the effects of programming style on performance, we now summarize some of the results published by B. Brawn and F. Gustavson in 1968. Their experiments were done on the experimental IBM M44/44X system at the T.J. Watson Research Center in Yorktown Heights, N.Y. They selected three problems for the experiment—matrix inversion, data correlation, and sorting. For each of these, three programming styles were used. The first, termed "casual," was programmed giving no attention to the paging environment. The second style, called "improved," took into account the paging environment, but only in a rather simple way. In the third style, termed "most improved," an attempt was made to produce the best structuring possible for the paging environment. Each program was run alone on the machine. Figure 10-7.2 shows the results for the matrix inversion problem coded in FORTRAN. The second style used some of the simple techniques of matrix access discussed earlier. This program processes the matrix in column order, which results in substantial improvement (as a smaller parachor). Similar results were obtained for the data correlation and sort problems by going from a casual code to programs tuned for a paging environment. Part (a) of Fig. 10-7.2 demonstrates that a change in programming technique results in better locality and smaller working sets. Figure 10-7.2(b) shows that a change in programming techniques results in substantially better improvements than those obtainable by fixing the program and using even the optimum MIN page-replacement algorithm (described in Sec. 10-6). The MIN

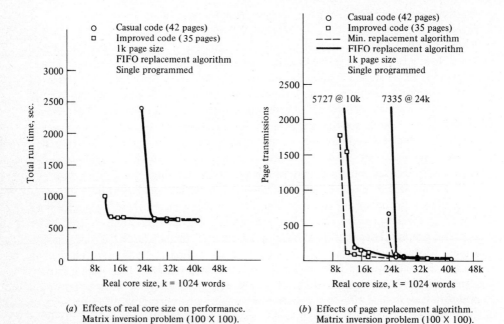

(a) Effects of real core size on performance. Matrix inversion problem (100 × 100).

(b) Effects of page replacement algorithm. Matrix inversion problem (100 × 100).

Fig. 10-7.2 Some results from the Brawn and Gustavson study.

algorithm results were obtained by an interpretive execution of the matrix inversion programs.

In their study, Brawn and Gustavson also ran programs in carefully controlled multiprogramming environments and compared systems with and without thrashing monitors. Although virtual-storage systems automatically fold a program's address space, this study (and others like it) demonstrates that the programmer can have a significant effect on performance in a virtual-storage environment.

10-8 CPU-DESIGN CONTEXT: IBM S/370 MOD 155
[CO3,GI,IB2,IB3,IB4,IB5,IB6,IB7,LI2,SI]

The problem of designing a fast CPU requires a fast small store between the fast processor and the much slower main store. Traditionally, the fast store is used in a special way, e.g., in "instruction look-ahead." Virtual storage is another more general way of managing a buffer-main store hierarchy. Its justification rests on several address-stream studies (Refs. GI,SI).

The Mod 155, along with Mod 165, used the CPU context of virtual storage to achieve high speed. The Mods 158 and 168 did the same, but in addition, the system-design context was implemented. In the following discussion, we describe only the Mod 155.

The CPU storage hierarchy, shown in Fig. 10-8.1, is seen to consist of a main store of typically 1-million byte capacity, a 2100-nanosecond cycle time per module

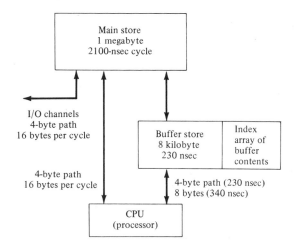

Fig. 10-8.1 IBM System/370 Mod 155 organization.

(four-way interleaved), and a small fast-buffer store of 8k bytes capacity and 230-nanosecond cycle time. In addition, there is the storage device containing the index array used for mapping processor effective addresses into buffer addresses.

During operation, whenever an instruction or data item is referenced, the Mod 155 checks it in the index store for buffer residence. If present in the buffer, execution is at buffer speed. If not present, a delay results while the 155 moves a block of 16 bytes containing the referenced item into the buffer (at main-storage speed). Store (as opposed to fetch) references by the CPU are made to *both* the buffer and main storage (*store-through*). This results in a current copy of the buffer contents always being in main storage, and hence eliminates the need to ever move changed information back from the buffer to main storage when replacement is required. This "store-through" procedure slows the effective reference rate. The slowing is likely to be statistically quite small, partly because store references are relatively rare (20 percent of total is typical) and also because a store operation causes no processing delay, unless an attempt is made to reference the same main-store module before the *write access* is complete.

I/O channel references in the Mod 155 are typically processed as follows: addresses of incoming data are used to check the buffer and, if present, the buffer presence bit is set to OFF and information is entered into main storage. The next CPU reference to such data will then result in a fetch of the latest copy from main storage to the buffer. Outgoing references need only come from main storage because the store-through principle ensures that the latest copy is in main storage.

To transfer information between main store and buffer store, the Mod 155 uses a kind of paging scheme that is controlled completely by hardware. The buffer store main-store organization is shown in Fig. 10-8.2. In Mod 155 terminology, a page is called a *storage block*. Each storage block is 32 bytes in size. Main storage is organized in rows, each row containing 128 blocks. A 1m-byte main storage contains 256 rows, as shown in Fig. 10-8.2. The buffer store is also organized into rows with 128 blocks

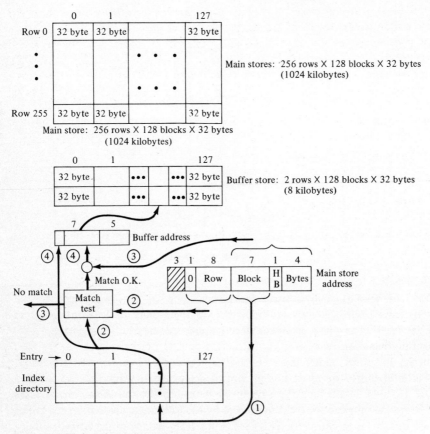

Notes: 1. Circled numbers indicate relative times during mapping.
2. Match test includes check of 2 validity bits in index for presence of data in buffer storage. No-match exit results in logic to replace a block in buffer with requested block of main store.
3. Since a block in column K of main store must be in column K of buffer, at most 2 blocks of any one main store column can be in buffer at once.

Fig. 10-8.2 Mapping main-store address into buffer address in Mod 155.

to a row. Being 8k bytes in size, the buffer has two rows. A many-to-one mapping scheme is used between main store and buffer store. Thus, blocks in column $\emptyset$ of main store may only be placed in column $\emptyset$ of the buffer store; column 1 of main store may only be placed in column 1 of the buffer, etc. This many-to-one scheme maps 256 blocks onto two blocks for the 1m-byte storage in Fig. 10-8.2. A buffer replacement strategy involves a decision concerning only two blocks for the column involved, making it rather easy to implement an LRU algorithm. Referenced blocks not in the buffer (page faults) require block replacement actions by the hardware. Transferring blocks from buffer back to main store (page-outs) are never required because of the store-through property).

During Mod 155 operation, all generated storage addresses refer to main storage. In a 1m-byte Mod 155, the processor will generate 20 significant bits of address for each reference, and this must be translated (mapped) into a 13-bit address to the 8k-byte buffer. Some details of translation are shown in Fig. 10-8.2. The effective address, generated as usual in System/360/370 machines, is considered to be composed of several fields. The block (column) field refers to the buffer index store used for mapping. It has as many entries as buffer blocks (256). Each index entry identifies the main storage row whose block contents are currently stored in the buffer. During translation, the block field of the effective address is used to address the index; the two index entries (for that column) are then checked for match with the row field of the effective address (and presence bits). If the match is successful, the column number (from the index) is used to access the buffer, together with the "half block" and byte address that precisely locate the referenced byte or bytes. Not shown in Fig. 10-8.2, updated with each reference, are activity bits of last reference for each buffer block. These will be later used to decide which block (of two) is to be replaced when a replacement is necessary. At replacement time, although a block in the buffer is reserved, only a half block (16 bytes) containing the referenced information is moved at once.

Performance of the buffer-backing store arrangement is indicated by the manufacturer's statement that in several experiments with actual programs, over 90 percent of main-storage references were found in the buffer.

The Mod 155 is representative of the other IBM CPU-design context models. There are variations in mapping schemes, system speeds, and capacities; however, the implementation principles are very similar.

The CPU-design contexts of the Mod 158 and Mod 168 are implemented by special additional hardware not found in other System/360/370 models. In addition, the Mod 158 and Mod 168 have separate hardware to implement the system-design context of virtual storage. This will be described in Chap. 11.

REFERENCES AND BIBLIOGRAPHY

1. [AH] Aho, A.V., P. J. Denning, and J. D. Ullman: Principles of Optimal Page Replacement, *Journal of the ACM 18*, no. 1, pp. 80-93, January, 1971.
2. [AR] Arden, B. W., B. A. Galler, T. C. O'Brien, and F. H. Westervelt: Program and Addressing Structure in a Time-Sharing Environment, *Journal of the ACM 13*, no. 1, pp. 1-16, January, 1966.
3. [BA1] Batson, A., S. M. Ju, and D. C. Wood: Measurements of Segment Size, *Second ACM Symposium on Operating System Principles*, Princeton University, pp. 25-29, October 20-22, 1969.
4. [BA2] Baylis, M.J.H., D. G. Fletcher, and D. J. Howarth: Paging Studies Made on the I.C.T. ATLAS Computer, *IFIP Proc. of the 1968 Congress 2*, pp. 831-837, 1968.
5. [BE1] Belady, L. A.: A Study of Replacement Algorithms for a Virtual-Storage Computer, *IBM Systems Journal 5*, no. 2, pp. 78-101, 1966.
6. [BE2] Belady, L. A., R. A. Nelson, and G. S. Shedler: An Anomaly in Space-Time Characteristics of Certain Programs Running in a Paging Machine, *Comm. of the ACM 12*, no. 6, pp. 349-353, June, 1969.
7. [BE3] Belady, L. A. and C. J. Kuehner: Dynamic Space-Sharing in Computer Systems, *Comm. of the ACM 12*, no. 5, pp. 282-288, May, 1969.
8. [BO] Bovet, D. P. and G. Estrin: A Dynamic Memory Allocation Algorithm, *IEEE Transactions on Computers C-19*, No. 5, pp. 403-411, May, 1970

9. [BR1] Brawn, B. S. and F. G. Gustavson: Program Behavior in a Paging Environment, *AFIPS Conference Proc., Fall Joint Computer Conference 33*, pp. 1019-1032, 1968.

10. [BR2] Brawn, B. S., F. G. Gustavson, and E. S. Mankin: Sorting in a Paging Environment, *Comm. of the ACM 13*, No. 8, pp. 483-494, August, 1970.

11. [BU] Burroughs Corp.: The Descriptor—A Definition of the B5000 Information-Processing System, *Burroughs Corp.,* 1961.

12. [CO1] Coffman, E. G. and L. C. Varian: Further Experimental Data on the Behavior of Programs in a Paging Environment, *Comm. of the ACM 11*, No. 7, pp. 471-474, July, 1968.

13. [CO2] Coffman, E. and P. Denning: "Operating System Theory," Prentice-Hall, Englewood Cliffs, N.J., 1974.

14. [COM] Comeau, L. W.: A Study of the Effect of User Program Optimization in a Paging System, *ACM Symposium on Operating System Principles*, Gatlinburg, Tenn., October 1-4, 1967.

15. [CON] Conti, C. J.: Concepts for Buffer Storage, *IEEE Computer Group News*, vol. 2, No. 8, 1969.

16. [DE1] Denning, P. J.: The Working Set Model for Program Behavior, *Comm. of the ACM 11*, No. 5, pp. 323-333, May, 1968.

17. [DE2] Denning, P. J.: Virtual Memory, *Computing Surveys 2*, No. 3, pp. 153-189, September, 1970.

18. [DE3] Denning, P. J.: On the Management of Multilevel Memories, *Proc. of the 3rd Princeton Conference on Information Science and Systems*, Princeton University, pp. 162-165, 1969.

19. [DE4] Dennis, J. B.: Segmentation and the Design of Multiprogrammed Computer Systems, *Journal of the ACM 12*, No. 4, pp. 589-602, October, 1965.

20. [DO] Doherty, W. J.: Scheduling TSS/360 for Responsiveness, *Proc. AFIPS, FJCC*, 1970.

21. [FE] Fenichal, R. R. and J. C. Yochelson: A LISP Garbage-Collector for Virtual-Memory Computer Systems, *Comm. of the ACM 12*, No. 11, pp. 611-612, November, 1969.

22. [FI1] Fikes, R. E., H. C. Lauer, and A. L. Vareha, Jr.: Steps Toward a General-Purpose Time-Sharing System Using Large Capacity Core Storage and TSS/360, *Proc. of the 23rd National Conference of the ACM P-68*, pp. 7-18, 1968.

23. [FI2] Fine, G.H., C. W. Jackson, and P. V. McIsaac: Dynamic Program Behavior Under Paging, *Proc. of the 21st National Conference of the ACM P-66*, pp. 223-228, 1966.

24. [FO] Fotheringham, J.: Dynamic Storage Allocation in the Atlas Computer, Including an Automatic Use of a Backing Store, *Comm. of the ACM 4*, No. 10, pp. 435-436, October, 1961.

25. [FR] Freibergs, I. F.: The Dynamic Behavior of Programs, *AFIPS Conference Proc., Fall Joint Computer Conference 33*, pp. 1163-1167, 1968.

26. [GI] Gibson, D.H.: Considerations in Block-oriented Systems Design, *AFIPS Conference Proc. SJCC*, pp. 75-80, 1967.

27. [GR] Greenfield, M. N.: FACT Segmentation, *AFIPS Conference Proc., Spring Joint Computer Conference 21*, pp. 307-315, 1962.

28. [GU] Guertin, R. L.: Programming in a Paging Environment, *Datamation 18*, No. 2, pp. 48-55, February, 1972.

29. [HA1] Hatfield, D. J. and J. Gerald: Program Restructuring for Virtual Memory, *IBM Systems Journal*, Vol. 10, No. 3, 1971.

30. [HE] Hellerman, H.: Complementary Replacement, a Meta Scheduling Principle, *Proc. ACM Conference on Operating System Principles*, Princeton, N.J., 1969.

31. [IB1] IBM Corp.: "Introduction to Virtual Storage in System/370," No. GR20-4260, IBM Corp. Data Processing Division, White Plains, N.Y. 10604.

32. [IB2] IBM Corp.: "IBM System/360 Model 85 Functional Characteristics," No. GA22-6916, IBM Corp. Data Processing Division, White Plains, N.Y. 10604.

33. [IB3] IBM Corp.: "IBM System/370 Model 155 Functional Characteristics," No. GA22-6942, IBM Corp. Data Processing Division, White Plains, N.Y. 10604.

34. [IB4] IBM Corp.: "A Guide to the IBM System/370 Model 155," No. GC20-1729, IBM Corp. Data Processing Division, White Plains, N.Y. 10604.

35. [IB5] IBM Corp.: "A Guide to the IBM System/370 Model 158," No. GC20-1754, IBM Corp. Data Processing Division, White Plains, N.Y. 10604.

36. [IB6] IBM Corp.: "IBM System/370 Model 165 Functional Characteristics," No. GA22-6935, IBM Corp. Data Processing Division, White Plains, N.Y. 10604.

37. [IB7] IBM Corp.: "System/370 Model 168 Functional Characteristics," No. GA22-7010, IBM Corp. Data Processing Division, White Plains, N.Y. 10604.

38. [JO1] Jodeit, J. G.: Storage Organization in Programming Systems, *Comm. of the ACM 11*, No. 11, pp. 741-746, November, 1968.

39. [JO2] Jones, R. M.: Factors Affecting the Efficiency of a Virtual Memory, *IEEE Transactions on Computers C-18*, No. 11, pp. 1004-1008, November, 1969.

40. [JO3] Joseph, M.: An Analysis of Paging and Program Behavior, *Computer Journal 13*, No. 1, pp. 48-54, February, 1970.

41. [KA] Katzan, H.: Storage Hierarchy Systems, *AFIPS Conference Proc., Spring Joint Computer Conference 38*, pp. 325-336, 1971.

42. [KE1] Keefe, D. D.: Hierarchical Control Programs for Systems Evaluation, *IBM Systems Journal 7*, No. 1, pp. 15-21, 1968.

43. [KE2] Kernighan, B. W.: Optimal Segmentation Points for Programs, *Second ACM Symposium on Operating System Principles*, Princeton University, pp. 47-52, October 20-22, 1969.

44. [KI1] Kilburn, T., D.B.G. Edwards, M.J. Lanigan, and F. H. Sumner: One-level Storage System, *IRE Transactions EC-11*, No. 2, pp. 223-235, April, 1962.

45. [KI2] King, W. F.: Analysis of Paging Algorithms, *IBM Thomas J. Watson Research Center Report RC-3288*, Yorktown Heights, New York, March 17, 1971.

46. [KN] Knuth, D. E.: "The Art of Computer Programming," Vol. 1, Fundamental Algorithms, Addison-Wesley, Reading, Mass., 1968.

47. [KU1] Kuck, D. J. and D. H. Lawrie: The Use and Performance of Memory Hierarchies: A Survey, *University of Illinois at Champaign-Urbana, Dept. of Computer Science Report No. 363*, December 4, 1969.

48. [KU2] Kuehner, C. J. and B. Randell: Demand Paging in Perspective, *AFIPS Conference Proc., Fall Joint Computer Conference*, vol. 33, pp. 1011-1018, 1968.

49. [LE] Lewis, P.A.W. and P. C. Yue: Statistical Analysis of Program Reference Patterns in a Paging Environment, *IEEE Computer Society Conference*, Boston, Mass. pp. 133-134, September 22-24, 1971.

50. [LI1] Lindquist, A. B., R. R. Seeber, and L. W. Comeau: A Time-Sharing System Using an Associative Memory, *Proc. of the IEEE 54*, No. 12, pp. 1774-1779, December, 1966.

51. [LI2] Liptay, J. S.: Structural Aspects of the System/360 Model 85, Part II, The Cache, *IBM Systems Journal*, vol. 7, No. 1, pp. 15-21, 1968.

52. [MA1] MacKenzie, F. B.: Automated Secondary Storage Management, *Datamation 11*, No. 11, pp. 24-28, November, 1965.

53. [MA2] Mattson, R. L., J. Gecsei, D. R. Slutz, and I. L. Traiger: Evaluation Techniques for Storage Hierarchies, *IBM Systems Journal*, Vol. 9, No. 2, pp. 78-117, 1970.

54. [MC1] McGee, W. C.: On Dynamic Program Relocation, *IBM Systems Journal*, vol. 4, No. 3, pp. 184-199, 1965.

55. [MC2] McKellar, A C. and E. G. Coffman, Jr.: Organizing Matrices and Matrix Operations for Paged Memory Systems, *Comm. of the ACM*, vol. 12, No. 3, pp. 153-165, March, 1969.

56. [MO] Morganstein, S. J., S. Winograd, and R. Herman: SIM/61: A Simulation Measurement Tool for a Time-Shared, Demand Paging Operating System, *ACM SIGOPS Workshop on System Performance Evaluation*, Harvard University, pp. 142-172, April 5-7, 1971.

57. [NE] Nelson, R. A. and G. S. Shedler: An Anomaly in the Space-Time Characteristics of Certain Programs Running in Paging Machines, *Comm. ACM*, vol. 12, No. 6, pp. 349-353, June, 1969.

58. [ON] O'Neill, R. W.: Experience Using a Time-Shared Multiprogramming System with Dynamic Address Relocation Hardware, *AFIPS Conference Proc., Spring Joint Computer Conference*, vol. 30, pp. 611-621, 1967.

59. [RA1] Randell, B. and C. J. Kuehner: Dynamic Storage Allocation Systems, *Comm. of the ACM*, vol. 11, No. 5, pp. 297-306, May, 1968.

60. [RA2] Randell, B: A Note on Storage Fragmentation and Program Segmentation, *Comm. of the ACM 12*, No. 7, pp. 365-372, June, 1969.

61. [SA] Sayre, D.: Is Automatic "Folding" of Programs Efficient Enough to Displace Manual? *Comm. of the ACM 12*, No. 12, pp. 656-660, December, 1969.

62. [SH1] Shedler, G. S. and S. C. Yang: Simulation of a Model of Paging System Performance, *IBM Systems Journal*, vol. 10, No. 2, pp. 113-128, 1971.

63. [SH2] Shemer, J. E. and S. C. Gupta: On the Design of Bayesian Storage Allocation Algorithms for Paging and Segmentation, *IEEE Transactions on Computers C-18*, No. 7, pp. 644-651, July, 1969.

64. [SI] Sisson, S. S. and M. J. Flynn: Addressing Patterns and Memory-Handling Algorithms, *AFIPS Conference Proc., Fall Joint Computer Conference 33*, pp. 957-967, 1968.

65. [TH] Thorington, J. M. and J. D. Irwin: A New Philosophy in Dynamic Memory Allocation, *Proc. of the 4th Hawaii Conference on Systems Science*, University of Hawaii, pp. 431-434, January 12-14, 1971.

66. [VA] Vareha, A. L., R. M. Rutledge, and M. M. Gold: Strategies for Structuring Two-Level Memories in a Paging Environment, *Second ACM Symposium on Operating System Principles*, Princeton University, pp. 54-59, October 20-22, 1969.

67. [VE] Verhoef, E. W.: Automatic Program Segmentation Based on Boolean Connectivity, *AFIPS Conference Proc., Spring Joint Computer Conference 38*, pp. 491-496, 1971.

68. [WA] Wallace, V. L. and D. L. Mason: Degree of Multiprogramming in Page-on-Demand Systems, *Comm. of the ACM 12*, No. 6, pp. 305-308, June, 1969.

69. [WE1] Weil, J. W.: A Heuristic for Page Turning in a Multiprogrammed Computer, *Comm. of the ACM*, vol. 5, No. 9, pp. 480-481, September, 1962.

70. [WE2] Weizer, N. and G. Oppenheimer: Virtual Memory Management in a Paging Environment, *AFIPS Conference Proc., Spring Joint Computer Conference 34*, pp. 249-256, 1969.

CHAPTER 11

Virtual Storage: System-Design Context

Virtual storages composed of a memory hierarchy whose members have access times in the ratio of 1000:1 (or more) characterize the system-design context. Typically, the faster member is main storage and the slower is a device like a disk or drum. As discussed in Chap. 10, supervisory functions are provided primarily by system software, with special hardware assistance for very frequent operations such as mapping and the recording of reference and change activity.

We now turn to some architecture choices, each with its own set of flexibilities and cost-performance characteristics. One fundamental issue is whether the system supplies the available address space as a single large unit shared by the currently active user tasks, or whether *each* user is given the large available address space. The first option is easier to implement, especially on small systems, and complete problem-program compatibility can easily be maintained with an existing conventional system. These traits should help explain why the first virtual-storage operating systems for the IBM System/370 (called OS/VS) use this scheme.

At the opposite end of the complexity and compatibility spectrum is *Multics*, which was designed from scratch for maximum generality and sharing in a timesharing user environment. Multics supplies each user with his own very large address space and makes extensive provisions for sharing programs and data, including an elegant storage-security mechanism.

Another major architecture option is represented by the IBM VM/370 operating system that provides each user with not only virtual storage, but also with a *virtual machine* (VM), which is the precise functional equivalent of a physical S/370 computer configuration. Each VM has all CPU instructions, including the privileged ones, as well as virtual I/O and other devices. VM multiprograms entire *operating systems* rather than only multiprogramming several programs. VM systems can simultaneously accommodate several operating systems by sharing the host system's resources, and this is done without reprogramming any of the operating systems.

In this chapter we shall examine in some detail the major classes of existing virtual systems using the IBM VS, VM, and GE-MIT Multics as timely examples.

11-1 SYSTEM DESIGN CONSIDERATIONS   [Refs. GE,GL,HA1,IB2,JO,LE]

Assume a segmented and paged address space, i.e., the address space is divided into segments of the same maximum size and each segment is subdivided into pages. As discussed in Sec. 10-3, segments permit information to be shared among several users with less space overhead (than a page-only system) for mapping tables. The variable-sized segments also serve as a convenient and flexible unit for address-space allocation. The paging structure results in simplicity and flexibility in main-storage management, since main storage can then be considered as a pool of page frames for use by a relatively simple replacement algorithm (relative, that is, to the complexity of managing segmented nonpaged main storage).

As mentioned earlier, a fundamental architecture consideration is whether the system maintains a single large address space that is shared by all users in much the same logical manner that physical main storage is shared in a conventional multiprogrammed operating system, or whether each user should be given his own large address space. The first of these options shall be called an AS(1) type system, while the second shall be termed as AS(n) system. In AS(1), the supervisor, resident system functions, and all scheduled executing jobs share the same large address space. A major incentive for the AS(1) approach is compatibility with a "conventional" operating system, already in widespread use, whose main storage now corresponds to the single system address space.

AS(n) systems provide each executing user with his own AS. "User" in this context may, for example, be a batch job, a timesharing task, or a teleprocessing application.

Mapping in AS(1) requires one segment table (to map the address space) with page tables to map all allocated segments, one page table for each segment. We assume that these tables reside in main storage, as they do in most cases. A special-purpose machine register, sometimes called the Segment Table Origin Register (STOR), identifies the main-storage origin of the segment table; each segment-table entry identifies the main-storage origin of the segment's page table; page-table entries identify page-frame locations for each page resident in main storage (see Fig. 10-3.2).

In an AS(n) system, each user has his own address space mapped by its own segment and page tables. To activate a program, the supervisor loads the machine's STOR register with the address of the program's segment table. Theoretically, the number of address spaces that can be created in an AS(n) system is almost unlimited.

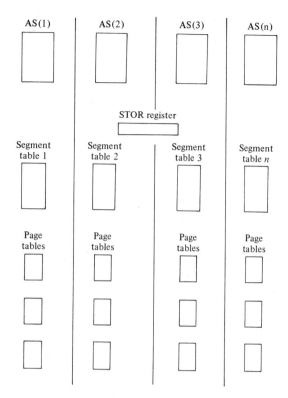

Fig. 11-1.1 An AS(n) mapping scheme.

The mapping scheme outlined in Fig. 11-1.1 indicates this possibility.* As a practical matter, the number of address spaces (or users) that are permitted to coexist is limited by available resources. For example, mapping tables use part of main storage; for each new AS, this increases. Main storage available for demand paging and limited auxiliary-storage size and speed are also only capable of supporting a certain level of activity. This also limits the number of users, but not in a simple way, since working sets differ greatly from program to program. Some disk space is also required for each new AS.

Fundamental parameters for an address space include: (1) address-space size, (2) segment size, and (3) page size. Many considerations affect value selections for these parameters. Among these considerations are the purpose of the operating system (multiprogramming, timesharing, or both), whether it is to be AS(1) or AS(n), the mapping-hardware and supervisory-software sophistication, and the range of speeds and sizes of available resources.

The addressing structure of the CPU determines AS size. Examples for the IBM Systems/360/370 and Multics are shown in Fig. 11-1.2. Each added bit of CPU effective address doubles AS size. In addition to AS capacity, the number of segments

*See Ref. IB10, p. 41.

and segment size are also important considerations. For a given AS size, segment size determines the number of segments within an address space, at least in those systems in which all segments have a fixed maximum size. (The Burroughs scheme is more flexible in this respect.) As indicated in Fig. 11-1.2, Multics has the largest address space—up to 256,000 segments of up to 256k words each. Choosing an appropriate segment size depends on the intended use-environment and mode of the system. In AS(1), address space can be conveniently allocated to jobs being scheduled in multiples of segments, thus making effective use of a large number of relatively small segments. The 64k-byte segments of the System/370 (Fig. 11-1.2) are particularly appropriate for this use-environment, as will be shown later. In an AS(n) system, a smaller number of very large segments (for example, 1m-byte segments) may be appropriate. If, in such a system, segments are allocated to program modules and data structures based on logical requirements, a 1m-byte segment can accommodate potentially large modules and data structures. The number of large segments provided in an AS(n) system can affect implementation considerations. If there are more logical program and data requirements than segments available, the system must "force" these logical requirements into the available segments. To avoid this problem, a system (with more expensive hardware) can implement a larger effective address to provide each AS with many large segments. Multics and the Mod 67 with 32-bit addressing are examples. When considering these alternatives, one must remember that virtual storage is an address space created by a mapping structure. During system operation, unused virtual

	Address size	AS size	Segment size	Page size
System/360	24 bits	16 mbytes	1 mbyte	4k bytes
Model 67	32 bits	4096 mbytes	1 mbyte	4k bytes
System/370	24 bits	16 mbytes	64k bytes	2k bytes or 4k bytes
	24 bits	16 mbytes	1 mbyte*	2k bytes or 4k bytes
MULTICS	36 bits	256k segments	256k words	1k words

* System/370 hardware supports two segment sizes; however, no IBM VS systems implement 1m-byte segments.

(a) Address, segment, and page sizes.

S/360 Mod 67 (32-bit address)

Segment I.D.	Page I.D.	Byte address
— 12 bits —	— 8 bits —	— 12 bits —

S/370 (24 bit-address, 64k-byte segments, 2k-byte pages)

Segment I.D.	Page I.D.	Byte address
— 8 bits —	— 5 bits —	— 11 bits —

MULTICS (36-bit address)

Segment I.D.	Page I.D.	Word address
— 18 bits —	— 8 bits —	— 10 bits —

(b) Virtual-address structures.

Fig. 11-1.2   Address space sizes and virtual-address structures.

storage results in little or no waste of physical system resources. Therefore, a system like Multics gives each user a very large potential storage without a corresponding commitment of physical system resources. The effect of *page size* was discussed in Chap. 10. Small pages result in less internal fragmentation, and possibly less page replacement, but require larger page tables (in main storage). Larger pages improve transfer efficiency between auxiliary and main storage and require smaller page tables. However, with larger pages, more instructions and data that don't belong to a program's current working set may reside in main storage. A typical commonly used page size is 4k bytes, which is a compromise among the above considerations (we know of no published justification for this choice).

Various mapping techniques to translate virtual addresses to main-storage locations were described in Chap. 10. When an AS has a segment and page structure, the mapping process must identify the segment number and page number of the AS location being addressed. Translation may then proceed through segment and page tables (or some of their images held in a fast associative store). The number of bits in the effective address interpreted by the mapping device as segment number, page number, and displacement within a page reflect the address-space structure for a particular implementation. In Fig. 11-1.2, the logical structures of several systems' virtual addresses are illustrated.

The segment-page combination helps to reduce the main storage needed for mapping tables when compared to a paged-only nonsegmented scheme. Page tables need not be constructed for unallocated segments. A presence bit in each segment table entry can be tested by the mapping device in a manner analogous to the presence bits used in the page tables. In this way, an attempt to reference an unallocated segment results in a segment fault that causes an interrupt to the supervisor system program. Another saving in mapping storage is possible in the common case where only some of the pages in a segment have information in them. With the restriction that all occupied pages of a segment are placed contiguously in the segment's address space, starting at its origin, only page-table entries for the pages used need be supplied along with the number of such used pages. This latter number is inserted as a limit number in the segment-table entry for the page table. During mapping, the page address will be checked against the limit, and if exceeded, a page-table fault interrupt is generated.

An example can best illustrate the savings in main-storage table space using the above ideas. Suppose AS size is 16 megabytes with 64k-byte segments and 4k-byte pages. Each entry in a segment or page table will be here assumed to require 2 bytes. Assume that only 2 megabytes, or 32 complete segments, are currently holding AS information. Under these conditions, the storage required for mapping is

$$
\begin{aligned}
\text{32 segment table entries} \times \text{2 bytes} &= \text{64 bytes} \\
\text{32 page tables} \times \text{16 entries per table} \times \text{2 bytes} &= \underline{\text{1024 bytes}} \\
\text{Total mapping bytes} &= \text{1088 bytes}
\end{aligned}
$$

In a nonsegment system, the single page table would contain one entry per page, or 4096 entries requiring 8192 bytes for mapping, no matter how little of the AS was actually occupied.

11-2 MULTIPROGRAMMING IN AN AS(1) ENVIRONMENT   [Ref. SM]

The AS(1) type of virtual-storage system is, in many ways, the simplest to understand. First consider a conventional multiprogramming operating system such as was described in Chaps. 7 and 8. The idea of an AS(1) scheme is to retain the same *logical* structure for users, but to substitute a large virtual address space for the much smaller physical main storage. The single large address space is shared by all active users and system programs in the same manner that such programs conventionally shared physical main storage. An AS(1) system is, therefore, typically designed to be completely program compatible with a conventional (nonvirtual) operating system.

Because of AS(1)'s similarity in function to a conventional system, we briefly summarize some of the latter's characteristics:

1. All system programs reside on auxiliary storage, usually direct-access storage.
2. Certain system programs—at least the supervisor—are held in main storage throughout normal operation.
3. Some system functions, like SPOOLing, may be made main-storage resident or scheduled when main storage is available.
4. Scheduling algorithms attempt to keep hardware resources active by multi-programming as many jobs as possible.
5. High thruput is the most common performance objective.

A typical structure for a nonvirtual multiprogramming system is shown in Fig. 11-2.1(*a*). Because main storage is also the entire address space and is relatively small, typically ranging in current systems from 64k to 4096k bytes, careful attention is given to the organization and management of this precious resource. A fixed-size partition or variable-size region scheme is typically used for job space allocation. In either case, system programmers and operators attempt to select jobs and tasks to run together so as to avoid main-storage fragmentation. Main storage may be allocated to SPOOLing functions, shareable programs like access methods, and service programs like supervisor calls or error recovery routines. However, this space commitment must be justified, generally by frequency-of-use, for each function and balanced against the alternative of using the space for job processing. Selection of a proper mix of jobs and system programs to share the limited main store concurrently depends on such factors as the installation's workload, the installation's objectives (e.g., thruput, response time, critical-job scheduling, etc.), and of course on the observed and constantly changing resource-use pattern. Much of this typically requires continuous human effort in observing system activity and making scheduling decisions of how the system's address space, which is also its main storage, should be allocated.

Figure 11-2.1(*b*) shows a typical AS(1) virtual-storage configuration, which is seen to be almost identical in structure to the conventional system of Fig. 11-2.1(*a*), except AS(1) has a much larger address space. Such system functions as job scheduling, program relocation at load time, and program loading need not change, although changes to improve performance may be possible because of the large system address space. Just as in a conventional system, user and system programs must reside in the system's address space to execute. However, in AS(1), the address space is

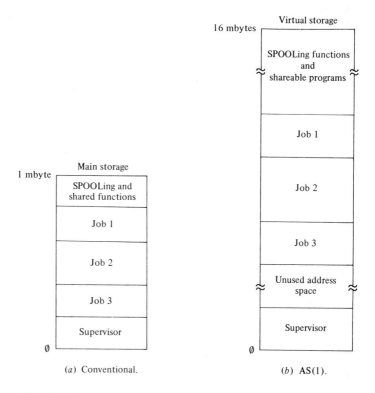

(a) Conventional.   (b) AS(1).

Fig. 11-2.1   Conventional operating-system structure compared to AS(1) structure.

virtual storage (not main storage), and the latter's size becomes primarily a performance factor rather than an operator or user-programmer concern.

Implementing an AS(1) multiprogramming operating system requires both hardware and software extensions to conventional multiprogramming. The CPU must have a mapping device for address translation. Part of auxiliary storage is used to "back" the address space. The supervisor contains additional functions (referred to as the *paging supervisor* in Chap. 10) that control demand-paging activity. Since mapping techniques were described in Chap. 10, we shall concentrate here on AS organization and allocation, the relationships between virtual, main, and auxiliary storages, paging supervisor functions, and other aspects of system operation.

Segmentation is a convenient means for address-space allocation in an AS(1) environment. As mentioned in the previous section, a 16m-byte AS with 256 segments of 64k bytes results in a substantial number of (relatively) small segments that can be allocated to system programs and user jobs. The supervisor (including the paging supervisor) would reside in the first n segments (n depends on supervisor size). All remaining segments can be allocated to other system functions and user jobs under supervisor control. Figure 11-2.2 illustrates the segment-allocation technique just described. For the example in Fig. 11-2.2, supervisor size is assumed to be 128k. Thus, segments $\emptyset$ and 1 are allocated to the supervisor. If a resident system function—such as

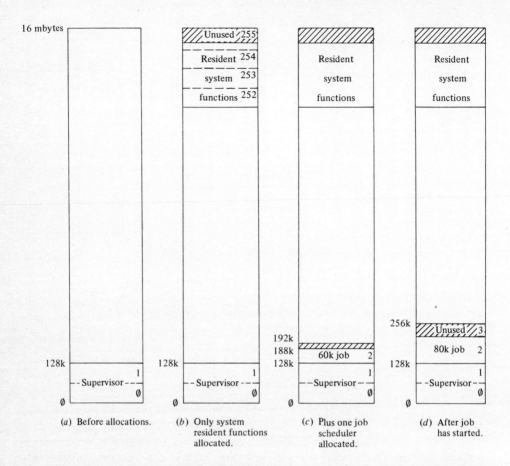

Fig. 11-2.2 Segment allocation technique in AS(1) system.

a SPOOLing program—requires say 150k, it would be allocated 3 segments (192k). Loaded at the top of the address space, these functions would appear as shown in Fig. 11-2.2(b). To process jobs, a job-scheduling program is started. In a system that uses dynamic regions, this effectively starts a region. If the scheduling program requires say 60k, a one-segment region is assigned, as shown in Fig. 11-2.2(c). If an 80k job is scheduled, region size is increased to two segments; the system then appears as shown in Fig. 11-2.2(d). While one job scheduler is active, one job stream is processed. To begin multiprogramming, a second scheduler would be started. As with conventional systems, the degree of multiprogramming depends on the number of active schedulers in the system.

Considering address-space limitations only, job schedulers may be started in an AS(1) environment so long as segments are available. Jobs must be allocated contiguous segments, and both internal and external fragmentation can result; that is, entire segments and parts of segments may be unused. However, the corresponding waste is of virtual (*not* physical) main or auxiliary storage. In an AS(1) scheme, the degree of multiprogramming is typically not limited by the large address-space size,

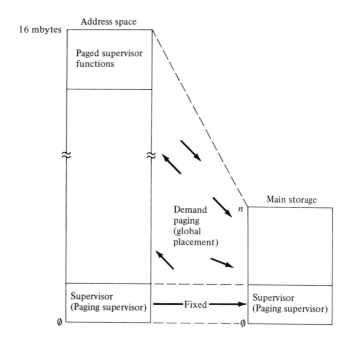

Fig. 11-2.3 Relationship between address space and main storage in an AS(1) system.

but rather by physical main-storage size, CPU speed, and the I/O device configuration. Although Fig. 11-2.2 shows a dynamic-region approach to AS organization, a partitioned system would simply define partitions as some multiple of segments; all of our other observations about the AS(1) environment would then apply.

The next item of interest in an AS(1) system is the relationship between address space and main storage. Figure 11-2.3 shows this relationship. Notice that a copy of certain critical parts of the supervisor resides in both the system's area of address space and main storage. These are fixed in main storage for the following reasons:

1. The supervisor controls all executing user jobs and all system resources; delays caused by paging might intolerably degrade performance.
2. An area within the supervisor, or a workspace area controlled by it, contains the mapping tables; these tables must be main-storage-resident during address translation.
3. The paging supervisor controls the remaining main storage using a demand-paging algorithm. It is usually executed so frequently that to maintain satisfactory system performance, it is fixed in main storage.

Only critical control functions within the supervisor need be fixed in main storage. Other supervisory functions for program loading, SPOOLing, error recovery, supervisor-call services, and so forth can reside in another area of the address space. Usually, they are paged (Fig. 11-2.3). The demand-paging mechanism should ensure that only currently used functions will occupy main storage.

The main storage that remains after the supervisor is fixed serves as a pool of page frames available for demand paging. As the system runs, program addresses (including the supervisor's) are translated. When a page fault occurs, the paging supervisor must place the referenced page in main storage; therefore, a *page-placement* operation is always required and, when all page frames are filled, a *page-replacement* operation is required. Figure 11-2.3 represents a *global-placement* strategy; that is, a referenced page not in main storage can be placed in any available page frame. Pages from all programs then contend for one page-frame pool. If replacement is required, all page frames are potential candidates presented to the replacement algorithm. An alternative to the global strategy is a *local-placement* strategy that assigns a subpool of page frames to each scheduled job. For a particular job, all placement and replacement operations would occur within the job's page pool. Although a local-placement scheme provides better system protection—jobs with high paging rates, and thus poor locality, don't contend with and possibly affect other jobs—its implementation is difficult. Users must somehow assess a job's page-pool requirements, in effect, its average working-set size, before execution begins. This is quite difficult in itself and would also have to be augmented by a penalty for poor estimates. Because of these problems, most systems use global placement and replacement policies.

The mechanics of page placement and replacement were highlighted in Chap. 10. The paging supervisor must create and maintain a table (or set of tables) that identifies the status of each page frame. When a placement operation is necessary, the page-frame table(s) is referenced to identify an available page frame. The paging supervisor can then initiate a page-in operation and update the appropriate page-table and page-frame table entries. When the page-in is complete, program execution can resume. If page replacement is first required, the paging supervisor references the page-frame table(s) to select a candidate for replacement. Typically, an LRU replacement algorithm is used which is implemented through special management of the page-frame table(s). Hardware assistance is usually provided by a *reference* and a *change* bit associated with each page frame. When any reference is made to the frame, its reference bit is turned ON. A frame's change bit is turned ON only when information in a page is changed (stored). The replacement algorithm's prime candidates are pages not recently referenced (reference bit OFF), or (among those with reference bit ON) those with change bit OFF. When all reference bits are ON, they are then all turned OFF.

Although demand paging is the usual technique for main-storage management in an AS(1) system, we have already seen one class of exceptions—certain supervisory functions are fixed in main storage. Also, provision is sometimes made to permit users to fix certain job pages to main-storage page frames throughout execution. Some variations are

1. User specification that certain functions, and therefore pages, be fixed in main storage during a job's execution.

2. User specification that an entire job be fixed in main storage during its execution. A certain small class of jobs cannot execute in a demand-paging environment, due to timing or I/O dependencies.
3. User specification that a number of page frames be reserved for a particular job's use, a variation of local placement strategy. The job would be demand paged; it would use the reserved page frames first and could contend for the remaining page frames with other executing jobs.

Prepaging or *context paging* is still another feature that can be implemented in AS(1). With this feature, a programmer can specify that a certain "context set" of pages should coexist in main storage. The first reference to any page in the context set causes all other members to be prepaged into main storage. If a programmer knows the reference pattern for all or parts of a program, he can in effect prepage the working set(s). Each feature just described serves a special-purpose situation. The normal mode of execution in an AS(1) environment is demand paging.

During the discussion of page placement and replacement strategies, we referred to page-in, page-out activity. Physically, this involves transmission between main storage and auxiliary storage. Figure 11-2.4 shows two techniques to establish the relationship between AS and auxiliary storage so that paging can occur in an AS(1) environment:

1. The first technique, Fig. 11-2.4(*a*), establishes a bulk one-to-one relationship between all of AS and auxiliary storage.
2. The second technique, Fig. 11-2.4(*b*), uses mapping tables that are called *external page tables*.

In the introduction to Chap. 10, it was suggested that virtual storage be visualized as a contiguous area in auxiliary storage. The bulk one-to-one correspondence technique shown in Fig. 11-2.4(*a*) for the AS, auxiliary-storage relationship is just that. The paged area of AS is mapped one-to-one with an area in auxiliary storage. No external mapping tables are required. When a page-in operation is required, the auxiliary-storage page location is determined from the virtual address of the referenced page. Page-out operations must return pages to their fixed auxiliary-storage locations. The bulk-correspondence approach is suitable only for AS(1) implementations. Address-space fragmentation results in auxiliary-storage fragmentation. This waste of auxiliary storage would be intolerable in an AS(n) system.

As mentioned in Chap. 10, external page tables may be used to map AS page addresses into physical locations on auxiliary storage. There is one such external page table for each internal page table. When a page fault occurs, the paging supervisor uses the corresponding external page-table entry to locate the referenced page in auxiliary storage. After a page frame has been allocated, the page-in process can begin. During replacement operations, the paging supervisor can "page out" a changed page to any available auxiliary-storage location, not necessarily the current location of the affected page. Location-selection algorithms that reduce access time can be used. After page-out, the paging supervisor updates the affected external page-table entry to reflect the

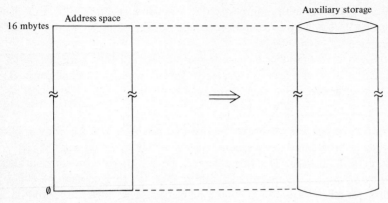

(*a*) Method 1   One-to-one bulk storage mapping where auxiliary storage is allocated to entire address space.

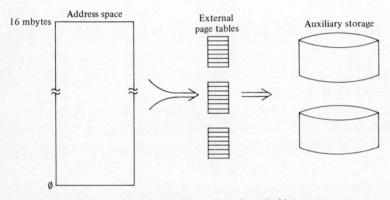

(*b*) Method 2   Auxiliary storage allocated to only used address-space pages.

Fig. 11-2.4 Address space/auxiliary storage relationships in an AS(1) system.

new auxiliary-storage location. External page tables, along with page tables, are constructed when segments are allocated. Auxiliary storage then need not be reserved for unallocated segments. This is a valuable feature in an AS(1) environment, but as we shall see, it is imperative in an AS(n) system.

Thus far, we have discussed main-storage management and paging. We now turn to two other vital operations—starting the system and loading programs.

During IPL, the supervisor is fixed in real storage. After IPL, the system operator may start SPOOLing operations and load paged supervisory functions. The operator controls the level of multiprogramming by starting job schedulers. With say three active job schedulers, three jobs can be multiprogrammed.

When a job step is scheduled, it is allocated a region of the AS and also I/O devices. It is then loaded into AS (*not* into main-storage frames). Assuming load-time (static) relocation as in OS/MVT, the loader program treats the program to be loaded

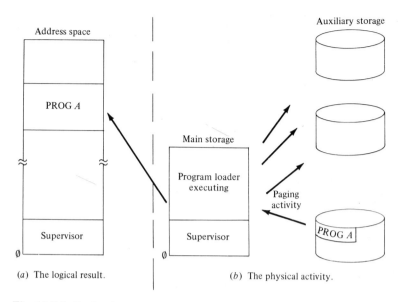

Fig. 11-2.5 Static relocation program loading in an AS(1) system.

as data, modifying its address constants and symbol dictionaries (Fig. 11-2.5) to bind the storage references to some region of address space.* The program modules are also given a page format, and the processed modules are paged out to auxiliary storage. After the loading into AS is complete, control is transferred to the loaded program, which then starts to execute in the demand-paging mode. Pages of the program can, of course, be placed in any available page frames. Note that we do *not* refer to the relocation process inherent in mapping or page-fault response as *loading*. The loading process can be simplified, and even made dynamic, if programs are stored in libraries in a page format. With *dynamic loading*, the first time a page is referenced during program execution, a copy is read from the program library and placed in main storage. Address constants are relocated at this time. If the page is subsequently replaced, it is paged out to the area of auxiliary storage used for demand paging. Initial program loading simply requires constructing external page tables to reflect program-library page locations.

We now summarize AS(1)'s advantages over a nonvirtual system with similar functions:

1. Region or partition sizes can be much larger with resulting user convenience and system flexibility in job scheduling.
2. More supervisory functions can be made "resident" and should be paged efficiently according to actual (rather than estimated) needs, thus relieving the installation of the need to make difficult physical residence decisions.
3. Physical main storage will be more nearly used by truly active parts of programs.
4. All of the above advantages are available without any user or installation reprogramming.

*See Ref. IB10, p. 39.

11-3 AS(n) VIRTUAL-STORAGE SYSTEMS   [Ref. MA2]

The concept of a virtual-storage system that permits multiple address spaces was introduced in Sec. 11-1. In such an AS(n) implementation, each executing user has his own address space. A "user" may be a batch job being multiprogrammed, a timesharing user session, or a teleprocessing application that may support a network of several terminals. The AS(n) scheme provides the basic design structure for systems like Multics, OS/VS2 Release 2, and VM/370. We now enlarge our discussion of the principles of an AS(n) type of system.

Reasons to choose an AS(n) over an AS(1) type of system include:

1. Several virtual machines, each with all the logical properties of the physical machine, may run concurrently.
2. System activities such as SPOOLing can be assigned a unique address space.
3. Program modules and data structures can be conveniently shared among users using segmentation.
4. Providing a large address space presents more direct solutions for more problems, with much less user-explicit I/O folding operations.

Figure 11-3.1 shows a kind of AS(n) system in which there are multiple address spaces with the supervisor mapped into the same segments in every address space; also, critical portions of the supervisor are fixed in main storage. The supervisor is mapped by a set of page tables that are common to each AS. Therefore, when the first AS is created, the first k segments are used for the supervisor (k depends on supervisor size). The first k page tables then map the supervisor. When a second AS is created, its first k-segment table entries point to the existing page tables. This technique is used to map the supervisor into every subsequent AS. Its common segments are mapped by one set of common page tables, as shown in Fig. 11-3.1(b). The mechanics of this mapping process permit more general segment sharing. Two approaches may be used: (1) an area common to all address spaces can be reserved for shareable programs or data, and (2) program modules and data structures may be shared by two or more users in different segments of address space. The first approach, reserving an area common to all address spaces, is like the one described above for part of the supervisor. It requires one set of page tables referenced by common segment table entries in each address space. Typically, system programs such as "supervisor calls" or error-recovery procedures, frequently used access methods, compilers, and frequently required user functions would occupy this common area. The address space available to each user is reduced by the size of the shared area. The shared common programs must be reentrant, and individual users cannot place problem programs in the shared area. This kind of approach was used in the IBM Research M44 and in the IBM VS2/2 systems.

A more general sharing scheme that is somewhat more difficult to implement allows general segment sharing between two or more users. Reentrant program modules or data structures are mapped in different segments in two or more user address spaces. The mechanics are similar to sharing in a common area, as shown in Fig. 11-3.2. Again a common page table is referenced by two or more different segment table entries. However, now conventions must be established for access rights to data structures and authorization to use program modules that assure adequate user

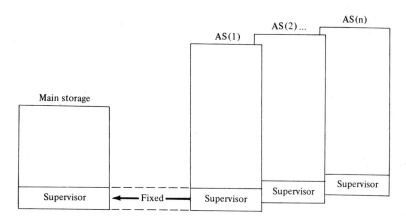

(a) The supervisor is mapped into the same segments in each AS.

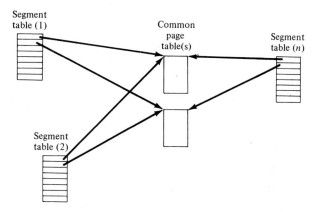

(b) A single set of page tables maps the supervisor in all address spaces.

Fig. 11-3.1 Sharing an area common to all address spaces in an AS(n) system.

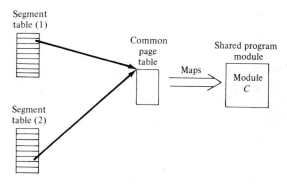

Fig. 11-3.2 Sharing a common program module or data structure mapped in *different* segments of two or more address spaces.

and data protection. With this approach to sharing, when a user with access rights references a shareable module currently being executed by one or more other users, the existing copy is mapped into the new user's AS through the latter's segment table. Logically, each user has a copy in his AS; physically, only one copy is paged in main storage and is mapped by one page table and one external page table.

As discussed earlier, the number of address spaces that may be created in an AS(n) environment is limited only by practical considerations: (1) the amount of auxiliary storage dedicated to paging, (2) how much main storage can be used for mapping tables, and (3) the size of the page frame pool (i.e., main storage size for pages). Aside from resources directly related to virtual-storage support, CPU speed and I/O device availability also affect the degree of multiprogramming and timesharing activity that can be efficiently run in an AS(n) system. For performance protection reasons, the paging supervisor must monitor the paging rate. Unless the proper awareness is built into the supervisor program, it is possible that the system may activate more address spaces than can be efficiently handled with a given main store. The result is then a very high paging activity as each program seeks to acquire enough pages for its parachor (with very little work getting done), a condition called *thrashing*. Some measures to control thrashing in an AS(n) system will be discussed in Sec. 11-5.

Early AS(n) implementations were originally used in timesharing environments. The IBM TSS (Time Sharing System) by its name implies this; Multics was similarly designed with a timesharing emphasis. The objective was to give a terminal user the full logical resources of a general-purpose computer with a large main store. Giving each user his own large address space greatly facilitated this objective. However, timesharing is not exclusive to virtual-storage systems, AS(1), or AS(n) implementations, nor is the opposite true. Virtual storage significantly enhances both timesharing and multiprogramming environments.

11-4 I/O OPERATIONS IN VIRTUAL-STORAGE SYSTEMS

Because channels or I/O processors execute I/O programs, they are really special-purpose computers. In a conventional operating system, channel programs and I/O buffer areas reside in main storage, where they are referenced during channel execution. In an AS(1) or AS(n) operating system, channel programs and I/O areas reside in virtual storage. However, they must be main-storage resident during channel execution. It follows that like the CPU, I/O channels require a mapping process to translate virtual addresses. Two methods to map channel programs are: (1) a hardware-software translation process, and (2) an all-software translation technique.

Hardware-software channel mapping would require a mapping device in each channel. During channel program execution, all referenced addresses would be translated. The same mapping tables used for CPU translation could also be used for channel mapping. If a page fault occurred, it would be necessary to interrupt the I/O program and service the page fault, say by moving a page from disk to main storage, before the I/O operation could resume. This is where the difficulty lies in a hardware-software mapping approach. Aside from a mapping device, channels would need hardware to interrupt an I/O operation, possibly serve other I/O requests during page-fault processing, and then resume the interrupted I/O to completion. There are also timing and other problems with this approach arising from the sequential nature of data transmission with most I/O devices. The complexity and expense involved in these functions has inhibited using this approach.

With an all-software translation technique, the operating system does all I/O mapping. The additional software is an extension to the I/O supervisory functions. For each I/O operation, the related channel program is translated *before* the operation begins. The functions involved include:

1. Translating channel program virtual addresses into their current main-storage addresses.
2. Reserving all pages that contain I/O buffers in main storage (if not currently resident) and *fixing* these pages.
3. Starting the I/O operation that is then executed by the channels using the translated channel program.
4. Releasing the fixed pages containing I/O buffers when I/O completes. They are then again subject to the page-replacement algorithm.

The mapping functions required for software translation are done completely by the CPU, thus adding somewhat to system overhead. Any techniques that reduce the number of I/O operations reduce this overhead. Large I/O buffers result in less I/O operations. However, to prevent possible data overrun, the buffer area must be fixed in main storage for the duration of I/O, and a balance must be achieved between buffer size and available main storage. It is usually advantageous to design programs so that they place as much data as possible within a program's address space. Data movement then occurs through system-directed paging I/O rather than user-directed file processing I/O.

The static nature of channel software mapping places a certain limitation on the type of I/O programming practices that may be processed in a paging environment. If a channel program dynamically modifies an address location(s), (for example, for a buffer area) *during I/O execution*, it cannot be detected in advance by the software premapping process. As a result, an attempt may be generated to transmit data to or from an incorrect location in main storage. Such an attempt must be detected and aborted by the channel's storage-protection mechanism. Dynamic channel program modification can, however, be permitted with some severe restrictions. The program must be assigned to an area of virtual storage whose addresses are identical to the main-storage area where the program is loaded, and the program must be fixed during its entire execution. In conventional (nonvirtual) systems, a major reason to modify channel programs dynamically was to conserve the address space used for buffer areas. Although a valid consideration when the address space is main storage, this is not as important in a virtual-storage system. The need to permit modification of channel programs arises primarily if it is desired to maintain compatibility with those programs written for nonvirtual systems that self-modify channel addresses.

11-5 MULTIPROGRAMMING AND THRASHING   [Refs. BR,BU,DE2]

In a multiprogramming system, several programs space-share main storage. In a virtual-storage environment using a global page-replacement strategy, all of these programs contend for the single pool of page frames. Each executing program has a working-set (parachor) size that, as seen earlier, depends on its pattern of executed storage references. The composite of these working-set sizes may be considered as the size of the *system working set*. Whenever this exceeds the size of storage in the page frame pool, a type of instability arises called *thrashing*. Its cause is the intense competition for page frames among the programs in main storage as they attempt to expand to their parachors. As a simple example, assume say two programs, X and Y, whose pages at the moment use all available frames, but with neither program at its parachor. Assume X is currently running. Since it is below its parachor, there is a high probability that it will not execute for long before one of its addresses generates a page fault. Since main storage is completely occupied, a page must be replaced. Suppose the paging supervisor finds that the "best" frame to replace currently holds one of Y's pages. After initiating the page-turning process, the system may well assign the CPU to program Y, since X cannot proceed until page-in is completed. Note however that Y is below its parachor to an even greater extent than a moment ago, since one of its pages was in effect given to X to satisfy X's page fault. We can therefore expect that with high probability, Y will very shortly encounter a page fault, at which point the same situation as before now exists, except for the reversal of roles for X and Y. This competition for the limited number of page frames results in a very high rate of page faults, low CPU utilization, and hence little useful work as the programs thrash in fruitless attempts to reach their parachors.

Means to detect thrashing are not difficult to envision. First, it is relatively easy for system programs to monitor the page-fault rate and CPU idleness and to detect when these are abnormally high (beyond some preset threshold). However, although thrashing can be detected easily, it is difficult to determine the specific reason, such as:

1. The total execution load, i.e., the number and size of executing user jobs and system programs, may be unreasonable for the system's main-storage size.
2. A particular job (or jobs) may have a "bad" reference pattern, i.e., a large working set.

With judgments based on workload knowledge and some operating experience, an installation can estimate the total load that is reasonable for its main-storage capacity. Measurement of the locality of particular programs in advance of production running is a different matter (discussed in Chap. 10). If an installation tries to premeasure program locality as a precaution to prevent thrashing, the resulting cost in terms of human effort and machine time may be prohibitive. Also, tools designed to measure locality are not generally available. If the paging supervisor tries to dynamically determine the contribution of each executing job to the total system paging rate, the overhead during execution may be prohibitive. For these reasons, the basic thrashing algorithms that have been reported typically do not identify which jobs or programs are most responsible for thrashing. The prevention of thrashing is important for system-performance protection. Algorithms for this purpose are called *thrashing monitors* or *load levellers*.

In an AS(1) system, the simplest load-levelling technique is to deactivate the lowest priority job or jobs when the system paging rate exceeds a specified threshold.

This threshold may be fixed within a system's design or either directly or indirectly specified by the installation. When job *deactivation* occurs, all of the deactivated job's pages in main storage are paged out to auxiliary storage under the control of the paging supervisor. The page frames recovered through this procedure are then available to the remaining active jobs and paged system programs. The system must of course protect deactivated jobs by reactivating them later. Also, to maintain a multi-programming level for best thruput, the paging supervisor continually monitors the paging rate and attempts reactivation of deactivated jobs when possible. This monitoring process to prevent thrashing and reactivate jobs adds some overhead to system operation. If deactivation and reactivation operations are attempted too frequently, the resulting thruput could be less than when operating an AS(1) system with a lower maximum degree of multiprogramming. Although an AS(1) system can prevent thrashing and allow useful work to be accomplished, an installation should not attempt an unrealistically high degree of multiprogramming.

The effectiveness of the load-levelling technique in preventing thrashing was demonstrated by R. O'Neil, the designer of system programs for the experimental IBM M44 system. Carefully controlled experiments to explore the relationships between programming style, degree of multiprogramming, load levelling, main-storage size, and other factors were reported by Brawn and Gustavson. Their experiments in a single-program environment were discussed in Sec. 10-7. In the multiprogramming tests, n copies of the same sorting program was the system load. Time per job (thruput) was the selected performance measure. As might be expected, the effects of programming style in the multiprogramming environment were similar to those in the single-program case. As seen in Fig. 11-5.1(*a*) for the casually coded program, some thrashing is already discernible, even for the case of two programs running at once (since time per job is poorer than in the single-program case). As the multi-programming level increases, so does the thrashing, and at four programs in contention, it is very severe. The same figure also shows the effect of multi-programming the "most-improved" sort program, where it is seen that for this case, there is no thrashing for up to five programs being multiprogrammed.

The addition of the load leveller (the thrashing monitor that deactivates programs) is dramatically illustrated in Fig. 11-5.1(*b*). The case of no load levelling is also plotted for comparison. Some of the results of these studies may be summarized as follows:

1. Thrashing control is feasible and effective.
2. A load leveller cannot completely compensate for poor program locality, such as may be due to poor programming style.
3. A load leveller can help ensure a measure of performance protection by preventing some combinations of jobs from unduly degrading system performance so that other jobs cannot complete in a reasonable time.

Other experiments (not shown) demonstrated that as in the case of monoprogram-ming, the page-replacement algorithm in a multiprogramming system is not a primary factor in thruput performance.

The job-deactivation technique of the load-leveller program was seen above to be effective in preventing thruput degradation due to thrashing. However, in a

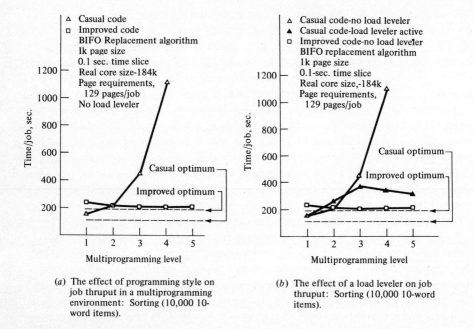

(a) The effect of programming style on job thruput in a multiprogramming environment: Sorting (10,000 10-word items).

(b) The effect of a load leveler on job thruput: Sorting (10,000 10-word items).

Fig. 11-5.1 Multiprogramming and load levelling in an AS(1) system [Ref. BR].

virtual-storage system that is also serving timesharing users, deactivation can result in intolerable response times. An AS(n) system typically services say 40 connected timesharing users in addition to the batch workload. If several timesharing users contend for main storage on a demand-paging-only basis, paging rates can become quite high. For this reason, some virtual-storage timesharing systems use a *block-paging* technique whereby the activation of a user program involves the scheduling and movement of several pages of that user's program. Although this is a type of swapping (as discussed in Chap. 9), it is much more efficient than the swapping in a conventional system. For one thing, the virtual-storage system ensures that only fairly active regions of the program are involved. Also, when a job must be bulk-paged out, only changed pages since last "swap in" need be moved to auxiliary storage; in a conventional system, all of a program's occupied address space (including portions unreferenced since last swap in) are swapped to auxiliary storage. The block-paging strategy can provide acceptable response times in a timesharing virtual-storage environment. Of course, if paging rates become too high, even when block paging is used, the system must protect itself. One strategy is to refuse "log on" to any new users.

The dynamic operations of the thrashing monitor involve some system overhead. This may be reduced by installation planning based on observation and measurement of its workload characteristics. Such information can be used to control the maximum degree of multiprogramming that will be attempted for various job mixes. An installation can also do much to encourage programmers to follow simple guidelines in order to improve programming style for the virtual-storage environment.

System	Implementation	Predecessor	Address space size	Segment size	Page size	S/370 models
DOS/VS	AS(1)	DOS	Up to 16 mbytes	64k	2k	Small to intermediate
OS/VS1	AS(1)	OS/MFT	Up to 16 mbytes	64k	2k	Intermediate to large
OS/VS2-Rel 1	AS(1)	OS/MVT	16 mbytes	64k	4k	Intermediate and large
OS/VS2-Rel 2	AS(n)	OS/MVT or OS/VS2-Rel 1	16 mbytes each *user*	64k	4k	Large
VM/370	AS(n)	CP/67	Up to 16 mbytes each *user*	64k	4k	Intermediate and large

Fig. 11-6.1   The IBM System/370 virtual-storage operating systems.

11-6   IBM VIRTUAL-STORAGE (VS) SYSTEMS
[Refs. AU2,IB1,IB2,IB3,IB4,IB5,IB6,SC]

In mid 1972 IBM announced virtual storage for most models of their System/370. Mapping hardware was added to most existing System/370 models and included in two new models (Mod 158, 168). Four new virtual-storage systems were produced to support these new configurations. In this section, we shall begin with a brief summary of the new operating-system characteristics, proceed to a description of System/370 mapping hardware, and then describe the IBM Operating System/Virtual Storage 2 (OS/VS2).

Design of the IBM VS systems is based on the IBM Operating System (OS) and Disk Operating System (DOS) architectures that were developed for System/360. To enhance compatibility, an AS(1) type of implementation was used for the DOS/VS and OS/VS systems, replacing main storage with virtual storage as the system's address space.* This is shown in Fig. 11-6.1. Notice that System/370 hardware permits two page sizes, 2k and 4k. The VS systems intended for small and intermediate machine models use the 2k page size, which, theoretically, can result in smaller working sets. All of the VS implementations support 64k segments and 24-bit addressing.

All System/370 virtual-storage models have a common logical Dynamic Address Translation (DAT) function for mapping. However, the hardware required to implement the DAT function varies among models, for speed-cost trade-off. Effective address size on all models is 24 bits, resulting in a 16m-byte address space. The DAT provides a segment-page address-space organization; however, the extent of segmentation varies with each VS system. The hardware permits a segment size of either 64k or 1m-byte, although none of the VS operating systems use 1m-byte segments, as indicated in Fig. 11-6.1. A machine control register indicates the segment

*More information on these systems is contained in Ref. IB10, pp. 49-83.

size and page size being used. This register may only be altered by a program executing in privileged mode, in this case, the VS control program. During execution, address translation (mapping) occurs as described in Chap. 10 for a segment-page structured address space. As in conventional operation, effective addresses are generated from System/370 base-displacement addresses. The effective address is then translated by the DAT function, the result being either the main-storage location of the referenced address or a page fault. The STOR register function is supplied by a System/370 control register. The segment table and page tables are built and maintained by the VS operating system. System/370s may operate in conventional mode—no address translation—or with the DAT function essential to a VS operating system. The DAT function can be turned ON or OFF by a privileged instruction.

Functionally, the DAT process is the same in all System/370 models. Address translation is performed by a table lookup procedure (with the tables resident in main storage). A special fast translation device translates all recently referenced virtual addresses with little or no loss in execution speed. Physically, there are implementation differences in the DAT function between small and large System/370 s. Smaller models use mostly microcode to implement the DAT function. A small associative store, similar to the one described in Chap. 10, is used for fast translation. The larger System/370 models use hardware circuitry to implement the DAT function for increased execution speed. Translation of recently referenced addresses is done in a fast buffer store called the Translation Lookaside Buffer (TLB). System/370 channels have no DAT facility. Channel programs are mapped by software techniques, as described in Sec. 11-4.

Of the three new IBM VS operating systems, Operating System/Virtual Storage 2 (OS/VS2) is the largest and contains the most functions. OS/VS2 was designed for intermediate-large systems (Mod 145 to 168) and is intended to replace OS/MVT (see Chap. 8). OS/VS2 has been implemented in two versions that are significantly different:

VS2 Release 1 (VS2-Rel 1) is an AS(1) implementation that was developed as an OS/MVT replacement.

VS2 Release 2 (VS2-Rel 2) is an AS(n) system intended for use with large System/370s.

There are several reasons why we wish to discuss OS/VS2:

1. To contrast VS2 with its predecessor OS/MVT with regard to function.
2. To identify the software additions necessary to implement virtual storage starting with MVT as a base for comparisons.
3. To examine the performance potential added to OS by virtual storage and contrast this with the additional resources required for VS2 implementation.

We shall first discuss VS2-Rel 1 and then note the differing functions in VS2-Rel 2.

In Fig. 11-6.2, MVT's address-space structure is compared with VS2-Rel 1. The two systems have only slightly different structures. The most significant difference is address-space size: 16m bytes of virtual storage in VS2 compared with the physical main-storage size in MVT. Because of the large AS in VS2, rather large segments (64k) are used as the basis for space allocation. Thus, SQA, PLPA, user regions, and so forth,

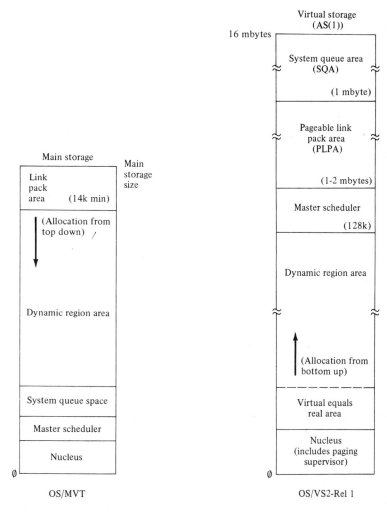

Fig. 11-6.2 OS/MVT and OS/VS2-Rel 1 AS contents and structure.

are multiples of 64k. The segment table, besides its use for address translation, indicates segment-allocation status.

The main advantages of VS2 stem from its large address space. The System Queue Area (SQA), for example, can be given 1m byte of AS with little impact on the remaining system structure. SQA is used as a VS2 work area to hold VS2 system queues and tables, including the segment table and the page tables that map all of virtual storage (except the dynamic region area). Although SQA size may be 1m byte, it is only allocated SQA pages that reside in main storage. The VS2 Pageable Link Pack Area (PLPA) includes the entire SVC library. SVC's are demand paged in VS2, and the need for a main-storage transient area (as found in MVT) is eliminated. As a result of using the demand-paging strategy, active frequently used SVC's will tend to remain effectively main-storage resident. I/O access methods may also be placed in the PLPA and shared by two or more active users. In fact, any shareable reentrant program may be placed in the PLPA. PLPA size can become quite large, perhaps 2 mbytes, but its contents affect main-storage utilization only according to their demand-paging activity. Besides the PLPA, the master scheduler and SPOOLing functions are also paged in VS2. With fewer space restrictions than in MVT, more consideration has been given to required and desirable system functions in VS2.

The nucleus, or supervisor, in VS2 and MVT performs an identical function, i.e., the control of system resources and basic system activity. In VS2, however, the control of main storage and I/O activity is more complex because of demand paging. Nucleus size in VS2 is therefore larger because of the addition of a *paging supervisor* and because of the need for channel-program-translation functions to the Input-Output Supervisor (IOS). The VS2 paging supervisor maintains the system's page tables, services page faults, and controls main-storage allocation through page-placement and page-replacement algorithms. VS2 tries to keep currently referenced pages in main storage through an implementation of the LRU replacement algorithm. Page placement is performed on a global basis, i.e., any available page frame is a candidate for placement selection, no matter what user or system function caused the page fault.

Because System/370 channels have no translation hardware, VS2's IOS must do channel program translation as described in Sec. 11-4. The vital control functions performed by VS2's nucleus require that the nucleus be fixed in main storage during system operation. Delays caused by page faults during nucleus execution could not be tolerated without reducing overall system effectiveness.

In a similar manner, VS2 provides a facility to allow user job steps that cannot tolerate page-fault delays to be fixed in main storage during their execution. It is called the *Virtual Equals Real* ($V = R$) option. Part of VS2's address space that falls within the range of main-storage size is reserved for this option above the nucleus (see Fig. 11-6.2). When a user designates a job step $V = R$ (as a JCL parameter), VS2 will allocate space for the job step from the $V = R$ area, providing it can load and fix the job step in corresponding main-storage locations. This job step has the advantage of execution without competing for pages or the overhead of channel program translation. These benefits to the $V = R$ job result in a penalty for other jobs, that is, a reduction of the page frames available to the remainder of the system. Job steps with critical timing dependencies or I/O functions that can't be translated through the IOS channel translation function require $V = R$ treatment.

Normally, VS2 jobs are demand paged and are scheduled in the VS2 regions starting at the bottom of the dynamic-region area, as indicated in Fig. 11-6.2. Region structure is shown in Fig. 11-6.3(a). Address space is allocated to jobs in multiples of segments from the bottom up. Each region uses one or more segments for a Local System Queue Area (LSQA) that is used as a workspace for queues and tables that pertain to the particular job that is executing, including the page tables for that region. LSQA segments are allocated to regions from the top down. Figure 11-6.3(a), then, depicts VS2 operation with one active region (one active job scheduler). If a job requests 90k, it is allocated two segments (128k); a 150k request results in three segments (192k). Figure 11-6.3(b) shows the address-space layout for three active regions, assuming jobs of 90k, 60k, and 200k. Each region has an LSQA of one

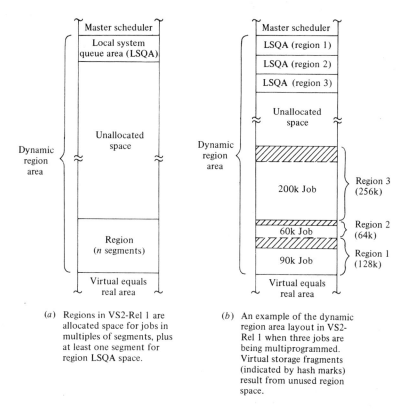

(a) Regions in VS2-Rel 1 are allocated space for jobs in multiples of segments, plus at least one segment for region LSQA space.

(b) An example of the dynamic region area layout in VS2-Rel 1 when three jobs are being multiprogrammed. Virtual storage fragments (indicated by hash marks) result from unused region space.

Fig. 11-6.3 Region structure and allocation in VS2-Rel 1.

segment. Notice that the segment-allocation unit results in fragmentation, but the resulting waste is in virtual storage, not in main storage.

Job scheduling in VS2-Rel 1 is very similar to MVT. Jobs are assigned a class and priority, using JCL, and there is a scheduling queue for each job class. The system operator starts initiator-terminator programs (job schedulers) through the master scheduler, assigning one or more job classes to an initiator. Each active initiator-terminator is associated with a region. Thus, the degree of multiprogramming within the system is determined by the number of active job schedulers. Storage protection for user jobs in VS2 is not implemented through storage-protect keys, but rather through protection bits in the system's segment table entries. When the protect key in the PSW is 0 (the supervisor state), the nucleus may access all of virtual storage. This is done by accessing one of two segment tables that we may call the *supervisor segment table*. For the PSW key nonzero (the problem program state), VS2 uses a second segment table for address translation. Only segments that belong to the executing user have their protection bits turned off. An attempted access to any other segment results in a "protection" interrupt. Because storage keys are not used for protection, VS2 is not limited to fifteen regions, as is MVT; the limit for VS2 is 256 regions. The 16m-byte address space in VS2 will thus place little if any logical restriction on the degree of multiprogramming. However, main-storage size and CPU power will limit the practical extent of multiprogramming. Starting too many initiators will result in thrashing and subsequent job deactivation by the VS2 thrashing monitor until the paging rate subsides to a productive level.

The TSO functions in VS2 are identical to TSO/MVT (see Chap. 9). The virtual-storage environment, however, allows for a different implementation. In MVT, TSO user areas are swapped between main storage and auxiliary storage. In VS2-Rel 1, paging is used. When a TSO user "logs on," he is assigned to a region, just as in MVT. During execution, TSO users share main storage with any active background jobs and system functions through demand paging. In TSO, multiple users may be assigned to a single TSO region. At the end of a major time slice, a user occupying a TSO region may be deactivated and moved to auxiliary storage (swapped) to allow another user to be scheduled in the region. Instead of swapping, VS2 uses a *block-paging* technique to transfer the user's main-storage-resident pages to VS2 external page storage. This includes the user's page tables, contained in LSQA. Block paging, which swaps only changed pages, involves significantly less data transfer when compared to MVT. When users are reactivated—scheduled for their next major time slice—their previously resident set of pages are block paged into main storage.

VS2's external page storage, or paging data sets, may reside on various IBM direct-access storage devices. In a batch environment, low paging rates can be expected, although too many active regions can produce a high paging rate and, possibly, thrashing. Device selection for external page storage is not too critical. However, a TSO system can result in high paging rates. In the timesharing environment, device selection for external page storage can have a significant effect on performance, in particular upon response time for trivial transactions.

The discussion of VS2 has thus far related to Release 1, an AS(1) system having good compatibility with its predecessor, OS/MVT. Since this initial VS2 version, VS2's architecture has been expanded significantly with the Release 2 version. VS2-Rel 2 is an AS(n) system. Certain system components and each VS2 user, batch or TSO, have their own 16m-byte address space. Thus, each time the operator starts a new job initiator, a new address space is created; each time a TSO user logs on, he receives his own address space. Certain VS2-Rel 2 subsystems also reside in their own AS. This is true of the HASP Job Entry Subsystem (JES2) and the Attached Support Processor (ASP), called JES3 in Rel 2. With VS2-Rel 2, the requirement for regions is eliminated. The structure of each VS2 address space is the same as shown in Fig. 11-6.4. The nucleus is fixed in main storage and mapped in each address space through a set of common page tables. This technique was described in Sec. 11-3. The *common area* is mapped in the same manner. The remaining area, *the private area*, is controlled by the system function, batch job, or TSO user assigned to the address space. This typically represents about 8 to 10m bytes. Theoretically, the number of address spaces that may coexist in a VS2-Rel 2 system is unlimited. However, practical limitations are imposed by CPU power and main-storage size.

The VS2 systems, especially VS2-Rel 2, represent a compatible yet significant departure from OS/MVT. The large address space and virtual storage allow many system design, operational, and programming advantages. Certain costs are, however, encountered:

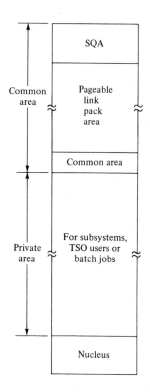

Fig. 11-6.4 Structure of each VS2-Rel 2 address space.

1. Nucleus size is increased, due mainly to the addition of a paging supervisor.
2. Address translation adds some overhead to execution time, although this is somewhat reduced by fast translation hardware.
3. Channel program translation must be performed by software (IOS) because System/370 channels have no translation hardware.
4. Some auxiliary storage, called external page storage, is required for demand paging.

To the extent that virtual storage allows easier system use for programmers, operators, system designers, and users, the advantages of virtual storage tend to justify these costs.

11-7 IBM VIRTUAL-MACHINE (VM) SYSTEMS
[AO1,AO2,AU1,BA1,BA2,CA,FI,GO1,GO2,GO3,IB7,MA1,ME,PA1,PA2]

With VS2-Rel 2, each user has a private address space, shares the CPU with other executing users, and controls a set of allocated resources. In a sense, each user has a private machine. However, this machine is not a System/370, since certain System/370 instructions are privileged and available only to the VS2 control program, not to each user. This imposes certain limitations on the types of programs and systems that a user may develop. In the Virtual Machine Facility/370 (VM/370) system, each user is provided an address space, a set of I/O resources, and a share of CPU time; the user may also execute in a *pseudoprivileged state*. The result is a virtual System/370 that

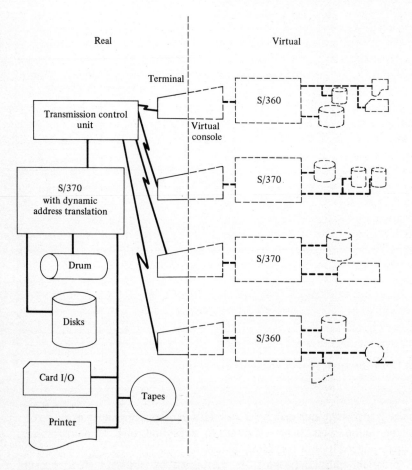

Fig. 11-7.1 The virtual-real machine relationship in the IBM VM/370 system.

may execute any program or system executable on a real System/370. Figure 11-7.1 shows the VM organization that is capable of multiprogramming entire operating systems, not just user programs.

VM/370 is a successor of Control Program/67 (CP/67) that was developed for the System/360 Model 67. With VM/370, each terminal user has a virtual-machine configuration of virtual storage, virtual I/O devices, and a CPU (the same CPU model as that under the control of VM/370). The virtual I/O configuration is mapped through tables to either real devices or partitions of real devices. For example, a virtual card reader or printer can be represented by a disk "extent." A virtual direct-access device can be mapped by an entire disk device or a disk extent, a concept called a *minidisk*. However, virtual tape drives must be represented by a real tape drive, one to one. Each virtual machine, like a real machine, requires a console device. In VM/370, the console is the user's terminal. After "logging on" to VM/370, a user can IPL any system that would execute on a real System/370, providing he has the proper configuration. During operation, the user may communicate as an operator would through his terminal (the VM system console) by a set of special commands.

These functions are all made possible by the VM/370 control program, which is fixed in main storage during system operation. The control program controls all mapping for virtual storage and virtual I/O devices, SPOOLs system I/O for virtual card readers and printers, controls CPU scheduling, and intercepts and then services all privileged instructions and virtual interrupts. This last facility allows virtual machines to operate in a pseudoprivileged state. When a privileged instruction is issued in a virtual machine, it causes an interrupt that passes the instruction to VM/370, where it is serviced, and control is then returned to the user's virtual machine. The same type of service is provided for virtual machine interrupts.

In a VM/370 system, several VM's can be running concurrently; for example, OS/MVT in one virtual machine, VS2 in another, and in others, several timesharing users each under the control of a *Conversational Monitor System* (*CMS*). This is a simple but effective operating system designed for good performance in the VM environment. When a VM/370 user IPL's CMS, he has a variety of System/370 program facilities at his disposal. Programs and text can be entered from the terminal, edited, and stored in private user data-sets. Several System/370 compilers may be executed under CMS, including ANS COBOL, PL/I, and FORTRAN. Program execution test and debug facilities are also available.

VM/370 facilities allow for a variety of concurrent activities such as:

1. Operating system development or maintenance
2. Testing of complex systems
3. Interactive program development

However, VM/370 has one serious shortcoming—execution speed. The overhead incurred in providing a virtual-machine environment is reflected in the degradation of execution speed of complex systems like OS/MVT. Under VM/370, OS/MVT might execute at only one-half of its speed on a real System/370. This tends to limit the usefulness of VM/370 in a batch processing production environment. To help offset performance abuses, the VM system has several features that allow an installation to favor a specific virtual machine by guaranteeing main storage and CPU availability, thus making it a privileged virtual machine.

11-8 THE MULTICS SYSTEM [Refs. BE,CO1,CO2,DA,OR,SA]

Multics (Multiplexed Information and Computing Service) was designed jointly by MIT and the General Electric Company. The hardware is basically a GE645 with the additional hardware necessary for a system-design context virtual storage. The operating system is complex, and it is noteworthy that it was decided to write its programs in a high-level language (PL/I).

The primary objective of Multics was to build a general timesharing and virtual-storage facility whose users could share all information in the system (with appropriate security and protection safeguards). This sharing objective is central to many of Multics' most interesting features. It is best described by the following quotation from the designers:

"Many contemporary systems permit some degree of sharing. Usually, sharing is accomplished by allowing several users to share data via input and output of information stored in files kept in secondary storage. Through the use of segmentation, however, Multics provides direct hardware addressing by user and system programs of all information, independent of its physical storage location. Information is stored in segments each of which is potentially shareable and carries its own independent attributes of size and access privilege."

Multics uses an AS(n) virtual-storage scheme. Each user has a segmented address space that may contain up to 2^{18} (262,144) segments. Segment size is variable and may become as large as 2^{18} words (approximately equivalent to 1m bytes). The selection of such a large address space was made to accommodate the objective of allowing a user to map many program and data segments into a single address space. Many such segments may be shared with the system or other users. In practice, a user may operate with relatively few segments, but the potential is almost always available to add more segments to the address space. If Multics used segmentation only, the system could experience a main-storage fragmentation problem and, if segments are large, could accommodate relatively few segments coresident in main storage. For these reasons, and others, Multics subdivides segments into 1024-word pages and allocates pages using a demand-paging strategy.

The GE645 includes the rather complex mapping hardware designed specifically for Multics' requirements. In principle, if not in detail, it is similar to the mapping schemes discussed earlier. In our short summary of Multics' highlights, we shall concentrate on its unique or near-unique features.

Each Multics user's address space is mapped by a *descriptor segment* (*DS*). DS length depends on the number of segments mapped in an address space, with one entry for each segment. When a user is active, the GE645 *descriptor base register* (*DBR*) identifies the main-storage location of his DA. All addresses in the GE645 processor consist of the integer pair $[s,i]$, where s identifies segment number and i the location referenced within the segment. Element i is further reduced to page number p and word location using modulo 1024 arithmetic. Address translation in the GE645 follows the process shown in Fig. 11-8.1. Notice that the DS itself is mapped by a page table and, thus, can be paged. This is important because the number of segments in an address space can become very large, resulting in a large DS.

The Multics supervisor is sophisticated and complex; it contains functions for segment control, page control, and a directory control function that controls allocation of segments using a protection scheme. The supervisor is mapped into each user's address space using a segment-sharing scheme where each user's supervisor segment entries point to a common set of page tables. In fact, this scheme for segment sharing is used throughout the system. Because the supervisor is mapped into each address space, users can request the service of supervisor functions, while the supervisor is protected against unauthorized references by a ring protection scheme. With the exception of the page control function, most supervisory functions are paged.

Multics, like other paging systems, controls main storage using a demand-paging algorithm. Pages are moved into main storage only when referenced and not already present. When replacement is required, an LRU algorithm is invoked for page

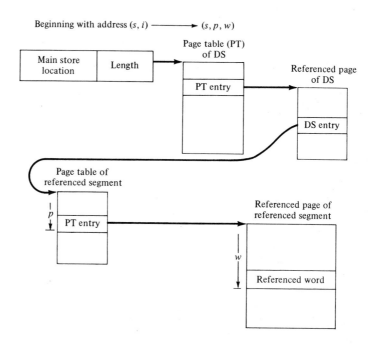

Fig. 11-8.1 Address translation process in the GE645 under Multics.

selection. Multics also deactivates and reactivates segments to conserve page-table space. A fixed area of main storage is used for the page tables that map active user segments. This area is usually smaller than the space required to map all segments that have been referenced, many of which may be currently *idle*. To avoid using unnecessary space for tables, page tables may be paged in and out of main storage. If page-table space for a newly referenced segment is not available, an inactive segment is selected for replacement based on the number of its pages residing in main storage. Hopefully, there will be some inactive segments with no pages in main storage. The system then removes the selected segment's page table from main storage, noting this deactivation in all address spaces that have been using the segment, and activates the newly referenced segment. In effect, Multics attempts to implement an LRU algorithm for page-table replacement.

In this introduction to Multics we have tried to place emphasis on its unique features, primarily program and data sharing. Many details and similarities to other virtual-storage systems have been omitted. Multics has been successfully used at MIT in a predominantly timesharing environment for several years.

REFERENCES AND BIBLIOGRAPHY

1. [AD1] Adair, R. and Y. Bard: CP-67 Measurement Method, IBM Corp. Cambridge Scientific Center, *Report No.* G320-2072, May, 1971.

2. [RA2] Adair, R.J., R.U. Bayles, L.W. Comeau, and R.J. Creasy: A Virtual Machine System for the 360/40, IBM Corp. Cambridge Scientific Center, *Report No.* 320-2007, May, 1966.

3. [AN] Anacker, W. and C.P. Wang: Performance Evaluation of Computing Systems with Memory Hierarchies, *IEEE Transactions on Computers*, EC-16, No. 6, pp. 764-773, December, 1967.

4. [AU1] Auroux, A. and C. Hans: Le Concept de Machines Virtuelles, *Revue Francaise d'Informatique et de Recherche Operationelle* 15, no. B3, pp. 45-51, December, 1968.

5. [AU2] Auslander, M.A. and J.F. Jaffe: Functional Structure of IBM Virtual Storage Operating Systems Part I: Influences of Dynamic Address Translation on Operating System Technology, *IBM Systems Journal*, vol. 12, no. 4, pp. 368-381, 1973.

6. [BA1] Bairstow, J.N.: Many from One: The "Virtual Machine" Arrives, *Computer Decisions*, vol. 2, no. 1, pp. 29-31, January, 1970.

7. [BA2] Bard, Y., B.H. Margolin, T.I. Peterson, and M. Schatzoff: CP-67 Measurement and Analysis, I: Regression Studies, IBM Corp. Cambridge Scientific Center, *Report No. G320-2061, June, 1970.*

8. [BE] Benoussan, A., C.T. Clingen, and R.C. Daley: The Multics Virtual Memory—Concepts and Design, *Comm. ACM*, vol. 15, no. 5, May, 1972, p. 308.

9. [BR] Brawn, B. and F. Gustavson: Program Behavior in Paging Environment, *Proc. AFIPS 1968 FJCC*, vol. 33, pp. 1019-1032, 1968.

10. [BU] Buzen, J.: Optimizing the Degree of Multiprogramming in Demand Paging Systems, *IEEE Computer Society Conference*, Boston, Mass., pp. 141-142, September 22-24, 1971.

11. [CA] Callaway, P.: Performance Considerations for the Use of the Virtual Machine Capability, IBM Corp. Thomas J. Watson Research Center, Yorktown Heights, N.Y., *Report RC*-3360, May 12, 1971.

12. [CO1] Corbato, F.J.: A Paging Experiment With the MULTICS System, *Massachusetts Institute of Technology Project MAC Memorandum*, MAC-M-384, July 8, 1968.

13. [CO2] Corbato, F. and V.A. Vyssotsky: Introduction and Overview of the MULTICS System, *AFIPS Conference Proc., Fall Joint Computer Conference 27*, Part I, pp. 185-196, 1965.

14. [DA] Daley, R.C. and J.B. Dennis: Virtual Memory, Processes, and Sharing in MULTICS, *Comm. ACM*, vol. 11, no. 5, pp. 306-312, May, 1968.

15. [DE1] DeMeis, W.M. and N. Weizer: Measurement and Analysis of a Demand Paging Time-Sharing System, *Proc. of the 24th National Conference on Systems Science*, University of Hawaii, pp. 449-451, January 12-14, 1971.

16. [DE2] Denning, P.J.: Thrashing: Its Causes and Prevention, *AFIPS Conference Proc., Fall Joint Computer Conference*, vol. 33, pp. 915-922, 1968.

17. [FI] Field, M.S.: Multi-Access Systems—The Virtual Machine Approach, IBM Corp. Cambridge Scientific Center, *Report No.* 320-2033, September, 1968.

18. [FU] Fuchel, K. and S. Heller: Considerations in the Design of a Multiple Computer System with Extended Core Storage, *Comm. ACM*, 11, no. 5, pp. 334-340, May, 1968.

19. [GE] Gelenbe, E.: Optimum Choice of Page Sizes in a Virtual Memory with a Hardware Executive and a Rapid-Access Secondary Storage Medium, *ACM SIGOPS Workshop on System Performance Evaluation*, Harvard University, pp. 321-336, April 5-7, 1971.

20. [GL] Gluck, S.E.: Impact of Scratchpads in Design: Multi-functional Scratchpad Memories in the Burroughs B8500, *AFIPS Conference Proc., Fall Joint Computer Conference*, 27, Part I, pp. 661-666, 1965.

21. [GO1] Goldberg, R.P.: Hardware Requirements for Virtual Machine Systems, *Proc. of the 24th Hawaii Conference on Systems Science*, University of Hawaii, pp. 449-451, January 12-14, 1971.

22. [GO2] Goldberg, R.P.: Virtual Machine Systems, *Massachusetts Institute of Technology, Lincoln Laboratory Report*, MS-2687, September 4, 1969.

23. [GO3] Goldberg, R.P.: Virtual Machines: Semantics and Examples, *IEEE Computer Society Conference*, Boston, Mass., pp. 141-142, September 22-24, 1971.

24. [HA1] Hatfield, D.J.: Experiments on Page Size, Program Access Patterns, and Virtual Memory Performance, *IBM Journal of Research and Development*, vol. 16, no. 1, pp. 58-66, 1972.

25. [IB1] IBM Corp.: "IBM System/370 System Summary," No. GA22-7001, IBM Corp. Data Processing Division, White Plains, N.Y. 10604.
26. [IB2] IBM Corp.: "IBM System/370 Principles of Operation," No. GA22-7000, IBM Corp. Data Processing Division, White Plains, N.Y. 10604.
27. [IB3] IBM Corp.: "IBM System/370 Advanced Function Bibliography," No. GC20-1763, IBM Corp. Data Processing Division, White Plains, N.Y. 10604.
28. [IB4] IBM Corp.: "OS/VS1 Planning and Use Guide," No. GC24-5090, IBM Corp. Data Processing Division, White Plains, N.Y. 10604.
29. [IB5] IBM Corp.: "OS/VS2 Planning and Use Guide," No. GC28-0600, IBM Corp. Data Processing Division, White Plains, N.Y. 10604.
30. [IB6] IBM Corp.: "Introduction to OS/VS2 Release 2," No. GC28-0661, IBM Corp. Data Processing Division, White Plains, N.Y. 10604.
31. [IB7] IBM Corp.: "IBM Virtual Machine Facility/370—Introduction Manual," No. GC20-1800, IBM Corp. Data Processing Division, White Plains, N.Y. 10604.
32. [IB8] IBM Corp.: "IBM Virtual Machine Facility/370 Planning and System Generation Guide," No. GC20-1801, IBM Corp. Data Processing Division, White Plains, N.Y. 10604.
33. [IB9] IBM Corp.: "IBM Virtual Machine Facility/370: Release 2 Planning Guide," No. GC20-1814, IBM Corp. Data Processing Division, White Plains, N.Y., 10604.
34. [IB10] IBM Corp.: "Introduction to Virtual Storage in System/370," No. GR20-4260, IBM Corp. Data Processing Division, White Plains, N.Y. 10604.
35. [JO] Johnson, O.W. and J.R. Martinson: "Virtual Memory in Time-Sharing System/360, TSS/360 Compendium," IBM Corp. Data Processing Division, White Plains, N.Y., 1969.
36. [LE] Lett, J.S. and W.L. Konigsford: TSS/360: A Timeshared Operating System, *AFIPS Conference Proc., Fall Joint Computer Conference*, 33, Part I, pp. 15-28, 1968.
37. [MA1] Madnick, S.E.: Time-Sharing Systems: Virtual Machine Concept vs. Conventional Approach, *Modern Data*, vol. 2, no. 3, pp. 34-36, March, 1969.
38. [MA2] Martinson, J.R.: Utilization of Virtual Memory in Time-Sharing System/360, IBM Corp. Systems Development Division, Yorktown Heights, N.Y., *Technical Report TR* 53.0001, October 28, 1968.
39. [ME] Meyer, R.A. and L.M. Seawright: A Virtual Machine Time Sharing System, *IBM Systems Journal*, vol. 9, no. 3, 1970.
40. [ORG] Organick, E.I.: "The Multics System," MIT Press, Cambridge, Mass., 1972.
41. [PA1] Parmelee, R.P.: Preferred Virtual Machines for CP-67, IBM Corp. Cambridge Scientific Center, *Report No.* G320-2068.
42. [PA2] Parmelee, R.P., T.I. Peterson, C.C. Tillman, and D.J. Hatfield: Virtual Storage and Virtual Machine Concepts, *IBM Systems Journal*, vol. 11, no. 2, 1972.
43. [SA] Saltzer, J.H.: A Simple Linear Model of Demand Paging Performance, *Comm. ACM*, vol. 17, no. 4, April, 1974.
44. [SM] Smith, J.L.: Multiprogramming Under a Page on Demand Strategy, *Comm. ACM*, vol. 10, no. 10, pp. 636-646, October, 1967.
45. [SC] Scherr, A.L.: Functional Structure of IBM Virtual Storage Operating Systems Part II: OS/VS2-2 Concepts and Philosophies, *IBM Systems Journal*, vol. 12, no. 4, pp. 382-400, 1973.

appendix A
Probability Functions

Some discrete probability functions

Function name	Distribution function	Mean	Variance	Meaning
Binomial	$B(k;n,p) = C(n,k)p^k(1-p)^{n-k}$	np	$np(1-p)$	Probability of k successes in n trials; p = probability of success in one trial
Multinomial	$P(k_1,\ldots,k_n;p_1\ldots p_n) = m!\prod_{i=1}^{n}\frac{p_i^{k_i}}{k_i!}$ where $\sum_i^n k_i = m$	mp_i	$mp_i(1-p_i)$	Probability of k_1 outcomes of first type, k_2 of second type, etc. in m trials
Geometric	$G(k;p) = p(1-p)^k$	$\dfrac{(1-p)}{p}$	$\dfrac{(1-p)}{p^2}$	Probability of *first* success on the $k+1$ trial
Negative Binomial (Pascal)	$N(k;r,p) = C(r+k-1,k)p^r(1-p)^k$	$\dfrac{r(1-p)}{p}$	$\dfrac{r(1-p)}{p^2}$	Probability of the rth *success* occurring at trial $r+k$ (also k failures)
Poisson	$P(k;\lambda) = \dfrac{\lambda^k e^{-\lambda}}{k!}$	λ	λ	Probability of k successes

Some continuous probability functions

Function name	Probability density	Mean	Variance
Exponential $0 \leqslant x < \infty$	$p(x) = \lambda e^{-\lambda x}$	$\dfrac{1}{\lambda}$	$\dfrac{1}{\lambda^2}$
Uniform over a,b $a \leqslant x \leqslant b$	$p(x) = \dfrac{1}{b-a}$	$\dfrac{a+b}{2}$	$\dfrac{(b-a)^2}{12}$
Normal $-\infty \leqslant x \leqslant \infty$	$p(x) = \dfrac{1}{\sigma\sqrt{2\pi}} e^{-(x-\mu)^2/2\sigma^2}$	μ	σ^2
Standard normal $-\infty \leqslant z \leqslant \infty$	$\phi(z) = \dfrac{1}{\sqrt{2\pi}} e^{-z^2/2}$	0	1

appendix B
Principles of Continuous Probability Functions

FUNDAMENTALS

A continuous random variable x can take values over a continuum. Many of its properties are closely analogous to those of discrete random variables (see Chap. 3). The probability of x falling between x and $x + dx$ is $p(x)dx$, and the certainty axiom is then expressed as the sum of all of these infinitesimals by integration

$$\int_{-\infty}^{\infty} p(x)\,dx = 1 \tag{1}$$

Note that $p(x)dx$, not simply $p(x)$, corresponds to the discrete probability function. It follows that the probability of x between a and b is

$$P(a \leqslant x \leqslant b) = \int_{a}^{b} p(x)\,dx \tag{2}$$

The cumulative distribution is a similar integral, only the lower limit is the smallest possible x value and the upper limit is a running variable z

$$P(z) \equiv P(x \leqslant z) = \int_{-\infty}^{z} p(x)\,dx \tag{3}$$

Note from Eq. (3) (and the calculus) that $p(x)$, called the *probability density function*, is the derivative of the cumulative

$$p(z) = \frac{dP}{dz} \tag{4}$$

Since $p(x)dx$ is the probability of x between x and $x + dx$

$xp(x)\,dx$ = the weighted value of x

Summing these by integration, the result is the *expectation* or *mean* of x

$$\mu_x = E(x) = \int_{-\infty}^{\infty} xp(x)\,dx \tag{5}$$

The *variance* is the integral of the squared differences from the mean weighted by the probabilities

$$\sigma_x = \int_{-\infty}^{\infty} (x - \mu)^2 p(x)\,dx \tag{6}$$

Most of the properties of discrete random variables have their counterparts in the continuous case, using principles illustrated above.

THE NORMAL DISTRIBUTION

The normal distribution (also called gaussian or laplacian) is the most important one in probability theory. The reason is threefold: (1) many processes in nature seem to fit this distribution, (2) the normal distribution can be represented by simple tables and used to approximate other distributions requiring more cumbersome tables, and (3) the central limit theorem states that the distribution of the sum of sample values from almost any distribution tends towards the normal distribution.

In actual problems, our variable is x, but it is very convenient to translate it to the standard variable z

$$z = \frac{x - \mu}{\sigma} \tag{1}$$

where μ is the mean of x and σ is the standard deviation. The standard normal distribution is

$$\phi(z) = \frac{1}{\sqrt{2\pi}} e^{-z^2/2} \tag{2}$$

Note that x values smaller (or larger) than the mean yield negative (or positive) z values. The transformation of x to z, using Eq. (1), shifts the x curve so that $x = \mu$ is $z = 0$ and scales the $x - \mu$ values by division of the standard deviation. Figure B-1 shows $\phi(z)$ to be a bell-shaped curve symmetrical about $z = 0$. In other words, each positive z value is weighted identically by a negative z value. It follows that the mean of z is zero. It is also easy to show that the variance, and hence the standard deviation, of the standard normal distribution is 1.

$$\mu_z = 0 \quad \text{and} \quad \sigma_z = 1 \tag{3}$$

The cumulative normal function, also called the *error function*, is the area under ϕ

$$\Phi(t) = \Phi(z \leqslant t) = \frac{1}{\sqrt{2\pi}} \int_{-\infty}^{t} e^{-z^2/2}\,dz \tag{4}$$

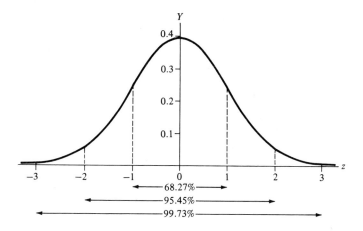

Figure B-1 Standard normal curve with percent areas at intervals of standard deviation.

Values of $\Phi(t)$ (or closely related ones) are given in tables. This is done in a few different ways. For example, Appendix Table C3 gives areas under $\phi(t)$ from 0 to t (see the little drawing accompanying the table). If the table values are called $T(t)$, then these are related to the cumulative normal distribution by

$$\Phi(t) = 0.5 + T(t) \quad \text{for } t \geq 0 \tag{5}$$
$$= 0.5 - T(t) \quad t \leq 0$$

Also, since $\Phi(a \leq t \leq b)$ is the area of $\phi(t)$ between a and b,

$$\Phi(a \leq t \leq b) = \Phi(b) - \Phi(a) \tag{6}$$

A little algebra with Eq. (1) shows that a distance of 1 in z on Fig. B-1 corresponds to a distance of the standard deviation (σ) on the normal curve of x. As seen from the figure, the area drops off very rapidly from the center so that, for example, 95.45 percent of the area is within two σ's of the mean of x.

The normal distribution approximates the binomial closely when k and n are both very large and $(k - \mu)^3 / \sigma$ is small. Of primary interest is the standard normal approximation of the binomial *cumulative distribution*. The approximation is

$$\sum_{j=k_1}^{k_2} C(n,j) p^j (1 - p)^{n-j} = \Phi\left(y_2 + \frac{1}{2\sigma}\right) - \Phi\left(y_1 - \frac{1}{2\sigma}\right) \tag{7}$$

where

$$y_1 = \frac{k_1 - np}{\sigma} \qquad y_2 = \frac{k_2 - np}{\sigma}$$
$$\sigma = \sqrt{np(1 - p)}$$

Example: Given 100 Bernoulli trials, each with success probability of $p = 1/5$. What is the probability of more than 24 successes?

Solution:

$np = (1/5)(100) = 20; \sigma = \sqrt{20(.8)} = 4$

$k_1 = 24 ; y_1 = (24-20)/4 = 1$

$k_2 = 100 ; y_2 = (100-20)/4 = 20$

From Eq. (7), the right side is

$P(k \geqslant 24) = \Phi(20+1/8) - \Phi(1-1/8)$

Using Appendix Table C3, calling the table values $T(t)$, and interpolating where necessary:

$\Phi(20+1/8) = .5 + T(20.125) = 0.5 + .5 = 1$

$\Phi(1-1/8) = .5 + T(.875) = 0.5 + 0.3092 = 0.8092$

Hence,

$P(k \geqslant 24) = 1 - 0.8092 = 0.1918$

One of the reasons that the normal distribution is so important is the following theorem, which is stated without proof (there are several such theorems).

Central limit theorem 1 If $X_1, X_2, \ldots, X_n$ are independent and identically distributed random variables with mean μ and standard deviation σ, as n increases without bound, the cumulative distribution of the *sum* $X_1 + X_2 + \ldots X_n$ approaches the standard normal distribution

$$\lim_{n \to \infty} P\left(\frac{X_1 + X_2 + \cdots X_n - n\mu}{\sigma\sqrt{n}} \leqslant a\right) = \Phi(a)$$

The remarkable thing about this theorem is its independence from the form of the distribution of the random variables. This has great significance, since we usually observe the combined effects of many elementary "micro" events. If these are independent and combine as a sum, the central limit theorem says that the observed sum will be normally distributed independent of the distribution of the elementary events. For example, consider a large collection of computer users, each submitting many jobs per month. The total processing time per user per month is the sum of the times of each user. It may well be that the distribution function for monthly time per user may be normally distributed, even though the distribution of individual job times is not.

THE CHI-SQUARED TEST

This widely applicable nonparametric test measures the probability that differences between any two frequency distributions are due to random fluctuation. We first sketch the theory, then give a computation procedure for doing a chi-squared test.

Consider a sample space with an alphabet of n points and associated probabilities $p_1, \ldots, p_n$. Suppose an experiment is done m independent times and we record their outcomes as a long string of sample-point labels. We also record the count of the number of times each point occurs as the frequency vector f. The probability of any such vector is then given by the multinomial distribution [Eq. (7), Sec. 3-15]

$$P(f_1, f_2, \ldots, f_n) = \frac{m!}{f_1! f_2! \ldots f_n!} p_1^{f_1} \, p_2^{f_2} \, \ldots \, p_n^{f_n} \tag{1}$$

where

$$\sum_{i=1}^{n} f_i = m \tag{2}$$

Suppose now that the experimentally obtained f_i values are to be compared to say a theoretical model whose p_i is used to estimate frequencies by

$$f_i' = mp_i \tag{3}$$

Since these will usually differ from the f_i, to see how much they differ, we use a measure of the differences called *chi-squared*

$$\chi^2 = \sum_{i=1}^{n} \frac{(f_i - f_i')^2}{f_i'} \tag{4}$$

The differences $f_i - f_i'$, and hence χ^2, may be due to two kinds of causes: (1) a true departure, since the assumed theoretical distribution is not a good model of the observed process, and (2) a random departure, due to the fact that any particular frequency vector f need not equal the vector mp. To attempt to separate these, we use the statistician's idea of the *null hypothesis* H_0: the measured frequency vector f matches the theoretical one $f' = mp$ in the sense that

$$P_n(> \chi^2) < Q$$

meaning that the probability of the deviation measure being larger than chi-squared is less than some "confidence or significance" level Q. If for a given Q level, the inequality is satisfied, we accept the null hypothesis; otherwise we reject it.

The key analytic problem is the form of the function $P_n(> \chi^2)$. This is a very tedious algebra-calculus problem, so we only sketch the theory here. The multinomial of Eq. (1) is first approximated by the multivariable normal function

$$P(f_1, f_2, \ldots, f_n) = \frac{1}{\sqrt{2\pi n}^{\,n-1}\sqrt{p_1, p_2, \ldots, p_n}} e^{-\chi^2/2} \tag{5}$$

where the approximation is valid if $f_i \gg 1$. Then the integral of the P's are taken over all sets of f_i vectors for which χ^2 is greater than the one calculated for the given data. These sums, i.e., the cumulative distribution for $P(\chi^2)$, are tabulated in Appendix Table C4 for various χ^2 values and also for various *degrees of freedom* v. The value v is the number of sample points diminished by the number of constraints, i.e., relations used to compute various parameters of the theoretical distribution from the data. For example, since $\Sigma p_i = 1$, this constraint means there are not more than $n - 1$ degrees of freedom. If the data is used to approximate the mean value of the theoretical distribution, we use $v = n - 2$ in the chi-squared table.

The following conditions must be satisfied in order for the chi-squared test to be valid: (1) each observation must fall into one and only one frequency interval, (2) the outcomes of the m observed trials must be independent, and (3) the number of trials must be large. The first two conditions are required for the multinomial distribution, which is the basis of the chi-squared test. The third condition is needed for approximating the distribution of chi-squared with the usual tabulated functions.

We now summarize the *computational steps* for actually doing a chi-squared test for "goodness of fit."

Given: Two data vectors as follows:
  (*a*) Theoretical probabilities obtained from some distribution function thought to fit the measured frequencies.
  (*b*) Measured frequencies.
  Note that the measured frequencies may be used to compute some needed parameter of the theoretical distribution (like its mean).
Find: Whether the deviations between the two data vectors are accountable by purely random fluctuation due to sampling. The question is to be answered *yes* or *no* with a significance level Q.
Procedure:

1. (*a*) Form the null hypothesis H_0, which is the statement: The measured distribution matches the theoretical one with significance Q; deviations are due to random fluctuations associated with sampling.
   (*b*) The alternative hypothesis to H_0 is H_1: Reject the null hypothesis; the experimental distribution does not match the theoretical distribution at the Q level of significance because the deviations are too large.

2. Compute χ^2 from the f and p vectors

$$\chi^2 = \sum_{i=1}^{n} \frac{(f_i - mp_i)^2}{f_i}$$

3. Determine the number of degrees of freedom df. At most, $df = n - 1$, but if the data was used to estimate one parameter of the theoretical distribution, $df = n - 2$; if used to estimate two parameters, like mean and standard deviation, $df = n - 3$.

4. Enter the chi-squared table with

   row value = df
   column value = Q

   Read the table value at the intersection. Call this x^2. This means that with probability Q, deviations larger than x^2 may be expected due to sampling alone.

5. If

   case 1. $\chi^2 > x^2$ reject the null hypothesis
   case 2. $\chi^2 \leqslant x^2$ accept the null hypothesis

   For case 1, the actual measure of deviations computed in step 2 is larger than the measure that can be expected from random sampling fluctuation alone; for case 2 it is equal or smaller. If, for example, case 1 applies for a significance level of 5 percent ($Q = 0.05$), then the chances are less than 1 in 20 that the measured distribution fits the theoretical model. This is a common criterion. In the event that the null hypothesis is rejected, we may well study the cases in the data that contributed most to χ^2 in order to help determine possible sources of deviation from the hypothesized model.

In framing hypotheses for statistical tests like the chi-squared tests, the hypothesis that is most easily proved false is taken as the null hypothesis. There are two types of error possible in the test process, which are designated in statistics as,

Type 1. Our test rejects the null hypothesis when it is in effect true.
Type 2. Our test accepts the null hypothesis when it is in effect false.

In a practical sense, the value of the significance level Q will determine what type of error is made (or whether no error in acceptance is made). If the significance level is set too stringent, then a Type 1 error is more likely than a Type 2 error, and conversely.

appendix C
Tables of Probability Functions

Table C1. Poisson distribution $P(k;\lambda) = (\lambda^k/k!)e^{-\lambda}$

k	0.100	0.200	0.300	0.400	*Lambda* λ 0.500	0.600	0.700	0.800	0.900	1.000
0	0.90484	0.81873	0.74082	0.67032	0.60653	0.54881	0.49659	0.44933	0.40657	0.36788
1	0.09048	0.16375	0.22225	0.26813	0.30327	0.32929	0.34761	0.35946	0.36591	0.36788
2	0.00452	0.01637	0.03334	0.05363	0.07582	0.09879	0.12166	0.14379	0.16466	0.18394
3	0.00015	0.00109	0.00333	0.00715	0.01264	0.01976	0.02839	0.03834	0.04940	0.06131
4	0.00000	0.00005	0.00025	0.00072	0.00158	0.00296	0.00497	0.00767	0.01111	0.01533
5	0.00000	0.00000	0.00002	0.00006	0.00016	0.00036	0.00070	0.00123	0.00200	0.00307
6	0.00000	0.00000	0.00000	0.00000	0.00001	0.00004	0.00008	0.00016	0.00030	0.00051
7	0.00000	0.00000	0.00000	0.00000	0.00000	0.00000	0.00001	0.00002	0.00004	0.00007

k	1.000	2.000	3.000	4.000	*Lambda* λ 5.000	6.000	7.000	8.000	9.000	10.000
0	0.36788	0.13534	0.04979	0.01832	0.00674	0.00248	0.00091	0.00034	0.00012	0.00005
1	0.36788	0.27067	0.14936	0.07326	0.03369	0.01487	0.00638	0.00268	0.00111	0.00045
2	0.18394	0.27067	0.22404	0.14653	0.08422	0.04462	0.02234	0.01073	0.00500	0.00227
3	0.06131	0.18045	0.22404	0.19537	0.14037	0.08924	0.05213	0.02863	0.01499	0.00757
4	0.01533	0.09022	0.16803	0.19537	0.17547	0.13385	0.09123	0.05725	0.03374	0.01892
5	0.00307	0.03609	0.10082	0.15629	0.17547	0.16062	0.12772	0.09160	0.06073	0.03783
6	0.00051	0.01203	0.05041	0.10420	0.14622	0.16062	0.14900	0.12214	0.09109	0.06306
7	0.00007	0.00344	0.02160	0.05954	0.10444	0.13768	0.14900	0.13959	0.11712	0.09008
8	0.00001	0.00086	0.00810	0.02977	0.06528	0.10326	0.13038	0.13959	0.13176	0.11260
9	0.00000	0.00019	0.00270	0.01323	0.03627	0.06884	0.10140	0.12408	0.13176	0.12511
10	0.00000	0.00004	0.00081	0.00529	0.01813	0.04130	0.07098	0.09926	0.11858	0.12511
11	0.00000	0.00001	0.00022	0.00192	0.00824	0.02253	0.04517	0.07219	0.09702	0.11374
12	0.00000	0.00000	0.00006	0.00064	0.00343	0.01126	0.02635	0.04813	0.07277	0.09478
13	0.00000	0.00000	0.00001	0.00020	0.00132	0.00520	0.01419	0.02962	0.05038	0.07291
14	0.00000	0.00000	0.00000	0.00006	0.00047	0.00223	0.00709	0.01692	0.03238	0.05208
15	0.00000	0.00000	0.00000	0.00002	0.00016	0.00089	0.00331	0.00903	0.01943	0.03472
16	0.00000	0.00000	0.00000	0.00000	0.00005	0.00033	0.00145	0.00451	0.01093	0.02170
17	0.00000	0.00000	0.00000	0.00000	0.00001	0.00012	0.00060	0.00212	0.00579	0.01276
18	0.00000	0.00000	0.00000	0.00000	0.00000	0.00004	0.00023	0.00094	0.00289	0.00709
19	0.00000	0.00000	0.00000	0.00000	0.00000	0.00001	0.00009	0.00040	0.00137	0.00373
20	0.00000	0.00000	0.00000	0.00000	0.00000	0.00000	0.00003	0.00016	0.00062	0.00187
21	0.00000	0.00000	0.00000	0.00000	0.00000	0.00000	0.00001	0.00006	0.00026	0.00089
22	0.00000	0.00000	0.00000	0.00000	0.00000	0.00000	0.00000	0.00002	0.00011	0.00040
23	0.00000	0.00000	0.00000	0.00000	0.00000	0.00000	0.00000	0.00001	0.00004	0.00018
24	0.00000	0.00000	0.00000	0.00000	0.00000	0.00000	0.00000	0.00000	0.00002	0.00007
25	0.00000	0.00000	0.00000	0.00000	0.00000	0.00000	0.00000	0.00000	0.00001	0.00003
26	0.00000	0.00000	0.00000	0.00000	0.00000	0.00000	0.00000	0.00000	0.00000	0.00001

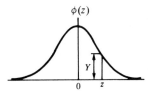

Table C2. Ordinates (Y) of the standard normal curve at z

z	0	1	2	3	4	5	6	7	8	9
0.0	.3989	.3989	.3989	.3988	.3986	.3984	.3982	.3980	.3977	.3973
0.1	.3970	.3965	.3961	.3956	.3951	.3945	.3939	.3932	.3925	.3918
0.2	.3910	.3902	.3894	.3885	.3876	.3867	.3857	.3847	.3836	.3825
0.3	.3814	.3802	.3790	.3778	.3765	.3752	.3739	.3725	.3712	.3697
0.4	.3683	.3668	.3653	.3637	.3621	.3605	.3589	.3572	.3555	.3538
0.5	.3521	.3503	.3485	.3467	.3448	.3429	.3410	.3391	.3372	.3352
0.6	.3332	.3312	.3292	.3271	.3251	.3230	.3209	.3187	.3166	.3144
0.7	.3123	.3101	.3079	.3056	.3034	.3011	.2989	.2966	.2943	.2920
0.8	.2897	.2874	.2850	.2827	.2803	.2780	.2756	.2732	.2709	.2685
0.9	.2661	.2637	.2613	.2589	.2565	.2541	.2516	.2492	.2468	.2444
1.0	.2420	.2396	.2371	.2347	.2323	.2299	.2275	.2251	.2227	.2203
1.1	.2179	.2155	.2131	.2107	.2083	.2059	.2036	.2012	.1989	.1965
1.2	.1942	.1919	.1895	.1872	.1849	.1826	.1804	.1781	.1758	.1736
1.3	.1714	.1691	.1669	.1647	.1626	.1604	.1582	.1561	.1539	.1518
1.4	.1497	.1476	.1456	.1435	.1415	.1394	.1374	.1354	.1334	.1315
1.5	.1295	.1276	.1257	.1238	.1219	.1200	.1182	.1163	.1145	.1127
1.6	.1109	.1092	.1074	.1057	.1040	.1023	.1006	.0989	.0973	.0957
1.7	.0940	.0925	.0909	.0893	.0878	.0863	.0848	.0833	.0818	.0804
1.8	.0790	.0775	.0761	.0748	.0734	.0721	.0707	.0694	.0681	.0669
1.9	.0656	.0644	.0632	.0620	.0608	.0596	.0584	.0573	.0562	.0551
2.0	.0540	.0529	.0519	.0508	.0498	.0488	.0478	.0468	.0459	.0449
2.1	.0440	.0431	.0422	.0413	.0404	.0396	.0387	.0379	.0371	.0363
2.2	.0355	.0347	.0339	.0332	.0325	.0317	.0310	.0303	.0297	.0290
2.3	.0283	.0277	.0270	.0264	.0258	.0252	.0246	.0241	.0235	.0229
2.4	.0224	.0219	.0213	.0208	.0203	.0198	.0194	.0189	.0184	.0180
2.5	.0175	.0171	.0167	.0163	.0158	.0154	.0151	.0147	.0143	.0139
2.6	.0136	.0132	.0129	.0126	.0122	.0119	.0116	.0113	.0110	.0107
2.7	.0104	.0101	.0099	.0096	.0093	.0091	.0088	.0086	.0084	.0081
2.8	.0079	.0077	.0075	.0073	.0071	.0069	.0067	.0065	.0063	.0061
2.9	.0060	.0058	.0056	.0055	.0053	.0051	.0050	.0048	.0047	.0046
3.0	.0044	.0043	.0042	.0040	.0039	.0038	.0037	.0036	.0035	.0034
3.1	.0033	.0032	.0031	.0030	.0029	.0028	.0027	.0026	.0025	.0025
3.2	.0024	.0023	.0022	.0022	.0021	.0020	.0020	.0019	.0018	.0018
3.3	.0017	.0017	.0016	.0016	.0015	.0015	.0014	.0014	.0013	.0013
3.4	.0012	.0012	.0012	.0011	.0011	.0010	.0010	.0010	.0009	.0009
3.5	.0009	.0008	.0008	.0008	.0008	.0007	.0007	.0007	.0007	.0006
3.6	.0006	.0006	.0006	.0005	.0005	.0005	.0005	.0005	.0005	.0004
3.7	.0004	.0004	.0004	.0004	.0004	.0004	.0003	.0003	.0003	.0003
3.8	.0003	.0003	.0003	.0003	.0003	.0002	.0002	.0002	.0002	.0002
3.9	.0002	.0002	.0002	.0002	.0002	.0002	.0002	.0002	.0001	.0001

Table C3. Standard normal curve areas

This table gives areas under the standard distribution ϕ between 0 and $t \geqslant 0$ in steps of 9.01

$\Phi(z)$

t	0	1	2	3	4	5	6	7	8	9
0.0	.0000	.0040	.0080	.0120	.0160	.0199	.0239	.0279	.0319	.0359
0.1	.0398	.0438	.0478	.0517	.0557	.0596	.0636	.0675	.0714	.0754
0.2	.0793	.0832	.0871	.0910	.0948	.0987	.1026	.1064	.1103	.1141
0.3	.1179	.1217	.1255	.1293	.1331	.1368	.1406	.1443	.1480	.1517
0.4	.1554	.1591	.1628	.1664	.1700	.1736	.1772	.1808	.1844	.1879
0.5	.1915	.1950	.1985	.2019	.2054	.2088	.2123	.2157	.2190	.2224
0.6	.2258	.2291	.2324	.2357	.2389	.2422	.2454	.2486	.2518	.2549
0.7	.2580	.2612	.2642	.2673	.2704	.2734	.2764	.2794	.2823	.2852
0.8	.2881	.2910	.2939	.2967	.2996	.3023	.3051	.3078	.3106	.3133
0.9	.3159	.3186	.3212	.3238	.3264	.3289	.3315	.3340	.3665	.3389
1.0	.3413	.3438	.3461	.3485	.3508	.3531	.3554	.3577	.3599	.3621
1.1	.3643	.3665	.3686	.3708	.3729	.3749	.3770	.3790	.3810	.3830
1.2	.3849	.3869	.3888	.3907	.3925	.3944	.3962	.3980	.3997	.4015
1.3	.4032	.4049	.4066	.4082	.4099	.4115	.4131	.4147	.4162	.4177
1.4	.4192	.4207	.4222	.4236	.4251	.4265	.4279	.4292	.4306	.4319
1.5	.4332	.4345	.4357	.4370	.4382	.4394	.4406	.4418	.4429	.4441
1.6	.4452	.4463	.4474	.4484	.4495	.4505	.4515	.4525	.4535	.4545
1.7	.4554	.4564	.4573	.4582	.4591	.4599	.4608	.4616	.4625	.4633
1.8	.4641	.4649	.4656	.4664	.4671	.4678	.4686	.4693	.4699	.4706
1.9	.4713	.4719	.4726	.4732	.4738	.4744	.4750	.4756	.4761	.4767
2.0	.4772	.4778	.4783	.4788	.4793	.4798	.4803	.4808	.4812	.4817
2.1	.4821	.4826	.4830	.4834	.4838	.4842	.4846	.4850	.4854	.4857
2.2	.4861	.4864	.4868	.4871	.4875	.4878	.4881	.4884	.4887	.4890
2.3	.4893	.4896	.4898	.4901	.4904	.4906	.4909	.4911	.4913	.4916
2.4	.4918	.4920	.4922	.4925	.4927	.4929	.4931	.4932	.4934	.4936
2.5	.4938	.4940	.4941	.4943	.4945	.4946	.4948	.4949	.4951	.4952
2.6	.4953	.4955	.4956	.4957	.4959	.4960	.4961	.4962	.4963	.4964
2.7	.4965	.4966	.4967	.4968	.4969	.4970	.4971	.4972	.4973	.4974
2.8	.4974	.4975	.4976	.4977	.4977	.4978	.4979	.4979	.4980	.4981
2.9	.4981	.4982	.4982	.4983	.4984	.4984	.4985	.4985	.4986	.4986
3.0	.4987	.4987	.4987	.4988	.4988	.4989	.4989	.4989	.4990	.4990
3.1	.4990	.4991	.4991	.4991	.4992	.4992	.4992	.4992	.4993	.4993
3.2	.4993	.4993	.4994	.4994	.4994	.4994	.4994	.4995	.4995	.4995
3.3	.4995	.4995	.4995	.4996	.4996	.4996	.4996	.4996	.4996	.4997
3.4	.4997	.4997	.4997	.4997	.4997	.4997	.4997	.4997	.4997	.4998
3.5	.4998	.4998	.4998	.4998	.4998	.4998	.4998	.4998	.4998	.4998
3.6	.4998	.4998	.4999	.4999	.4999	.4999	.4999	.4999	.4999	.4999
3.7	.4999	.4999	.4999	.4999	.4999	.4999	.4999	.4999	.4999	.4999
3.8	.4999	.4999	.4999	.4999	.4999	.4999	.4999	.4999	.4999	.4999
3.9	.5000	.5000	.5000	.5000	.5000	.5000	.5000	.5000	.5000	.5000

Table C4. Percentile values (χ_p^2) for the chi-square distribution with ν degrees of freedom (shaded area $= p$)

ν	$\chi^2_{.995}$	$\chi^2_{.99}$	$\chi^2_{.975}$	$\chi^2_{.95}$	$\chi^2_{.90}$	$\chi^2_{.75}$	$\chi^2_{.50}$	$\chi^2_{.25}$	$\chi^2_{.10}$	$\chi^2_{.05}$	$\chi^2_{.025}$	$\chi^2_{.01}$	$\chi^2_{.005}$
1	7.88	6.63	5.02	3.84	2.71	1.32	.455	.102	.0158	.0039	.0010	.0002	.0000
2	10.6	9.21	7.38	5.99	4.61	2.77	1.39	.575	.211	.103	.0506	.0201	.0100
3	12.8	11.3	9.35	7.81	6.25	4.11	2.37	1.21	.584	.352	.216	.115	.072
4	14.9	13.3	11.1	9.49	7.78	5.39	3.36	1.92	1.06	.711	.484	.297	.207
5	16.7	15.1	12.8	11.1	9.24	6.63	4.35	2.67	1.61	1.15	.831	.554	.412
6	18.5	16.8	14.4	12.6	10.6	7.84	5.35	3.45	2.20	1.64	1.24	.872	.676
7	20.3	18.5	16.0	14.1	12.0	9.04	6.35	4.25	2.83	2.17	1.69	1.24	.989
8	22.0	20.1	17.5	15.5	13.4	10.2	7.34	5.07	3.49	2.73	2.18	1.65	1.34
9	23.6	21.7	19.0	16.9	14.7	11.4	8.34	5.90	4.17	3.33	2.70	2.09	1.73
10	25.2	23.2	20.5	18.3	16.0	12.5	9.34	6.74	4.87	3.94	3.25	2.56	2.16
11	26.8	24.7	21.9	19.7	17.3	13.7	10.3	7.58	5.58	4.57	3.82	3.05	2.60
12	28.3	26.2	23.3	21.0	18.5	14.8	11.3	8.44	6.30	5.23	4.40	3.57	3.07
13	29.8	27.7	24.7	22.4	19.8	16.0	12.3	9.30	7.04	5.89	5.01	4.11	3.57
14	31.3	29.1	26.1	23.7	21.1	17.1	13.3	10.2	7.79	6.57	5.63	4.66	4.07
15	32.8	30.6	27.5	25.0	22.3	18.2	14.3	11.0	8.55	7.26	6.26	5.23	4.60
16	34.3	32.0	28.8	26.3	23.5	19.4	15.3	11.9	9.31	7.96	6.91	5.81	5.14
17	35.7	33.4	30.2	27.6	24.8	20.5	16.3	12.8	10.1	8.67	7.56	6.41	5.70
18	37.2	34.8	31.5	28.9	26.0	21.6	17.3	13.7	10.9	9.39	8.23	7.01	6.26
19	38.6	36.2	32.9	30.1	27.2	22.7	18.3	14.6	11.7	10.1	8.91	7.63	6.84
20	40.0	37.6	34.2	31.4	28.4	23.8	19.3	15.5	12.4	10.9	9.59	8.26	7.43
21	41.4	38.9	35.5	32.7	29.6	24.9	20.3	16.3	13.2	11.6	10.3	8.90	8.03
22	42.8	40.3	36.8	33.9	30.8	26.0	21.3	17.2	14.0	12.3	11.0	9.54	8.64
23	44.2	41.6	38.1	35.2	32.0	27.1	22.3	18.1	14.8	13.1	11.7	10.2	9.26
24	45.6	43.0	39.4	36.4	33.2	28.2	23.3	19.0	15.7	13.8	12.4	10.9	9.89
25	46.9	44.3	40.6	37.7	34.4	29.3	24.3	19.9	16.5	14.6	13.1	11.5	10.5
26	48.3	45.6	41.9	38.9	35.6	30.4	25.3	20.8	17.3	15.4	13.8	12.2	11.2
27	49.6	47.0	43.2	40.1	36.7	31.5	26.3	21.7	18.1	16.2	14.6	12.9	11.8
28	51.0	48.3	44.5	41.3	37.9	32.6	27.3	22.7	18.9	16.9	15.3	13.6	12.5
29	52.3	49.6	45.7	42.6	39.1	33.7	28.3	23.6	19.8	17.7	16.0	14.3	13.1
30	53.7	50.9	47.0	43.8	40.3	34.8	29.3	24.5	20.6	18.5	16.8	15.0	13.8
40	66.8	63.7	59.3	55.8	51.8	45.6	39.3	33.7	29.1	26.5	24.4	22.2	20.7
50	79.5	76.2	71.4	67.5	63.2	56.3	49.3	42.9	37.7	34.8	32.4	29.7	28.0
60	92.0	88.4	83.3	79.1	74.4	67.0	59.3	52.3	46.5	43.2	40.5	37.5	35.5
70	104.2	100.4	95.0	90.5	85.5	77.6	69.3	61.7	55.3	51.7	48.8	45.4	43.3
80	116.3	112.3	106.6	101.9	96.6	88.1	79.3	71.1	64.3	60.4	57.2	53.4	51.2
90	128.3	124.1	118.1	113.1	107.6	98.6	89.3	80.6	73.3	69.1	65.6	61.8	59.2
100	140.2	135.8	129.6	124.3	118.5	109.1	99.3	90.1	82.4	77.9	74.2	70.1	67.3

Source: Catherine M. Thompson, Table of percentage points of the χ^2 distribution, *Biometrika*, vol. 32 (1941), by permission of the author and publisher.

Problems

Chapter 1   The Nature of Computer-Performance Evaluation

1. Explain why the generality of the computer is the source of fundamental difficulties in performance studies.

2. Characterize each of the following situations as adaptive or nonadaptive:
   - (a) A user must declare the amount of main storage his program requires.
   - (b) Management of storage space in a typical modern string or list-processing language (e.g., SNOBOL or LIST).
   - (c) Jobs are processed in the order of user-declared priority.
   - (d) Jobs with shortest-measured run times are processed first.
   - (e) Program P is run on system A and system B, which are both identical, except that B has more main storage. The systems, during this test, run only P. B runs faster.

3. Briefly discuss the important distinction between thruput and response time and give examples where each is the more appropriate performance measure (see Sec. 4-5 for a further discussion).

4. Two systems are to be compared with the same two job streams. The following table was obtained by measurements of run times:

Run times

Stream	No. Jobs	System 1	System 2
1	25	2.50	5.00
2	10	0.67	1.00

   - (a) Compute the thruputs for each stream for each system.
   - (b) Compute the ratio of thruputs for each stream; compute the difference of the ratios.
   - (c) Compute the ratio of the thruput differences; compare result with (b).

5. Given the following records of three account numbers:

Account no.	No. jobs	Ave. run time	% of jobs	% of run time
0001	300	30 sec		
0002	50	20 min		
0003	150	2 min		

   - (a) Fill in the rightmost two columns of the above table.
   - (b) Discuss the questions: Which account number accounted for most use of the system; which served most jobs?

6. Describe in your own words the major characteristics of a timesharing system. Emphasize those features that are unique to this type of system.

7. Briefly define the nature of a virtual-storage system. Draw on your fundamental knowledge of the nature of a storage hierarchy (e.g., core storage and disk) to speculate about the relative importance (from a performance viewpoint) of including *only one* of: *timesharing* or *multiprogramming* in a virtual-storage system.

Chapter 2 Principles of Statistics

1. The number of punched cards read by five successive job decks was measured as

80, 19, 276, 58, 712

(a) Find the range of deck size.
(b) Find the average deck size.
(c) Find the coefficient of variation.
(d) Find the median.

2. Suppose that only the average run times of jobs processed by a certain computer center are available for January, February, and March.

(a) Is it possible from only this data to compute the average run time for the three-month period?
(b) If the answer to (a) is no, specify what additional information is needed.

3. Derive the formula for the mean value of three sets of numbers (similar to Eq. (9) of Sec. 2-1).

4. Write a program to accept data X and compute and print
(a) Range
(b) Mean
(c) Standard deviation
(d) Coefficient of variation
(e) Median

5. Write a program to produce a frequency-grouped distribution function for data X. It must request the user to specify (at his option) either the number of buckets, or else the bucket range desired. The program must compute and print:

(a) All the results of Prob. 4 (include that program in the current program)
(b) A table of frequency groupings which is to look as follows (for example)

Bucket no.	Bucket range	Freq.	Relative freq.	Cum. freq.	Cum. relative freq.
1	0 to 0.5	10	0.0500	10	0.0500
2	0.5 to 1.0	50	0.2500	60	0.3000
etc.	etc.	etc.	etc.	etc.	etc.

6. Use the program for the flat random-number generator given in Fig. 2-5.1 (or any other random-number generator available) to generate 1000 values.

(a) Run your program of Prob. 5 on this data. Compare values with what you expect intuitively.
(b) Consider the first 500 values as X values, the second as Y values, and compute the correlation coefficient.

7. Given the following relative frequency function of main-storage sizes (in kbytes) of several observed programs

kbytes	0	8	16	32	64
Rel. freq.	0.00	0.80	0.10	0.06	0.04

(a) Compute the cumulative relative frequency function.
(b) Generate 1000 random samples using this function.
(c) Use your program of Prob. 5 with appropriate bucket size (=8) to obtain the relative frequency function of the generated numbers.

(*d*) Compare the results of (*c*) with the table given above, using the root-mean-square difference of the two relative frequency functions as a measure of the differences.

8. Several kinds of data can (and should) be gathered in a computer installation. Examples include: run (execution) time, wait-to-run time, and numbers of jobs and their times in various categories (compile, run, utilities, etc.). Such data helps to tell us "what the system is doing" and is an essential first step in evaluating and later improving any computer system.

This problem and Probs. 9, 10, and 11 illustrate the idea of analysis of job data with a very simple example—statistics of job execution times. Given the following 50 execution times (in minutes) of jobs observed at a computing center (vector Y):

$$Y = \begin{array}{cccccccccc}
10 & 18 & 91 & 42 & 13 & 11 & 32 & 17 & 4 & 152 \\
\hline
23 & 13 & 36 & 101 & 1 & 14 & 2 & 23 & 34 & 15 \\
\hline
27 & 1 & 57 & 17 & 3 & 29 & 53 & 4 & 62 & 47 \\
\hline
4 & 11 & 20 & 13 & 38 & 54 & 46 & 12 & 5 & 26 \\
\hline
18 & 19 & 3 & 10 & 5 & 13 & 24 & 3 & 2 & 11
\end{array}$$

(*a*) Display the above data as a sorted vector (for visual inspection).

(*b*) Use the programs developed in the previous problems to compute and print the five statistics of Prob. 4 for the above execution time data.

(*c*) Compute and print a relative frequency and cumulative relative frequency table of this data using some convenient bucket scheme.

(*d*) Plot a histogram.

9. From the computations of Prob. 8 (plus any others) and considering the jobs in nondecreasing time order:

(*a*) What longest of the shortest job times accounted for 20%, 40%, 60%, and 80% of the number of jobs executed?

(*b*) What longest of the shortest job times accounted for 20%, 40%, 60%, and 80% of the total *time* to execute all jobs?

(*c*) What percents of the number of jobs accounted for the following percents of total execution time: 20%, 40%, 60%, and 80%?

10. The jobs whose execution times are given in Prob. 8 are found to require the following corresponding number of kbytes of main storage (vector S):

$$S = \begin{array}{cccccccccc}
80 & 120 & 250 & 200 & 90 & 50 & 60 & 100 & 20 & 160 \\
\hline
100 & 90 & 60 & 64 & 18 & 160 & 36 & 80 & 180 & 76 \\
\hline
90 & 24 & 48 & 120 & 44 & 170 & 220 & 20 & 260 & 190 \\
\hline
100 & 76 & 120 & 80 & 128 & 200 & 190 & 128 & 100 & 64 \\
\hline
100 & 120 & 64 & 80 & 16 & 90 & 80 & 68 & 36 & 76
\end{array}$$

(*a*) Give the scatter plot for S vs. Y. Write a program for computing and printing the following parameters for analysis of execute time and storage space data.

(*b*) Determine a_0 and a_1 for the best least-square line and plot the line on the scatter plot.

(*c*) What is the standard error of estimate?

(*d*) What is the correlation coefficient?

(*e*) What do you conclude about the relationship between time and space demands of the particular job stream represented by the given data?

11. Write a report (one or two pages) summarizing the results of Probs. 8 to 10.

12. *Card-compaction study*: Obtain several decks of punched cards (or their images on tape) by collecting several (say 50) student and other jobs.

(*a*) Write a program to measure used length of each card defined as the number of characters from column 1 to the last nonblank character.

(*b*) Construct frequency and cumulative frequency functions for the decks. Also compute relative frequencies and relative cumulative frequencies.

(*c*) What is the average used length of a card?

(*d*) Consider a compaction program that, upon read in of each card into a buffer area, determines the used length and then stores this length in one byte (followed by the card characters to the last nonblank character). Estimate the savings of characters stored (over storing the entire 80 columns of each card). Also compute the percent savings.

Chapter 3   Topics in Discrete Mathematics and Applications

1. Most computers use the internal symbols 0 and 1 in their circuitry.
   (*a*) If a byte consists of 8 bits and each byte represents one character of the character-set, how large a character-set is possible?
   (*b*) The address register of a certain computer has 24 bits. How many addressable cells are there (express as decimal number)?
   (*c*) A certain computer is to have a character-set of 56 distinct characters. How many bits per character is required?

2. From a set of seven jobs, in how many ways can a stream of four jobs be selected if:
   (*a*) Streams consisting of different orderings of the same jobs are counted as distinct.
   (*b*) Different orderings are not counted as distinct.

3. The character-set of a certain computer system has 48 characters and it uses a standard IBM punched card of 80 columns and 12 rows.
   (*a*) How many holes are required, at most per column in a punched card, to represent this character-set?
   (*b*) If the punched card has 80 columns, how many different possible character configurations can be represented in the punched card (assume one character per column) with this 48-symbol character-set? (You don't have to calculate the result; just show its mathematical representation.)

4. The common IBM punched card has 12 punch positions per column. Usually, the hole configuration in a column represents a character of data. Construct a 12-row table listing $N(h)$, the number of possible characters (i.e., the size of the character-set), obtainable by permitting *at most* h holes, where $1 \leqslant h \leqslant 12$.

5. A computer manufacturer makes the following line of models for a particular system:

CPU	3 Models
Main Storage	6 Sizes
Disk Drives	4 Models
Tape Drives	4 Models
Card Reader	
Punch (CRP)	1 Model
Printer	3 Models

How many different system configurations are possible with:
   (*a*) One CPU, one main storage, two disk drives, two tape drives, one CRP, one printer?
   (*b*) One CPU, two main storages, at least two disk drives, at least one tape drive, one CRP, up to two printers?

6. How many possible nine-person task forces, each consisting of three engineers, four programmers, and two salesmen, can be formed from a group of candidates consisting of 10 engineers, 15 programmers, and 12 salesmen?

7. A company needs to assign a distinct part number to each item in its inventory for use in data processing. They have 80,000 different parts in stock.
   (*a*) Will a number with two alphabetic characters and two numeric characters, in that order, produce enough distinct numbers?
   (*b*) Suppose part numbers could be represented with two alphabetic and two numeric characters in any order. How many part numbers could be represented?

8. Some computer operating systems divide main storage into partitions and assign jobs to partitions as a technique of job scheduling. If main storage is divided into five partitions (P) it might appear as follows:

$$\left| \; P_1 \; \left| \; P_2 \; \right| \; P_3 \; \left| \; P_4 \; \right| \; P_5 \; \right|$$

Each partition may be assigned a class symbol A, B, or C for scheduling jobs of different classes.

   (a) If each partition is assigned one class symbol, with repetitions allowed, how many distinct class assignments are possible?

   (b) If each partition is assigned one class symbol and each class (A, B, and C) must be represented in every class assignment, how many distinct class assignments are possible?

9. A certain computer has a main storage composed of 32 independently accessible modules. The address references to this main storage are as likely to be to any one module as to any other. Assume the main-storage control references the modules from an ample stream of requests.

   (a) How many possible distinct reference configurations are there for a stream of two requests?

   (b) Of the number of reference configurations in (a) with 20 requests, how many configurations will allow eight different modules to be referenced during the first memory cycle?

   (c) In a reference stream with 20 requests, how many configurations will allow eight different modules to be referenced during one memory cycle of the memory cycles needed to service the 20 requests? Note this is a very difficult problem. It has been included so that you might give its solution some thought. It demonstrates how a small change in a problem statement can make a large difference in the complexity of the problem.

10. A certain computer center has 100 users of which 50 use FORTRAN or COBOL (or both) and 20 use FORTRAN only. Answer the following, if possible, from the information given. If no answer is possible in a given case, suggest additional information needed.

   (a) Number using neither FORTRAN or COBOL

   (b) Number using COBOL

   (c) Number using COBOL only

11. A certain programming job has been divided into four modules A, B, C, and D. The available programmers are to work in teams on the modules; each team may be assigned one or more modules.

   (a) In how many ways can the job be assigned? (*Note*: The number of teams need not be the same for each way.)

   (b) Enumerate the ways.

   (c) If the job were divided into six modules, how many ways are there?

12. The formula for the amount of each of n *equal* payments required to retire a loan of initial amount A at interest r is

$$P(n) = \frac{Ar(1 + r)^n}{(1 + r)^n - 1}$$

   (a) Derive formulas for N_A, N_M, N_D, the number of operations of addition-subtraction, multiplication, and division as a function of n. Assume $n - 1$ multiplications to compute $(1 + r)^n$.

   (b) Using the formulas of (a) estimate the number of each operation required to produce a table of p vs. n (such as used to determine mortgage payments) where $n = 1, 2, \ldots, 30$.

   (c) Derive the following recursive form for p

$$P(1) = A(1 + r)$$

$$P(n + 1) = \frac{P(1)P(n)}{A + P(n)}$$

   (d) Repeat (a) and (b) for the recursive form and compare with the nonrecursive form.

13. Show algebraically that a recursive form of the binomial formula is

$$B(0; n, p) = (1 - p)^n$$

$$B(k + 1; n, p) = \left(\frac{p}{1 - p}\right)\left(\frac{n - k}{k + 1}\right)B(k; n, p)$$

for $k = 0, 1, \ldots, n$. Compare the number of addition-subtractions, multiplications, and divisions for $n = 10$ using the recursion and nonrecursion forms for B.

14. In a certain computer system, there are six on-line users; each can be in one and only one state at a time:

State	Probability
B (busy)	1/3
T (thinking)	1/3
W (waiting)	1/3

(a) Give the sample space for each user.

(b) How many sample points are there in the state of the system? Write down at least four examples of system sample points.

(c) Consider the sample space for "n users are busy," where $n = 0, 1, \ldots, 6$. Compute the sample point probabilities.

(d) Compute the mean number of users that are busy.

(e) Repeat (c) and (d) if the state probabilities for each user are 0.1, 0.3, and 0.6.

15. A collection of 100 programs are available to all users of a certain special-purpose system, and each user must be running one and only one of these at any one time (all with the same probability). What is the probability that if 10 users are connected, no two of them require access to the same program?

16. In a given computer system, there are only two storages, a fast one with cycle time t_f, and a slow one with cycle time t_s. If the probability of a reference to the fast store is p

(a) Derive a (simple) formula for the average cycle time of the system.

(b) Assume that the fast store is 10 times faster than the slow store. If the average speed of the system is to be only four times slower than the fast store, what must be the probabilities of any given access being in each store?

17. A system contains a CPU, a core memory, and a card reader-punch. Each of these components can either be operational or failed, with the probabilities of being operational during a given time period of 0.98, 0.90, 0.85, respectively. What is the probability that the system will fail in the time period? (*Note*: The system fails if any of its components fail.)

18. Measurements show that the probability that a disk access references drive A is 0.4. Assuming a binomial distribution, what is the probability that in four accesses

(a) There are two access to drive A?

(b) Drive A is not accessed?

(c) There is at least one access to drive A?

(d) There are at least two accesses to drive A?

19. A certain computer system can have the following types of units:

	Reliability
Arithmetic unit, AU	0.95
Core storage module, CSM	0.92
I/O channel, CH	0.85
Disk file, DF	0.80
Tape unit, TU	0.80
Card reader/punch, CRP	0.78

(a) What is the reliability of a system consisting of one AU, two CSMs, two CHs, two TUs, and one CRP? Assume all units must work for the system to work.

(b) Repeat part (a), except now assume four TUs are present, but that any two of these will suffice to keep the system working.

20. (a) Repeat Prob. 19, but now assume two AUs are present, only one of which need be working for the system to be working. Compare the reliability to that of Prob. 18.

(b) If the improvement due to adding the additional AU is not great, discuss other factors that might still suggest a two AU system.

21. Assume exponential forms for all reliability functions.

    (a) A system has a mean time to failure (MTF) of 14 hours. What is the probability that it will survive 3 hours?

    (b) What is the probability it will survive 14 hours?

22. Assume exponential reliability functions. If the MTF of a certain component is 100 hours, what is the MTF of:

    (a) Two components in parallel?

    (b) Four components in parallel?

    (c) Six components in parallel?

23. A certain computer is to contain 50,000 transistors and is to have a MTF of 50 hours. Assuming exponential distribution, what must be the MTF of each transistor?

24. Consider a component standby system with $n - 1$ components in standby, each containing a switch for connecting the standby component in the event of failure. Show that if r is the reliability of each component and w is the reliability of each switch, the system reliability is given by

$$R = 1 - (1 - r)(1 - wr)^{n-1}$$

    (a) Take $n - 2$, plot a curve of R vs. r for each $w - 0.5, 0.8, 0.9, 0.95, 1$.

    (b) Repeat (a) for $n - 3, 4, 5$.

25. The price of improved reliability by redundancy is the cost of the additional redundant equipment. Suppose a system has a mean operational time of 100 hours and a mean repair time of 4 hours. Using the model of Sec. 3-2, Eqs. (11) and (12)

    (a) What is the system reliability?

    (b) If two systems are installed and become one supersystem, what is its reliability?

26. Starting with Eq. (10) of Sec. 3-2, derive the formula for the reliability of an n machine system, assuming that the repair rate is independent of the number of machines that are down. Compare this formula with Eq. (13).

Chapter 4 Job Processing Models: Informal and Simulation Viewpoints

1. Explain why a simulation model can be more general than a mathematical model of job processing? What advantages do analytic (mathematical) models have over simulation models?

2. Define and explain the term "job" in job processing models.

3. In your own words, explain the distinction between job-stream performance and resource performance.

4. What general criteria (at least three) should be considered in selecting jobs for a test or simulated workload?

5. What is a synthetic workload? What are its advantages over a selected-job workload? What are its disadvantages?

6. Assume a conventional type of computer center as is found at many universities. Jobs are submitted at a special window and returned in bins arranged alphabetically by user name.

    (a) Name at least three factors other than machine-software performance that influence job-stream performance of this system.

    (b) Consider the installation of a card reader and printer at the job-submission window in which users can place their cards in the reader and receive output from the printer. Discuss how this is likely to affect performance, giving reasons for your statements.

7. Given a job stream where all jobs arrive at the same time (e.g., gathered into a batch at the same time). Assume FCFS scheduling with arbitrary selection for tie breaking.

    $X = 10, 1, 4, 2, 1, 5$

    (a) Compute the thruput.

    (b) Compute the average elapsed time.

    (c) Compute the F value (short-job-figure-of-merit).

    (d) Change the ordering of the above X so that they are in ascending order of X values. Repeat (a) to (c).

(e) Change the ordering of X to descending order and repeat (a) to (c).

(f) Prepare a table including the results of (d) and (e) and comment on the comparison of each performance parameter.

8. Given the following Type II workload where all setup and setdown times are equal (to 0.2).

A	0	0	0	0	0
X	8	1	4	2	1
S	0.2	0.2	0.2	0.2	0.2

(a) For FCFS scheduling, compute average elapsed time, thruput, F, and percent of total time consumed in setup/setdown.

(b) Assuming a time slice of 1.0, compute the performance parameters of (a), only now assuming a round-robin scheduler.

(c) Compare the results of (a) and (b) for each parameter.

9. The mean queue length of a server system may be defined as:

$$\bar{Q} = \frac{\text{Total (wait + service) time of jobs}}{\text{Elapsed time for job stream}}$$

Show that mean queue length is related to average elapsed time and thruput by

$$\bar{Q} = \bar{t}_e H$$

10. A hardware monitor applied to a system with one CPU and two channels for 100 hours shows CPU utilization of 60 hours, channel A of 20 hours, channel B of 30 hours, unoverlapped CPU time of 10 hours, both channels overlapped with the CPU for 8 hours, and 20 hours of idle time.

(a) How long was the CPU in the "wait state" (awaiting a "channel end")?

(b) How long was the CPU overlapped with only one channel?

11. Derive the following general results for a k segment pipelined system with t_i = service time for the ith segment

(a) Time for a single job to be serviced

$$T_1 = \sum_{i=1}^{k} t_i$$

(b) Time for n jobs serviced through the pipe

$$T_n = \left(\sum_{i=1}^{k} t_i \right) + (n-1) \text{Max} (t_i)$$

(c) Speed improvement of pipelined over strictly sequential nonpipelined service

$$I = \frac{n \sum_{i=1}^{k} t_i}{\left(\sum_{i=1}^{k} t_i \right) + (n-1) \text{Max} (t_i)}$$

(d) If all pipe segments require equal service time, the above formula becomes

$$I = \frac{nk}{n+k-1}$$

12. Using the SIMJOB SIMULATOR, one server with a speed factor of 1, time slice of 2, and the job stream:

A	0	0	0	0	0	0	0	0	0	0
X	1	3	8	2	5	1	3	9	2	4
SU	0	0	0	0	0	0	0	0	0	0

(a) Compare thruput, average stretch factor, and setup utilization for the FCFS, RR, and SJFS schedulers.

(b) How can the performance results of RR and FCFS be explained?

(c) What X_i reordering can best improve performance for the three schedulers; what reordering causes worst performance?

(d) What scheduler(s) are least affected by X_i reordering; what scheduler(s) most improved, and why?

13. Repeat Prob. 12 only with a setup time of 0.5 for each job. Comment on the effect of setup time on the performance of each scheduler compared to the others.

14. Using the job stream and schedulers from Prob. 12, process the stream with two parallel servers, each server having a speed factor of 0.5.

(a) How do the performance results compare with Prob. 12?

(b) Why is there a difference?

15. Repeat Prob. 14, only now assume a setup time of 0.5 seconds for each job.

Chapter 5   Queuing Theory

1. Assuming purely random (Poisson) arrivals with a mean interarrival time of 10 seconds, what is the probability of at least one new arrival in the following intervals: 2, 5, 10, 20, and 100 seconds? What are the probabilities of two or more new arrivals in these intervals?

2. Assume Poisson interarrival and service times with

Interarrival mean = 10 seconds
Service mean = 5 seconds
Max. queue length = 4 seconds

Find:

(a) Traffic intensity

(b) Mean queue length

(c) Variance of queue length

(d) Utilization

3. Repeat Prob. 2 for the case where the queue length is permitted to grow indefinitely large.

4. A certain computer installation shows an average job wait time of 5 minutes and the system is 40% utilized. Assuming exponential (Poisson) functions, what is the mean service time?

5. A computing center is known to have a mean execution time for jobs of 3 minutes. It is suggested that the distribution function of execution times might be exponential. Suggest a simple calculation to be used with your intuition to investigate the feasibility of the exponential function.

6. The ratio of mean wait time to mean service time may be considered to be a "stretch-factor-of-means." Assuming Poisson functions and steady-state conditions with infinite maximum queue length, plot a curve of stretch-factors-of-means for values of traffic intensity in the range $0 \leqslant r < 1$.

7. Discuss critically the value of mean wait (response) time as an adequate measure of the responsiveness of a timesharing system. See Chap. 9 for a full discussion of timesharing systems.

8. In a certain system using a first-come-first-served scheduler, the arrivals are random with a mean of 6 seconds. The service-time distribution is unknown, but its mean is 2 seconds with a coefficient of variation of 0.3.

(a) Find the mean wait time.

(b) Assume now the same interarrival and service means as above, only the distributions are exponential. Find the mean wait time.

9. Given a timesharing system with

25 = No. of signed-on users
15 seconds = mean think time
1 second = mean compute time

(a) Find the mean wait time.

(b) How many users may be permitted to sign on if the mean wait time is to be only five times the mean compute time?

Chapter 6 Single-Component and Single-Job Performance

1. Explain briefly the distinction between access and cycle time of a magnetic-core memory.

2. Discuss the significance of bandwidth as a measure of memory performance. Explain why it is a better single number than access or cycle time.

3. Given a 16-module core-storage subsystem with a 1-microsecond cycle time and width of 16 bits per module
   (a) What is the single module bandwidth?
   (b) What is the maximum system bandwidth?
   (c) What is the minimum system bandwidth?
   (d) Estimate the effective bandwidth.

4. Given a core storage module of width 32 bits and cycle time of 800 nanoseconds. How many interleaved modules are required to achieve a 400-nanosecond effective cycle time?

5. A certain computer working on a given job stream shows instruction execution statistics as follows:

Instruction type	Time/instruction, µseconds	Relative frequency
LOAD/STORE	1	0.40
ADD/SUB/COMPARE	1	0.30
BRANCH	1	0.25
MULTIPLY	8	0.04
DIVIDE	12	0.01

   (a) What is the mean instruction time? Call its reciprocal the mean instruction speed.
   (b) What percent speed improvement results if DIVIDE time is improved by a factor of 4?
   (c) What percent speed improvement results if ADD time is improved by a factor of 4?
   (d) Note that in (c), improvement of ADD time usually also improves MULTIPLY and DIVIDE time. Assume that with an ADD time improvement of a factor of 4, MULTIPLY and DIVIDE are improved by a factor of 2. Compute the percent speed improvement under those conditions.

6. Give one advantage and one disadvantage of the mix over the kernel method.

7. Describe an experimental technique for identifying information to be microcoded.

8. Discuss the nature and importance of emulation.

9. A certain report-generator program handles equal-length 80-byte problem records and requires 2 milliseconds of processing time per record. The records are read from two magnetic-tape units with 10 milliseconds access (start-stop time) and a flow rate of 100 kbytes/second. After processing, the records are stored back on tape.
   (a) If the blocking factor is 20, how much data storage is required, and what is the average time per record in a strictly sequential system?
   (b) Repeat (a) for a system that can overlap input, output, and compute.

10. Determine the best blocking factor and the total space and time per record for this optimum for the configuration of Prob. 9.

11. Explain at least two reasons why an in-core compiler can be faster than a folded compiler.

12. Since the code produced by a compiler cannot be faster than the best code written by an Assembler-language programmer, why shouldn't programming be done predominantly in Assembler language?

13. Discuss the following optimizing tactics:
   (a) Jamming
   (b) Unrolling
   (c) Invariance

14. What is an execution profile analyzer (EPA)? Discuss and contrast two ways to construct an EPA: building it into a compiler or transforming the source code.

15. Discuss some ways that features of a programming language can aid the compiler in producing an optimum code.

Chapter 7   Operating Systems: Evolution and Fundamentals

1. Describe the distinction between a program's symbolic name space and its address space (object module).

2. Describe the characteristics of open-shop and closed-shop scheduling in an environment with no operating system.

3. What is a "bootstrap" loader, and why is it necessary?

4. What advantages and disadvantages result from binding the following at compile time (rather than later):
  (*a*) Names to addresses?
  (*b*) I/O device names to I/O devices?

5. Using the ideas of *binding-time* and *address space*, discuss and compare the following:
  (*a*) Absolute programs
  (*b*) Static relocation
  (*c*) Object modules
  (*d*) Load modules
  (*e*) Linkage editor (a systems program)
  (*f*) Loader (a systems program)

6. What are the primary functions of a job control language?

7. What is the job-input stream in a monoprogrammed operating system? Where does it typically reside in the system?

8. What scheduling algorithm is typically used for job scheduling in a monoprogrammed system?

9. What are the primary functions of the control-program nucleus and of the job scheduler program in a monoprogrammed operating system?

10. What is system residence in a monoprogrammed system? Where does it usually reside?

11. What is a JCL procedure library? What is its function?

12. Describe what occurs during the IPL process in a monoprogrammed operating system.

13. What are the two primary functions of a linkage editor? Discuss the question in terms of binding times and address space.

14. What is the primary objective of a SPOOLing system?

15. (*a*) Describe the functions of the *system reader* and *system writer* in a SPOOLing system.
  (*b*) Where does the job-input stream typically reside in a SPOOLing system?
  (*c*) What type of job scheduling algorithms are possible in a SPOOLing system, but are impractical in a system that does its system I/O in strict sequence with problem program execution?
  (*d*) Describe how the CPU is typically scheduled (dispatched) in a SPOOLing environment.

16. Discuss the *advantages and disadvantages* of a multiprogrammed system relative to a monoprogrammed system from the viewpoint of:
  (*a*) An individual system user
  (*b*) An installation manager

17. Describe briefly the need for each of the following in a monoprogrammed and in a multiprogrammed system:
  (*a*) Real-time clock
  (*b*) Interval timer

18. Discuss briefly the following aspects of storage protection in a multiprogramming system:
  (*a*) Why is it needed?
  (*b*) Is it usually provided by hardware for main storage? Why?
  (*c*) Is it usually provided by hardware for disk storage? Why?
  (*d*) How is main-storage protection done in the IBM System/360?

(e) Discuss at least one other type of hardware method for main-storage protection and give relative advantages and disadvantages.

19. (a) Why are privileged instructions often provided in a multiprogramming system?

(b) The CDC-6600 system does not have privileged CPU instructions. Study this system from articles in the literature and explain how it achieves the same kind of results.

20. What is the purpose of a supervisor-call (SVC) interrupt?

21. How does an interrupt scheme allow preemptive CPU dispatching?

22. Describe how fragmentation appears in a system with static (load-time) program relocation.

23. (a) When does program relocation occur in a multiprogramming system with dynamic relocation?

(b) What special hardware is required? (Describe at least one scheme.)

(c) What flexibility in main-storage allocation is available with dynamic relocation, but not with static relocation?

24. What functions are involved in job scheduling in a multiprogramming system?

25. (a) Compare the types of information available from a software and a hardware monitor.

(b) Discuss the effects of the software monitoring process itself on performance and what may be done to minimize such effects.

26. Endless looping is a fundamental problem in computing systems. Explain why and what practical means are used to combat it.

27. Test-and-set is a type of instruction found in many multiprocessor systems. Discuss its purpose.

28. What is a serially reusable resource?

29. List the four conditions sufficient to cause deadlock.

30. Compare the advantages and disadvantages of combatting deadlock by:

(a) Prevention

(b) Detection

(c) Avoidance

31. (a) Write a program that simulates the deadlock avoidance algorithm discussed in detail in Sec. 7-7.

(b) Construct at least three examples illustrating the algorithm's ability to avoid a deadlock. (The examples must not simply request more resources than are connected in the system.)

32. This project is designed to explore and evaluate, by simulation, some job-scheduling and dispatching rules in multiprogramming configurations that do and do not include dynamic relocation. The system objective is maximization of thruput. You are to write a simulator for the system described below. The system resources for modelling purposes are: one CPU, one I/O resource, and a main store with a capacity of 300 kbytes. The workload model characterizes each job, on input, by four numbers:

Required CPU time, C
Required main store space, S
Mean time between I/O requests, R
Mean duration time of an I/O request, D
(See part D for the source of data on these.)

Any given job can be in one of six states at any given time. State progression is described by the following table (you may wish to draw a state diagram to help visualize the process).

Present state	Next state	Transition event
INITIAL	READY	Job scheduler selects job
READY	CPUTIME	Dispatcher selects job
CPUTIME	JOBEND	End-of-job
CPUTIME	IOQ	I/O requested
IOQ	IO	I/O available
IO	READY	I/O ends

(a) Job-scheduling rules to be explored
  Class S Static relocation only
    S.1 – FCFS (first-come-first-served)
    S.2 – Smallest (storage) jobs first
  Class R Dynamic relocation
    R.1, R.2 like S.1, S.2
    R.3 – Construct your own rule
(b) Dispatching rules
    D.1 – Job first into main store (among READY jobs)
    D.2 – Job with most accumulated I/O time
    D.3 – Job with least accumulated CPU time
    D.4 – Construct your own rule
(c) Data should ideally be obtained from actual computer system. For test purposes, use
    the space-time data of Chap. 2, Probs. 8 and 10, where time is now taken as C, the CPU
    time. Generate the R and D data from exponential distributions with means as follows
    (see above for notation):

$$R = .1C \quad \text{and} \quad D = .2R$$

(d) The simulator should include at least the following outputs:
    (1) Thruput, mean elapsed time
    (2) Storage utilization (mean space-time product)
    (3) CPU utilization
    (4) I/O utilization
(e) Write a report describing the simulator logic, how you tested its validity, the results
    from the above cases, plus others you decide are useful.

Chapter 8   The IBM OS/360 Operating System

1. (a) What are the three major kinds of statements in OS JCL, and what are their major
functions?
  (b) Name and discuss briefly at least four JCL parameters designed to influence space-time
      allocation.
  (c) Ponder and discuss the questions: In what ways is the OS/360 JCL like other
      programming languages and in what ways is it different? Use this to discuss possible
      improvements in JCL structure.

2. (a) What is a cataloged procedure (CP)?
  (b) Describe briefly how the system handles a reference to a CP during job processing.

3. Distinguish between a file name and a data-set name and how and when they are related.

4. Identify and briefly describe the major classes of functions in OS/360.

5. What functions do the following perform:
  (a) System residence?
  (b) Transient area (for SVC's)?
  (c) What is the alternative to using a transient area?
  (d) What is the effect of using the alternative on performance?

6. Compare OS/MFT and OS/MVT according to the following:
  (a) Main-storage allocation: consider both the problem program and the system
  (b) Job scheduling
  (c) Dispatching (of the CPU)

7. What usually determines the degree of multiprogramming possible with OS/360?

8. When are programs finally bound in OS/360? Could they conceivably be bound later in this
system? Why? What effect does this have on performance?

9. What is multitasking in OS/MVT? Why and when is this desirable?

10. Describe the function provided by the OS/MVT link-pack area.

11. (a) Briefly describe the rollout-rollin option in MVT.
    (b) Why might it be used?
    (c) What are its limitations and disadvantages?

12. What basic scheduling algorithm does the MVT time slice option implement? Is this desirable in a multiprogramming environment?

13. How does HASP SPOOLing differ from SPOOLing with OS readers and writers?

14. (a) Describe the HASP heuristic dispatching option.
    (b) Contrast this to basic scheduling algorithms described earlier in the text (Chap. 4).
    (c) Contrast this to conventional OS/MVT dispatching.

15. (a) What are the major advantages and disadvantages of software compared to hardware monitors?
    (b) Describe briefly the basic operation of a software monitor.
    (c) Give at least two major uses of a software monitor.
    (d) What is meant by "levels" of trace? Give examples from OS/360.

16. Compare the types of events that may be monitored by SMF and GTF.

17. Consult the literature (you may start with our Bibliography for Chaps. 1 and 7) and write a report on the scheduling functions of at least one non-IBM operating system. Compare these with OS/MVT. Suggestions: CDC 6600, UNIVAC 1108, Burroughs 5500. (*Note*: Sufficient detail may only be available from manuals rather than published articles.)

18. If a software monitor is available, use its output to
    (a) Describe (say) one month of system activity.
    (b) Compute *thruput* and mean elapsed time.
    (c) Describe utilizations of channels and CPU.
    (d) Describe utilizations of various compilers.
    (e) Produce a stream of job descriptors suitable for driving a job simulator.

19. (a) Write a simulator to be driven by the streams of Prob. 18*d*.
    (b) Compare its outputs to those produced in Prob. 18*b*.

Chapter 9 Timesharing Systems

1. (a) What are the major unique advantages of a timesharing system?
   (b) What are the disadvantages relative to a batch system?

2. Identify and describe the following as needed by a timesharing system over and above what is needed by a modern multiprogramming system:
   (a) CPU features
   (b) Other system hardware

3. Swapping is an often used tactic in timesharing systems.
   (a) What is it?
   (b) What are its advantages and disadvantages?

4. Discuss the distinction between a *dedicated* and nondedicated timesharing system.

5. (a) What are user commands? What is their counterpart in a batch system?
   (b) What types of commands are most needed?

6. (a) What types of program-interruption facilities require special compiler organization in a timesharing system that are not needed in a compiler for a batch system?
   (b) Briefly describe the needed compiler facilities.

7. Contrast the fundamental organization and performance properties of interpreters and compilers, including advantages and disadvantages of each. When does binding time occur for each?

8. (a) What are two pertinent performance measures for timesharing systems?
   (b) What scheduling algorithm(s) can help satisfy these criteria?

9. (a) Discuss considerations in choosing the time slice(s) in a timesharing system.
   (b) What two types of time slices are often used?

10. Why were two storage units of equal size used in the CTSS system?

11. Describe the "exponential" scheduling algorithm used in CTSS. How did this algorithm prevent long-running tracts from being locked out? How did CTSS identify trivial tracts?

12. What are some of the facilities, advantages, and disadvantages that result from the fact that the APL language processor is an interpreter?

13. How can APL I-beams be used to obtain data on:
   (a) The APL translator's performance?
   (b) An APL program's performance?
   (c) The APL system's performance?

14. What is the purpose of using main-storage resident terminal-message buffers for signed-on APL users? (The alternative would be to include terminal buffering only in each user's workspace.)

15. Describe the characteristics and differences between internal and external performance-measurement techniques for timesharing systems.

16. Describe how a "snooper terminal" can be used to measure performance in a timesharing system.

17. What is a *script*, and how is it used in timesharing performance studies?

18. (a) What is the admission rule when scheduling a timesharing system, and how is it applied?
   (b) What is complimentary replacement?

19. What must be done to establish confidence in a simulator?

20. Define the term *reaction time* as used in a timesharing system.

21. How can a TSO terminal user create his own commands?

22. Describe what happens in TSO
   (a) When the operator starts the system (IPL)
   (b) When a terminal user logs-on

23. Discuss the performance issue involved in the selection of modules for the extended link-pack area in TSO.

24. Describe the function of the major time slice and the minor time slice in TSO scheduling.

25. (a) What TSO scheduler feature is designed to handle long-executing transactions?
   (b) What TSO scheduling parameters are designed to ensure rapid response to trivial transactions?
   (c) What TSO scheduler features are designed to handle the background (batch) workload?

26. What are line concentrators, and why are they important in some timesharing systems?

27. Consider yourself a manager of an organization that requires (say) 20 timesharing terminals. Contrast the services available from a system like (say) TSO and from a utility-type system like the GE network. Some factors to be included in your discussion are:
   (a) Generality of functions
   (b) Likely dependability of services (admittedly hard to estimate, but speculate anyway)
   (c) Ease of use
   (d) Ability to implement customized subsystems
   (e) Degree of control over system resources
   (f) Costs

28. In Sec. 5-8, a simple mathematical model of a timesharing system was developed, resulting in the performance equation, Eq. (13), or its recursive form, Eqs. (14) and (15), plotted in Fig. 5-8.1. Use these to answer the following:
   (a) If 40 users are signed on, their mean think time is 20 seconds and their mean CPU time is 0.5 seconds. What is the average wait time?
   (b) In the above system, how many users can be permitted to sign on before the average wait time becomes 3 seconds?
   (c) What does the model say about the trivial response time?

(d) List some of the factors that affect timesharing-system performance that are *not* included in the model.

29. Consult the literature (see Bibliography to start with) and write a report on the topic: A comparison of programmer productivity in batch vs. timesharing environments. (Be sure to include a critique of the methodology used, as well as your own conclusions about the comparisons.)

30. This project requires that a timesharing system be actually available. Design and conduct a "snooper-terminal" study including the following:
    (a) Select and define the test scripts (include both trivial and nontrivial tracts).
    (b) Measure CPU, elapsed, and print times.
    (c) Take measurements at several hours during the day and over several days.
    (d) Arrange your data in tabular form and use the techniques of Chap. 2 to analyze the results.
    (e) Write a report on your findings and conclusions.

31. Report on a timesharing system other than one in the text. Compare it to APL or TSO discussed in the text.

Chapter 10 Virtual-Storage Principles

1. Discuss the concept of folding and give examples of the following in a nonvirtual-storage system:
    (a) Folding of programs
    (b) Folding of data

2. What are the two contexts of virtual storage and how do they differ?

3. Contrast the following mapping methods for an address space of 2^n words with page size of 2^p words. In each case, give the number of mapping cells required by
    (a) Associative mapping
    (b) Mapping by addressing
Also comment on other advantages and disadvantages of each method.

4. Discuss a mapping scheme using page tables in main storage and a small associative store.

5. What is a page fault, how is it detected, and what is done about it?

6. Contrast a paged-only virtual store with a segmented-only virtual store.

7. What information is contained in the PRT of the Burroughs B5500 and how is it used?

8. Discuss the following terms and the type of system where each occurs:
    (a) Internal fragmentation
    (b) External fragmentation

9. Describe the purpose of each of the following control bits often included in mapping mechanisms:
    (a) Presence bit
    (b) Change bit
    (c) Activity bit

10. Discuss the appropriateness of hardware or software implementations of the following:
    (a) Mapping
    (b) Page-fault detection
    (c) Page-fault response
    (d) Input/output control

11. Describe the address-translation process in a typical system using both segmentation and paging.

12. Suggest at least two items of information that should be captured in each recording of an address-stream trace.

13. Define the following as precisely as you can:
    (a) Locality of reference

(b) Working set

(c) Average working-set size

(d) Parachor

14. (a) Why is page replacement such an important operation in a virtual-storage system?

(b) What is the most important single measure of replacement algorithm performance? On what does this depend?

15. Briefly describe the MIN and LRU replacement algorithms and how they are related.

16. What is a stack algorithm and why is it an important class of algorithm?

17. Briefly describe at least two techniques of programming style that can be used to improve virtual-storage performance.

18. From the experiments cited, which seems to influence performance the most: replacement algorithms or programming style?

19. (a) What context of virtual storage is implemented on the IBM Mod 155?

(b) Describe the mapping method in the Mod 155.

(c) What is the "store-through" principle and where is it appropriate?

(d) Describe the logical relationship between I/O transmissions and movement of data to and from the buffer and main stores in the Mod 155.

20. Assume a CPU-context system with a buffer having a 100-nanosecond cycle and a main store with a 1000-nanosecond cycle. If the average effective speed must be 80% of the speed of the buffer, what must be the probability of a buffer "hit"?

21. This major project requires capturing an address stream. This can be done by modifying an existing machine or language interpreter. Assuming this is done, program a few "standard" problems such as matrix inversion, text processing (such as word counting in a text string), a bubble or merge sort, etc., and capture the address streams for each. Then write stream-analysis programs to include at least the following:

(a) For page sizes of (say) 8, 16, 32, or 64 words, the relative frequencies of read, write, and total references to each page. Plot the four histograms.

(b) Write a simulator to determine the number of page replacements for each of the above page sizes, assuming the LRU replacement algorithm (recall this is a stack algorithm) and a fast-store size of 1/8, 1/4, 1/2, and 1/1 of maximum program-plus-data-size.

(c) Write a report summarizing your findings.

22. If a virtual-storage system is available, reproduce the Brawn-Gustavson type of experiments with programs and data of your own selection. Take care with the following:

(a) After debugging, timings of the test programs must be done with *only* these programs running on the system.

(b) For single-program tests, be sure the program(s) plus data are large enough to induce significant paging.

(c) It is usually not possible to vary the available size of main storage. However, comparisons of programming-style effects for the same problem can still be done.

23. Consult the relevant IBM manuals and literature to discuss the various CPU-context implementations of S/360 Mod 85, S/370 155, 165. Emphasize similarities and differences.

Chapter 11   Virtual Storage: System-Design Context

1. (a) What is the distinction between an AS(1) and an AS(n) virtual-storage system?

(b) Compared to AS(1), what additional hardware or software is needed to implement an AS(n) system?

(c) Under what conditions might an AS(1) organization be most appropriate?

2. Briefly discuss the effects of the following architecture features on mapping (hardware and software and main storage for tables), and assume a fixed address space size for:

(a) Page size

  (*b*) Segment size

  (*c*) Segment-page organization vs. page-only organization

3. What are the functions of a paging supervisor in a virtual-storage system?

4. Why is a global page-placement strategy typically used in a virtual-storage system?

5. What are some reasons for page fixing in a virtual-storage system?

6. Contrast prepaging (or context paging) to the demand-paging technique. What is the inherent danger of prepaging?

7. Contrast the bulk one-to-one management of auxiliary storage to the use of external page tables. Would the one-to-one approach be suitable for an AS(n) environment? Why?

8. What program-loading techniques can be used for an AS(1) system? How does this compare to program loading in a conventional multiprogramming environment?

9. From the single-user viewpoint, what is the advantage of an AS(n) over an AS(1) system?

10. How can the supervisor and other system programs be shared in an AS(n) implementation? How many physical copies of the supervisor exist?

11. What parameters limit the number of address spaces that may be created in an AS(n) system?

12. IBM (and most other systems) use software only for mapping main-storage references due to I/O channels. Discuss the difficulties in handling such references in the same way as is done for CPU references.

13. Describe the functions necessary for software translation of channel programs. What pages must be fixed during this process? Why?

14. What are two approaches to reduce the overhead required for channel program translation?

15. (*a*) Describe the condition called *thrashing* in a virtual-storage environment. What conditions cause thrashing to occur?

  (*b*) Describe briefly some typical tactics of a thrashing monitor.

16. Contrast block paging to the demand-paging technique. How can block paging be used effectively?

17. Describe the similarities and differences between OS/VS2 (Rel 1) and OS/MVT.

18. How is storage protection achieved in OS/VS2 Rel 1 and in OS/VS2 Rel 2?

19. How are TSO users "swapped" in VS2 Rel 1?

20. How are system programs shared in VS2 Rel 2?

21. (*a*) What is the fundamental nature of the virtual machine offered each VM/370 user?

  (*b*) What advantages accrue from (*a*)?

  (*c*) Discuss the compatibility of VM/370 architecture with sharing of user files and programs.

22. What is the purpose of providing a large number of segments for each user in the Multics system?

23. What is the purpose of the descriptor-base register during address translation in Multics?

24. What selection process does Multics use to page page-tables?

25. Write a report describing the objectives, functions, algorithms, etc., for a virtual-storage system not described in this chapter; for example, the TSS/360, Burroughs, etc.

26. Compare OS/MVT to OS/VS2 considering the functions available, ease of use, amount of system overhead (including size of system programs and time in supervisor state), etc.

Index

Index